SUGAR BARON

UNIVERSITY PRESS OF FLORIDA

Florida A&M University, Tallahassee
Florida Atlantic University, Boca Raton
Florida Gulf Coast University, Ft. Myers
Florida International University, Miami
Florida State University, Tallahassee
New College of Florida, Sarasota
University of Central Florida, Orlando
University of Florida, Gainesville
University of North Florida, Jacksonville
University of South Florida, Tampa
University of West Florida, Pensacola

Sugar Baron

Manuel Rionda and the Fortunes of Pre-Castro Cuba

Muriel McAvoy

University Press of Florida

Gainesville/Tallahassee/Tampa/Boca Raton
Pensacola/Orlando/Miami/Jacksonville/Ft. Myers/Sarasota

Copyright 2003 by Muriel McAvoy
All rights reserved
Published in the United States of America

First cloth printing, 2003
First paperback printing, 2025

30 29 28 27 26 25   6 5 4 3 2 1

Library of Congress Cataloging-in-Publication Data
McAvoy, Muriel, 1919-
Sugar baron: Manuel Rionda and the fortunes of pre-Castro Cuba / Muriel McAvoy.
p. cm.
Includes bibliographical references (p.) and index.
ISBN 978-0-8130-2613-8 (cloth)
ISBN 978-0-8130-8107-6 (pbk.)
1. Sugar trade—Cuba—History—20th century. 2. Rionda y Polledo, Manuel.
3. Businessmen—Cuba—Biography. I. Title.
HD9114.C882 M33 2003
338.7'664122'092—dc21   2002033850
[B]

The University Press of Florida is the scholarly publishing agency for the State University System of Florida, comprising Florida A&M University, Florida Atlantic University, Florida Gulf Coast University, Florida International University, Florida State University, New College of Florida, University of Central Florida, University of Florida, University of North Florida, University of South Florida, and University of West Florida.

University Press of Florida
2046 NE Waldo Road
Suite 2100
Gainesville, FL 32609
http://upress.ufl.edu

GPSR EU Authorized Representative: Mare Nostrum Group B.V., Mauritskade 21D, 1091 GC Amsterdam, The Netherlands, gpsr@mare-nostrum.co.uk

Contents

List of Illustrations and Maps   vii
Acknowledgments   ix

Merchant at the Crossroads   1
1. Business with Aliens   7
2. Head of the Mouse   30
3. Tarafa and the Genial Shark   57
4. Cuba Cane   81
5. A Fixed Price   104
6. Tail of the Lion   128
7. The Steel Gray Battleship   159
8. Visible Hands   182
9. Receivership and Reorganization   207
10. Empty Saddlebags   232
11. From the Wolf, a Pelt   259
The Roads Taken   282

Notes   299
Bibliography   319
Index   329

Illustrations and Maps

All illustrations are reproduced by permission of the University of Florida's George A. Smathers Libraries, Department of Special and Area Studies Collections.

Fig. 1. Rionda on horseback 3
Fig. 2. Manolo Rionda Benjamin, Cosme de la Torriente y Peraza, José Rionda y de la Torriente, Leandro Rionda y de la Torriente, Bernardo Braga Rionda 29
Fig. 3. J.I.C. Clarke and Mrs. Clarke, Manuel and Harriet Rionda, unidentified 49
Fig. 4. Ellen and Manolo Rionda, Maude and Bernardo Braga, unidentified, Manuel and Harriet Rionda, unidentified 69
Fig. 5. Czarnikow-Rionda headquarters building 130
Fig. 6. Alfonso Fanjul Estrada, Higinio Fanjul Rionda, Bernardo Braga Rionda, Antonio Barro 273
Fig. 7. Manuel Rionda 287

Map 1. Cuban mills, 1901 39
Map 2. Cuban mills, 1913 67
Map 3. Cuba Cane mills, 1917 89
Map 4. Cuban mills, 1939 277

Acknowledgments

This book could not have been written without help from the New York Public Library, the Library of Congress, and the National Archives. Still less could it have been written without the generosity of the Baker Library at Harvard Business School, which let me into its subterranean stacks to explore its superb sugar collection, or without the able staff and resources of the New Hampshire State Library in Concord. Least of all, it could not have been written without the Braga Brothers Collection in the University of Florida at Gainesville and without Carl van Ness's helpfulness and mastery of the wealth of material it contains.

I am grateful to all of them, to Wayne Gallup for the maps and to Dr. César Ayala, Dr. Franklin Knight, and Dr. Caroline Murphy for their suggestions and encouragement.

I am grateful, too, to the late Ernest M. Law of Boston University for teaching me how specific the history of agricultural commodities should be; to the late Andrés Ramos Mattei of the University of Puerto Rico for his enthusiasm for sugar in particular; and to Keith Laurence of the University of the West Indies, St. Augustine, for asking me the question this book has tried to answer.

Merchant at the Crossroads

The Cuba Cane Sugar Corporation was incorporated in New Jersey on December 31, 1915. In Europe, there had been a second wartime Christmas, and the armies were stalled in cold French mud. Although those in the sugar trade often expressed their regret at the carnage, the Allies desperately needed all they could produce, and raw sugars were up to 3⅝ cents a pound from barely 2 cents a pound in early 1914.

The new corporation had an authorized capital of $50 million, which was more than two and a half times the capital of the Cuban-American Sugar Company, the largest existing U.S.-Cuban sugar company to date, and sixteen and a half times greater than the $3 million with which E. Atkins and Company had launched the Punta Alegre Sugar Company four months earlier.

Capital was being raised by the sale of 500,000 shares of 7 percent cumulative preferred stock, par $100. An additional 500,000 shares of common stock, no par value, were also being issued, to be distributed to those who acquired the preferred stock or who were otherwise useful, both common and preferred carrying the same voting rights. The shares were being underwritten by a syndicate, with most of the big Wall Street firms taking shares and with the private investment banking firm of J & W Seligman as syndicate manager.[1] So impressive was the venture that, even before the company had a legal identity, rumors had flown through Cuba, raising for some the hope of profits and for others a dread specter of engobblement by an insatiable Sugar Trust.

President of the giant new corporation was Manuel Rionda y Polledo, Spanish-born master of two important Cuban mills and chair of the major U.S. sugar brokerage firm of Czarnikow-Rionda.[2] At age sixty-one he was arguably the greatest of Cuba's sugar barons, riding over his own acres every *zafra*, general of that fierce and hard-fought harvest, commanding the machines that pressed his family's cane in their own mills. The rest of every year he spent on his Hudson River estate, commuting to his Wall Street office. Surrounding him were his nephews, whom he had raised to be his lieutenants, bound to him by iron family ties of affection and duty.

At the turn of the twentieth century, three forces had come together in the Cuban cane fields: Spanish, Cuban, and North American. Manuel embodied them all, united them, and played them off against each other, and it is this diversity of functions, this contradictoriness, that makes him so interesting a figure. To the end of his very long life, he described himself as a merchant, knowing the merchant's craft was honed to forge mutually profitable alliances among men of different nations. But he would learn, chiefly from Cuba Cane itself, that he was a merchant at the crossroads of forces that were perhaps irreconcilable. He had cultivated Wall Street's financiers, charming them with Don Quixote proverbs and Spanish courtesy. He came at times, secretly, to hate them.

Rionda went north to the lawyers, the investors, and the con artists to raise from English-speaking men of a different world the money he needed to dominate the world of Cuban sugar. With his success, money's claims would press on him. In a time of depression and glut, they would thrust him into the world of international politics among the bounties and tariffs of the nationalism that he would fantasize of controlling with a "League of Nations of Sugar."

This is the story of a merchant among bankers and of the creation, existence, and eventual metamorphosis of a sugar company. As such, it is an object lesson in the geopolitics of sugar. We can trace much of the story through a stroke of luck, the donation of his clan's papers to the University of Florida at Gainesville in 1981. As a result, 730 linear feet of accounts, blueprints, records, and correspondence spanning some eighty years—from the first Spanish family letters from Matanzas in the 1880s to the documents of the early 1960s—were trucked down from a Brooklyn, New York, warehouse where they had been stored and hero-

Fig. 1. Rionda on horseback

ically cataloged. Known as the Braga Brothers Collection from the two grandnephews of Manuel Rionda, whose generous gift they were, they open up an intimate record of individuals living through historic times. Because of the close family ties of the men involved in this network of enterprises and because some were based in Havana while others operated out of New York, there are almost daily letters detailing business transactions of great scope. In addition, the correspondence is supplemented by two typed manuscripts: "Personal and Business Experiences" by Bernardo Braga Rionda, one of Manuel's nephews, and "A Bundle of Relations" by Bernardo's son, George Atkinson Braga, who was a little boy at Czarnikow-Rionda's zenith. While neither of these accounts always conforms exactly with the historical record, they show how the family itself remembered its history, and they recount the family legends.

If it never crossed Manuel Rionda's mind or those of his nephews that half a century after their deaths their communications with each other would be the concern of scholarly curiosity, they were aware that among their clerks might be spies for rival firms. Since Rionda was close to Henry Havemeyer when the full fury of popular indignation against the Sugar Trust was hammering down on Havemeyer, they also knew that they might face government subpoenas. Thus they utilized codes, some transparent, some merely nicknames, others unfathomable. They were not always candid or fully honest. They instructed their confidential secretaries from time to time not to save copies of certain letters, and they engaged in transactions with political authorities better kept off the record. Yet if these concerns shadow the clarity of understanding that the documents in the Braga Brothers Collection provide, they do not obliterate it. There are too many records.

If we must take into account the human propensity to consider one's own actions in the best light, as when Manuel Rionda writes of the generosity of his motives, we need not take his opinion at face value. We can measure his protestations of selflessness against what he did, for the documents are self-correcting in their fullness. When he described how fortunate the *colonos* on his lands were, he could go on, without self-consciousness, to recount in the next paragraph that he had requested the president of Cuba to check their attempts at organization.

There is much to explore in the records. The Riondas' home plantation, *Tuinucú*; their pioneering *Francisco*, a giant plantation in eastern

Cuba, conceived even before the United Fruit Company built its *Boston* or Robert Hawley his *Chaparra*; their *Manatí*, for a time Cuba's greatest mill; and crowning and uniting them, the brokerage firm of Czarnikow-Rionda, at the harbor end of Wall Street in Manhattan, which sold much of Cuba's total sugar crop and was closely tied to the world's greatest sugar broker, the London firm of C. Czarnikow Ltd. There is also the Cuban Trading Company near Havana's docks, middleman for hemp bags and coal and for machinery and political contacts with Cuba's presidential palace.

Finally, there is the Cuba Cane Sugar Corporation, Manuel's most ambitious business undertaking. In its time, it was the single greatest sugar company on the island, perhaps in the world. Conceived in boom times and bringing together a number of existing mills, and thus built upon the expertise of an earlier generation of Spanish-speaking entrepreneurs, for a time it put into the hands of the Riondas the production and marketing of a quarter of all the sugar the island produced. In studying it, one follows the fortunes of the crop in prosperity and through times when demand dropped so low that corporations lost money harvesting and cane fields were abandoned to weeds. One sees the frictions and conflicts of interest between men of different cultures. One touches the effects of vertical combination when the refineries purchased their own mills to supply their raw material. One observes through six decades the roles the Cuban and the U.S. governments played, both officially and behind the scenes. One sees how other sugar producers from the Elbe to Java to Salt Lake City influenced it, their interactions often as chaotic and intangible as a Tokyo butterfly's wings, and one traces the conception of a worldwide agreement that Rionda supported, almost fathered.

This is the story of sugar companies told from the inside. Because of the vast sums of money their operations required, much of it deals with how that capital was raised, what profits accrued, and who benefited financially. Many volumes analyze neocolonial dependency. This work instead details the day-to-day interrelations of one entrepreneur with his investors.

Between the sugar on the grocers' shelves and the tropical plantations stretched a network of connections from Havana east to Santiago de Cuba and north to the Brooklyn docks, to the Atlantic Coast refineries, to banks and offices in New York and London, to the marble antechambers and the smoke-filled back rooms of the politicians of several nations. For a long time, Manuel Rionda was at the center of this web.

Rionda brushed aside allegations, when Cuba Cane was launched, that he had acted as part of a conspiracy on behalf of the Sugar Trust. "I don't see any grounds for the great hullabaloo they are making in Cuba," he wrote one of his Havana nephews. "That the refiners are interested is absolutely absurd—no refiners have ever spoken to me on the subject." And again, "There are no refiners in this scheme—no one started the ball rolling but myself. The bankers themselves would never have thought of it."[3]

He may well have convinced himself that this was true.

I

Business with Aliens

Manuel Rionda y Polledo first saw Havana in 1870, when he was sixteen. He had been born in Noreña, northern Spain, near the Bay of Biscay, on August 3, 1854, one of the nine children of Bernardo Rionda and of Joséfa Polledo de la Mata and the youngest of their three sons. His two brothers, Francisco, called Pancho, ten years older, and Joaquín, six years older, went off to America when he was a child, leaving him behind with his sisters. "I had no boyhood," he reminisced in his old age. "I was a lad of 12/13 years of age, with my two brothers in America making money and I plowing the fields. I always felt that my brothers were going to get the advantage of me, and as a consequence of that I was always anxious to leave Spain and come to America." But he, too, in his turn was summoned across the Atlantic.[1]

The young Riondas followed a classic Asturian pattern. Their uncle on their mother's side, Joaquín Polledo y Alvarez, was established in western Cuba as a merchant, with connections branching from Havana to Matanzas, the center of abundant sugarcane lands and rich *ingenios*. Merchants, often Spanish-born, functioned as local brokers for plantation owners, making cash advances, attending to business details, finding buyers, and arranging for warehousing, shipping, and credit until final payments cleared. Cuba lacked a modern banking structure and merchant advances of cash, albeit at high interest rates, kept the system spinning. Through such services, hard work, and thrift, and also because they benefited in several ways from the favoritism of the Spanish government, many became, as did Joaquín Polledo, owners of plantations.

Francisco joined his uncle and by the early 1870s had become a partner in what became Polledo, Rionda y Cía. By 1875, he had married Elena de la Torriente y Hernández, whose father, Cosme de la Torriente, was patriarch of a family empire, one of three brothers who, in an earlier wave of adventuring Spaniards, had emigrated to Cuba in the early 1820s. They had profited from the African slave trade and now owned, at the height of their wealth, the *Amistad, Carlota, María, Elena, Isabel, Progreso*, and *San Pablo* plantations. In the early 1860s, Baring Brothers of London had loaned Cosme $500,000 and a Hamburg bank an additional $250,000 to erect the largest warehouse in Matanzas.[2]

There was more to building a fortune in Cuban sugar than laden oxcarts. It was the quantities sold and the prices received that determined profits. Not much Cuban sugar was absorbed by Spain itself, for cane had grown in Granada since Moorish times. Some went from Cuba to the Continent, some to England. But the closest market, and increasingly the dominant one, was the republic to the island's north.

Cuba's brokers established ties with the Yankee merchants. Their contacts bound them to the refineries of Portland, Maine, and Brooklyn and Boston. They bargained terms, chartered ships, and arranged the necessary bills of sale. They oversaw the clerks who still wrote with pen and ink in the ledgers. They took care of the weighing on the docks and of the invoices and the duties to be paid. If reality required, they also took care of the bribes to various officials. They supplied Cuba with dried fish and barrel staves and horses; they talked with salesmen hawking improved machines for sugar ingenios.

Most important, they courted the refiners. Good connections in the States were as important as good cane land in Cuba. There was a fine art to selling, and New York was the best place to master it. Joaquín, the middle Rionda brother, was assigned there. By 1873, he was partner of the commission merchant Lewis Benjamin in Manhattan's bustling financial district, and he had married Benjamin's daughter, Sophie.

Manuel, summoned at last into this expanding world, was sent first to Havana, seeing from the ship's side the Caribbean port with its red-tiled roofs and forts and its stone and iron warehouses. Inland were miles of cane, black African slaves and amber indentured Chinese, overseers on horseback, and the elegant carriages of the hacendados, high-wheeled to surmount the mud. He saw a productive Cuba, with the price of sugar high and demand for it rising, and the men with whom his uncle Polledo and his brother Pancho did the shrewd and hardworking business of the flourishing ports.

The Ten Years War for Cuban Independence was being fought, but it was far away, in the eastern Sierra Maestra. Manuel instead saw Havana and Matanzas Provinces, where some 400 ingenios were linked to ports by railroad networks built with British capital. In the five years since Lee's surrender at Appomattox, U.S. imports of sugar from the Spanish West Indies had doubled. In another five years, they would almost triple.

From this tropical exuberance, Manuel was consigned to Portland, Maine, entrusted to George S. Hunt, manager of Portland's Eagle Sugar Refinery. For two centuries, logs had been floated down the cold Maine rivers to be made into the shooks and staves out of which hogsheads were fashioned. The ships that carried them south had returned heavy with molasses to nourish the loggers and make the rum to sustain the Labrador fishermen. Between 1856 and 1861 alone, 1,040 vessels had carried lumber out of Maine ports, and only 17 of them had not sailed for Cuba. Hunt himself had gone to the island several times, had made contacts and "entered into an arrangement . . . to handle their exports to the United States and in return export American products to Cuba." Manuel's uncle must have been among Hunt's connections, for one of Hunt's ships was named the *Noreña* and another the *Isidora Rionda*. First incorporated in 1866, Hunt's refinery could process some seventy to eighty hogsheads of moist, raw Cuban *muscovado* sugar a day into twenty tons of sugar of eleven different grades, ranging "from nearly white down to dark yellow."

After Manuel had admired the refinery's steam boiler, its vacuum pans, and its centrifugal machinery, he was dispatched inland to the frugal mercies of the Little Blue School in small-town Farmington, Maine. Shivering through four years of Down East winters and plain Yankee fare, he mastered the merchants' tools: English, bookkeeping, and good penmanship, the severe routine tempered by high spirits, by girls, and skating parties.[3] For the rest of his life, or at least until the 1930s sobered his natural generosity, Manuel was to be a faithful contributor to the school.

In 1874, when he was twenty, his formal education completed, he left Portland to join Joaquín in New York. The East River, still white with sailing ships, echoed to the sound of hammers of those building the Brooklyn Bridge, and Manhattan's banks grouped beneath the spire of Trinity Church. Only the building on the corner of Wall and Broad Streets, built the previous year for the new private banking firm of Drexel, Morgan, towered as high as six stories, its two allegorical statues in togas flanking the thirty-seven-year-old J. Pierpont Morgan's entrances. The New York City Bank at 52 Wall Street still occupied its three-story, remodeled lodging house where white-side-whiskered Moses Taylor presided. Taylor had built a fortune out of the Cuban trade, bankrolling ingenios and cannily accumulating stock in the Bank of Havana.

Wall Street was scarcely half a mile long, but it joined Alexander Hamilton's grave in the Episcopal Church Yard to the East River and the harbor, ending at the docks where warehouses filled the salt air with the smells of coffee and molasses. Walking the Street, passing at 98 Wall Street the offices where Henry O. Havemeyer conducted the business dealings of the sugar refiners Havemeyer and Elder, Manuel could observe the bankers, operators, the promoters, lawyers, and stock manipulators. On the New York Stock Exchange, hundreds of daring ventures were being schemed, telegraph and telephones lines radiating out to make it the financial center of the nation's expanding industrialization.[4]

In Cuba, despite the Ten Years War, total sugar production had reached a record high of 775,000 tons in 1873, almost 42 percent of world cane production. In 1875, the rebel forces were driven back from a foray into the central cane zone, and the war wound down until February 1878, when the Peace of Zanjón ended hostilities.

In Cuba, Francisco was put in charge of the de la Torriente estate *Elena*. In July 1876, his first son, a second Francisco, was born. Two more sons, José and Leandro, followed two and four years later. In New York, Joaquín became the senior partner of the rechristened Rionda, Benjamin and Company. Only the death of Joaquín's wife, Sophie, in childbirth on November 2, 1877, brought a note of sadness. Her son, Manuel Enrique Rionda Benjamin, who would be known as Manolo, survived, and he was sent to be raised in Cuba.

By now, the Polledo uncle had acquired the sugar mill *China* in Matanzas, and the three brothers entertained high hopes for its development. In 1877, through Rionda, Benjamin and Company in New York, the firm of Polledo, Rionda y Cía. in Cuba contracted with a crusty mechanical genius, Franklin Farrel of the Farrel Foundry and Machine Company of Ansonia, Connecticut, for considerable new machinery.

Inventors and manufacturers like Farrel were now striding more importantly through the brokers' offices. The new machines they flourished, with their double and triple crushing, would yield not only more but drier sugar from Cuba's rich cane, which could thus with considerable savings be shipped in jute bags instead of wooden hogsheads.

Meanwhile, slavery was inevitably doomed, the slaves daily less and less pliable, empowered by the opportunities and promises the Ten Years War had brought them. With abolition imminent, the Riondas saw an added necessity for the improved technology. Machinery, however expensive, would become the genie in the bottle that Cuba must now summon forth—improved steam-driven mechanical feeders, double-bottom defecators, multiple-effect evaporators. Cuban cane growers must afford and master them. Here, the three Rionda brothers saw their opportunity.

Franklin Farrel submitted his bids for *China*, and by the end of August 1878 he was ready to ship "the engine mill and machinery." "We want to build them a big mill for the island," he wrote.

Farrel, an impatient, tinkering creature who had gone to work in his father's machine shop when he was fourteen, was beginning to cast revolutionary chilled iron rolls and heavy castings. He was also devoting some attention to "mines, smelters, metal refineries, forges, foundries, machine shops, brass and copper rolling mills, railroads, banks, hotels and sugar plantations." In 1876, he had purchased a worthy silver and copper mine in Butte, Montana, and his scrawled letters giving directives to his scattered henchmen were apt to be dashed off on the engraved stationary of Chicago's Parker House en route to or from this highly profitable venture. "I conclude to save a few cents," he once wrote to explain why he had not telegraphed.[5]

But his machinery was dear, and as orders were placed for it and Manuel began his career in Manhattan, sugar prices began to decline. European beet fields were multiplying, mountains of the muddy vegetables piling up from the Rhine to the Elbe. In 1860, European fields had yielded only 20 percent of the world's sugar. By 1878, their production had reached 1,615,934 tons—46 percent of the world total and three times Cuba's 533,000 tons.

Politics had stimulated the rise. Wherever Europe's beets grew—in

France and Belgium, in the sprawling Austro-Hungarian and Russian domains, in the Hohenzollern Empire—laboratories and field research were supported and bounty systems put in place, as governments paid the price of domestic contentment with agricultural subsidies. In a cruel contrast, all of Spain's imperial glory, as it faded, fed on its colonies. As Cuban sugar sales to the United States rose, Madrid's bureaucrats piled bribes on top of pyramiding charges. The Court sold gaudy new titles to Spain's prospering émigrés and taxed their foodstuffs and imports and exports.[6]

The Riondas ambitiously purchased Farrel's latest new machinery for the *China* plantation. But Polledo soon realized, as prices fell, that his nephews had been too bold. In December 1878, Polledo, Rionda of Havana, more than $400,000 in debt to Rionda, Benjamin of New York, was declared insolvent. Rionda, Benjamin of New York acquired Polledo's share in the *China* as well as dominance in his Matanzas branch in an apparently bitter financial settlement. "*Carrajo*," swore the uncle, "they are incorrigible."[7] But the New York firm was also in trouble, dragged down by Cuban losses. On November 5, 1879, to further burden the firm's future, Spain abolished slavery in Cuba without compensation to either the slaves or their owners.

The brothers hung on, looking to Washington, D.C., where a new tariff bill was pending and where domestic interests influenced tariff legislation. For Cuba, nothing—not machinery, not weather—was more decisive in determining the fate of its crop than was the U.S. tariff.

In 1883, the Morrill Act would cut the tariff on foreign sugar from 2.75 cents per pound to 2.24 cents. But the reduction, applying equally to European beet sugar, gave Cuba no special advantage. Prices continued to rise, and throughout the island ingenios failed. The de la Torrientes lost *Soledad* and *Elena* for debt. Joaquín went to Cuba to try to save the *China*, and Manuel joined him to reinforce the Matanzas commercial firm, leaving an employee, Hugh Kelly, in charge of their New York office.

Kelly, the son of Irish immigrants, had gone to work when he was thirteen. In 1880, at age twenty-two, he now had to cope with the firm's creditors and an "*ugly*" Farrel, who, he reported, "blows hot and cold" despite, as he wrote Manuel, "the big things in the way of broadgauge railroads, cars, vacuum-pans, machinery and electricity," which the brothers were "successfully [carrying] into effect." In 1883, Rionda, Benjamin followed Polledo, Rionda into insolvency. Farrel took over the *China* for the debts and acquired Kelly's talents. The New York Sugar Manufacturing Company, with Farrel, Kelly, and Lewis Cooke as founders, was established to manage it. In May 1886, Farrel and Kelly also bought about 9,000 acres of undeveloped territory near Manzanillo in the shadow of the Sierra Maestra. There, presumably with Farrel's copper mine profits, they erected the central *Teresa* with a "nominal" capital of around $300,000.[8]

The 1880s taught the Rionda brothers bitter lessons. They had been right to seek the latest technology, but they had gambled without sufficient capital for backup when worldwide market forces turned against them. The *Elena* gone, they had no alternative but to fall back upon the plantation *Tuinucú* near Sancti Spiritus, which they had acquired. Despite its good cane land, railroads ran no farther east than Santa Clara, and its inland location was a serious disadvantage. The shallow Tuinucú River had transported the plantation's small yields of sugar since the 1830s but was not adequate for its expansion to profitable scale. Lacking railroad connections, it would have to depend on lumbering oxcarts and impossibly muddy roads. But it was all they had, and Francisco settled in to do his best. His family was growing, and *Tuinucú*'s spreading plantation house could, at least, shelter them. There, the motherless Manolo, Joaquín's son, was raised along with Francisco and Elena's own three sons, who soon were joined by three younger siblings—Elena, in 1882; Salvador, in 1888; and Esperanza, in 1890.

In Noreña, Spain, four Rionda y Polledo sisters had been married, Bibiana to José Braga, to whom she bore a son, Bernardo Braga Rionda, in 1875. Maria had married Alonso Fanjul, giving birth to Higinio Fanjul Rionda in 1877, while Gregoria had married Nicasio Fernández, and Ramóna had wed Pedro Alonso.

Among the villagers of Noreña, José and Bibiana Braga were relatively prosperous. Bernardo later remembered his mother as managing the family's affairs while his father guided a mule train on long missions over the Pyrenees. But Bibiana died when Bernardo was eight or nine, leaving him to a stepmother's carelessness. He milked the cows, helped carry water from the well, and served as an altar boy. When he was ten or eleven—family accounts differ slightly—his uncle Manuel fetched him to America and entrusted him in his turn to the Little Blue School in Farmington, where he, too, would submit to Protestant sermons and the rules of English grammar. If Manuel cheerfully remembered skating parties and gregarious companions, Bernardo's memories, written down at the end of his life, are bitter tales of persecution.

By 1886, having failed to salvage what was left of the Polledo, Rionda operation in Matanzas, Manuel had returned to New York to stay, entering into partnership with Juan M. Ceballos, a naturalized U.S. citizen born in Spain, who was of some prominence in New York sugar brokerage circles. Manuel's fortunes finally began to improve. He was by then in his early thirties, with "flashing dark eyes, framed by black hair and trim Van Dyke beard," a small man, wiry and vital. He boarded at a Mrs. Coventry Wardell's, and it was at her establishment that he became acquainted with Harriet Clarke, "who, to support herself, gave lessons in Portuguese and French, piano and singing." Dublin-born of a family of Irish rebels, the Paris-educated Harriet was the sister of the editor of the *New York Herald*, Joseph Ignatius Constantine Clarke. Gallantly, Manuel was to swear in a 1935 affidavit that he knew neither her year of birth nor when she emigrated to the United States, but his grandnephew is authority for the statement that she was divorced, a professional singer, and thirteen years Manuel's senior. Victor Herbert, the account goes on, became Manuel's rival for her hand.

In New York, on January 17, 1889, his long courtship was crowned with their marriage. If George Braga's account is accurate, she was forty-eight to Manuel's thirty-five at the nuptials. All the evidence seems to indicate their mutual love and devotion throughout their marriage. They were to be childless, but, like her husband, Harriet was part of a large family clan, fiercely loyal to her varied kin. The fortunes of their Spanish and Irish connections were fused in their futures, as nieces and nephews clustered, to be evaluated, educated if found worthy, and absorbed, if still worthy, into the network of Rionda enterprises. As Manuel was to be "the Uncle," so Harriet as his consort was to be "the Aunt."

With the marriage, the 1880s would have ended in triumph had not Manuel's brother Joaquín drowned when, family legend recounts, "having dined and wined too well," he was "attempting to ford the Tuinucú River on horseback." Orphaned thirteen-year-old Manolo was sent to

New York and put, like his cousin Bernardo, in Manuel and Harriet's charge. He was old enough to begin his training to be useful.[9]

The Ceballos office was at 80 Wall Street, a short walk from the bankers' sanctuaries. There Manuel would center the rest of his life. He and his brothers had failed in their early ambitions by not having enough capital to carry them through a depression. Next time, they must have a stronger financial base. Also, he knew, the depression of the 1880s had its causes and could therefore have its remedies. They must be partly political, and there were political stirrings.

Prices had fallen in large part because of German subsidies, which had made beet sugar for export so cheap on the Hamburg market that England no longer bothered with its colonial cane. But in the British Isles, where ships out of the Clyde, out of Bristol and Liverpool, had once connected the Antilles with flourishing English and Scottish refineries, a campaign for an international pact to end European bounties was gaining adherents. Manchester Free Traders, Tory imperialists, West Indian interests, and British refiners were forming the parliamentary alliances that would eventually lead to the Brussels Agreement of 1902, a pact among European governments to end the subsidies of exports.

In the North American market, Cuban sugar had suffered, despite all its geographic advantages of proximity and soil, not so much from cheap European beets as from Spanish political levies, which had kept Cuban production costs uncompetitively high. The machinery Cuba must buy from North America and the salt fish, rice, and oil were heavily taxed by Spain. In addition, the port charges for the Yankee ships that brought them into colonial harbors were burdensome. In 1882, the Spanish government had added an export tax on Cuban sugar. The decline in trade then accelerated as the United States retaliated by imposing an additional 10 percent ad valorem duty on imports from Cuba in Spanish ships.

Far better placed than Manuel to evaluate and influence political affairs within the United States was Edwin Farnsworth Atkins of Boston, whose family firm, Elisha Atkins and Company, had acquired, for debt, the de la Torrientes' *Soledad*. Other North Americans (Farrel and Kelly among them) also owned Cuban plantations, but it was Atkins whom history would appoint as the archetypical North American investor. It was a role he played to perfection, not least in the halls of the U.S. Congress, and which he was to immortalize for himself in his book of reminiscences, *Sixty Years in Cuba*. His political and social connections were of the best and steadfastly utilized.

Four years Manuel's senior, Edwin had begun his Cuban apprenticeship at sixteen, when he had been shipped to Cienfuegos to learn Spanish and the Cuban folkways, as Manuel would be sent to Maine a few years later to master English and the American ways. The Atkins family, of Cape Cod origins, had been doing business with Cuba since the 1820s, ferrying slaves from Africa, then establishing a commission house in 1838. By the 1870s, the family was earning over $100,000 in a season in sugar. In 1875, when Edwin was twenty-five, his father, Elisha, put him in charge of affairs on the island, while Elisha himself shrewdly diversified his investments into Boston wharfs, the Bay State Sugar Refinery, and the Union Pacific Railroad. It was well he did, for the 1880s hit even the Atkins's sugar profits hard.

By 1884, as a presidential election pended, young Atkins was at work in New York and Washington promoting reciprocity with Spain. Cuba, he argued, was close to the East Coast refineries. Its fertile soils were unequaled. Should America grant Cuban sugar free entry in return for Spanish concessions on North American foodstuffs, lumber, and machinery, costs in Cuba would tumble and plantation profits would rise, American machine tool manufacturers would work around the clock filling new orders, and the prices consumers paid for sugar would decline. If the Yankee ships no longer faced Spain's discriminatory port charges but gained equal treatment with vessels out of Barcelona and Cádiz, Maine shipyards would ring with hammers as new ships slid down their ways.

Atkins saw reciprocity as dependent upon a Republican victory in the 1884 presidential election. James G. Blaine, the Republican candidate for the White House, had long been a senator from the state of Maine, with its Cuban connections, and Atkins had briefed him on the heavy burdens U.S. and Spanish tariffs alike imposed on the business owners of both countries, Blaine seeming much interested. Reciprocity was a word Blaine liked. But Blaine was defeated by Democrat Grover Cleveland. Cleveland withdrew a trade treaty with Spain from Senate consideration, and the United States continued levying duties on Cuban sugar while

Spain went on penalizing U.S. goods and shipping. Yankee business with the West Indies declined, and Cuban planters struggled to survive.[10]

By the 1880s, with falling prices, the slaves freed, and the high costs of improved machinery forcing them into debt, the Spanish and Cuban planters were beginning to evolve a new form of production, the *colono* system. In the majority of cases, this was a sharecropper arrangement whereby men with more land than money to pay wages turned over small plots to their former field hands and where working families kept starvation at bay by toiling for a share of the yield. But there was also evolving another, upper layer of *colonías* whereby the owners of ingenios divided the tasks of future development. In his own account, written in 1925, Manuel credited its invention to the owner of a Matanzas estate, Francisco Feliciano Ibáñez. Ibáñez's plan, Manuel wrote, "was for the smaller, outlying plantations to shut their factories and send the cane . . . to the larger, more central ones. These logically soon became known as *centrales*." The result, he continued, was a reduction in the number of plantations "from 1,000 to some 200."

The social results of so great a change were complex. Because of it, the owners of the 800 former ingenios who now engaged only in the agricultural side of the business were able to remain on their estates. That they were spared the problems of manufacture was, in many ways, a relief. Nevertheless, it seemed a step down the social scale, and Rionda, half a century later, remembered and sympathized. They were, after all, "men of local importance and standing whose position they felt would suffer once . . . their holdings were classified as colonías [sugar cane farms] instead of ingenios."

Ibáñez then hit on the idea that the mill owners should pay the colonos in kind, a proportion of the sugar produced by each ton of cane delivered. This, Manuel wrote, was "more attractive to the planter . . . because it permitted him to remain a factor in the community as a holder of sugar, he thereby enjoyed a greater prestige."[11] If the new division of production, forced by necessity, enhanced the standing of the 200 ingenio owners who went on to mechanize, it also permitted in western Cuba the continued existence of a group of men not too far below them with their own pride and ability. The centrale system took hold, their owners sharing with their colonos according to agreed-upon formulas, a sensible allocation of resources for both manufacturers and agriculturalists if the ratios were fair and prices high enough for there to be enough to go around.

In due time, the 1888 elections brought Benjamin Harrison and the Republicans back into the White House, and in October 1890 a far more promising decade for the Cuban hacendados opened when the McKinley Tariff passed a Republican Congress. Although in other respects a high tariff measure drafted to protect the manufacturing interests, it granted raw sugar (the refiners' raw material) free entry into the nation. This, the cynics muttered, had been a reward for the Sugar Trust's lavish campaign contributions. Originally, free entry for foreign sugar had been unconditional. But Blaine, who had become Harrison's secretary of state, recognized this as a gratuitous surrender of bargaining chips and saw it remedied by a provision that allowed the president to reimpose duties on the raw materials of any country unjustly taxing U.S. imports. Blaine was thus able to negotiate with Spain a reciprocity agreement that dropped prices drastically for North American imports into Cuba, so that the benefits of the McKinley Tariff went far beyond free entry. Reciprocity was not free trade—rather, a shrewd Yankee swap—but with it all of Spain's impediments to U.S. products came crashing down. "The cheapness of things," a leading Cuban planter was to testify, was "almost a revolution." Edwin F. Atkins claimed credit. "I had been working," he wrote, "to put through some such law for some years and the reciprocity features were framed on almost the exact lines that I had outlined to Blaine a few years before." Again, complacently reminiscing about his tutelage of the senator in his father's office: "Little I thought then that I should be instrumental in changing the aspect of this world commerce."

There was, to be sure, a cloud on the horizon for Cuba since the McKinley Tariff, by granting a two-cents-a-pound bounty on sugar produced within the United States, had bowed to the Louisiana cane growers and to those few domestic interests beginning to explore local sugar-beet possibilities. But the cloud seemed small. Between 1890 and 1894, Cuban sugar production rose from 632,000 to 1,054,000 long tons, feeding the refineries the Sugar Trust had meanwhile consolidated.[12] Every logic of geography and climate turned Cuba, with its sugar, to the United States and fated them to be partners. Not only did the spreading republic need the cane fields' offerings, it was needed in return, as had been obvious since the halcyon days of Moses Taylor's National City

Bank, for the financial resources without which no wheel could turn, no ship could raise anchor. Supply and demand rose in tandem. Demand's name was Henry O. Havemeyer.

A short, portly man with a walrus mustache and a taste for antique Japanese tea jars, Henry O. Havemeyer was the most famous of a family of refiners. A descendant of two sugar boiler brothers who had emigrated from Schaumburg-Lippe at the end of the eighteenth century, he had inherited a controlling share in the Havemeyer and Elder refinery on the Brooklyn docks, a genius for business, and a dislike of waste. Just as the mechanization of milling was revolutionizing the cane fields, simultaneously the rapid pace of technological improvement was driving the refining industry. Eager to seize the economies it made possible, he rode its wave into the future.

In 1887, just as Manuel Rionda was beginning again in New York, Havemeyer confronted refining's prospects. Overcapacity had bred cutthroat, wasteful competition, and he talked the majority of America's refiners into joining a pooling arrangement famous then and thereafter as the Sugar Trust. A small board of trustees would manage everyone's rationalized holdings, weeding out duplication and instituting economies of scale, new business methods, and imaginative corporate structures.

Hunt's little Portland refinery joined in, as did Atkins's Bay State Sugar Refinery in Boston. Within a year, twenty competing plants, through dismantling and consolidation, became ten, their former owners rewarded by generous bundles of stock that would pay handsome dividends.[13]

Since the price of sugar in the grocery stores simultaneously dropped (facilitating increased consumption) the Sugar Trust was also arguably helpful to consumers. "Reduction in price to consumers," Mrs. Louisine Havemeyer was to point out, "was the blessing of trusts." To the merchants, however, it meant that a single buyer now bought at least three-quarters of the raw sugar. Rionda and his competing brokers (for the supply end of the equation was as scattered as the demand end was centralized) must wait on Havemeyer. They could only undercut each other, and the savings consumers enjoyed arguably came from the lower prices that Havemeyer was thus able to pay for the Trust's raw material. In 1880, granulated sugar scooped out of the grocer's barrels sold for 9.6 cents per pound. In 1894, it sold for 4.1 cents, down 5.5 cents. Meanwhile, the price the trust paid for its raw sugar dropped from 8.2 cents to 3.2 cents per pound.[14]

In 1890, the year the McKinley Tariff gave sugar free entry, Henry O. Havemeyer himself, his wife, and Mr. and Mrs. Charles Senff went to Cuba and inspected the growing cane, Charles Senff being a Havemeyer relative important in the trust. They visited Mr. and Mrs. Atkins at *Soledad*, enjoying its shaded verandas, and bought land on the island's southern coast. There they began a central, the *Trinidad*, incorporating it in 1892 in New Jersey where, in the meantime, their trust arrangement had metamorphosed into the American Sugar Refining Company. Havemeyer and Senff each furnished 40 percent of *Trinidad*'s $600,000 capital and Atkins the balance. Havemeyer scarcely needed to be concerned about his source of raw material, for Cuba's many producers had no alternative but to compete for his patronage. Rionda, reminiscing forty-one years later, conjectured *Trinidad* was acquired because the women had "fallen in love with the scenery." But it was, with its smokestacks rising into the Santa Clara sky, like Farrel's *Teresa* six years earlier, a trial balloon, although not a particularly significant one since Havemeyer testified in 1902 that it had a capacity of only some 8,000 tons annually at a time when the American Sugar Refining Company was consuming 2.4 million tons a year.[15]

A year before *Trinidad*'s papers were filed in New Jersey, Manuel Rionda had joined with Ceballos and Juan M. Clark of Havana to incorporate the Central Tuinucú Sugar Cane Manufacturing Company, with a capital of $150,000. In 1895, its crop was about 27,000 (325-pound) bags. Thirty-seven years later, Leland Jencks, in his study of U.S. investment, would write it was incorporated by a "group of New York sugar merchants, chiefly members of the Rionda family." This gives the incorrect impression that indigenous U.S. entrepreneurship deserves the credit (or blame). Rather, the gamble was taken by Spanish-born entrepreneurs, although Ceballos had by then become a U.S. citizen. Clark, of Hispanic origin, was the Havana representative of the Krajewski-Pesant Company, Pittsburgh-based manufacturers of heavy machinery.[16]

The process of incorporation, as much as vacuum pans, centrifugals, and electricity, was one of the new tools of the rising industrialism, a legal innovation that offered improved ways to obtain capital. Few mill owners in Cuba, as they built up their centrals, had sufficient private funds to do a proper job of it. Loans would have to be repaid in full, at high interest rates. Selling shares in a company, on the other hand, would cost only future dividends paid out of future profits, and as long as a hacendado held a majority of the shares, he could keep control in his own hands. Francisco began to try—although with little immediate success—to convince his planter friends to raise funds through stock companies. To incorporate in the United States might also ensure some degree of U.S. protection. A number of Cubans were believing it to be practical, just then, to acquire citizenship in the northern republic. This would be a similar, pragmatic tactic.

With the Reciprocity Treaty, Cuban sugar production mounted swiftly—820,000 tons in 1891; 977,000 tons in 1892; 1,054,000 tons in 1894—while U.S. exports to Cuba rose in value from $11 million to $17 million to $23 million in these same years. U.S. manufacturers of machinery entered many profitable orders—Hugh Kelly alone sold $600,000 worth in 1894. Improved techniques were shining ever brighter, and in 1889 a Calumet mill in Louisiana reached an unprecedented yield of 200 pounds of sugar per ton with a milling plant of five rolls. Two years later, the Fulton Iron Works's first nine-roll mill, driven by common gearing and a single engine, yielded 800 tons in twenty-four hours.

Yet the golden time proved short. In 1894, the Democrats retook the U.S. Congress, and Grover Cleveland was reelected president. Their Wilson-Gorman Tariff in 1894 reimposed a duty of 40 percent ad valorem on Cuban sugar, and the Reciprocity Treaty with Spain was consequently abrogated. "[M]any plans were dropped," Louis Ponvert, master of the central *Hormiguero*, later commented, "and everything came to a standstill."

Worse than a standstill, it was a disaster. "Spain retaliated," wrote Atkins, "by returning to her old discrimination against United States imports into Cuba; the cost of living in Cuba advanced and the price of sugar dropped, credit became impaired, the estates upon finishing their crop in 1895 discharged their hands, and unrest flamed into insurrection." On February 24, 1895, the poet-journalist José Martí, Major-General Máximo Gómez, and General Antonio Maceo launched the revolution for Cuban independence. Martí, who was a year Rionda's senior, had been in exile in New York, and the shabby room from which he sent out his dispatches was not too far from Rionda's offices. But even if they passed each other on the streets, their interests were different. Rionda might, if he heard it, have nodded at Martí's phrase that "the people who buy command; the people who sell obey," but investors in flammable crops expected only trouble from fiery manifestos.[17]

This time the rebel victories were extensive. In less than a year, the insurgent campaign had swept through the major plantation areas. In 1896, as cane fields burned, production dropped to only 225,000 tons —a quarter of the previous year's output. *Tuinucú* was threatened. The Ceballos firm faced ruin.

Yet luck smiled on Manuel amid the general chaos, and 1896 marked the defining chance of his life when he was asked to join Czarnikow, MacDougall and Company, the newly established New York branch of the world's greatest sugar brokers, C. Czarnikow Ltd. of Mincing Lane, London. The sugar business has always been international, and this has never been more clearly illustrated than by the Czarnikow firm. Its founder, Julius Caesar Czarnikow, was the Polish-Jewish son of the court agent to the prince of Schwartzenburg, a small principality not far from Magdeburg. Preferring "the wide open spaces of commercial life rather than the oppressive forests of his youth," Julius had, at eighteen, left the ghetto confines of his birth and moved to London in 1854. No pushcart peddler but well connected, he shortly became a sworn colonial broker, married the daughter of a nonconformist Scottish minister in Clapham Common, and shortly "bought a carriage and pair, laid down a cellar and kept a good table." A little later, there was a house on Eaton Square and a country estate in Surrey, where he collected exotic animals. Six keepers from the Zoological Gardens at Regent's Park would be among the mourners at his funeral.

Czarnikow built on strong Anglo-German banking connections—notably with the private London banking firm of J. Henry Schroeder, and his firm had its office on Mincing Lane. Just as Wall Street geographically and symbolically linked investors to the New York harbor and thence to world markets, so in the late Victorian harvest time of empire, Mincing Lane was in the shadow both of the Tower of London and the Thames docks.

He had begun his trading with the Teutonic beets. It is even "not improbable," relates his firm's official history, that he was the intermediary in the very first sale of beet sugar to London refiners in the early 1860s. "The extra-ordinary impetus of the beet sugar industry during Caesar Czarnikow's lifetime," the history continues, "undoubtedly helped him to sustain and enlarge what has since become a world-wide enterprise." But Czarnikow, not content to be bound to central Europe, wove connections with Java and Egypt, Australia and Mauritius. By 1891, he had two partners, Charles Lagemann, a melancholy, meticulous North German, and Julius Charles Ganzoni, son of a Swiss banker.[18]

In 1891, when U.S. tariffs ceased to impede the entry of Cuban sugar and promised great developments, Czarnikow visited New York. He called on Henry Havemeyer, with whom he considered himself on friendly terms, and launched a New York office, bringing over a Glasgow man, George MacDougall, to head it. Observing the crisis from London's heights, the turn in U.S. sugar policy after the 1894 election and the Cuban revolt did not discourage him. He also realized that momentous changes in German bounties on exports from the European continent were in the offing. The burning of Cuban cane fields made those hundred or so hacendados still able to harvest their crops all the more worth cultivating. Czarnikow needed a dynamic, intelligent representative from the island itself. He found Manuel.

For not only Manuel but also Francisco, Czarnikow's offer came at a very welcome time, as *Tuinucú* was being abandoned to the marauding armies. Francisco himself, the family account goes, had been seized first by guerrilla forces, then by Spanish troops, threatened with execution by each side. He had then rounded up Elena; their six children; Elena's personal maid, Concha la Negra; his sister, Aunt Isidora; and her maid, Teofilia. With only what valuables they could carry, they had ridden "under Spanish military escort" to the port of Tunas de Zaza and had hired a fishing boat to bear them to safety in the United States. Arriving eventually at New York (where Manuel and Harriet had recently acquired a brownstone on West 93rd Street), the bedraggled refugees took refuge in a house Manuel rented for them just across the Hudson River at Spuyten Duyvil. The three oldest boys were sent camping in Maine with their cousins Manolo and Higinio and Harriet's nephew Will Clarke, living on canned beans and fish. Francisco's ambitions had been checked, while for Manuel, circumstances in the Ceballos firm were gloomy. He was sorry, Manuel wrote in a letter, to leave Ceballos, who had always been a good friend, but "the Cuban War killed Cuban business and as our co-partnership expired on Jan'y 1 and Czarnikow made me very satisfactory terms," he seized his chance.[19]

Czarnikow's invitation changed his life, he wrote years later, recalling "the trip I made to London in 1895 when our dear Senior told me not to renew my contract with Ceballos at its termination (December 1896) without first communicating with him. That was the turn of my fortune—not only mine but that of the many depending upon me." "No one of you," he wrote Czarnikow's London partners, "owes Mr. Czarnikow as much as I do. No one of you had recognized this as much as I have. When I was at J. M. Ceballos & Co. I was worked to death and had nothing when I left."

He fell to work in his new position, soon enlisting his older brother's help. Czarnikow, MacDougall, propelled by Francisco's and Manuel's connections, quickly established a base in what was left of Cuba's sugar trade. As the 1897 zafra ended (what there was of it, since production had dropped still further to 212,000 tons), Manuel could point out to London that Czarnikow, MacDougall had handled one-tenth of all Cuban shipments and could well expect to handle a full quarter the following year. Caesar Czarnikow kept a close eye on Manuel as well as a tight grip on the purse strings, scrawling frequent letters, often outspokenly critical, but Rionda greatly respected "our beloved Senior" and wrote him gratefully, expressing his satisfaction with his position.[20]

The Republicans were by then once more in power, with McKinley president. At the end of July 1897, the Republicans' Dingley Tariff replaced an ad valorem rate of 40 percent on sugar imports with a specific tax (1.685 cents per pound) and placed countervailing U.S. duties equal to any European bounties on European beet-sugar imports. Less fortunately for Cuba, they also befriended domestic beets. Overabundance had sent wheat and corn prices tumbling for Midwest farmers, conjuring up Populist nightmares. The U.S. Department of Agriculture had therefore begun to devote itself to propagating the root vegetable as an alternate crop. But in 1896, U.S. domestic production of beet sugar was only 70,128,000 pounds, one-eighth domestic cane's 582,466,000 and only 1.5 percent of total consumption. In 1899, it reached only 77,930,000 pounds.

In the United States, the drums of war rolled, and accounts of Spanish atrocities swept the United States toward intervention in Cuba, while the Rionda family experienced a strange mix of loyalties. Bernardo later recounted that when the United States entered the war, he wanted to go to Cuba to fight for Spain, while his cousin Cosme de la Torriente, his aunt Elena's godchild, heroically joined the rebels in the field, and Francisco and Elena's daughters, "Espie aged eight, and Elena, fourteen, both earned local fame . . . by joining with the other children of the neighborhood in stoning their own house . . . crying 'Remember the Maine, to hell with Spain.'"[21]

Manuel, with so many dependent upon him and well aware of the importance of the U.S. market, kept his feelings to himself and attended to business, predicting in September 1896 the annexation of Cuba to the United States within six months. "Reciprocity," he wrote, "I think is the only remedy for the disease and should be promptly applied, it will settle all difficulties." Yet he went on: "For the Lord's sake, let us have peace, let each man yield a little on his part and stop so much misery in the country." "There is hardly sufficient cause for war," he wrote London, "but the press in both countries have been inflaming the feelings." When the *Maine* exploded in Havana harbor, he wrote a former schoolmate that it was "the most horrible thing that I have heard since 1893 and it has affected me immensely. I sincerely hope it was an accident." If war came, he asked, where would it end?

In March, in a business letter to the same friend and after a neatly typed paragraph about the business detail regarding the "Fancy Ponce Molasses business with Morales," he added three and a half pages in his own hand. "Are we going to fight? What is most surprising to me is that no one asks—if we put Spain out of Cuba is Cuba going to go on peacefully? Are we not going to have to go down there and put another or many other civil wars down? Are we not really running a risk of having, once Spain is out of Cuba, to take Cuba in? Are we willing to have Cuba in?"

The "we" is noteworthy, since Rionda would not renounce his Spanish citizenship for another forty years. An alien whose personal fortunes depended on doing business with the United States, a merchant at the crossroads, he now and for the rest of his long life faced the ambiguities of divided allegiance. "*Cuba cannot be independent,*" he continued, underlining. "Her inhabitants are not advanced enough." But then he shifted pronouns. "Why don't your statesmen look the matter over fairly and on all sides—Let them look at the gains from war and the losses it may bring." It would be better, he argued, to bring any number of starving Cubans to New York City and keep them in the Waldorf-Astoria than to go to war. "War we know where and when it starts but don't know how or where it will end."

He doubted there were as many idle fieldworkers as the papers said or that they needed to starve since some estates were still grinding and there should be work for those who wanted to work. The Americans had been so carried away by their sympathies "that they lose their heads and *their politicians* are driving them into a war that can bring no honor for Spain." If the Americans wanted to crusade, why didn't they "go to England and say free Ireland!! Why try to lick the small boy and not the big one!!"

Spain, he wrote, "merely wants to have the honor of having some land left her in the continent she discovered. Why not let her. Let autonomy be so absolute as to be really independence, but let Spain have control over Cuba as England over Canada." He concluded: "I gain by independence personally but I dread the consequences to this country. Goodbye. Yours Manuel." Then he added another line: "I did not mean to write so much stuff."[22]

But his business affairs went well. "It seems a pity," he wrote a Cuban associate nine days later, "that now we are getting on so nicely with ASR & Co [American Sugar Refining] . . . that this war business should interfere." But war, of course, it would be. On April 11, President McKinley submitted his message to Congress, requesting authority to intervene in Cuba. Manuel became an enemy alien, although the fact does not seem to have interfered with his business life.

The Americans, Manuel now wrote in Spanish on April 20, were "causando un atropello á España" (trampling Spain). Annexation or a Cuban republic would result. If America should "nos van sin razón ninguna [use force against us without any reason], then I say let them not abandon us." He had changed pronouns as well as language. This time he was writing to Ramón Pelayo, a fellow Spaniard, who had acquired the central *Rosario* in Havana Province. Another letter on the same day to the merchant Julio Rabel in Havana was businesslike in the extreme, concerned with bills of lading and quotations. And that April 20 he also wrote Francisco (who, having been engaged to look after Czarnikow's affairs there, had returned to Cuba) that he had had a long talk with a Mr. Lamb. "He thinks land in Cuba good property and wishes he had a million acres." It was time to place their bets. Francisco, accordingly, by early May acquired 50,000 acres on the south coast of Cuba, near Guayabal, some 200 miles east of the Riondas' *Tuinucú*.

It was uncleared territory. Czarnikow, when approached to take a quarter share, was dubious. It "might suit me," he wrote on May 21, 1898, even as troops took up position, "but before taking a decision I want to know whether this land is real sugar land." In general, he was optimistic: "You must be on the alert, as I foresee that Cuba once pacified will be the great field for our action." But on this specific venture, he questioned details. "You likewise remark that there is a wharf capable of taking steamers drawing 16 feet of water, but this is scarcely sufficient depth for 3 to 4,000 ton boats." Ten days later, he was more distant. "I note what your brother thinks about the land in Cuba, and am not surprised at his way in looking at the matter.... Scores of similar proposals are put before me at present from Egypt, the Sudan and Mexico, etc., but we cannot be in every corner of the earth."[23]

Francisco was fifty-four now, and his health was of concern to the family, but he eagerly pursued the advantages a U.S. victory promised. On July 8, 1898 (four days after Theodore Roosevelt's Rough Riders had charged up San Juan Hill and more than a month before the formal end of hostilities), he wrote a long letter to New York. He began by apologizing for his excessive cable expenses. Neither the U.S. nor the Spanish governments permitted cables in code, and there was sharp competition for what sugar Cuba still had in its ports. The rival brokers—Zaldo, Francke, and their "subagents"—were putting up as many obstacles as possible to keep Czarnikow, MacDougall from getting "any kind of footing." But MacDougall's prestige, he wrote, was very high, and Francisco believed he himself deserved credit for this. After the war, he commented, there would be "a large field for business and money making." Within two years, Cuba could be producing a million tons a year, and in three years it could supply the entire United States at from 1.25 cents to 2 cents a pound. He would, he projected, turn over *Tuinucú* and use his experience on "making sugar estates into stock companies and obtaining control of the sale of sugars therefore." With a banking house in Havana and given his "close relationships" with other merchants—T. Bea and Company in Matanzas, Rabel and Company in Cárdenas, Nicolás Castaño in Cienfuegos, Larrondo and Company in Sagua, Zosaya and Company in Caibarien, and another house in Manzanilla, plus Manuel's "New York and London houses"—he was sure "a mighty combination would be made." There would be large profits in the first two years, although he feared that in due time the "American manner of forming Syndicates and Trusts, issuing Bonds and Watered Stocks" might bring inflation.

His friend Castaño, he continued, was now the richest merchant in Cuba. If a syndicate could be formed to take $150,000 in bonds in the sugar estates in which he was interested, they could control the sale of 60,000 tons. The Spaniards, Francisco wrote, had been slow in accepting stock companies for their estates, but now they would no longer hesitate. Should Cuba be annexed, Francisco noted, Havemeyer, Howell, McCahan, and other refiners would buy up the centrals, railroads, and so forth. "We should anticipate this so we can sell to them when the time comes." He asked Manuel how New York and how Czarnikow in London would feel "so that when the time comes, we may be prepared to jump in and lose no time."

"Time." The word echoes. Hostilities ended officially by August 12, with U.S. forces taking charge in Cuba, Puerto Rico, and the Philippines. Frock-coated statesmen bargained at a Paris peace conference while the indebted owners of Cuba's battered ingenios took inventory. In London, Caesar Czarnikow still delayed and at the end of August wrote that he was "too busy" to discuss Francisco's plans, "wishing to defer until Mr. Lagemann returns." He apparently was still thinking it over when Francisco died on November 13, 1898.

Posthumously, Francisco was rewarded by London. "When my dear brother died," Manuel reminisced in 1906, "Mr. Czarnikow agreed to give his heirs a certain sum as commission in the business my brother had brought here. . . . When the boys became men, the same friend pushed them into the house of C MacD & Co."[24]

With both his brothers dead (an illegitimate son of his father by the cook seemed to hardly count, although Silvestre Rionda would be provided for with a colonía at *Tuinucú*), Manuel had now become the family

Fig. 2. From left, Manolo Rionda Benjamin, Cosme de la Torriente y Peraza, José Rionda y de la Torriente, Leandro Rionda y de la Torriente, and Bernardo Braga Rionda

patriarch, the classic uncle of Spanish Cuban custom. He was devoted to his sisters, but none of his brothers-in-law were involved as equals. He was, however, well supplied with young kinsmen. The eldest of Francisco's four sons would be confined for life to a mental institution, and Salvador, eleven, was not yet of useful maturity. But José, called Pepe, was twenty-one, Leandro was nineteen. Joaquín's son, Manolo, was twenty-two. All three of them were enrolled in Columbia College, Manolo about to receive a degree in electrical engineering. Among the sisters' children, Bernardo Braga Rionda was twenty-four, and Higinio Fanjul Rionda was twenty-two.[25] Manuel Rionda clearly was responsible for the survival and apprenticeship of a clan, and if the young men turned out to be industrious and obedient, he would have lieutenants he could count upon.

2

Head of the Mouse

Spurred by free entry into the United States, sugar imports from Cuba had more than doubled between 1890 and 1894. But when, with the hostilities of the Spanish-Cuban-American War, they had dropped by 75 percent, there nonetheless had been no shortage on the grocery shelves.

No single source had substituted. In 1897, imports from Germany and the Austro-Hungarian Empire had more than tripled from 1896's 218,609 to 716,495 long tons. The following year, when these Germanic sources fell to only 62,307 long tons, the British West Indies, British Guyana, and the Philippines filled in. Java's share rose steadily, from 49,968 long tons in 1890 to 274,504 in 1898. It would almost double (to 518,841) in 1900. Hawaii had accounted for less than 8 percent of U.S. imports in 1895. By 1898, it accounted for over 19 percent.[1]

Manuel himself sold much of the Dutch share—Czarnikow had fixed his attention on its faraway archipelago of Java. Like Cuba, Java had suffered in the 1880s from falling prices, the obsolescence of its machinery, and the cane disease *sereh*. In 1893, only 20 of its 190 sugar factories had been really profitable. But Javanese industry was now coping, reinforced by Dutch capital and agricultural science, changes in the tax system, and the importation of Chinese laborers. Sell Java sugar, Czarnikow instructed. Manuel did, and he was successful, too, with quantities from points as diverse as Peru and Egypt.[2]

But while the exotic supplies turned profits, the ready availability of sugar was disturbing. The Cuban mills must get back into production before rival producers had too firm a hold on the market. In addition,

Rionda must see if *Tuinucú* had survived and decide the fate of the wilderness Francisco had purchased. Taking Harriet with him, and with two nephews to follow, Manuel went to the island as the 1899 zafra got under way.

Armies had trampled Cuba, burned ingenios, slaughtered oxen, and starved workers. If, for the United States, it had been a short little war, for Cuba, it had been a long and great one, and the prevailing scene was one of desolation. Fields were clogged with weeds, machines with rust. The island would be able to ship to the United States in 1899 scarcely a quarter of what it had supplied in 1894.

Still, of the 574 mills there that had ground in 1894, 91 remained in operation, although only 29 could produce as many as 20,000 bags. The best-connected hacendados—the princes of Terry and the marquis de Apezteguía—had been able to defend their fields and had profited from rising prices. Other proprietors had survived: Díaz and Mendoza, Baró and Zulueta, Ponvert and Arenal, names that echoed through the Cuban sugar world. Rionda renewed acquaintances, cultivated new ties, and talked with ambitious men who appreciated that bureaucratic Spain would no longer hold them back and that their principal market was only ninety miles away. Wrecked structures could now be replaced by the most up to the minute factories and machinery. Only they would need money to bring it off.

Some funds would come from the Spanish merchants who retained their strongboxes and showed little inclination to return to their homeland but every indication of remaining where future profits promised. Manuel was on fraternal terms with many of these men. Chief of them all was Nicolás Castaño. Born in Vizcaya, Spain, in 1836, he had come to the island as a boy of thirteen. Starting out as a clerk, he scrimped and saved and made shrewd loans. By now he held mortgages on many of the greatest Cuban haciendas—the marquis of Apezteguía's *Constancia*, Ponvert's *Hormiguero*, the Fowlers' *Dos Hermanos* and their *Parque Alto*, *San Agustín*, and *Lequeito*. Castaño, who had been Francisco Rionda's old friend, now was Manuel's.

But there was a whole island of mills to rebuild. If Rionda could arrange financing promptly from C. Czarnikow Ltd. and from the Schroeders Bank in London, Cubans would have a future and he a grateful clientele. As for New York, he lacked contacts with investors and suspected (rightly) that the refiners, although they were anxious for cheap Cuban sugar, would play their own private game. In the United States, investment was held back by uncertainty about U.S. policy. If Cuba was to be annexed, its sugar would enter duty free, and there would be protection for investments. But if it were not annexed, how much should Wall Street gamble on the future of a society where so many dark-skinned men had learned to use weapons?

In the Wall Street offices of Rionda's former partner, Ceballos, Robert Percival Porter, a newspaper man whom President McKinley had appointed a special commissioner, had already begun an examination of America's stake in Cuba. The meeting had been attended by Ceballos, Hugh Kelly, W. D. Munson of the Munson Steamship Lines, and a number of commission merchants eager to sell their pork, coal, lumber, rails, machinery, and other goods, and especially by Edwin Atkins, who announced with Bostonian loftiness that he considered himself "called upon to speak for the sugar interests."

"Not very much can be done to put Cuba into a state of production," Atkins testified, "until the great question of annexation is taken up." It was a matter of protecting property. It was also the tariff. Cuban sugar, he warned, if it paid full foreign duty, might not long compete with the free sugar from already annexed Puerto Rico and from the Hawaiian archipelago he still called "the Sandwich Islands." Like Rionda, he had been impressed with the shiploads of sugar that had been unloading from other ports. "We [producers in Cuba] could get along," he granted, "until [they] increased their production . . . but matters would be getting worse and worse every year." "Until" not "if." And the Philippine Islands, when subdued, would be, he added, "almost unlimited in capacity."

Rionda did not testify in person but sent a letter stressing the need for economic aid. Cubans, he wrote, had not been "so dissatisfied with the political part of the Spanish Government as with the very low prices for sugar which arose from the fact that Spain discriminated against Cuban products when imported into Spain." If Cuban sugar and tobacco could be given favored treatment in the American market, he predicted "all other questions will settle themselves."[3]

Rionda did not express certain other private doubts. If the United States abandoned Cuba, he wrote Juan Clark, he would not be "inclined to make advances on cane that is in danger of being burned at any time."

It was a fear the marquis of Apezteguía expressed more openly. The United States, he wrote Porter, had a moral obligation to keep forces in Cuba, for the insurrection had "caused a great fraternity." The "distinction of race" that had reigned before 1895 no longer existed, and "the insurgent energy" must be checked by a strong American military force.

Ramón Pelayo and Juan Clark were among Manuel's closest associates now and were foremost among Cuban entrepreneurs. Pelayo, whose mother had been a sister of Francisco's father-in-law, was Manuel's attorney in Havana. He was also an important hacendado, owning a model sugar plantation, *Rosario*, by far the largest in Havana Province, which, in accord with Francisco Rionda's strategy, he had incorporated in 1896. A "notable exception" to the "general devastation," with "its great sugar mill, and tenant village adjoining . . . in the midst of thousands of acres of waving cane," it had come through the hostilities, and Pelayo sold its sugar through Czarnikow, MacDougall. Juan Clark, who represented the Krajewski-Pesant machine works from offices at 15 O'Reilly Street in Havana's crowded commercial blocks near the harbor, had recently hired Harriet Rionda's nephew Alfred J. Thompson to head a new electrical department. He scouted out investment opportunities for Manuel. "[I]f you can arrange with London," he wrote, "to give money . . . I can get you five or six of the best [planters] to be had."[4]

Manuel had come to Cuba that December to seize just such opportunities, but he also had family responsibilities. In late January 1899, the Rionda family legend recounts, Francisco's coffin was carried onto a chartered freighter in New York harbor. The vessel was loaded, it was related, with desperately needed "provisions, medicine, farm implements, pigs and chickens," with nephews Bernardo and Pepe in charge of corpse and cargo. It was Bernardo's first look at the island, while Pepe was returning home. Landing on the Havana docks, they watched U.S. officers supervising dark stevedores, barking orders, and blowing their trumpets beneath the Stars and Stripes. Only when they passed beyond the port into the countryside did they grasp the devastation: burned shells of what had been ingenios, weeds, whitened carcasses of cattle, crumbling machinery, an emaciated peasantry. Joining Manuel and Harriet, they watched Francisco's body duly committed to the family tomb in Matanzas and the poultry sold "at a profit." Then they went on to find out what was left of *Tuinucú*. Although its living quarters and ingenio were still standing, they were "ransacked and rank with weeds and vines," and not a chair or a bed survived, only a stray carpenter sleeping in a hammock. Still, the structure remained, and Manuel decided it could be put back together and the widowed Elena and her six children return to live in it. It would be home base once more and command post for Manuel's operations. "My beloved 'cielo' [heaven]," Manuel would refer to it in his old age, paying tribute to Harriet's bravery then among the rubble, "that my compañera and I saved." He suggested to Bernardo, as the oldest nephew, that he become its administrator, but Bernardo refused. Manuel accepted his refusal, deciding Bernardo was correct in pointing out that he knew nothing of the technical complexities of factories but only the merchant world. Manuel's sister Ramona's husband, Pedro Alonso, would therefore take charge while Francisco's sons were learning how to manage their inheritance. In a year, the spring of 1900, there would be 3,400 bags of sugar to sell.

Tuinucú's inland location, however, dooming it to high transport costs, made its improvement difficult. More promising were the thousands of isolated acres that Francisco had purchased near the primitive little port of Guayabal, on the edge of wilderness. Leaving Harriet behind, Manuel and Bernardo shipped there from Tunas on a leaky sailing boat. They passed the night on deck with "a cargo of canned goods and live pigs . . . a beautiful star lit night but a rough sea." The next day, hiring horses, they rode over the wild tract, and Manuel decided to build a central. In the saga of the family fortune, this is the key decision, the seizing of fate by the forelock, a gambler's move, for Czarnikow had already refused to help, and, except through the London firm, the Riondas had no viable contacts with rich men. A potentially excellent harbor (although it would have to be dredged) did not compensate for its location at the end of nowhere. And where was the labor to come from? There was only a scanty local population.

Manuel then decided that since Bernardo did not want to administer *Tuinucú*, he should be put in charge of an export department, which Czarnikow, MacDougall could profitably establish since all the local plantations needed almost everything. The nephew was accordingly dispatched on horseback through Santa Clara, Matanzas, and Havana, "visiting the sugar mills and stores, making friends and getting orders." The clan's future course settling into place, Manuel returned to Havana to resume building his network of contacts. He would carry out the strategy Francisco had outlined before his death, "obtaining control of the sale of sugars" of the expanded enterprises he would convince the hacendados to form into joint stock companies.[5]

In 1898, Cuba had been able to export only 305,543 long tons of sugar to the United States. In 1899, it exported only 335,668. Yet somehow, despite all the sacrifices that had transpired in the war, all the cane cutters starved and scattered, Cuba's ingenios began to lurch back into production. What money came in, their owners plowed back as down payments on new equipment. "There is nothing in history," Rionda claimed later, "relative to the rehabilitation of a country that compares with this, at least not to my knowledge. All was done without any outside assistance for Cuba had no outside financial support." Years later, he wrote with pride that Czarnikow, MacDougall had been "the first foreign house to enter the Cuban field . . . advancing money to the many needy Cuban planters . . . when no one else would." Thus he gave credit to those who spoke his native tongue and in writing "no outside financial support" counted himself (and for that matter, apparently his English associates as well) among the Cubans. "Those Americans," he went on, "who went there during the American occupation entered the Eastern section: their capital did not go toward rebuilding the old section." It was these local men with whom Rionda worked who somehow bagged their harvest even as the politics of the time dragged along their torturous way.

On March 1, 1899, Rionda took the ferry from Manhattan to Jersey City, New Jersey, and incorporated the Francisco Sugar Company. Three men were present—Manuel; Harriet's brother, the journalist Joseph I. C. Clarke; and Trenton attorney G. H. Atkinson. Atkinson was a family friend, and the Riondas spent some summer vacations at Merriwold, an inn run by the Atkinson family. Bernardo, in love with the daughter, Maude, had written "I love you with all my heart" in Spanish on her fan. But launching *Francisco* proved hard. London once more, for the final time, refused to participate, and Manuel wrote John Craig, a Philadelphia sugar broker with connections to Philadelphia's McCahan Refinery, in mid-April: "About capitalizing the company, that is one of the points at which I am entirely at sea. I don't know how to do it." He could only struggle to reassure possible investors. "Anyone who has followed developments in Cuba can realize that the Americans are determined to maintain peace for the present, and I am a firm believer that the ultimate result will be full annexation, probably before our Company makes the first crop."[6]

Meanwhile, discretely, North American investment nibbled at independent possibilities. In May, Juan Clark informed Manuel that Havemeyer had bought the estate *Lugareño* in Camagüey and *San Manuel* in Oriente. It was reported, he went on, that $800,000 had been paid for *Lugareño*, and he had no doubt the price had been at least $700,000. Rionda himself had planned to advance $125,000 to *Lugareño*'s owner on a first mortgage and was annoyed that he had withdrawn from the transaction to negotiate with the refiner instead. He wrote Havemeyer a mild "I believe it is my duty to inform you" letter, but Havemeyer and his American Sugar Refining Company were far too crucial for any sugar broker, especially an ambitious Czarnikow associate, to become irate. Besides, there was a silver lining. It would help with *Francisco*, he informed Craig, "for if Mr. Havemeyer has bought property in Cuba, why not others? He seems to be satisfied that the country is safe."[7]

How inadequate Rionda's contacts still were, compared to his aspirations, is proven by the fact that it was June 1900 before he finally succeeded in selling enough shares in *Francisco* to get it under way. The venture was pulled through only by conceding a dominant position to the McCahan Sugar Refinery interests when Rionda convinced its founder, William J. McCahan Sr., to put up a large part of the capital and to become its president. The old man, grumbling, pleaded ignorance of cane fields, but Rionda duly promised to take care of the practical details.

They were details on a huge scale. *Francisco*'s great advantage was its apparently limitless territory, but the remoteness that thus endowed it brought with it a lack of available workers and infrastructure. Boatloads of laborers had to be recruited elsewhere from the demobilized ranks of the uprooted. They were duly unloaded at a temporary dock to fell the trees; to string the telephone lines; to build the new embarcadero facilities, barracks, and living quarters; and to lay eleven miles of railroad connections between fields and factory, all of which must be in place before planting could begin. Occasional battles, too, must be fought with officialdom. While sugar machinery paid only 10 percent ad valorem in duties, the U.S. authorities assessed *Francisco* a $14,500 tax on an iron building. It was worse than under the Spanish, Manuel exploded. "The iron building is as much a part of the machinery as the grinding unit or the vacuum pans and engine, for it should not be expected to put the apparatus out in the wilderness." He appealed to Louis V. Placé to persuade Colonel Tasker Bliss, collector of customs in Cuba during the first American occupation, to correct the grievance. Placé, a general commission merchant and agent for the Ward Steamship line in Havana, was another close friend, ally, and confidant.

Also, eastern Cuba required colonos. In western Cuba, where the colonía system had evolved, there had been a ready network of experienced agriculturalists and penniless freed workers. Here, pioneers must be lured in and staked to tools and rations while they cleared the land on which they would plant. Among the recruits, nephew Higinio Fanjul, twenty-two years old, was assigned "to build and manage a . . . colonía, and to run the company store." Higinio convinced Wallace Risley, an Atkinson connection, to put in some money and become his partner. Risley's bride's letters home to her Philadelphia family tell of their honeymoon in a thatched hut ("bohio") with a "maja" rustling in the thatch overhead, a "maja," she calmly explained, being "a species of boa constrictor . . . rarely more than sixteen feet in length." The planting was begun, and in due time she could write of riding through a cane field: "The tall stalks of cane are far above one's head as one sits on the horse and the sharp leaves reach out and slap at one, cutting hands and face if they happen to strike edgewise. To look down the 'guardo rayo' or fire lane between the fields make one think the whole world is a vast field of sugar cane for it waves on and on until the parallel lines seem to meet and one is imprisoned between the green walls."[8]

It was hard for Manuel to scrape up funding for his planter connections, harder still for him to finance *Francisco*. But although Cuba's relationship with the United States was still in question, North Americans were scouting out the island's jungles. Two months after Francisco had been incorporated, Juan Clark reported to Manuel that "a Mr. R. B. Hawley" had called on him twice "about buying property on this island for, as I understand him, making a sugar plantation." "I guess," he continued dismissively, "he just wants to speculate, just like a good many that come to this country and think they can buy a sugar estate for a dollar." But Clark's visitor turned out to be a U.S. congressman, Robert Bradley Hawley, Republican of Galveston, Texas, and with Hawley's entrance, North American expansion began in earnest.

Five years Manuel's senior, Hawley had been born in Memphis, Tennessee, and there, in his teens, he had survived its siege and the hungry years of the Civil War. In 1870, at twenty-one, he had moved to Galveston, going into business as a merchant. In 1896, he became its first Republican congressman. Somewhere in the interim, he had become involved in Louisiana sugar, acquiring an interest in the New Iberia Sugar Company. He was involved, as well, with certain New York refining interests.[9]

At the end of June 1899, James Howell Post told Rionda that "Howell's" was going into the Cuban raw sugar business. "Howell's" was B. H. Howell, Son and Company, sugar commission merchants, established since 1836 on lower Wall Street. Its founder, the patriarch of traders, still survived at eighty-eight years, but although his son, Frederick H. Howell, was also active, Post was now dominant. A kinsman, probably a nephew, Post had come to work in the firm as a boy and became a partner in 1887. He was simultaneously working at consolidating the new National Sugar Refining Company of New Jersey as an ostensible competitor to the American Sugar Refining Company. Since time would eventually reveal Henry Havemeyer's secret involvement with Post and in the National, it may be presumed that Havemeyer also had considerable input into Howell's parallel entrance into the Cuban cane fields.[10]

Post had already taken his first step in Cuba, investing $150,000 in Ernesto A. Longa's *Mercedita* in Pinar del Río, for which he had received a first mortgage and $100,000 in stock. (Rionda thought the terms very hard.) He now moved more boldly, on July 26, 1899, as one of a group of investors who incorporated the Cuban-American Sugar Company in New Jersey, to buy the remains of two more partly devastated plantations in Matanzas Province. The *New York Journal of Commerce* reported that the syndicate had acquired 20,000 acres and planned to spend $1.5 million. Cuban-American, it was announced, would build a mammoth new central, the *Chaparra*, on the north coast of Oriente Province. Even more remote than *Francisco* and on three times as grand a scale, it would launch a new Cuba. General Mario García Menocal y Deop, it was announced, would survey and build it.

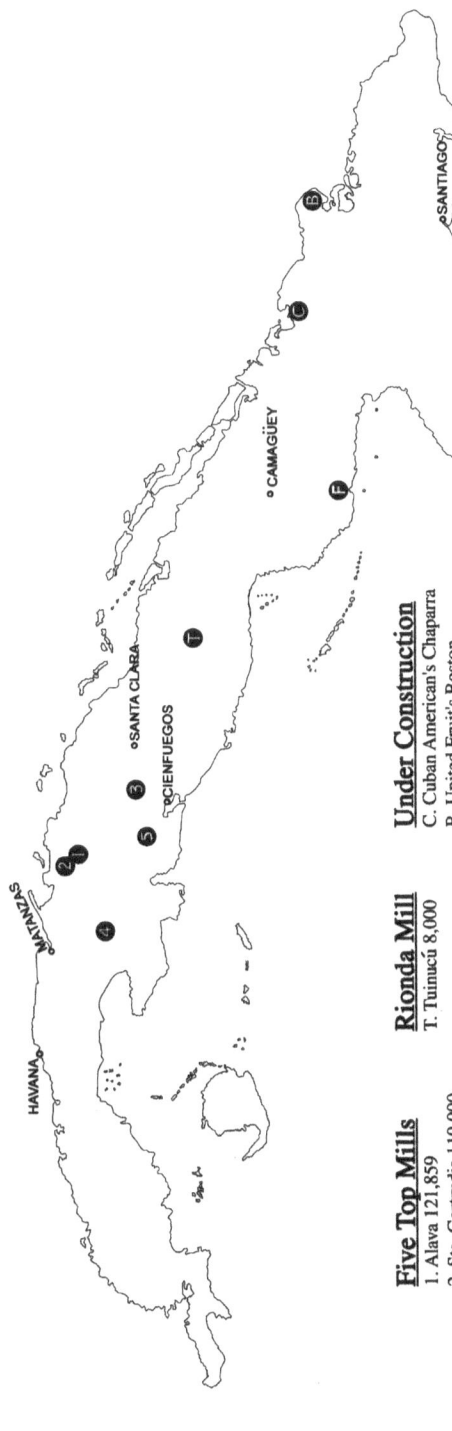

Map 1. Cuba mills, 1901. Production in 325-pound bags. Source: Wood Report, 1901.

Born at Jagüey Grande in 1866, Menocal had grown up in the United States and Mexico while the Cuban Ten Years War was raging, had studied engineering at Cornell, and had acquired experience in Nicaragua, where his engineer uncle was surveying a cross-isthmus canal for the U.S. government. He had fought for independence under Calixto García, commanding in the area where *Chaparra* would be, thus learning its terrain and potential. Ideally competent and bilingual, he would in due time become president of Cuba. Now, with his bride, he camped out in the high woods as the caibo, cedro, and majagua trees were felled and some 2,000 men (many who had fought under him) were enlisted for the great work.[11] The Chaparra Sugar Company was incorporated in New Jersey on October 18, 1899, with capital stock of $1 million, three times the amount that Rionda was unsuccessfully struggling to raise for *Francisco*. Hawley became its president, with Frederick H. Howell as vice president and James H. Post as treasurer. Its offices were at 109 Wall Street. With its capacity far greater than anything before it, *Chaparra* would be the first full-scale sugar operation in Cuba launched with ample American capital, the giant opening up the island's remote East, setting world records.

Rionda hoped his *Francisco* might grind 12,000 tons daily; *Chaparra* would grind 36,000 tons. Yet Rionda welcomed it, believing the U.S. market big enough for both. Like Havemeyer's *Lugareño*, *Chaparra* would signal investors, and money was the price of development. Rionda later put Hawley beside Ibáñez as the second of the two heroes who had created a new world for sugar. People knew it at the time. *Chaparra*, the *Louisiana Planter* prophesized, would herald "an industrial revolution . . . without precedent in the history of Cuba and probably of the entire world."

Meanwhile, some eighty miles even farther east, the newly incorporated United Fruit Company was buying the Dumois family's banana land and engaging Rionda's former partner Kelley to build the *Boston* plantation. An apparently separate, simultaneous venture was the newly incorporated Colonial Sugars Company's purchase of the famous *Constancia*, reportedly backed by Louisiana and by Illinois Central Railroad capital. The Colonial's strategy was to transport sugar across the Gulf (a shorter haul than to Brooklyn), refine it in New Orleans, and ship it via the Illinois Central to the Midwest market, again more economically than bringing it over the Appalachians from New York. In a few years, Colonial Sugars would be joined to the Cuban-American Sugar Company.[12]

No statistics record the production of individual centrals for the 1898–99 zafra, but for 1899–1900, the U.S. Military Government collected data for each of the 108 plantations in operation, 82 of them in Santa Clara and Matanzas Provinces, averaging only some 18,500 bags of sugar. Pelayo's *Rosario* produced 14,557 bags and accounted for a quarter of Havana's crop. Atkins's *Soledad* produced 59,000 bags, and the greatest single producer (the Terry brothers' *Caracas*), 86,000. A year later, 152 ingenios were counted for the 1900–1901 zafra, the greatest production (121,850 bags) from Zulueta y Gamiz's *Alava*.[13]

Finally, *Francisco* was under construction, but *Tuinucú* was still far from good order. Letters from a very young nephew of Aunt Harriet's sent there with Manolo, along with some boilers, tubes, and sixteen boxes of parts, reported finding "bearings all full of dirt and out of adjustment ... tools that would not cut, pulleys ... almost just as they ought not to be." Rather timidly the young man requested "a grinding machine for tools [about $12]" and "some up to date lathe tools [about $5]."

But in April 1900, with men carrying surveyors' gear and with a clatter of hammers of workers laying steel rails, the future arrived for *Tuinucú*. At the home plantation, U.S. hegemony was to reward the Rionda clan, as construction of Sir William Van Horne's Central Railroad began. Van Horne, his engineers, and his crews were ready to run their line from Santa Clara through the center of the island on to Oriente Province.

The Central Railroad was the project of the Cuba Company, incorporated on April 25, 1900, in New Jersey. It was an investment for the rich, 160 shares at $50,000 a share, all immediately subscribed by major U.S. investors, including Thomas Fortune Ryan, James J. Hill of the Northern Pacific, General Grenville M. Dodge of the Union Pacific (he who had once held the flank of Grant's army at Vicksburg), Henry M. Flagler of Standard Oil, and E. J. Berwind, the Pennsylvania coal magnate. Van Horne was already covered with glory from his construction of the Canadian Pacific, and although the Foraker Amendment supposedly barred the granting of franchises during the military occupation, Secretary of War Elihu Root, Military Governor General Leonard Wood, and even President McKinley himself were blessing and speeding its way. Influential politicians as well as capitalists were looking eagerly toward improving Cuba's eastern infrastructure. *Tuinucú* had labored under the disadvantage of its inland location, its sugar having to be transported by oxcart to Sancti Spiritus. Now, bound by a spur to the main track, it became, Manuel would write, "one of the first plantations, if not the very first, to haul sugar over the Cuba Company's railroad."[14]

The Yankee troops remained in Cuba, and for this Rionda was grateful. If Cuba could become part of the United States, U.S. soldiers and courts would safeguard investments in the island. But as statehood seemed more and more unlikely, what mattered even more was the tariff Cuba would pay. While Hawaiian, Puerto Rican, and no doubt Philippine sugar would now be entering the U.S. market duty free, the full Dingley Tariff rates still applied to Cuban exports, and capitalists, including C. Czarnikow Ltd., were still hesitant to invest.

In Washington, the situation was not promising. On Capitol Hill, Congress held back from annexing Cuba not only from a moralistic distaste for imperialism but also from concern for constituents who grew beets or bayou cane. Recent elections had brought in beet Republicans from western states to reinforce Louisiana's two Democratic senators in keeping the tariff high. The protectionist agricultural bloc was growing. To counter it stood the well-funded lobby of East Coast refiners, generous contributors to both political parties, but the farm vote was decisive in many congressional districts, "the Trusts" were suspect, and the battle lines were drawn.

Manuel wrote Pelayo that Cuba's hacendados must be represented on Capitol Hill. He was pleased when in early 1901 his friend Louis Placé checked into the Hotel Arlington, a few blocks from the White House, on behalf of a newly formalized Cuban Círculo de Hacendados. But he wrote individual letters to ten of his Havana contacts, warning they were too parsimonious. It would be well, he suggested, for them to employ his brother-in-law J.I.C. Clarke, who had many friends in Washington, and to collect some $40,000 or $50,000 for expenses for a Washington office "y para echar aceite a los eyes" (to grease the wheels). Nothing was done anywhere without money. His advice was not taken, and nothing had been accomplished when Congress adjourned in March 1901.

The tariff mattered far more to Manuel than the debates of Cuba's Constitutional Convention. He had little patience with the five commissioners sent to Washington in April 1901 "to set forth Cuba's objections to the [Platt] amendment and to seek a basis for establishing satisfactory commercial relations." "Mr. Post," he wrote, "wanted to give them a dinner but I told him that I did not think we ought to take any notice of them as they were not the real representatives of the country, they were politicians and not businessmen, and to treat them kindly would make them think they were considered more highly than they really were. . . . Had they looked more after the interests of their country and less after their own, I would have had more respect for them." A new Cuban Constitutional Convention, he thought, should be elected, "men who will look after the welfare of the country, and not poets."

But although the current Cuban Constitutional Convention eventually surrendered, voting sixteen to eleven with four abstentions, to accept the Platt Amendment, and although an assassin's bullet in September replaced McKinley with Theodore Roosevelt, the U.S. Congress stalled, while the charge circulated that reciprocity was "Havemeyer's benevolent scheme to get his raw material free." The Sugar Trust, it was alleged, had already purchased Cuba's harvest. Should the tariff be lowered, not an extra cent would go to the poor men who grew the cane but all into the rich refiners' pockets. In the spring of 1902, in connection with this allegation, Manuel was summoned to testify in Washington before a subcommittee of the Senate Committee on Relations with Cuba. There, cross-examined by Senator Orville Platt (of the Platt Amendment) and Henry Teller (of beet-sugar Colorado and author of the Teller Resolution, which had pledged the United States to an independent Cuba), he swore, despite his private suspicions to the contrary, that the contention that the Sugar Trust had already cornered the greater portion of that year's crop was absurd. "Mr. Havemeyer," he wrote after the hearings had concluded, "has nothing for which to be thankful to us! In working in Washington, we are doing it more for our own sake than his." Perfectly willing to make common cause with the refining interests with whom he carried on his profitable brokerage business, he had no confidence in politicians from either country. "I fear the Americans," he wrote, "have lost all sense of honor. They have cornered Cuba into accepting the Platt Amendment which gives Americans all the privileges as though Cuba was annexed and now they refuse to give Cuba anything in return." And, since the arguments for tariff concessions stressed pity for Cuba's starving people, he complained that the planters sent to lobby on Capitol Hill were "too prosperous looking to appeal to Congressmen."[15]

In Europe, meanwhile, on March 5, 1902, and with the active participation of Czarnikow's partner, Charles Lagemann, the Brussels Agreement had finally been negotiated, which would end continental subsidies on beet-sugar exports. Rionda had hopes that England (since its colonies could not produce enough for its own needs) might now turn to Cuba and that ships out of Liverpool and the Clyde would load in Matanzas and Cárdenas. Nor would these British ships arrive in ballast. Where Cuba sold, it would buy. Rionda reported to a nephew that he had written Senator Platt "in such terms that he will realize that unless they act quickly, Cuba will slip through their hands." Ten days later, Platt himself wired from Connecticut, saying that he would be in New York the next day and would call on Rionda about noon. What they discussed is apparently unrecorded. It could not have helped much, for in Washington the opposition of nineteen insurgent Republican senators (all but three from the beet-sugar West) sufficiently reinforced thirty Democratic Senators to checkmate changes in the tariff.

When in late May 1902 Cuba became at least nominally independent and Tomás Estrada Palma was installed as its first president, Rionda was annoyed by the celebration in Havana. "As far as I am personally, concerned," he wrote in June, "the sooner [the Americans] gobble up the Islands, the better for me." But once more there were satisfactory profits. In August, his client Pelayo was reported to have some 200 men planting new fields at his *Rosario*, while Pelayo and his family, the *Louisiana Planter* reported, were "now at San Sebastian in Spain where he owns a palace purchased from the profits of his Cuban sugar estate and he now has General Leonard Wood and family visiting him at the noted Spanish watering place." The account concluded with its highest praise: "Pelayo is a galvanized American."[16]

In the late fall of 1902, since Cuban independence opened the way for an end run around the U.S. Congress, Roosevelt sent General Tasker Bliss back to Havana to negotiate a reciprocity treaty. "No better man could be employed," Rionda decided, and he lunched with him on December 12, the day Bliss and the Cuban secretary of state signed the agreement, trading a 20 percent reduction in U.S. duties on sugar imports for reductions by Cuba of from 20 to 40 percent on its imports from America. Both reductions were to be greater than those either offered to any third country.

Admirable as the possibilities the treaty opened for those in the sugar business, it would, however, discourage Cuba's trade with third countries as well as any attempts by Cubans to produce manufactured goods or foodstuffs. McKinley's investigator Porter, of all people, reporting in 1898, had been concerned about something of the kind, pointing out that several machine shops already existed in Cuba and that admission of U.S. machinery would wipe them out. "[I]t is impossible to see in such a policy permanent benefit to the country," he had mused. "Above all things, Cuba needs diversified industries." Yet this was a consideration that apparently did not trouble Bliss or Rionda, Roosevelt or Estrada Palma, although Rionda did write New York, "It does seem as though the U.S. was having the best of the bargain but Cuba is satisfied." There was optimism in Havana that the treaty would be approved by the U.S. Senate in time for the 1903 zafra. But although the American Beet Sugar Association withdrew its opposition, a revolutionary switch traditionally explained as due to Havemeyer's purchases of beet-sugar companies, the Senate still dragged its heels. "[T]he only thing for us to do in Cuba is to make sugar as cheaply as possible," Manuel concluded in May. "If reciprocity or annexation comes, well and good, but let us get our chief support out of the ground." It was December 18, 1904, before the new tariff schedule finally went into effect.[17]

The Cuba Company's Central Railroad was by now rolling down the tracks that opened the center and eastern sections of Cuba. Engine whistles echoed over the cane fields. Reliability and efficiency, along with capital and technology, were what the Central provided Rionda. On January 3, 1903, he left *Tuinucú* on the 1:30 P.M. train and arrived in Havana the next morning. "A year ago," he wrote, "it took from Friday 7 A.M. to Sunday 6 P.M. . . . it has imparted to [Tuinucú] the advantages it needed of quick connections and cheap freight. . . . Castaño was saying to me today he thought Tuinucú property had increased 50 percent on its valuation."

But with such improvements came questions about his family's future relationships with the new economic powers. Manuel's letter to Bernardo and Manolo in New York continued that the Cuba Company was "very desirous of having a merger between the Tuinucú and a new plantation the Cuba Co. wants to put up." The New York investors did not "want to run plantations . . . and as they must do something to increase traffic they want to join with good people who . . . will take charge of the mills." The Cuba Company plan, he wrote, was "to take whatever machinery is good. . . . [Tuinucú's] lands, oxen, agricultural implements, etc., etc., at a fair value to form part of the capital of the new concern" and to buy enough additional machinery to make 100,000 bags at the new site, where they already possessed about 20,000 acres. Manuel had a two-hour discussion about it with a Mr. Ward, Cuba Company's manager, who "talked well and seemed very enthusiastic," and he had promised to put Ward's proposal to fuse *Tuinucú* into a new Cuba Company central before *Tuinucú*'s board. But he was lukewarm. "I cannot see," he wrote, "how this proposal can benefit Tuinucú stockholders. . . . Tuinucú having enough lands to make 50,000 bags, does not fear competition or nearby estates."

Although the new company would pay $350,000 for *Tuinucú*'s machinery and lands and would value the Cuba Company's own assets at only $100,000, Manuel suspected its capital might be increased in the future to perhaps $600,000 for "cash capital," leaving the clan with only a minority share. *Tuinucú* alone, he predicted, should be able to make 32,000 bags in 1904, which should mean a profit of $26,000, even after allowances for "interest of mortgages" and "deterioration of machinery." That would provide for his brother's widow and children. Also, *Tuinucú* would be a proving ground for Francisco's sons, Pepe, Leandro, and Salvador. "In other words, my brother's heirs will have a sure income and the young men is [sic] to be employed. By making this merger I run the risk of losing control and become only a small fraction among *big* people. We say in Spanish 'mas vale ser cabeza de ratón que cola de can'—So my personal decision is against this merger." It was better to be the mouse's head than the dog's tail.[18] Since the proverb usually refers to a lion's tail, his substitution of a less imposing animal might hint at his feeling as he wrote the letter.

If, for the Rionda clan, launching *Francisco* had been the heroic gamble, Manuel's decision to hold *Tuinicú* free and clear was no less decisive. Manuel would never deviate from this resolve to preserve an independent base in Cuba for his family, despite the lure of hundreds of thousands of American dollars. If he was expanding his ties to London and

New York, he still did not want a future where his heirs would not ride through their own acres and be masters of their own mill.

Van Horne's Cuba Company, having failed to buy Rionda's *Tuinucú*, then issued $4 million in bonds to finance the building of new centrals of its own. Its *Jatibonico* in Camagüey began production in 1906, bringing in 97,000 bags in 1907, and work then began on its *Jobabo* almost at the end of the Central Railroad line in Oriente. Railroads pioneering through unsettled areas had to find freight and passengers, and the railroad's profits would lie in bulk loads of sugar.

In September 1903, Bernardo married Maude. The next year, George Atkinson Braga was born, to begin the roster of Manuel's grandnephews, followed six years later by a brother, Ronnie. Manolo shortly married a New Yorker, Ellen Goin. The Cuban cousins also paired off, Leandro to Fanny, who had briefly acted on a Broadway stage; Pepe to Mercedes Chaumont; and Higinio, more indigenously, to María Estrada, daughter of the manager of *Tuinucú*.[19]

In 1904's zafra, Cuba's production finally equaled its highest previous prewar record, reaching 7,169,569 325-pound bags. Almost all the sugar still came from mills that had existed before independence. More capital was becoming available each harvest and with it much expansion. In Europe, the beets suffered from bad weather, driving world prices higher. *Francisco* came on line in 1904, producing more than 69,000 bags and showing a profit of $60,000. In the first years after the war ended, the Pelayos, Mendozas, Arenals, Díazes, Barós, Bernabé Sánchez, and their like had put things in place. Even in 1902, when *Chaparra* and United Fruit's *Boston* had begun production and when the Apezteguías' *Constancia* and the Terrys' *Caracas* had been acquired by the Howell interests, North American holdings totaled only 446,353 bags out of an all-island total of 5,859,709 bags. The world of Cuban sugar was still a Spanish-speaking world.[20]

Rionda was becoming established. He and Harriet had for some time admired land across from Manhattan, on the New Jersey palisades. Now they acquired a tract there at Alpine and built a spacious house overlooking the Hudson, which they christened Río Vista. Here, they would preside at family dinners, as many as forty around their table, with butler and maids, chauffeurs and gardeners, and a fine stable for Manuel, who rode his horse every morning over his acres. There was room to gather in the aunts after they were widowed and to house the Cuban kin when they came north to escape summer's heat, as well as space for impressive entertaining of business contacts.

When the zafras had ended and Cuba's inactive *tiempos muertos*, its "dead seasons," between crops closed in, Harriet and Manuel would sail annually to Europe. There were London musical evenings and talks with the Mincing Lane partners in Czarnikow's Eaton Square dining room, much cause there for pride. Lagemann had stood at Joseph Chamberlain's elbow during the crucial days for the Brussels Agreement, as Rionda had kept in touch with Platt and General Bliss. Rionda sat among the lords of the world's trade, one among equals.

As each zafra began, Manuel and Harriet would go to Cuba, to *Tuinucú*, the home plantation, to remain usually until April. Their annual migration became a train journey by private railroad car from vaulted Pennsylvania Station south 1,200 miles, then by sea to Havana and an overnight train east to Zaza del Medio, where their car was uncoupled from the Havana Special and hitched to a *Tuinucú* engine to meet a waiting carriage. Then "down the long avenue lined with laurel trees, palms and bamboo, interspersed with flowering vines" to the two-story, ochre yellow *casa vivienda* with its red-tiled roof, bougainvillea, and red poinsettias. "The perfume of jasmine and lumbago flowers mingled with the sweet smell of molasses, and in the house the smell of tobacco, cedar and sandalwood."

Their suite was "on the mill side" of the first floor—two bedrooms, dressing rooms and baths, and sitting room with upright piano. There they would hear, day and night, the "steady beat" of the grinding mill, broken by "shrieks from the whistle as the shifts were changed," hear unendingly the "frequent unexpected clangings of engine bells and the crash of cane as it was dumped from railroad cars and ox carts into the chutes." The carts, "their wheels groaning," passed "in a constant stream," pulled by teams of six straining oxen.[21]

Business was good. Louisiana, the sugar-beet Midwest, Puerto Rico, and Hawaii all together did not produce enough to satisfy half of the American demand, while guerrilla war and concessions to Spanish shipping delayed investment in the Philippines. With its 20 percent advantage in the tariff and closeness to the eastern refineries, Cuba need not fear foreign competition.

Fig. 3. From left, J.I.C. Clarke and Mrs. Clarke, Manuel and Harriet Rionda, unidentified

On September 19, 1906, an expanded Cuban-American Sugar Company was incorporated in New Jersey. A $20 million holding company, it joined Hawley and Menocal's *Chaparra* with five more modest mills, totaling some 280,000 acres and producing 546,000 bags of sugar. Hawley became its president, James H. Post its treasurer, and T. A. Howell its vice president. The Guantanamo Sugar Company, also controlled by the Howells, added another 55,000 acres and 127,000 bags.

This horizontal integration under North American control did not worry Rionda. Nor was he upset by rumors that Howell was the front man for Havemeyer and the Sugar Trust. Havemeyer was by far Czarnikow, MacDougall's best customer, and Manuel admired his competence. Consolidation was efficient, and Cuba needed North American allies with political influence. When a revolution erupted in Cuba just as the Cuban-American Sugar Company was launched, he was angry. "Your countrymen are not worthy of self-government," he wrote Placé. "[T]hey have frightened the capitalists . . . and without capital what can be done?" Why had the United States not sent in the marines immediately? If the capitalists were not reassured, all of them, all of them ("todos, todos") would abandon Cuba. He wrote his sister's husband at *Tuinucú* to move the horses lest *Tuinucú* fall to the insurgents. He was consoled only when the second American intervention of 1906–9 settled in under Provisional Governor Charles Magoon. The eruption had been, he wrote, a blessing after all because it showed the effectiveness of the Platt Amendment. He hoped the Yankee troops would remain "for many years to come." He still hoped for annexation.[22]

Despite the growth of U.S. investment, the overwhelming bulk of Cuba's sugar still came from Cuban mills. Cuban-American's *Chaparra* (259,000 bags) and its *Caracas* (193,000) led the pack in 1906, they were followed by Juan Pedro Baró's *Conchita* (184,000), while United Fruit's *Boston* was only in fourth place (161,000). There was ample market for expansion, and when Manuel Silveira, a Havana banker, failed in 1906, abandoning in its early stages a new central begun on Cuba's south coast, Manuel took the lead in salvaging the venture. The Mincing Lane firm put $100,000 into the bonds of what was now rechristened the Stewart Sugar Company in honor of the Glasgow manufacturer who had "designed and constructed it," with plans directed by the prominent Cuban hacendado Octavio Davis y Owen. Its sugar would be sold by "Czarnikow's New York house" for a commission of 1 percent of the gross proceeds. Additional capital was found on Wall Street, illustrating Manuel's progress there, for even as rebels rode in Cuba he now acquired the aid of Sullivan & Cromwell, the corporate law firm that had convinced the state of New Jersey to tailor its laws to favor corporations and had organized the United States Steel Company for J. P. Morgan. Founded in 1879, the firm also had excellent expansionist credentials. When Panama had been declared independent, a Waldorf-Astoria victory banquet had honored "four Panama Railroad officials and five Sullivan and Cromwell lawyers."

With impressive connections thus opening with Wall Street, $2.5 million in capital stock of the Stewart Sugar Company was sold plus $2.75 million in twenty-year bonds. Sullivan & Cromwell drew up for *Stewart* a complex "voting trust agreement" between the holders of the capital stock and three "voting trustees"—Manuel Rionda, Sir William Van Horne, and J. S. Fiske. Rionda became president of the company. "I . . . remained as such," he wrote later, "during the entire period of construction and uplifting, but resigned . . . when the Company had become prosperous. . . . Our house continued to finance the company and sell its sugars." Although *Stewart*'s first crop in 1908 was only 70,000 bags, it jumped to 162,000 bags the following year and to 215,000 in 1910. Meanwhile, Cuban-American's *Chaparra* and United Fruit's *Boston* had hit their stride, producing 337,000 and 282,289 bags, respectively, in 1907. Cuban-American's total for its six centrals reached 679,824 bags and Guantanamo's 194,236.[23]

In 1907, Juan M. Clark died. For some years he had served as Havana agent for Czarnikow, MacDougall's Export Department, which Bernardo headed in New York. Rionda now decided, since the profits of the Export Department were rivaling Czarnikow, MacDougall's own income, to replace it with an independent company, and the Cuban Trading Company was incorporated in Havana on July 20, 1907, by Victor Zevallos y Chiriboga. It had a capital of $20,000, all its shares owned by the New York parent company. Through this Havana office would flow subsequent contacts with Cuba's presidential palace and its Congress, as well as an extensive trade in machinery, jute bags from India, and plantation supplies. Victor Zevallos, until his retirement years later, was to be one of Manuel's innermost circle, as was Rafael Zevallos, presumably his brother, who was employed in Rionda's Wall Street office. Two years later, Manuel, without consulting Bernardo, transferred this oldest nephew to selling sugar. It was a job in which Bernardo's toughness would stand him in good stead.[24]

In the United States, 1907 was a year of financial crisis. One of the panic's casualties was Hugh Kelly, comrade-in-arms of Manuel's youth, worn out by "strain and worry." More notably, on December 4, 1907, death also came for Henry O. Havemeyer. His activities had long been under scrutiny by courts, congressional committees, and the press for a variety of reasons, including the illegality of his original trust, the magnitude of his contributions to candidates for political office, his alleged bribes to those already elected, his secret investments, his railroad rebates, and the dishonesty of the scales on his docks. At the end of 1907, he was facing a tangle of legal complications with which his loyal widow and his only son, Horace Havemeyer, aged twenty-two, were left to cope. The appraisal of Havemeyer's estate revealed the extent of his holdings. His largest Cuban raw sugar investment was 18 percent of Cuban-American's stock, "some $695,000," and together his Cuban holdings totaled slightly under $1.5 million, only a third his $4.5 million investment in U.S. beet-sugar companies.

Presidency of the American Sugar Refining Company passed to a Boston man, W. B. Thomas, with Edwin F. Atkins as vice president. At least some of the company's board of directors had for several years disapproved of Havemeyer's expensive expansion into beet-sugar companies and Cuban mills, and they now shifted the firm's attention to building up its core holdings in East Coast refining and promoting its own Domino brand, putting upon Havemeyer's dead shoulders responsibility for any alleged dishonesty. Without Havemeyer, the sugar-refining world in general settled down to become more of an oligopoly. The other refineries, which although nominally independent had been suspected of taking his orders, moved more freely, and even the *Louisiana Planter*, which still stormed at "the Trust," sometimes referred to it as a "Triumvirate." Rionda cultivated all existing refiners and was successful with all of them.[25]

By 1908, matters were progressing well at *Stewart* and at *Tuinucú*, but *Francisco* was far less satisfactory. It had come on line in 1902, made a

$60,000 profit in 1904, and in 1905 even declared a one-time dividend of $20 on its common stock, of which $1,277,700 was then outstanding. But then it had stalled, and although Manuel predicted production of 100,000 bags, it still made only 73,995 in 1907. He privately blamed the McCahans for asserting their authority in the choice of *Francisco*'s administrator and the type of boilers. In 1908, he tried to sell it to Post and in 1909 offered it to the Cuban-American Sugar Company and to various others, but no one seemed interested in the property.[26] His effort to salvage it or dispose of it was interrupted when, in April 1909, Julius Caesar Czarnikow's butler discovered him dead in his Eaton Square bedroom. It was a surprise—he had been at the office the previous day and had retired after a good dinner apparently in his usual health.

Three days later, Manuel sailed for London. He did not know how generous the four surviving London partners would be toward the New York firm—Lagemann and Ganzoni had been joined by Hubert Nieburg, a German, and by a Belgium, Theodore Westrik—but MacDougall (who had given notice he would soon retire) had offered Rionda his $150,000 accumulated life savings. Pelayo, informed of the crisis, immediately sold "some sugars he had" and put the proceeds, some $500,000, at Manuel's disposal. Since Czarnikow had, after all, been seventy-three, Rionda had already discussed the eventuality of his demise with Frank Tiarks at Schroeders, the London banking firm.

Mincing Lane proved cooperative, and it was agreed not only that Manuel would become a partner in the New York business, Czarnikow, MacDougall becoming Czarnikow-Rionda, but that he would guide its course. It would be a private company with five partners: Rionda, Lagemann, Ganzoni, and the two other partners of the London firm, Westrik and Nieburg. The Londoners would hold a total of $300,000 in common stock and Manuel $200,000. There would also be $1 million in 8 percent preferred shares, $250,000 in New York and $750,000 in London, but the common stock alone would carry with it "the full management of the company." When any one of the five common stockholders died or retired, his shares would also be retired.

Rionda sailed home highly satisfied. "When all of you came up handsomely," he wrote Lagemann later, "and subscribed 75 percent of the capital, my work was finished. The details and divisions of profits were nothing to me. All I wanted was the house to continue and capital to work with." But he was anxious (tail of the lion, head of the mouse) that his New York nephews should "not be entirely frozen out of the firm" in case of his death. "I was," he went on, "jealously guarding the places of Manolo, Braga and Zevallos, as I knew they were the only ones to second me." It was therefore agreed that $100,000 of Manuel's stock could be divided so that Manolo and Bernardo each held $35,000, Ralph Zevallos $20,000, and Victor Zevallos $10,000, while Lagemann and Ganzoni would be able to transfer their shares to their sons providing the sons should be "actively engaged in the business." Neither Fanjul nor the Rionda y de la Torriente nephews were included in the New York operation, Fanjul limited to his *Francisco* colonía and the de la Torrientes in line for their mother's inheritance from their late father, a major interest in *Tuinucú* and a share in *Francisco*.

Subsequently, Schroeders backed Rionda handsomely. The sums they advanced the New York firm annually rose from £85,000 in 1910 to £251,000 in 1913. The first figures available on Czarnikow-Rionda's operations are from 1912, when the accountants' consolidated balance sheets show "advances against sugar" for more than $1 million, a $30,000 dividend declared, and surplus and reserves of almost $700,000, rising a year later to over $1 million.[27]

Manuel returned to New York, resuming his effort to take over *Francisco*. The McCahans, who evidently had had enough problems with it, cooperated. On June 22, its board of directors elected the twenty-nine-year-old Leandro Rionda as its general manager to replace the McCahans' John Durham. Manuel wrote his nephew that his salary would be the same as Durham's had been, $9,000 a year. "Let me send you my congratulations and hope you will be worthy of it," he wrote, adding that Manolo, as soon as he formally became secretary of the company, would start the official correspondence. Then he warned Leandro not to expect him to make suggestions. "It is up to you to think [of] everything concerning Francisco. Heretofore I have done the thinking for the whole family." The officers and members of the board, who until 1908 had been exclusively Philadelphian except for a Mr. Parker of Boston and Manuel himself, gave way to Rionda family members. The corporate headquarters moved from Philadelphia to Czarnikow-Rionda's 110 Wall Street location.

Leandro's subsequent reports about *Francisco* communicated day-to-day disasters: an occasional cane fire; too much or too little rain; the need to stop grinding for an hour and a half to clean the mills; a break in a vacuum pump that could perhaps be patched up with bolts, plates, and other materials; the late arrival of steamers; jammed "trace plates"; and the unwillingness of the field hands to work on San José's Day. He made progress, however. In 1909, *Francisco* produced 107,469 bags. For the next three years, production hovered in the 120,000 zone. In 1913 came the leap to 257,140 bags, putting it ninth among Cuba's plantations in production.

Francisco—Rionda dream, Rionda creation—is an example of how contemporary listings of ownership by nationality are oversimplified, failing to give proper recognition to indigenous entrepreneurship, to engineering skill and management. *Francisco* appeared in *Cuba Review*'s listing of Cuban mills in 1904 as "American" and continued as "American." Perhaps that was a realistic recognition of the primacy of capital in the international world of sugar, a capitalist world par excellence, but it omitted much.

As he constantly extended his influence among Cuba's plantation owners, financing and selling their sugar, Manuel became more deeply tied to certain individual centrals. Between 1909 and 1912, he acquired through indebtedness the management of two more—the *San Vincente* and the *Washington*. *San Vincente* was small and old. "We should," Manuel instructed Leandro, "see if we can get it out of the mire." Its output then mounted steadily, if modestly. Under Leandro's management, between 1909 and 1913, *Washington*'s production tripled.[28]

Such accomplishments were solid, but meanwhile the few North American mills in eastern Cuba were growing into the true giants. The Spanish and Cuban plantations still produced a full 71 percent of Cuba's sugar, but their proportion had fallen 11 percent in four years. Cuban-American's total (1,108,446 bags) was now 8.9 percent of the island's output. If the Guantanamo Company's production was added, the Post/Howell interest controlled 11 percent. But 11 percent was not a monopoly and did not come close to filling the total needs of Post/Howell's National Sugar Refinery. The United Fruit Company's 7 percent was not a monopoly either and was far from enough to supply its Revere Sugar Refinery in Boston. The steady trend to vertical integration did not alarm

Rionda. Besides, even if its relative percentage of the island's production was diminishing, in 1910 Cuban production had increased in absolute terms by almost 1.5 million bags since 1907, bringing the local men who were Manuel's allies and clients higher incomes and increasing Czarnikow-Rionda's brokerage commissions.

3

Tarafa and the Genial Shark

In March 1909, a cordial but firm William Howard Taft replaced Theodore Roosevelt in the White House. Rionda preferred Taft, although Taft had been in charge in the Philippines and was feared to be sentimental about them. Rionda was not too concerned when, five months into Taft's administration, the Republican Payne-Aldrich Tariff allowed 300,000 tons of sugar a year to enter duty free from the Philippines, since Cuba kept its 20 percent advantage over all other foreign suppliers. Instead, he dispatched a man to Manila to investigate a possible Philippine Trading Company. Expansion was in the air.

Two months before Taft's inauguration, on January 28, 1909, Governor Magoon and the forces of the Second American Occupation had sailed out of Havana harbor, leaving José Miguel Gómez installed, with the blessing of the United States, as Cuba's president. Gómez, a dark-skinned man, was known as a genial shark, and the water he splashed when he gamboled in the government's pleasant sea of patronage gave pleasure to his favorites. Hundreds of favored constituents found gainful employment in selling lottery tickets, as thousands, buying them, dreamed of riches. An arrangement with the United Railways, called the Arsenal Lands swap, profitable for the politicians in charge, set carpenters hammering away to erect a new railway station for the United, while more construction gangs fell to expanding the harbor's warehouses. There was also a Port Improvement Act, and Royal palms were planted along avenues in city parks.

This freewheeling tropical exuberance disturbed London's financial circles, but merchants worried less than bankers about such expenditures. For Rionda and for other men with whom he collaborated, optimistic dreams began to assume concrete form. They were even more encouraged when in November 1910 there was a solid Democratic victory in the U.S. congressional elections.

Rionda reported to London that a lower tariff, possibly even free sugar, would be a Democratic battle cry in the 1912 election. Midwest beets, still less Louisiana cane, could never compete with Cuban sugar, and Cuba's future would be assured for all time. It was in this period, so promising for entrepreneurs with the right connections to Gómez, that Rionda's fortunes intertwined with those of José Miguel Tarafa.[1]

Tarafa was twelve years younger than Rionda, Matanzas-born, a "short, stocky" man with "browned features" and blue eyes, educated in Cuba and in the United States, apparently in engineering. He had fought for Cuban independence when he had been assigned (he, too, became a colonel) to the staff of General Calixto García in Camagüey. "I rode all over the province," he later told a *New York Times* reporter. "It was largely jungle then but I saw its possibilities. It needed railroads." Tarafa dreamed of owning sugar centrals along newly laid tracks. Chasing these conceptions, he would plunge over his head into debt, counting on his cleverness to bring him again to the surface. In Tarafa's ventures, Rionda would be, alternately, collaborator and critic.[2]

The British-owned United Railways monopolized Cuba's settled West, and Van Horne's Central Railroad ran down the middle of the island to its eastern end. Yet no line tapped the rich potential along the northeastern coast from Morón east to Nuevitas. Tarafa aspired to locomotives, freight, profits. He began, enlisting Manuel's aid in their financing, with two small Matanzas mills, the *Flora* and the *Central Cuba*. Rionda was given exclusive sale of their sugar, a connection fortified in 1911 when Tarafa joined Regino Truffin and Horatio Rubens in founding the Cuban Distilling Company and purchasing *Tuinucú*'s and *Francisco*'s molasses.

Truffin and Rubens were enterprising men. Regino du Repaire de Truffin y Amador, born in Santa Clara to a French father and Cuban mother, had been educated in Paris, returning to Cuba to become president of the Havana Yacht Club, marry Pepe Rionda's beautiful sister-in-law, and acquire and develop plantations, most successfully his *Mercedes*.³ Horatio Rubens, a graduate of Columbia Law School in 1891, had started out as Elihu Root's law clerk in 1892. Three years later, while apparently continuing with Root, he had also become legal counsel to the Cuban junta in New York. Settling in Havana, he served there as attorney for the New York banking firm of Speyer and Company.⁴

In 1911, with the purchase of a 2.5-mile railroad and a concession of land from his friend President Gómez that gave him control of railroad links to the port of Matanzas, Tarafa reached the takeoff point for his aspirations. He obtained Rionda's cooperation in approaching Mincing Lane; enlisted Walter Ogilvie, United Railway's legal counsel in Havana; and sailed for England with the banker Roland Conklin. A glimpse at how boldly he gambled is available in a furious letter that Lagemann wrote Rionda from Mincing Lane during the proceedings. "I wrote you," he dictated, "that for the sake of securing Tarafa sugar, we would take $100,000. . . . But what I refused to do was to have my name paraded everywhere . . . strongly recommending the property to investors. . . . I leave that to Mr. Conklin (a man, as you say, of not very high reputation)." Rionda, Lagemann thundered, was seeking funds "for a stranger who . . . would mortgage no security and intended to give skimmed milk only." But Tarafa went on to Paris, then back to London, where he was able, by a sort of railway blackmail, to obtain funds to launch the Central Cuba Sugar Company.⁵

Amid the ebullience of Tarafa's success, Lagemann's reproaches depressed Manuel. He saw his London associates holding him back from promising opportunities. Also, he feared President Gómez was not paying sufficient attention to the growing power of U.S. domestic sugar interests. Cuban politicians, he complained (not for the first or last time), had no real interest in the welfare of their country. The *remolacheros* (the U.S. sugar-beet men) were in Washington fighting tooth and nail for higher tariff protection. "You told me," Rionda wrote Tarafa, "that Cuba really gains very little from the 1903 Reciprocity Treaty and that is true in *pesos y centavos* but don't forget that the 20 percent preferential it grants keeps Cuba the United States' principal supplier of sugar."

Tarafa took up the cause of reciprocity, as eager a crusader politically as in high finance, discussing the matter with Edwin Atkins, who now filled Henry Havemeyer's chair as president of the American Sugar Refining Company. In matters concerning low tariffs, East Coast refiners and Cuban sugar magnates had every interest in common, and Atkins, Tarafa reported, had told him "the best way" to protect their joint interests. Accordingly, Tarafa was meeting the next day with President Gómez. "Tell me," Tarafa requested, "if you will accept the Cuban government naming you to negotiate in Washington, with another whom you may choose, to be also appointed by the Agrarian League, which will pay all your expenses etc." While he appreciated the honor of being named to represent the Cuban government, Rionda replied, he was too busy to serve, and he recommended instead Cuban-American's Robert Hawley along with Schaefer, the late Hugh Kelly's successor, as head of Hugh Kelly and Company. On such details of the delegation, a wiser, if Yankee, head prevailed, since Tarafa informed Rionda a week later that Atkins thought it would be more advantageous from a public relations point of view if Cuba's representatives should be Cuban instead of the American heads of American-owned sugar companies.[6]

When nothing came of the political negotiations, Rionda blamed Havana. The Cuban government had not acted "as energetically as the importance of the case demands." To Placé he growled: "As regards politics, that is something that I never hope to have satisfactory in that unfortunate island."[7]

But as the U.S. presidential election raged, he took another long step forward, incorporating the Manatí Sugar Company in New York on April 30, 1912. It was to build a completely new central on the northern coast of Oriente Province on a bay "more than twice the size of Havana harbor."[8] Obtaining the financing for his *Francisco* had been hard going among relatively small investors. *Stewart* had been financed by Schroeders before he had been involved. Now he himself approached the top echelons of North American financiers.

Wall Street was by 1912 very different from the modest neighborhood Manuel had first encountered, its taller buildings electric lit late into the night. The National City Bank had moved in 1908 across the street from its three-story lodging house to the site of the original Merchants' Exchange. It had preserved the historic Ionic colonnade from the 1863 U.S. Customs House and redesigned its interior to invoke the Roman Pantheon. The House of Morgan's gray-brown Drexel Building still held the corner of Broad and Wall Streets, but a Renaissance edifice was being planned to replace it, and J. Pierpont Morgan was shopping for marble columns in Italy. In some six square blocks where the banks clustered, bricks, mortar, granite, and marble attested to the success of American business.[9]

Simultaneously, a new generation was taking over. James Stillman of the National City Bank now spent most of his time in Paris, while a midwestern newspaper man, Frank A. Vanderlip, without banking experience, had become the bank's president in 1908. Stillman had picked Vanderlip almost on a whim, intrigued by his flair for public relations—Vanderlip had been assistant to President McKinley's secretary of the treasury, in which post he had sold the bonds that had financed the U.S. involvement in the Spanish-Cuban-American War. In the House of Morgan, lieutenants were closing ranks around J. Pierpont Jr. Jack looked like his father, but there was room beside him in 1910 for Tom Lamont, who, like Vanderlip, had begun his career as a newspaper reporter. None of the new men had business school book learning, but if they were less swashbuckling than their Robber Baron predecessors, the better to move swiftly, their banks were swollen with the excess capital of industrial advance. The railroads Morgan had rationalized had carried profits for a generation, oil money was spurting like geysers, and corporate deposits totaled unprecedented sums. National City was the largest bank in the United States, but George Baker's First National and Kuhn, Loeb were not far behind in financing new bond issues. As whole new industries called for enormous investments, the banks cooperated in bond underwriting, sharing risks and profits.

In many ways, this bankers' world, despite the anti-Semitism of the times, was a close-knit world. Boards of directors overlapped, and heads of one bank acquired important blocks of stock in the others. Five out of the nine directors of the Chase National Bank were also directors of First National. Morgan partners were First National directors; Jacob H. Schiff of Kuhn, Loeb sat on National City's board. Since national banks could not establish overseas branches or exercise trust functions while state-chartered banks and trust companies could, the great banks were also buying up impressive parcels of the latter's stock. Bankers Trust, the National Bank of Commerce, and Guaranty Trust were thus becoming

"Morgan banks." From 1909, when Morgan took it over, the Guaranty Trust Company was being built into the nation's largest trust and had two Morgan partners on its board.

There were also fraternal bonds between big business and what Progressives at the time called the Money Trust. The bankers sat on the boards of burgeoning American businesses, the captains of industry similarly on the boards of the banks in which they placed their deposits. National City was Standard Oil of New York's bank. William Rockefeller was a director, as were the Havemeyers, father and later son, and James Howell Post of the National Sugar Refinery and of the Cuban-American Sugar Company. Louis D. Brandeis, lawyer, trust buster, and future justice of the U.S. Supreme Court, pointed out that bankers on corporate boards served other functions than merely supervising how wisely the funds they had already invested were expended. They could, he wrote, encourage new bond issues and handsome loans at profitable interest rates.[10] But if such warnings reached Rionda's ears, he still must have money for *Manatí*. It could come only from the bankers. He was known on Wall Street by now, and Sullivan & Cromwell stood by with introductions.

Manatí's capitalization was for $1.5 million, three times what *Francisco*'s had been. This time money came quickly. Edmund Converse, president of Bankers Trust; Monsieur Hartjes of Morgan, Hartjes and Company of Paris; Captain Joseph Raphael DeLamar, the International Nickel Company's largest stockholder; and Sullivan & Cromwell each put up $100,000, with Czarnikow-Rionda contributing $150,000. Sullivan & Cromwell was represented by Alfred Jaretzki, who, born poor to immigrant parents in New York in 1861, had somehow made the vast social leap from City College of New York to Harvard, graduating there at age twenty magna cum laude. He had joined the fabled firm in 1881, simultaneously attending Columbia Law School, and became a partner in 1894, specializing in corporation practice. He had guided many large corporate reorganizations, including both the Illinois Central and the Northern Pacific, and was second only to William Nelson Cromwell in importance. Manuel also had hopes, he wrote Truffin, to interest a partner of J. P. Morgan and Company itself. "Con gente así, se puede ir a ciegas" [With such men, we can go the limit]. There was money in Cuba as well. Rionda and Jaretzki planned for Cubans to contribute

$350,000—$150,000 from Truffin, $100,000 from Eduardo de Ulzurrún (a wealthy Havana Spanish marquis), and $100,000 from Manuel Rafael Angulo, one of Rionda's Havana attorneys. Also, Rionda hoped that José H. Beola—who owned much of the land being purchased for *Manatí*—would accept $260,000 of his price in bonds and stock.[11]

Briefly, an Afro-Cuban rebellion in the field discouraged prospective investors. But in mid-May, Jaretzki wrote of his pleasure that Rionda had decided to increase his subscription from $150,000 to $250,000 and his expectation that within a few days the full $1.5 million would be subscribed. Rionda pressed McCahan and the Craigs to take some shares, reassuring them that "these 'Big' people in the Syndicate will see to it the syndicate makes money."[12] All ended triumphantly. A few months before the U.S. elections (Taft, Roosevelt, and Woodrow Wilson battling out their three-way race), the decisive meeting was held at the home of banker Isaac Newton Seligman of the investment banking house of J & W Seligman. Founded in 1862, with offices at 1 William Street in New York's financial district, Seligmans was a legendary private international bank, dominated by the brilliant Strauss brothers, Albert and Frederick. In their fifties, they were the sons of a couple who had left Germany in 1848 to go into candy making in New York. Both had started at City College of New York, dropped out for "lack of means," and gone to work as junior clerks for Seligmans in the 1880s, becoming partners by the turn of the century.[13]

Present at the meeting were Seligman, the Strausses, Jaretzki, Rionda, and Claus August Spreckels, president of the Federal Sugar Refining Company of Yonkers, New York. Seligman agreed to take a $200,000 share in *Manatí* and Spreckels $100,000. Never, wrote Rionda, had he seen a company as cooperative ("que tenga simpatías") and that brought together such rich men. It seems to me, he wrote, that we now have many open doors to accomplish great ventures ("hacer negocios grandes"). There was then some discussion of naming a North American as president of the company. "Neither you nor I want flowers," Rionda wrote Truffin. "I want not glory but dollars; let them have the Presidency then, if thus they desire." In the end, Regino Truffin was made president and Jaretzki, Frederick Strauss, and Rionda vice presidents. The marquis de San Miguel de Aguayo, Eduardo de Ulzurrún, became general manager, personally taking command of the construction. The venture was then and subsequently listed as "American" in the records, again leaving much entrepreneurship out of the account.[14]

By late 1912, overall Cuban expansion was progressing steadily. Two years of profitable prices had brought 1912 production up to almost 1.9 million tons, double what it had been in 1908, and poised it for a leap in 1913 to more than 2.4 million tons. Tarafa's Central Cuba Sugar Company spread out, acquiring the *Saratoga* and the modest *Santo Domingo*. Rionda was put in as the company's treasurer to watch out for the interests of the London investors and added some $500,000 of Czarnikow-Rionda's own money. Tarafa had also acquired his second railroad stepping-stone. Small and rickety, the little Júcaro and Morón controlled a crucial sixty-mile north-south right-of-way, from the Atlantic to the Caribbean. It was what was left of an old Spanish military road once called the Ferrocarril de la Trocha de Júcaro-Morón. He had also picked up control of the central *Jagueyal*, within sight of Rionda's central *Stewart*. Now he had his base for his railroad—the Cuban Northern. It would stretch eastward from Morón some one hundred miles to the port of Nuevitas. He began planting 400 *caballerías* of cane to supply *Morón*, a new central that he and his allies would also construct.[15]

Morón, the *Louisiana Planter* wrote, "represented Cuban, or at least 'Spanish-speaking' capital only." Laying its cornerstone in January 1912 involved a special train from Havana, a blessing by the bishop of Cienfuegos, bands, and champagne, as well as an address by Nicolás Castaño's son-in-law, Rogelio Díaz Pardo, a prominent lawyer and politician. The factory was to be equipped with four seven-foot, quadruple-effect mills from Grueber Stork and Company of Holland. Babcock and Wilcox of New York would furnish, among other equipment, nine boilers, four bagasse furnaces (representing 5,140 horsepower), and centrifugals. "Cuban and Spanish experience in sugar-making here will call to their assistance both European and American skill in machinery-making." Eight months later, as *Morón* was nearing completion, the *Planter*'s correspondent, Irene Wright, again stressed its Hispanicity, praising López Navarro, its contractor, as "a Spaniard of the best type.... His sort ... are the keenest business men in this island, reliable, accurate, and the way they work and make everybody else work leaves the average American and all his Yankee energy panting at the post." López

Navarro was an agent in Cuba for the U.S. machinery manufacturer Babcock and Wilcox. This was flood time for Cuban businessmen, a good price for sugar, adequate demand, and smooth identity of interests with the refining interests to their north.[16]

President Gómez arranged a generous Cuban government subsidy for the Northern Railroad. In October, he signed a decree granting it $6,000 per kilometer. "Once," wrote the *Planter*'s Miss Wright, "before the war of 1868 some of the most famous plantations in the colony were situated right in there. . . . War came and slavery was abolished and hard times endured. . . . Tropical vegetation overran all. The very names of the plantation houses which once stood for Creole wealth and enterprise dropped from memory."

Now the "unsurpassed cane lands" would come into their own again. The marvel, Wright thought, was that they should have been neglected so long "when we consider the size of profits bound to accrue . . . under the same keen business management."[17]

Expansion built its own momentum. Czarnikow-Rionda's profits rose, and Rionda concluded that free sugar was a real possibility in the next Congress. Although the United States was producing more and more at home and in its insular possessions (692,556 long tons of beet sugar in 1912 compared to 312,921 in 1905, and 862,798 tons of cane from Hawaii and Puerto Rico alone even before the Philippines came on-line), it was still supplying only half of what the nation consumed. Since mainland production costs for both cane and beet sugar were far higher than Cuban costs, even if sugar tariffs favoring domestic interests were not abolished altogether (which seemed possible) but merely slashed (which seemed inevitable), U.S. home production would be curtailed by at least some 1 million tons.

The U.S. election went as Rionda predicted, with Wilson triumphant. While Rionda would have preferred "a man of business and financial knowledge such as J. P. Morgan" rather than "these book-worms and judicial men," hopes for free entry for Cuba's sugar rose high.[18] Shortly thereafter, a Cuban election also took place, with guerrillas again in the bush. This year they were rather quickly crushed. "The black shadows of revolution," Wright was able to poeticize, "which swept anon over Cuba, dimming the green and gold of her tropical spectrum, seems to be passing away." And she concluded optimistically: "As industrialism invades

Tarafa and the Genial Shark

her solitudes, rends her silences and disperses her shadows, it lays a kindly touch upon her people and by giving them occupation leads them a long step toward sanity and poise.... Steam and smoke are fast making [the Pearl of the Antilles] uglier—and better."[19]

The Conservative Party was declared the winner of the Cuban presidency, and on May 20, 1913, in the Red Parlor of the palace where the Spanish captain-generals had once commanded, Mario García Menocal, builder and administrator of *Chaparra*, the world's greatest sugar factory, and a current member of the board of directors of the Cuban-American Sugar Company, swore to uphold the Cuban Constitution. He then received a message of congratulations from Woodrow Wilson, who pledged that the United States would seek only "the development of such personal and commercial relations between Cuba and the United States as will redound to the profit and advantage of both and interfere with the rights and liberties of neither." Menocal's reply was dignified. "Trade relations will," he promised, "be cultivated and favors granted to American products in proportion as our products are received in the northern market." On his own inaugural day, two months earlier, Wilson had called a special session of the U.S. Congress in the cause of free trade. "We must abolish everything," he had instructed it, "that bears even the semblance of privilege or of any kind of artificial advantage."

The Underwood-Simmons Tariff duly passed on October 3, 1913, decreeing that on March 1, 1914, duties on 96° polariscope sugar (the highest grade of sugar admitted as "unrefined") would be lowered 25 percent and that after May 1, 1916, all sugars "of whatever origin, color or degree of purity" (in other words, including refined) would enter the American market duty free. Free sugar, Rionda believed, would save American consumers at least $50 million a year and, by lowering prices, lift demand.

The air, that year of 1913, crackled with opportunities. Czarnikow-Rionda's surplus would rise to $300,000 for the year after paying the usual dividends, 8 percent on preferred and 10 percent on the common stock.[20]

Rionda was too assured now to be checked or reprimanded by his London partners, and in August he exploded with anger in a six-page handwritten letter giving them notice of withdrawal from their joint firm. He would start a new house on his own, without London having any role in its management. He had, he wrote, reached fifty-nine the day

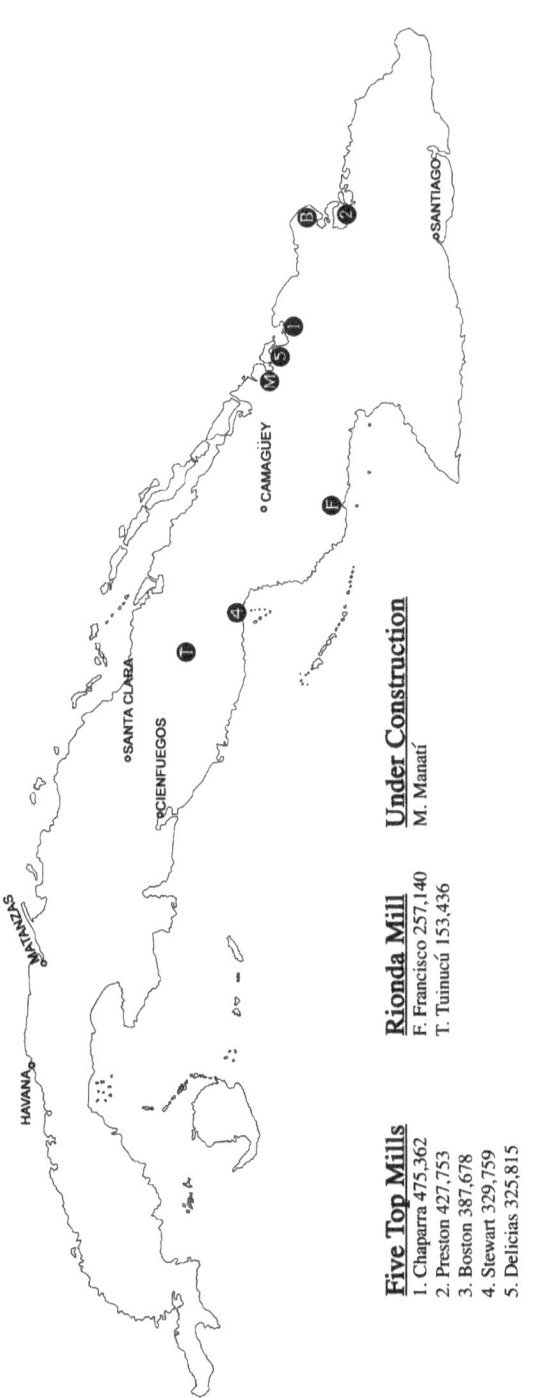

Map 2. Cuba mills, 1913. Production in 325-pound bags. Source: Cuba Review, 1915.

before. Since 1879, he had been hard at work. Though not a rich man "compared with any of you," he was comfortably "well supplied." "All my boys," he went on, "whom I have had the desire to help, are all able to take care of themselves. . . . Now it is up to them to continue the work commenced by me." If Lagemann's sons, Walter and Eric, who had been serving apprenticeships with him, wished to try their fortunes in New York, he continued, he would take them. But Lagemann Sr. and Ganzoni must place no capital with the new firm. "I want freedom for my nephews." (Mouse's head, lion's tail.)

He was proud of what he had accomplished. "My dear Lagemann, you and Ganzoni love money too much. You are always afraid of expending it and still more of loosing it. . . . I had much rather leave behind me Tuinucú—Francisco—Manatí—San Vincente & a New York house with boys of my own making at the head of all these enterprises than to leave $4 million to be thrown away by my sons, nephews or their children." If this was a variant of his reasoning when he had refused to sell *Tuinucú*, it also illustrated the loyalty he felt toward tangible cane fields. "Money is the curse to many an heir. I do not want to help idlers to increase. . . . My work will last longer than your millions."

He was still irate sixteen days later, writing to Westrik, another London partner: "I am not so bad as I am painted. Neither is the devil. I too want peace of mind. London business is pure & simple speculation. Ours is not so unless the advances made are so classified. But I would prefer to lose £10,000 in a bad a/c than £5,000 in a speculation. . . . I am not worried because money is at stake. It is only what we give that we carry away in our cold dead hands when we leave this world."

A second letter to Lagemann was equally firm. He would have "no one put money in the new company but people who if they have anything owe it entirely to me." "My plan," he wrote MacDougall, retired in Bournemouth, "is that my own boys will start a new house and play the game by themselves with assistance from me." After all, Manolo was thirty-six and Bernardo thirty-eight. Both were skilled in maneuvering through New York's financial and brokerage mazes. In Cuba, José, Leandro, and Salvador were supervising plantations to their uncle's grudging satisfaction, while their sister Elena's husband, Oliver Doty, was learning to manage *Tuinucú*. Surely, daily details could be trusted to the family team he had formed, if he supervised. He wrote Victor

Fig. 4. From left, Ellen and Manolo Rionda, Maude and Bernardo Braga, unidentified, Manuel and Harriet Rionda, unidentified

Zevallos that "the monument that has been erected shall be zealously guarded against demolition."[21]

Reinforcing his rebellious independence, his new moneyed contacts in New York were looking for further investments, and he guessed that, with free sugar scheduled for 1916, Texas and Louisiana sugar interests, as well as beet men, might move across the Gulf. The Oxnard brothers (one of them president of the American Beet Sugar Producers Association) were contacting him and approaching Kuhn, Loeb about funding. In May, one of them arrived in Havana with Van Horne "to secure lands where they can install machinery from several of their Louisiana sugar factories which they don't propose operate under present tariff conditions."[22]

He was apparently not too concerned that prices were less satisfactory, as Cuban production in 1913 jumped from 1912's 1.9 million tons to 2.4 million tons. From 1909 to 1912, the annual average price for sugar, C&F New York, duty paid, had not gone below 4 cents per pound. Yet in 1913, the price for sugar had opened at 3.73 cents per pound and moved almost steadily downward to 3.30 cents on May 15. Meanwhile, he became involved with adding sugar futures to the trading on New York's Coffee Exchange, placing Manolo on the committee that accomplished it.

"Selling futures" had voodoo overtones that made people uneasy. But the grain elevators of the North American Midwest had fortified the corn and wheat farmers, while speculators bid up grain prices in a trading pit at the Chicago Board of Trade. There were investors on Wall Street with money to gamble on sugar prices, three months, six months ahead, to help free Cuba from the exclusive clutches of the Sugar Trust.[23] This was a new game that Rionda and his nephews must learn to play.

But Rionda did not agree with other proposals that were being discussed. Some of Cuba's bolder hacendados—Rafael Fernández de Castro, Francisco Negra, and Froilán Cuervo apparently notable among them—were studying Brazil's efforts to market its coffee through a government body and how Russia, under the Romanov czar, was limiting sugar production in order to make that industry more "remunerative."[24] Also, since a lack of credit seemed at the heart of Cuba's dependency, these sugar men were now talking of a Cuban agricultural bank to make advances against crops, as well as of refining on their own plantations now that the Underwood Tariff promised them that when May 1916 dawned there would be free entry of even the whitest sweetener into the U.S. market. Double and triple presses, centrifugals, and all of the new, improved machinery had so improved the processing of the raw cane that only one more rather short step would produce a sugar so white and dry that—although it might not technically be classified "refined"—it could be sold directly to consumers.

Why, planters asked, had the Atlantic Coast refineries been able to pay handsome dividends while the Cubans themselves had scraped and borrowed? Because, they explained to each other, U.S. tariffs had been prohibitive on imports of sugar over a certain grade of purity. Now that Woodrow Wilson had taken charge, Cuba could supply its great market directly and sell its white cheaper with lower shipping costs and lower financing charges because of the shorter time from the cane field to the grocery shelf. There would also be more skilled factory jobs for Cubans. The Gómez Mena brothers, who had been among the first to completely electrify their plants, began a "boneblack refinery" at their *Amistad*.

Rionda held aloof from these aspirations. By now a valued client of the National City Bank and the Royal Bank of Canada, as well as of Schroeders in London, and with funds of his own to advance to his connections, he feared the paper money that, given their own agricultural bank, Cuban politicians might run off the presses. As for refining in Cuba, it would of course alienate the East Coast refiners in the United States. The Sugar Trust ran a powerful lobby in Washington, and the beet-sugar men, with their cry for protection for their own interests, would try to repeal the Underwood Tariff as soon as the congressional balance shifted in their favor. Cuban sugar needed allies under the eagle's wings.

Rionda shared these fears with both Nicolás Castaño and Laureano Falla Gutiérrez, who, when interviewed by the *Diario de la Marina*, pointed out with prosperous self-satisfaction the desirability of the status quo. Refineries, Laureano remarked, were expensive to build and the "combustibles" to run them 40 percent more expensive than in the States. The American refiners were not the enemies of the Cuban planters but their "natural allies." If Americans prospered, it was not because of a high "differential" between the price of raw sugar and the price of refined but because of the enormous quantities involved and an excellent selling mechanism which smaller, individual Cuban operations could not equal.[25]

Nevertheless, as sugar prices did not rise beyond August's 3.8 cents per pound but declined to end the year 1913 at 3.23 cents, calls for a stronger organization of sugar men, a more active Agrarian League, became louder. President Menocal, who was reported purchasing the remains of the old Elejalde estate in Havana Province to make into a model showplace, sat on the podium when a crowded meeting took place in November 1913. Rionda was skeptical of joint action, and although Hawley of the Cuban-American Sugar Company as well as the Gómez Mena brothers, the Mendozas, and Miguel Arango were involved, no member of the Rionda clan was seen attending, nor did the commissions appointed include a Rionda connection among their forty-four members. Only two commissioners were not Hispanic: Hawley and George Crawley, recently appointed by Menocal to head up a scientific research station.[26]

When in February a separate Association of Planters and Sugar Manufacturers was launched, Hawley reappeared as a member, but again neither Rionda nor his kinsmen came aboard. In June 1914, a joint meeting merged the association and the league, electing Tarafa president, with Ernesto Longa, Francisco Negra, G. R. Fowler, and Froilan Cuervo vice presidents. Longa was president of *Mercedita* (1913 production, 104,971 bags) in Pinar del Río, and Negra was a wealthy colono. Fowler, British on his father's side but Cuban-born, headed the *Constancia, Narcisa, Parque Alto*, and *Dos Hermanos*, all in Santa Clara and collectively producing about 400,000 bags in 1913. Froilan Cuervo controlled the *Nueva Paz* (Havana, 91,500 bags) and would shortly be involved with the new *Algodones* and *Arrojo Prieto*. These were solid, ambitious men.[27]

Manatí's construction meanwhile was going forward, and the mill, on schedule, began to grind on January 19, 1914. Manuel recounted the day's success: "When the first train came along whistling and decorated with flags, many were deeply affected and tears could be seen in eyes of men, not women. I do not know what the future of this plantation will be, but of one thing I am certain, that those who come after us will have to do justice to the work that was accomplished here. . . . From the car basculator up to where the juice runs, viz: the five defecators, there was not the slightest trouble. . . . There was no escape of steam and not a pipe burst."

"Sr. Rionda," the *Louisiana Planter* reported in early February, "invited the community to celebrate with him, at a free moving picture show in the little theater there. Cleopatra was the film shown." In late February, in a flurry of private railway cars and festivities, the New York investors—most of whom had never seen a cane field—were brought down to inspect what their funds had made possible. "They were very much satisfied," Manuel wrote back to his New York nephews, "and arrangements were made to increase the capacity as soon as possible to 500/600,000 bags for the crop 1916/17. An additional . . . $650,000 were subscribed on the spot. . . . This pleased me very much as it shows the confidence in the management by the capitalists, who are really no more than perfect strangers to me and have known me for such a short time."[28]

At the beginning of the 1914 zafra, as the carts began to dump the cane at his mills (*Francisco, Tuinucú*, and *Manatí*), Rionda had estimated his possible profits if production rose as much as it should (to a projected 785,833 bags) and if the price of sugar and molasses held. His figures show all the details that went into the calculations: prices for fuel, packing, freight, bags, and more. If all went as hoped, there should be an overall "operating profit" of $877,999.[29]

The cane cutters were at work, the mills ground the 1914 zafra, the bags were swung into the ships' holes. But when on March 1, 1914, the Underwood-Simmons Tariff dropped the duty on Cuban sugar from 1.348 cents to 1.0048 cents per pound, no benefit accrued to Cuba, since the price received dropped proportionately. By March 10, a sale was made that netted only 1.73 cents FOB. Meanwhile, in the United States and its possessions, production had gone up 630,000 short tons in five years; in Cuba, more than 1.2 million short tons; and worldwide, almost 5 million short tons.[30]

Nor was this the only threat to Rionda's interests. That June, a new U.S. Federal Reserve Act made it legal at last for American banks to open branches overseas, challenging his role as the major source of credit for his planter clients. In July, it was announced that the National City Bank was extending its field abroad. "I have decided," Manuel wrote Ogilvie, "to place the services of Czarnikow-Rionda Company at the disposal of the National City Bank because of our intimate relations with that Institution, where we keep our largest accounts, and because of my desire to keep well informed of what goes on in the Island of Cuba." Yet, he continued, if "foreign institutions of this caliber" should open Cuban branches, while they would have "exceptional opportunities for investment" and be "of great benefit to the planter," they would at the same time "tend to make it more difficult for us, in the future, to enter upon such profitable and extensive business as is offering now." "After these big guns, like City Bank," he wrote Lagemann, "are well rooted in the Island, business will not be so easily had." That year, Czarnikow-Rionda would sell some 7 million bags, 40 percent of Cuban production, but Rionda believed he had "real" control over the sale of only 3 million bags. "Can I be easy," he pleaded, "when I see so many capitalists going into Cuba!! . . . give me $10 million and I will give even the City a good run!"[31]

He was also well aware that the new trading of sugar futures on the New York Coffee Exchange was bringing not only opportunities but a larger potential for speculation. At the harvest's peak, when sugar brought only 2.03 cents for immediate delivery, the speculators had been willing to pay 2.06 cents to 2.09 cents for June and July shipment. Still, trading was a rigged game. Prices jumped too suddenly ("2⁷/₁₆ths July") and then too quickly receded. "You can have no idea," he wrote,

> of the ways and means some refiners (No. 100) employ to manipulate the market. . . .
>
> That is, Nos. 101 and 102—who separated in business last year—now are made the tools of No.150 and it was only a few days ago that No. 160 put out some of their own sugars through 170 and rebought them through No. 180, thus putting the market down to 2⁵/₁₆ cents. [The numbers were part of a code. A slip of paper would have been enclosed in the letter, or even mailed under separate cover, telling to whom they referred.]
>
> If there is anything I should like to see result from the Options in Futures on the Coffee Exchange it is the abolition of the modern methods that have been introduced into sugar circles—as one man put it the other day, the ethics employed in the sugar trade are far below those in any other community.
>
> There are some parasites in this business that live by selling the article short and taking advantage of the financial situation of the planter to buy! I could name 4 or 5 of these people who live by such a means.[32]

Price rigging, competition from the great banks threatening his hold over his clients, falling prices—such were Rionda's worries in July 1914. But in remote Sarajevo, a student's bullet changed his prospects.

On August 1, 1914, the day Germany declared war on Russia, the *Louisiana Planter*'s new Havana correspondent pounded out his copy for his weekly "News Letter." There were, he typed, "prospects that the sugars to be made will obtain much better prices than for a long time past."[33] It was a considerable understatement, for in all the markets of the world, prices quickly soared. On July 30, 1914, 96° centrifugal sugar had sold for 3.29 cents per pound, duty paid, in New York. On August 6, it sold for 4.14 cents.

On August 3, the day Germany declared war on France (and his sixtieth birthday), Rionda wrote his Hamburg-born London partner, Lagemann. This "awful catastrophe," he observed, "only proves that civilization is a farce, and that while great armies and navies exist . . . we cannot claim to be civilized and sons of God." He had, he went on, been trying "to lighten Lagemann's account" in the New York firm but perhaps, after all, it would be better for Lagemann to keep his capital in the neutral United States rather than in England since Lagemann, it must now be realized, was German.[34] Rionda himself had been an enemy alien sixteen years earlier. He sympathized with his associate, although they were personally on strained terms.

On August 7, 1914, sugar sold in New York for 4.26 cents a pound. In all his experience, Manuel wrote Victor Zevallos, he had never seen anything like it. He was, he added, cabling everyone to be cautious, not to get excited and not to speculate. Prices might possibly go up another ¾ cents, but it was like playing with dynamite to hold sugar at these prices. "War is a thing," he warned, "of which we merchants know nothing."[35]

But his clients, reading their newspapers, decided it might be a long war. They calculated that even on a sale of only 20,000 bags, if they waited a little longer a rise of ¾ cent a pound would bring them an additional $48,750. Even Pedro Laborde refused to take Manuel's advice, although Rionda had recently advanced him $400,000. He had already received $60,000 more this year than he had ever hoped for, Manuel grumbled.

Such rebellion as Laborde's boded ill. Although in 1914 Czarnikow-Rionda would sell more than 40 percent of Cuba's 18 million bag production, the sugar came from many hacendados. Manuel sold for Galban y Cía of Sagua la Grande; for Sobrinos de Bea y Cía of Matanzas; for Manuel's former competitor, Francke, Hijos y Cía of Havana; and for Ferrer and Rabassa of Cienfuegos. These four brought him over 2 million bags. Not far behind (quantities sold for the Stewart Sugar Company and for Tarafa's Central Cuba Sugar Company intervening) were the Gómez Mena brothers, whose three mills in Havana Province supplied 362,980 bags. Within the family circle, Manuel sometimes referred harshly to the brothers, but he courted their business, of which in 1914 he had only some two-thirds. They had been among the first in Cuba to completely electrify their mills, and they had recently invested heavily in modern irrigation methods. Czarnikow-Rionda also sold sugar for Gutiérrez, Pelayo, Truffin, Laurentino García, Nazabal, and Castaño. Each of these clients might at will assert his independence. "I would prefer peace and 2½ to War and 4½—Cubans will make so much money it will spoil them," he commented.[36]

On August 18, he was sure the market had reached its zenith. He was correct, for 1914's high was 6.32 cents per pound on August 13. Thereafter prices, with some wavering from day to day, slid downward to end the year at 4.01 cents per pound. The giddy rise had lasted less than two weeks.

War had brought a quick, unprecedented demand, but now the classic forces of supply and demand would no longer run rampant. On August 4, when Great Britain declared war on the German and the Austrian-Hungarian Empires, His Majesty's Government had resurrected its mercantilist traditions and seized control first of Britain's armaments industries, then of its railroads, and next of its sugar, supplies of which would be exhausted, it was realized, in two months. The chickens Adam Smith had hatched were home to roost. With bargain prices abroad and with the blessing of the Manchester School of Economics, Great Britain had for over half a century relied on Germanic imports to fill its sugar bowls, while the Empire's Caribbean islands were abandoned to decline. In 1913, 67.5 percent of the raw sugar it had consumed and 72 percent of the refined sugar had come from Germany and Austria. Now the beets along the Elbe were enemy crops; armies were trampling those of Belgium and northern France. Java was half a world away, and the ships that might have fetched its cane must become the troopships of the far flung empire.

Overnight, Great Britain seized what supplies there were within the kingdom or on the high seas. On August 7 and 8, it purchased 57,000 tons of Cuban sugar on the New York market and in the next ten days rounded up the rest of available supplies worldwide, including the 211,904 tons that were all Cuba had remaining. It was this urgency that for ten days impelled the soaring market of early August. Then, despite the increasing brutality of the conflict, as Rionda had predicted, prices stopped rising and receeded.[37]

On August 20, the United Kingdom regularized its control by establishing the Royal Sugar Commission under the Home Office, with civil servants from the Board of Trade and the Ministries of the Exchequer and Agriculture and a single professional sugar man, Robert Park Lyle. One of the six sons of a ruddy Scottish sailing ship owner, Lyle had been brought from the Clyde to help with the family's refinery on the London wharfs and in its Mincing Lane head office, where he was neighbor to

Czarnikow.³⁸ Henceforth, in a world at war, there would be new confines, not least for the world's merchants, although His Majesty's Government bought through competing firms of brokers, C. Czarnikow Ltd. doing well with the arrangement. As the German armies flanked France's Maginot Line, it was obvious that Cuba's mills must reach maximum output as soon as the next zafra began.

The situation underlined Rionda's need for capital. He had always borrowed from Mincing Lane and from Schroeders to fund his clients, and Cuba had planned on $30 million from Europe for the expenses of the dead season. Now, with the war disrupting international financial exchanges, all credits there were canceled. They would have to finance the Cuban crop alone "with," he wrote Zevallos, "only what little assistance we can get from the U.S."

Rionda wrote Lagemann on August 13 that Czarnikow-Rionda could not repay C. Czarnikow on schedule without sacrificing business in Cuba. If he could retain £150,000 from the London firm and borrow £50,000 from Lagemann and £30,000 from Ganzoni until January 1915, he could pull through since he had a pledge of $1 million from the National City Bank and the National Bank of Commerce. On August 31, as the French were beginning to slow the German advance on the western front, Manuel wrote his thanks for London's cable confirming loans totaling $1,325,000 against the zafra, payable in April 1915. He had been talking angrily of breaking his ties with Mincing Lane, but this was not the time to be difficult.³⁹

From Mincing Lane, young clerks marched off to war, some not to return. Younger sons of the firm's correspondents from Buenos Aires to Melbourne and Vancouver passed through New York on their way to the war and were entertained and wished godspeed. Lagemann's sons, Eric and Walter, had already come to New York as trainees with the New York firm and remained. Ogilvie's son, George, had been on the point of leaving to serve his apprenticeship at C. Czarnikow Ltd., but on August 7 Manuel had instructed Leandro and Oliver Doty at *Tuinucú* that George would now go to Cuba instead. "You know," he wrote his nephews, "how closely associated we are with Mr. Ogilvie and I am going to consider his son as one of us. . . . I want him to be treated as one of the family." And again, "I wish you would put at his disposal my horse, Rajah, and let him ride out in the fields with Mr. Tucker, with Swift and yourself."⁴⁰

At Schroeders, under suspicion as a German firm and with its capital heavily committed in Berlin and Frankfurt, Frank Cyril Tiarks, a partner and a director of the Bank of England, took charge while the baron Bruno von Schroeder kept out of sight in his country house, carrying on with the Schroeder orchids. On November 18, Manuel penned him a handwritten note. "I want you to know that you have my sympathy in these hard times when your feelings must be sad. . . . Let us pray we may see an end . . . & wishing you patience and good cheer." In December, there was a letter of thanks to Tiarks and the baron. Realizing the many difficulties under which they were laboring, he replied that he appreciated their offer for £50,000 credit. He had, however, made other arrangements for financing the crop, but whenever Schroeders was ready to do business in the old way, he would be ready for them. He had not bound himself to his present financiers for the future, for his relations with Schroeders were too long-standing and pleasant for him to want to change.⁴¹ To the Scottish MacDougall, Manuel wrote the conventional thing: he was "very glad" that Great Britain had jumped into the breach "as it was her duty." But to the Swiss Ganzoni, he was wistful. "I am one of those who believe that there should be no nationality but the earth that we inhabit & that there should be no strifes but those of commercial rivalry, for after all it is commercial supremacy that should prevail, it is brains, not might, that must conquer." To the German Lagemann, he commented that he didn't know enough of European politics to judge but that the war would "have to be paid for by the poor" in "high prices and misery." And two months later: "[T]he poor will be the greatest sufferers—crowned heads never starve."⁴²

"I am glad," Manuel had written Lagemann, "that you made such handsome profits. For myself, I prefer not to have made any out of this awful catastrophe."⁴³ But at the end of 1914, Czarnikow-Rionda had been able to pay its usual generous dividends and have $370,000 left to "pass on to surplus." As "New York managers," the Riondas had been entitled to "from seven to ten percent" of the year's profits as well as the returns on their own shares. And they shared as well the profits of the clan's plantations, *Francisco, Washington,* and *Tuinucú,* which Manuel had predicted would be over $800,000 if sugar sold at 2.10 cents a pound. They also shared in the Cuban Trading Company's commissions on the purchases for their clients. With the war's high prices, every hacendado had gone into high gear, and the Cuban docks were piled high with new machinery.

Manuel's sister's son, Higinio Fanjul Rionda, was now receiving his uncle's closer attention. Up to now, he had been entrusted first with two colonías at *Francisco*, then with a third at *Manatí*. Between Higinio and his uncle, as between Higinio's father, Alonso Fanjul, and Manuel, there had occasionally been friction—the Fanjuls must have had an independent streak. But in 1914, Higinio, while retaining his colonías, was brought in to join Zevallos in the Cuban Trading Company in Havana and in 1915 he was made its vice president.

Manuel briefed Higinio, walking with him on the grounds of the Rionda estate at Alpine, New Jersey, during one of the visits, every dead season, when Manuel drew his kin around him. In the fall of 1914, Manuel wrote Higinio several times a week. He wanted, he wrote on October 20, "the names of all the plantations doing business with #3," for this man was "our greatest competitor."

In Cienfuegos, Rionda wrote, "[Y]ou say we've 114,000 bags—48,000 of Miguel Díaz and 66,000 of Castaño and Laureano Falla Gutiérrez. We've always had difficulty in Cienfuegos because of the competition, and I hope now that we have you in Cuba you can go there to see if we can do more with Don Nicolás." They had sold 30,000 bags for Bea and 30,000 for Arenal, Rionda noted. They had advanced Pedro Laborde $500,000. He enclosed a list of the sales to date. "[T]here are rumors," he continued, "that machinery manufacturers will not now be willing to grant long terms of payment for orders. Naturally, there may be some difficulty in securing loans for payrolls and other expenses that the ingenio owners must meet during the dead season."[44]

Cuba's hacendados continued restive through the long months when the European conflict stalled in the mud and the predictions of a quick victory gave way to grim endurance. Britain's Royal Sugar Commission, in competition with the U.S. refineries, purchased all the sugar Cuba offered, and through 1915, prices continued high, always in the range of 4 cents per pound.

Since July 1914, Manuel had been negotiating with Lagemann and Ganzoni to detach Czarnikow-Rionda from the London firm. But in May 1915, he wrote them that he needed $5 million so that Czarnikow-Rionda, not Wall Street, could finance moving 8 million to 10 million bags of sugar, worth $100 million to $120 million, in less than ten months. He must be strong enough, he commented, not to need to borrow from local banks since such borrowing would "mean our very life depends on them." Therefore he was willing to agree that there should henceforth no longer be a restriction on the transfer of Czarnikow-Rionda's common shares. He had insisted on that restriction in 1909 to protect his family legacy. That concern was still important, but the need for funds now overrode it. To his old associates he was honest. "My greatest ambition," he confessed, "is that in my family there shall continue that unity of interest and perfect harmony that has existed for generations. This idea of mine may be impossible, especially now that the family has branched out and there is more over which to create discord."

Now he wanted to be free to transfer his personal stock. If the common stock could be transferred, it would open the danger of outside interests coming in, but if his nephews would not be willing to look after the business, they would not be worthy of it. His Cuban nephews Leandro, José, and Salvador, he went on, were largely interested in *Francisco, Tuinucú,* and *San Vincente* but had no stake in Czarnikow-Rionda, although the Rionda plantations contributed nearly $100,000 in commissions to Czarnikow-Rionda's yearly profits. Bernardo and Manolo had, on the contrary, only small shares in the plantations but large shares in the brokerage house. Perhaps in the future this division would be a bone of contention, unless each nephew should be interested in every enterprise. And he added that since Lagemann would have $100,000 in common stock, his sons could come in as directors when age and experience would qualify them. On August 1, 1915, Lagemann and Rionda entered into a contract for a five-year copartnership under which Lagemann acquired 20 percent of Czarnikow-Rionda's common shares and would receive 20 percent of the firm's profits.[45]

The U.S. and Canadian banks were enthusiastically opening their own branches in Cuba just as his traditional London sources were constrained. He now needed to risk his exclusive control of Czarnikow-Rionda to finance his clients' harvests, while hitherto respectful clients grew increasingly independent. War had its costs and dangers, although its sacrifices were handsomely rewarded financially. But at this juncture, there seemed to open a new route for the Riondas to a still greater future.

4

Cuba Cane

The Cuba Cane Sugar Corporation was incorporated on December 31, 1915. Three years later, Rionda described its genesis as rather by chance, recounting "a casual conversation I had had with Mr. Strauss in September 1915 when quite accidentally I told him that Cuban plantations might be purchased at favorable prices. . . . The idea seemed to strike Mr. Strauss favorably and that same evening we called on Mr. Sabin." Charles H. Sabin was president of the Guaranty Trust Company.[1]

Yet when Manuel, at sixty-two and in the midst of a world war, launched his clan on its most fateful gamble, it was not accidental at all but long premeditated. The idea of a great combination bringing a significant number of existing centrals under a single control—his own—had been in his thoughts for years. As early as September 1911, he had written his nephew Pepe that he had discussed it with Isaac Seligman. But nothing had come of it then, nor of similar dreams by others, although assorted capitalists were reliably reported considering such moves. It had been August 3, 1915, before, at Edwin Atkins's bidding, the Punta Alegre Sugar Company was incorporated. Backed by Boston capital, it put a thousand men to work clearing 4,200 acres to build a new facility on Cuba's north coast, at double prewar wages.[2]

Atkins had been chiefly involved outside Cuba since his father's death, not only with the American Sugar Refining Company of which he was a director and sometime president but also with the Union Pacific Railroad, the American Trust Company, the National Shawmut Bank, the Bank of Boston, with the Aetna Mills, the Boston Wharf Company, and Westinghouse Electric, of which he had also been president. But his family's origins were in Cuban sugar, and the romance of his youth, of sailing ships and the whole exotic, un-Boston enterprise, as well as his expertise in analyzing future profits, had led him, when his elder son, Robert, graduated from Harvard in 1910, to encourage the young man to "enter the sugar business in Cuba." It had been Mr. and Mrs. Atkins's considered decision to raise their sons in a cultured Boston suburb, and thus Bob had not been steeped in the cane fields as were all the Rionda nephews from their infancy. But "Bob seems as interested as if it were a theater," his father wrote home from Havana in 1910. "[H]e is investigating something every moment, in the sugar house, laboratory, or on the colonías as well as in the office. I think he will learn rapidly."

In 1915, when Edwin Farnsworth Atkins Jr. also graduated from Harvard and when prices were very profitable, the Punta Alegre Sugar Company was launched, in the expectation a third generation of Atkinses would find this sizable capitalization of their plantation heritage worthwhile. Bob organized it, his father wrote. But the twenty-six-year-old Bob was well reinforced. The Boston investment firm of Hayden, Stone and Company assumed its promotion. Eugene V. R. Thayer, president of Boston's Merchants National Bank, took charge of its finances while Edwin Atkins Sr. accepted its presidency. Shortly, the stockholders of the private Trinidad Sugar Company, which Havemeyer, Senff, and Atkins had founded in 1892, would vote to join Punta Alegre, as would the owners of *Florida*, a new plantation in Camagüey.[3]

Rionda, in contrast to Atkins's expansionary aspirations, did not plan to clear jungle to plant cane that would take fifteen months to ripen. The war could not last forever, and the sooner wartime profits were secured, the safer. Also, wartime prosperity threatened his base. The National City Bank and the Royal Bank of Canada were wooing his clients away with their easy loans.

The morning after Rionda and Strauss met with Charles Sabin, Rionda was ready to spring into action. He wrote Strauss (with a copy to Sullivan & Cromwell's Alfred Jaretzki) listing eleven plantations for possible purchase. They would, he estimated, cost between $25,400,000 and $28,950,000 and would produce about 2.6 million bags. The undertaking, he believed, would be profitable if sugar brought even 2.5 cents a pound. He would not, he promised the Guaranty Trust, buy any estate that would not make at least 10 percent profit a year on invested capital. But since most of the plantations were already selling through Czarnikow-Rionda (paying it commissions) and making their purchases through the Cuban Trading Company (involving more commissions), it would be "very essential to make some arrangement as to the sale of sugars and shipment of merchandise in order that we may not lose a hold on the business we have already had for many years."[4]

Bankers and lawyers conferred. It was agreed the Cuba Cane Sugar Corporation would have an authorized capital of $50 million, to be raised by the sale of 500,000 shares of 7 percent cumulative preferred stock, par $100. An additional 500,000 shares of common stock, no par value, would also be issued, which would pay dividends only after there was a sufficient amount in the treasury to ensure two years' dividends on the preferred stock. Both common and preferred stock would carry voting rights. They would be sold through a Wall Street syndicate whose members would receive free of charge a bonus of 70 shares of common stock for every 100 shares of preferred they underwrote. The Strauss brothers and Jaretzki then offered Rionda $1.5 million for his services in "buying the plantations and assisting in the organization of the Company." He refused it and demanded stock instead. "I refused," he wrote, "to accept the cash although I was told that my refusal might jeopardize the whole scheme." Thirty thousand common shares were then allotted to him and Truffin.

Why the refusal and the counterdemand? One explanation might be that he refused $1.5 million because he did not want to be an employee working for the financiers but preferred to be one among equals. Thirty thousand common shares would bring him 3 percent of the voting stock and ensure him a seat on the board of directors. Better the head of the mouse than the tail of the dog. While he believed he could trust to the New York bankers' ignorance of practical matters in the cane fields to ensure his dominance, stock ownership would fortify his position.

The venture agreed upon, the clan got down to details. Victor Zevallos and Higinio Fanjul in Cuba were instructed to collect options on about twenty-five plantations and Leandro to check on their condition. A burst of follow-up correspondence soon expressed Manuel's growing irritation at Cuban expectations. Since the Riondas had long-standing ties with most of the properties and since their owners were friends from Manuel's young manhood, they rather logically expected him to get them the best possible prices. One of Manuel's assorted explanations for the launching of Cuba Cane was, after all, his desire to aid his old friends. "I tell everybody here," he wrote Higinio, "that those who really started the ball rolling were Pedro Arenal and Pedro LaBorde who approached me at various times to assist them in the sale of their plantations." LaBorde, he complained to Higinio, had come to him two years earlier "with tears in his eyes," wanting to sell his *La Julia* and *Jobo*. Now LaBorde as well as Arenal, owner of *Socorro*, had "ridiculous pretensions. . . . I'm rather a fool in going into it to help [them] to get rid of their properties. . . . They merely unload their burdens on my shoulders." The interests of the investors must come first.

> Naturally, as the success of the company will depend upon me I am going to defend it to the utmost every way I can. . . . Supposing Pedro Arenal does ask my advice as to whether he should sell for $5,000,000 or $5,250,000. . . . I would be inclined to decide in favor of the company. . . . While the new company faces a very successful year and will make large profits, it is equally true that Pedro Arenal gets rid of his plantation—which in the event of his death would be very difficult for his heirs to handle—whereas the new company with one successful year might have to contend with 20 to 30 bad years.

This ratio of good to bad years sounded more pessimistic than was warranted. The two Pedros must have thought so. Manuel had planned to pay LaBorde between $3.4 million and $3.9 million. He ended up paying him $4 million. He paid $5 million for Arenal's *Socorro*, which he had estimated from $4 million to $4.5 million. He had planned to acquire the *Mercedes* for between $3.5 million and $4 million. Its chief owners, Regino Truffin and Miguel Arango (the latter its manager since the Spanish-Cuban-American War, and of the great Cuban family who had founded it in the 1840s), expected more, and Manuel tried to divide the two men. Writing Truffin, he held out promises that "naturally you will form part of the Company as its representative in Cuba." He also made a veiled threat. The new company might never come into existence if plantations were too expensive. His maneuvers worked in this case, as he obtained the *Mercedes* for $3.9 million. Not only Truffin but also Arango would become part of Cuba Cane's management. Five other sellers were persuaded to reduce the price of their options a total of $535,000.

The selling prices take into account commissions Rionda was paid by the sellers but which, unknown to them, he passed on to the corporation. "Whatever commission these people allow us," he informed Higinio, "will have to be given to the Syndicate because I would not care to have anyone think that I or anyone connected with me made anything in this behind their backs. While I say this to you, at the same time it is not to be disclosed to the sellers—the more commissions we get the cheaper the purchasers secure the plantations."[5]

There was no problem in finding investment bankers to underwrite the corporation. Manuel wrote Lagemann on December 27 that the preferred stock had been oversubscribed by the syndicate, "nearly doubled." The chief banker, he wrote, "was J. P. Morgan & Co., although their name does not appear in the syndicate for reasons of their own." Czarnikow-Rionda, which had planned to subscribe $1,650,000 "to show confidence," found its share reduced to $485,000 because of the demands from "our friends" to be let in. Eugene Meyer Jr. and Company headed a group of investment houses to handle the preferred at 97.5 in return for a selling commission of 2 percent, plus the bonus of common shares.[6]

Cuba Cane was incorporated on December 31, 1915, and Rionda left for Cuba on January 1, 1916. The new year was dawning auspiciously for his project at least, and it was not his fault that men were dug into their trenches in Flanders. On the contrary, he saw himself as supplying the sugar that cheered the troops, thus contributing to the war effort. By January 4, he was at the Hotel Inglaterra in Havana, writing the Strauss brothers and Jaretzki. Matters were rapidly moving forward. "My nephew Leandro and Miller Smith," he wrote, "left by special train last night on visit to 'Progresso,' 'Santa Gertrudis,' 'Alava,' 'España,' 'Lequeito,' 'Reforma' and 'San José.'" Haste was spurred by possible rivals. "Un stockbroker llamado Baruch" was said to be forming a $10 million syndicate, and there were rumors Tarafa was flirting with a rival endeavor. "Mr. Tarafa, together with Mr. Vidal Morales (the politician) and

Mr. Julian Linares, are obtaining options on sugar plantations here; in view of this fact I do not think we should have Mr. Tarafa on our Board of Directors, even if we buy Moron."

In his eagerness to close the purchases of the mills, Manuel threw some of his own shares into the bargaining. Of the 30,000 he had been given, he later reported, "17,382 were distributed gratis amongst those who had been of assistance to Mr. Truffin and myself . . . and to those who later became General Managers . . . and General Superintendents." One thousand each were given to Ogilvie and W. A. Merchant, head of the Banco Nacional, followed by 250 to Enrique Zulueta and 500 each to Pedro LaBorde and José Miguel Tarafa. Manuel explained the last three in a letter to Jaretzki. Zulueta had taken over the management of *Avila* and LaBorde that of *Socorro*. Tarafa's 500 shares had been promised when *Morón* was secured "in appreciation of his having reduced the purchase price." Truffin received 12,000 shares. With par for the common shares at $50, distributing 17,242 shares to others had cost Manuel, in theory, $862,100. Again, why? Why did he work so fervently to have the corporation pay as little as possible for each plantation, passing on his own commissions, then compensating the sellers from his own pocket? Pride, which kept him from admitting he had estimated prices too low? A sincere desire to build a successful company? The need to make haste?

Starting January 14, several cables a day informed New York of deals closed and contracts signed. "With . . . sugar prices going higher," he summarized later, "there was nothing to do but hurry and close the bargains."[7]

The syndicate members handling the sale of the preferred stock put about two-thirds of the shares of the common stock they had been given up for sale on the curb. First appearing on January 11 at $44 a share, the stock climbed as both the *New York Times* and the *Wall Street Journal* front-paged the opportunity they were said to offer, the last available share selling on March 15 at $64. Financiers had that day found the new corporation headlined on the front page of the *Wall Street Journal*: "Cuba Cane Sugar's Firm Investment Foundation—Plantations Secured at Bottom Prices on Options Beginning before the War's Outbreak." The text amplified the good if not entirely truthful news.

No new industry was ever introduced into Wall Street with as solid an investment foundation under it as that which entered last year under the name of the Cuba Cane Sugar Corporation.

Never before in an industrial flotation were the leading technical talent and the leading investment talent combined upon the buying side. . . . There has been a false assumption in some quarters that these purchases must have meant investment based upon the advanced price of sugar and therefore enhanced land claims. Decidedly the contrary is the fact.

Turning to page seven, readers would find a map stretched across eight columns showing the properties with an explanation why original estimates of returns were far too small.

The *New York Times* put its account on its inside financial page but compensated by a poetic headline: "Riches in Romance of Cuba Cane Sugar. Wall Street Adds $32,000,000 in Three Months to Promoter's $50,000,000 Estimate. War Puts $21,000,000 Profit into Sight before the End of This Year." "Mr. Rionda," the *Times* concluded, "enlisted banking support on the theory that, with sugar at 3¼ cents, the new company would earn $11,000,000. Cuban centrifugals sold yesterday at 5¾ cents."[8] On March 24, when J & W Seligman announced the syndicate closed, the underwriters would have already cleared, collectively, over $10 million if they had all sold their bonus common shares on the curb, even at the opening $44 a share. None of this windfall went to increase Cuban Cane's capitalization but represented transfers among investors.

In one hectic month, Rionda had purchased sixteen plantations.[9] Ten of these had been on his original list, estimated to cost $26 million. They had cost $29,850,000. The additional six properties brought the total to $44,595,000. Pedro Arenal and José López Rodríguez—the "Pote" of Cuban legends who had come to Cuba from Spain and made a fortune in printing, contracting, sugar, politics, and banking—received the highest prices, $5 million each for the *Socorro* and the *Conchita*, Pote, having bought the latter the preceding August for less than $3.5 million.[10] Tarafa had sold his *Morón*—that Cuban venture just launched with such a flourish about its Cubanness—for $4,350,000.[11]

Included in the purchases were sugar mills and cane lands (334,100 acres owned, 164,766 leased) and also machine shops, stores, workers' houses, offices, residences for the managers, cane carts, oxen, and about 396 miles of railway, with 83 locomotives and 2,234 cane cars. Included, too, was all the sugar currently being harvested. The preceding owners had borne the costs of the 1915 dead season.[12]

Thirteen mills were in Cuba's western provinces, only three in the east. In the first year, the western ones would produce five times as much as the eastern.

Almost all of the purchased centrals were long established; only Tarafa's *Morón* was new. Although only the *Socorro* and the *Mercedes* had produced more than 300,000 bags in 1915, all had recently increased their production. The *Feliz*, for example, had increased production from 64,054 bags in 1911 to 145,438 bags in 1915, the *María Victoria* from 36,670 to 90,481. Rionda estimated that the sixteen plantations would produce 3.7 million bags of sugar a year, one-sixth of the entire Cuban output.[13] An empire was being established, with Cuban-owned estates becoming the property of a single huge Wall Street corporation.

At that moment, both labor and cane were in short supply, and therefore the effect of the transaction on farmers and wage earners was minimal. The more immediate impact was on those who voluntarily, even eagerly, sold their holdings. With Cuba Cane's purchases, some $45 million was transferred to the former owners.

What, then, of them? Of Pedro LaBorde and Pedro Arenal, of Truffin and Miguel Arango, of Pote and Dolores Viuda de Fernández, of Salvador Guedes, the Zulueta y Gamiz brothers, Miguel Mendoza, B. Urbiztonto, and Domingo Nazabal? What of Tarafa, Miguel Díaz, Moises B. de Marchena, Luis Galbán, and Melchor Bernal?[14] For one thing, except for Arango, who was named the new corporation's general manager, and for Truffin, who became one of its officials, they played no part in the new venture. Six months after its founding, despite stock bonuses from Manuel, only sixteen retained shares. Perhaps, unlike Manuel, they had sold them while the price was high.

Manuel had written Galbán that as part of the negotiations for Galbán's *Lugareño*, he would get 500 shares of preferred stock at par with the additional 70 percent of their value in common stock thrown in as a "bonificación." A Canary Islander, Galbán was building up the Havana

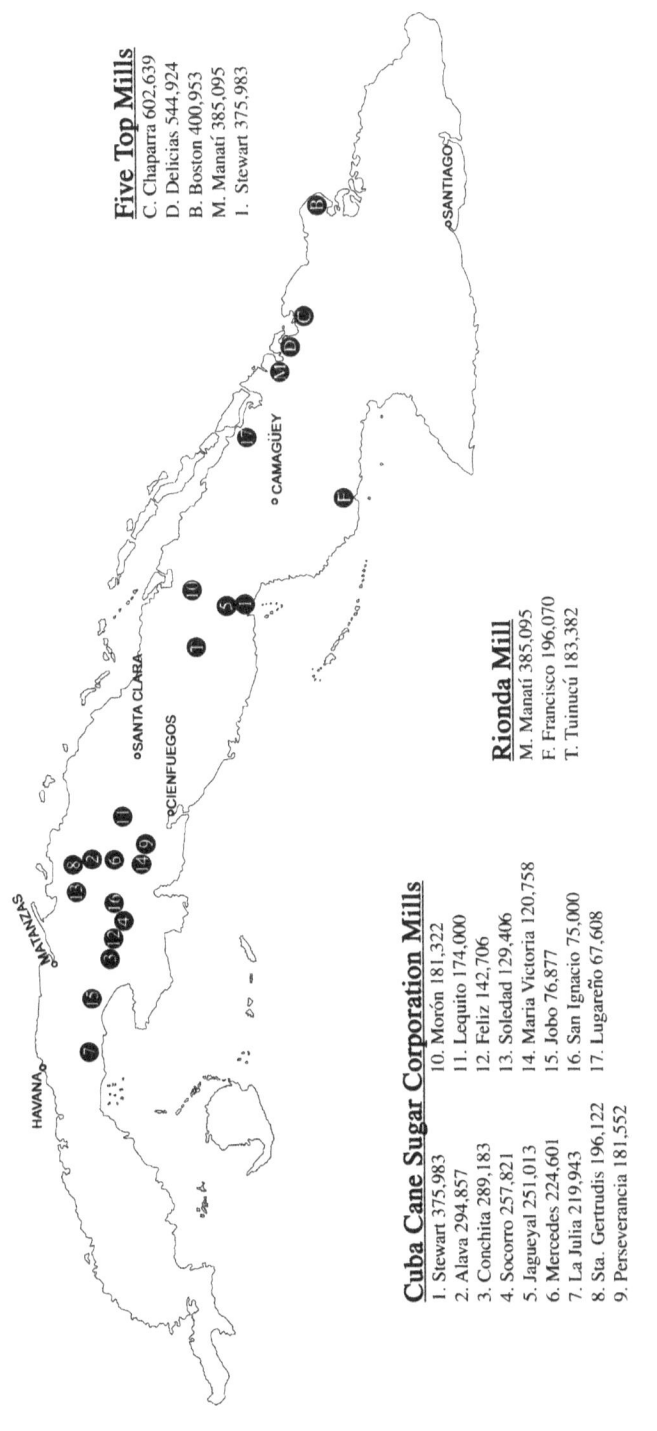

Map 3. Cuba Cane mills, 1917. Production in 325-pound bags. Source: Cuba Review, 1920.

commercial firm of Galbán, Lobo, together with Heriberto Lobo, who had come from Venezuela at the turn of the century and whose son, Julio, was studying sugar engineering in Louisiana. Presumably, Galbán must have sold about half his shares, for in September he held only 250. Only three other sellers held preferred shares: Arango, 408; Nazabal, 1,000; and Marchena, 4,900. Since the preferred paid 7 percent, they would receive an assured income as long as dividends continued: Arango, $2,856 a year; Nazabal, $7,000; and Marchena, $34,300. Of the common shares, LaBorde held 500; Arango, 3,430; Enrique Zulueta, 250; Nazabal, 500; Tarafa, 400; Miguel Díaz, 1,000; Marchena, 400; and Galbán, 210.[15]

While continued participation in the New York company was thus small scale, the sales of their properties did not mean that all the sellers then retired from the sugar business. While some of their proceeds obviously went to settling old debts, two years of wartime high prices had already decreased their obligations. Manuel's venture did not decapitate Cuba's entrepreneurial bourgeoisie. On the contrary, Cuba Cane's beginnings further empowered some significant entrepreneurs and contributed to a general shuffling of ownerships of important installations.

One of the more significant shifts occurred on February 17, only six days after Rionda had concluded his purchases for the corporation, when Pote acquired the *España* in Matanzas. It would in the 1916 campaign produce only 147,283 bags, but the press soon carried enthusiastic stories of Pote's plans for its expansion. It would become, reports predicted, one of the largest mills in the world and would yield 600,000 bags by 1918 and more than 1 million the following season. Although these predictions were only half fulfilled, it produced 207,550 bags in 1917, 409,673 in 1918, and slightly over 500,000 in 1919.[16]

Others purchases followed. Colonel Tarafa, busy as ever with his railroads and plantations, merely continued improving his holdings, but before long Salvador Güedes, who had sold the *Feliz*, bought a share in the *Orozco* in Pinar del Río. Miguel Díaz put at least some of the $330,000 he received into a share in a new plantation to be erected in Camagüey. In this, he joined Miguel Mendoza and other Mendoza kinsmen, as well as Truffin and Miguel Arango. The result would be the *Cunagua*, "a completely electrified double tandem factory" with a capacity of 600,000 bags. It would be, the *Mundo Azucarero* would report, "netamente cubana" (totally Cuban). LaBorde, too, became a shareholder in *Cunagua* and in 1918 would also buy the *El Pilar* for $900,000. Thus at least eight of the sellers went on into expanding new sugar ventures. When capital ran low, they found the North American banks supplied it generously.[17]

The *Louisiana Planter*'s old editor had for half a century watched cane's ups and downs. Now, musing on the important sums that the buyers were spending, he warned that they might invest in new operations until there would be, after the war, a surplus of Cuban sugar. He was, as usual, a voice in the wilderness.

In addition to the economic consequences that Cuba Cane triggered, that monumental accomplishment also had political spin-offs, stimulating both patriotism and potential levels of corruption. Cuban newspapers resurrected fear of "the Trust," and members of the Cuban Congress, some inspired by love of country, others perhaps hoping for generous Yankee sums to quench their oratory, expressed concern at so many acres of Cuban soil being owned abroad. On the other hand, Cuba Cane could assist greatly in lobbying the U.S. Congress in the interest of Cuban sugar—far more effectively than the previous diverse noncitizen mill owners would have found possible.

Rionda had had to consider Cuban politics early in the operation. "Mr. Ferrara," he informed Jaretzki, "came to see me at the hotel the last day I was in Havana. . . . As some members of Congress are talking about introducing a bill prohibiting the sale of Cuban property to foreigners, we think it would be well to have Mr. Ferrara on our Board." Orestes Ferrara, the Naples-born colonel in the rebel army in 1898 and Liberal Party leader, was close to former president Gómez. He was also one of the founders of the Ports Company, owner of the newspaper *Heraldo de Cuba*, and president of the Cuban House of Representatives. "While Ferrera is not intimate with Menocal," Rionda continued, "they do not antagonize each other." Ferrara was thus elected a member of the board of directors.[18]

As for the results for Manuel Rionda himself, he had joined forces with New York's greatest capitalists, his allegiances to them, and presumably theirs to him, strengthened. As he saw it, they were partners in a joint patriotic and profitable task.

Cuba Cane's future effects upon its host island inspired little if any concern abroad, and congratulations poured in upon Rionda. "The whole thing," wrote Lagemann from London, "reads almost like a dream.... You will leave behind a magnificent record." "When you come back to New York, you will find yourself *famous*," Jaretzki assured him. And, later, "Your name is now one to conjure with in the financial community." Yet Rionda himself was unsure. Wall Street had already profited, but the operation of so many mills was still to be tested. He replied to Jaretzki on April 8, less than a week before he formally became president of the company: "[I]n reality, this success, i.e.—the commercial success of the Corporation, is yet to come." "I fear," he confided to Manolo and Bernardo, "that the stock . . . will become a regular football on Wall Street, going up and down with the sugar market—which is a thing I had always been fearing—while I think that they will be able to put it up to 75 or so, I must say that I do not see any intrinsic value in the property to make it go up like that."[19]

The front-page story in the *Wall Street Journal* had worried him. "It seems to me," he wrote Frederick Strauss, "that your friend Mr. Barron goes a little bit too far in his articles. . . . I do not believe it good policy to go so far beyond the mark—because, when the reality is known, there are apt to be a great many disappointments." Profits, he wrote back to New York, could not really amount to more than $15 million. Everywhere there were details to be ironed out. "It is no small job," he warned, "to get familiar with *one* plantation in one year, to say nothing of *sixteen* plantations during four months and those four months crop months."

Of the $50 million for which Cuba Cane was capitalized, some $45 million had already been spent on acquiring property and less than $5 million remained as working capital. Manuel, anxious to expand operations, was worried by rapidly rising prices. With the war pushing every factory, he had to pay almost $32,000 for an engine from the Fulton Iron Works, with only 5 percent off. "I know that the price I paid is exorbitant," he told New York, "but knowing . . . how difficult it would be to get delivery in May—I decided to clinch it. I tried to get 10 percent discount or even 7 percent—but could not succeed."[20]

In New Orleans, the editor of the *Louisiana Planter* contemplated the "anticipation of some of the parties . . . who are promoting the Cuban Cane" and was reminded by press estimates of $20 million profits a year "of our own expectations in sugar planting more than forty years ago. . . .

We wish them every success but we are led to think of the old Latin motto, *festina lente.*" *Festina lente*—make haste slowly. The editorial was translated into Spanish for the *Planter*'s monthly Spanish-language edition with an additional three lines: *"festina lente . . . no hagais á tontas y á locas lo que pide dentenimiento y reflexión"* (do not act like idiots and madmen in that which requires deliberation and reflection).[21]

Worried about rising costs, Rionda, as he took over the corporation, informed his New York nephews that he wished them to extend to Cuba Cane a freight contract held by Czarnikow-Rionda to ship its sugar to the United States at a lower rate than its competitors, although he realized that giving 25 cents freight to Cuba Cane sugars would be a "great sacrifice" to Czarnikow-Rionda. "I appreciate," he continued, "your desire to join and pull with me in order to make Cuba Cane a success. . . . I am so anxious to have the Cuba Cane Sugar Corporation successful that I would not only sacrifice C-R Co. but also Francisco and even Tuinucú." Yet he did have second thoughts—there were limits—and wrote Manolo and Bernardo again on February 5: "While of course I am more than willing to let CC have all the benefit possible from our freight arrangements, we . . . must not lean too much on the side of the Cane Co.—let them participate to the extent of ½ or even ⅔ of the profits—but not take them all." He pointed out that the colonos exchanged the cane they grew for a fixed percentage of the sugar. Since the price they received was "based on the *current prices*, and that includes the *current rates of freight* it would not be right to take *all* the sugars of the Cane Co. at say 25 cents freight when they are paying the colonos for their sugar on the basis of 50 cents freight. . . . In other words, I am perfectly willing that we should try very hard to carry about 60 percent of their 3.5 million bags . . . at 25 cents freight, but the balance, being Colono's sugars, should go at the current rates." The New York nephews must "explain this very clearly to Mr. Strauss and Jaretzki."[22]

In the spring of 1916, rainfall was sparse in Cuba, and the sugar content of the cane declined. By the end of March, as Wall Street optimism was being whipped ever higher, all of Cuba Cane's plantations were feeling the drought's effects. Rionda feared that *Socorro* might produce $80,000 less in sugar than anticipated and that *Morón* would be down about 50,000 bags. Yet there were ample profits for Cuba Cane to pay its first two quarterly dividends on the preferred stock, with a great deal left over. Although prices usually fell during the zafra months when supply was greatest and demand low after the Christmas holidays, this wartime year they rose from 4.5 cents a pound in January to 6 cents by mid-April and held through July at well over 6 cents.

There were charges that these unprecedented prices were not unconnected with Czarnikow-Rionda's simultaneous new power. With Cuba Cane added to the clan's own mills and those of its other clients, it could now control of "nearly 60 percent of all sales." Might this not have put it in a strong position to "rig" the market?

Manuel denied any such rigging, citing justifications for his new empire. He reassured MacDougall that while his company's aim was "naturally" to keep prices up, he especially wished to avoid the price fluctuations that had previously prevailed. "Whatever may be said to the contrary," he wrote Lagemann, "I assure you that the new company is not going to manipulate the market to its advantage and the disadvantage of the consumers—companies like that, with such a control of sugar, will be much better able to supply the consumer than individuals only controlling from 10,000 to 15,000 bags of sugar at a time." In other years, he pointed out, Cubans had needed quick cash to meet their promissory notes. Now, after two prosperous years, since they had been able to pay off their debts, they could afford to wait for a fair price. Had they still been in as straitened circumstances as before the war, five Cuba Canes could not have upheld the market.

Bernardo Braga wrote a formal letter to the same effect to J. P. Morgan and Company. "You have asked us our opinion," he began, "as to the causes underlying the present high price of sugar, and also as to whether, in our opinion, the formation of the CCSC [Cuba Cane] has been instrumental in bringing about those high prices." The actual causes were the war, the loss of European beet sugar, shortages of shipping, plus the Cuban drought. "The very aim of CCSC," he piously concluded, was "to avoid speculation in its product."[23]

Manuel himself spoke often of stabilizing prices. Since the 1890s, the Cuban planters had been forced to settle for prices far below the world's parity. Czarnikow-Rionda, he would write later, had tried to remedy that, but as long as there were a hundred sellers and only two or three buyers, success was impossible. Planters with strong banking arrangements might carry their sugars into the three months of the largest consumption to obtain fair prices; the smaller planters, however, could not wait and thus fixed the prices for all the producers.

Rionda had never participated in—or even sympathized with—any Agrarian League of hacendados. Such groups, he had explained to his nephews, were made up of the "lame ducks," and the important men would stay out of them. Now he argued the very size of Cuba Cane, under his avuncular tutelage, would make things better also for the small, independent planters. "We saw the opportunity," he would explain to Cuba Cane's shareholders, "to reduce the number of sellers and, thereby [improve] the possibility of securing a price for Cuban sugar closer to that obtained by European beets."[24]

Appeals for Cubans to show sympathy for the embattled Allies by accepting lower prices, fell on deaf ears. "The Cubans say," Manuel pointed out in another letter, "that when they were at war with Spain and their property all torn to pieces, not a single European, Chinese or Japanese came to their rescue. So they see no reason now why if they can get 5 cents and make up for the losses of the terrible war, they shouldn't. This may not be a very humane line of reasoning—but they certainly are right in a way—and you will remember that when their crop (1895–96) went from 1.2 million tons to 200,000 tons, nobody came to give them a helping hand."

He reminded London of economies of scale. "There are 100 other purposes for the formation of this Company than pushing up prices," he wrote indignantly, breaking into capital letters: "Amongst which I would point out: BETTER AGRICULTURAL METHODS, MODERN MACHINERY, MORE EFFICIENT RAILROAD SERVICES AND SMALL DISTANCES FOR HAULING CANES, IRRIGATION, CESSATION OF COMPETITION AMONG PLANTERS and many others."[25]

In a press release, he waxed eloquent:

The great improvements made in the Cuban sugar industry . . . have been confined almost exclusively to perfecting the machinery. . . . The cane fields have been largely left to themselves—that is, to the unaided forces of Nature. A rich and generous soil has permitted this, and the draft upon Nature has been greatly honored. . . . All, however, have been in the way of taking out; nothing has been restored. The science of agriculture has by now made plain that immense returns wait upon the application of intensive methods in Cuba and elsewhere. . . . In the new incorporation, deep steam-ploughing and extensive fertilizing, which is hardly known in Cuba, will be applied.[26]

In June 1916, in such an apostolic mood, the company's board of directors accepted the recommendation of its Executive Committee that a large part of its first year's profit should be used to further improve its holdings. Other sugar companies were riding high—paying off the accumulated unpaid dividends on their preferred shares and handsomely rewarding their common stockholders. The new Punta Alegre was only beginning to come on line and would not pay its initial dividend of $1.25 until October 1919, but Cuban-American's common shareholders were receiving 2.5 percent quarterly, and in October that company would issue stock dividends of 40 percent on both common and preferred, plus an extra cash dividend of 10 percent. In July 1915, Guantanamo had paid 12 percent plus a 10 percent stock dividend. *Manatí* would pay its common as well as its preferred shareholders 10 percent plus a 20 percent stock dividend in November. *Francisco*, most rewarding of all, had issued a stock dividend of 233.3 percent in 1915 and would pay 15 percent on these new shares in 1916.[27] But Cuba Cane's board of directors, as profits rolled in, now approved spending $331,000 for additional lands and an additional $420,000 for machinery and buildings. The board then, on the recommendation of its Executive Committee, voted to spend an additional $8.4 million to buy the *Stewart*.

There were twenty-two directors, and although ownership of the new corporation was technically vested in its stockholders, it was the board, meeting quarterly, that made such decisions. The board included eight bankers—with their assorted ambitions and obligations—representing six major banks: Grayson Murphy and Sabin of the Guaranty, the Strauss brothers of Seligmans, Stephen B. Fleming of the Chase, James N. Jarvie of the Central Hanover, William J. Matheson of the Bank of New York, and John D. Ryan of the National City. (J. P. Morgan's people, although they held 59,399 shares, were not represented directly.)[28]

On the board, too, sat spokesmen for Cuba's two major railroads— George Whigham, president of Cuban Central, and Walter Ogilvie of the United Railways of Cuba—plus an impressive roster of the leaders of

American business, including Cornelius Bliss, the opera-loving treasurer of the Republican National Committee, and Alfred Jaretzki for Sullivan & Cromwell. Manuel, Manolo, Bernardo, and Truffin were directors, but only two other directors were Cuban—the corporation's noted Havana attorney, Antonio de Bustamente, highly regarded for his academically noble legal abstractions and his close ties to Elihu Root, and Orestes Ferrara, a necessary concession to Cuban politics.

The true decision-making body, selected from among these directors, was the eight-member Executive Committee—William Ellis Corey (Charlie Schwab's successor as president of U.S. Steel, a determined-looking man with a receding hairline and a high, starched collar), Horace Havemeyer (bony son of that founder of the Sugar Trust whose rotund hobgoblin still haunted the trade), Jarvie (an associate of the Arbuckles in their sugar refining career, now "devoted . . . to managing his own substantial investments"), Claus Spreckels of the Federal Sugar Refining Company of Yonkers, Albert Strauss, Jaretzki, Sabin, and Manuel.

What seems impossible to tell from the surviving records is who suggested investing so much of the first year's profits in acquiring the *Stewart*. Surviving correspondence between Manuel and his nephews makes no reference to any discussion nor do the Executive Committee minutes until on June 12, 1916, when a proposal was made—it is not specified by whom—and approved. Nor is there any explanation why the purchase price of $8.4 million was $4.1 million more than *Stewart*'s appraised value.

Certainly, the purchase made sense. The *Stewart*, with its 500,000 bag capacity, nicely clustered near Cuba Cane's *Morón* and *Jagueyal*, moved the center of the corporation's holdings to the east. Also, J&W Seligman and Sullivan & Cromwell, as well as the Rionda clan, had been involved with the *Stewart* from its very inception. Very likely among its largest shareholders, they would not need to study it further. It is entirely probable that from the first discussion about founding Cuba Cane, it would have been accepted as given that when the 1916 zafra was over, *Stewart* would take its rightful place at the top of the new corporation's holdings. Given all these good reasons for the decision, it is still interesting that so major a purchase slid through without any recorded discussion of raising additional capital to fund it. Later, when things began to go bad and questions began to be asked, this would seem a puzzle.

In any case, the *Louisiana Planter*'s "Letter from Havana" in July detailed *Stewart*'s magnificence: "The property that is to change hands not only includes the three-tandem factory but also several hundred *caballerías* of land. . . . All the cane ground is drawn from the company's own colonías that are reached by the plantation railway lines or those of the Júcaro and Morón Company." The letter outlined plans for growth: "[T]here are now on order for delivery during the rest of the year five new plate and frame filter-presses that are being built in the shops of Messrs. Duncan Stewart & Co. of Glasgow; a 20,000 square foot quadruple effect . . . ; two 10,000 G.P.M. steam turbine driven Cameron centrifugal injection pumps; one Ingersoll Rand duplex steam-driven vacuum pan of the Imperial type." And so on and so on.[29] Management staked the corporation's future on expansion, and Cuba Cane's sixteen mills thus became seventeen. They stretched some 300 miles, across three-quarters of the length of Cuba.

Although all the existing managers and employees of the formerly independent plantations had been retained to complete the 1916 zafra, the problems the clan faced in managing so diverse an empire were daunting. Rionda removed Leandro from *Francisco* (which under his management had done extremely well) and made him general superintendent, and he put Pepe (who was said to be a genius with machinery) in charge of the *Stewart* and the other three eastern mills. He entrusted the thirteen older western mills to Arango.

Manuel's First Annual Report for Cuba Cane, dated September 30, 1916, was sober, without rhetoric. The corporation's operating profit (totaling $14,729,088, or 29.5 percent of the sum for which the corporation was capitalized) represented earnings from the sale of the sugar plus minor income from molasses and a few miscellaneous revenues, minus the immediate costs of production. Other deductions were then subtracted (for interest on loans and for conversions of foreign currencies), and money was also set aside for depreciation, taxes, and the next dead season. This left the net profit at $12,179,013. From the net profit, a total of $2,327,506 was paid in dividends on the preferred stock, and the remaining $9,851,507 was carried to the surplus account, almost 20 percent of the $50 million capitalization and almost $10 per share for the million shares authorized, even though an additional 7,500 acres plus the great *Stewart* property had been acquired with no additional securities issued.

Cuba Cane's directors, under Rionda's leadership, were thus building for the future instead of paying dividends on common shares, of which they were themselves the largest holders, although since Czarnikow-Rionda was guaranteed a 1 percent commission for selling all the sugar the seventeen centrals produced and since in addition the Cuban Trading Company received a 2 percent commission for handling its extensive purchases, the Riondas could afford to wait.

The annual report projected future production. In 1916, Cuba Cane had produced 3,174,168 bags, not including *Stewart*'s 489,054. In the future, with *Stewart* added, it expected, for 1917, 3.8 million to 4 million bags; for 1918, 4.4 million to 4.6 million; for 1919, 4.8 million to 5.1 million.

But Rionda's final paragraph, "Prospects for the Next Season," was not euphoric. There had been "many difficulties" in the shipment of machinery. There had recently been "unusually heavy rains." "If continued too long," he warned, "their effect on the crop will be adverse."[30]

Meanwhile, letters had been going back and forth between Wall Street and Mincing Lane. The patriotic drums were beating, and Lagemann was retiring since feeling in England against "the Hun" was rising with each casualty list. He had often grated on Rionda's nerves, and his retirement might have been, however politely unexpressed, a source of relief to Manuel had not it resulted in Lagemann moving to New York. This did not foretell serenity. "Old men should retire gracefully," Manuel advised. He "surmised" unhappily that the German would want "to meddle in our routine affairs." A year later, he was writing: "Mr. Lagemann's ideas of running a plantation do not coincide with mine but as I hold the majority of the stock . . . he will have to do what we decide."[31]

Meanwhile, there were political developments. The U.S. tariff, so recently condemned to extinction, was rising from its grave. If in the peacetime dawn of Wilsonian idealism the U.S. Congress had agreed free sugar would be phased in on May 1, 1916, it now had second thoughts. "I see by the press," Rionda wrote from Havana in April, "that there is some talk of not only leaving the present duty on sugar as it stands but increasing it one cent. I cannot see how the politicians have gotten around President Wilson . . . if the Democrats are 'Free Traders' as they often boast." The about-face, he suspected, was because Louisiana, in an election year, had "weakened a bit in its support of the Democratic Party." Yet Rionda believed the bayou was not the problem. Beets were. Continuing tariff support for them was "fostering a child that when it grows to manhood may create many difficulties. . . . Beet Production in the United States will increase to such enormous proportions that later an administration would not venture to remove the duty on sugar for fear of a panic in those states. It would be far better to kill that offspring now, than to allow it to reach dangerous manhood."[32]

In November 1916, as Cuba Cane was beginning its second year, voters in the United States reelected Wilson. There was also an election in Cuba, Menocal's ruling Conservative Party announcing its own victory. The Liberals protested they had been robbed, and in February, at the very height of the 1916–17 zafra, guerrilla armies once again took to the field, shadowed by the smoke of burning cane. In a ten-page handwritten letter to New York, Rionda spelled out a simple, if cynical, explanation for the controversy. "I am afraid," he wrote, "[Menocal] owes more money than they [sic] can pay if called. I am told he owes [West India Finance Co] 1½ million and 1 ½ million to [Howell]!! That is why [Menocal] does not want to accept defeat."

He was not optimistic three weeks later. "These troubles will not be over in a week nor in months. . . . All talk about politics and Menocal and Zayas and elections—what of planters, merchants and working men! . . . Pretty soon we will have strikes and famine somewhere and sugar at 4 cents. It is incomprehensible, unthinkable!!! The Cubans rebelling in the midst of this prosperity." "What surprised us," Ganzoni agreed from London, "was to see the names of such prominent and wealthy men among the opposing party."[33]

Both sides, Manuel wrote Strauss, had cheated in the election, but the Liberals had not been found out as plainly, although any sympathy he might have had for them had been lost when they commenced to burn the cane fields. Since all leaders of both parties were largely interested in sugar, tobacco, and cattle, he added to Ganzoni, "No one would expect them to run the risk of heavy losses. It was not like in 1896 or even 1906 when the men to start the wars had little to lose. . . . Good God! we, innocent of all these doings are the ones to be sacrificed." And he bewailed that Wilson did not intervene to protect the investments of U.S. citizens but had told Cuba to manage its own affairs.

Lagemann, now in New York exile, was even more irate:

> Messrs. Bliss, Corey, Ryan, Strauss, Sabin, Murphy, Childs, Spreckels, have gone into a foreign country exposed to revolutions, incendiaries, lawlessness, hurricanes, droughts, etc., in order to fructify and create a foothold by American capital, to bring here their earnings and pay heavy American taxes thereon in return for what? Not a finger was lifted here to protect them, when their plantations were burnt, railways destroyed—bridges blown up, factories on point of being wrecked and production at a standstill with expenses running up.[34]

In the end, the rebellion was nearly over by the last of April, and Rionda admitted that Menocal, despite his weakness as president, had shown he had been a general. But hostilities had lasted long enough to cut into Cuba Cane's second-year profits. The worst harm was at *Lugareño*, the westernmost central. There, operations had to stop for six weeks, and its total production as a result was only 67,608 bags, down from 153,971 in 1916. *Stewart*, near the center of military operations, lost some 75,000 bags, and *Morón*, too, suffered seriously.

Losses had been far greater at the Riondas' *Francisco*. There, there had been three days of "terrorism and destruction," wiping out "practically all the colonos" when the rebels, fleeing U.S. Marines and Cuban troops sent in to protect the mill, "scattered to the four winds and in their flight set fire to every field of cane that they passed." But at least only the cane burned. The buildings that housed the machines had come through unscathed.[35]

In the 1917 zafra, Cuba Cane's plantations produced 54 million pounds of sugar less than in its first year. Nor had the revolt been the only problem. Facing so many details in so huge an operation, there had been inefficiencies, despite the clan's best efforts. "We certainly have very little to be proud of," Manuel wrote Leandro in May. "You will have noticed that in my report to the Executive Committee. . . . I do not spare myself in assuming responsibility for the bad results of the Cuba Cane this year and all of you should adopt the same policy."

Lower output, however, pushed prices higher. From 4.83 cents per pound at New York, duty paid, on February 2, they had gone up to 5.39 cents on March 1 and to 5.98 cents on April 2. To Ganzoni, Rionda pointed out another silver lining. "I agree with you that the rebellion had put a setback on the development of the Island and, perhaps, after all, that is the best thing because we were going rather too fast in the production of Cuba which was exceeding the supply of laborers with the consequent continual advance in wages." Since the supply of beets in the United States was growing, he commented, "if Cuba had reached close to 4,000,000 tons, there would have been an enormous surplus after the war which would have had to seek foreign markets."

American involvement in the European war grew closer as German submarines sank American freighters in the mid-Atlantic. On April 6, 1917, the United States declared war on Germany. Rionda wrote soberly to London: "Now that at last the United States is in the struggle and willing to give financial support I trust we are coming to the end."[36]

With the declarations of war, sugar prices rose from 6.05 cents per pound on April 5 to 6.46 cents on April 13. It was the sort of situation out of which fortunes were made. It was also the sort of situation that encouraged Cuban hopes for even higher prices. Tarafa, who had been plunging boldly ahead not only with his ambitious railroad projects, his Júcaro and Morón and his Cuban Northern, but also with the development of his Central Cuba Sugar Company, tried in early April to buy 50,000 bags of sugar from Rionda for future delivery. Failing (in Rionda's opinion, his credit was at best shaky), he obtained them elsewhere. A month later, futures fell sharply, leaving Tarafa facing possible disaster. Rionda, Tarafa charged, had manipulated the market. "[Y]ou were the only man in the world," he wrote, "able to sell the sugars that had been sold short."

Rionda replied angrily, charging misrepresentations in Tarafa's sale of *Morón* and *Jagueyal* to Cuba Cane and adding a reminder of $56,000 due on the colonel's *Nueva Paz*. "[I]t would be, to say the least, most disastrous for this house to be selling short an article which its associates produce so largely . . . this house does not buy sugar for speculation nor does it sell it short. . . . [S]tocks in refiners' hands in U.S. are heavier than ever . . . the weather has been very unfavorable for the sale of refined and that the widespread rumors of Government control of foodstuffs, has had its influence upon consumption." And he concluded with fury that he was resigning from the boards of Tarafa's Central Cuba Sugar Company and Flora Sugar Company.

Tarafa immediately drew back: "I can assure you that . . . I had no intention of belittling the acknowledgment of my gratitude to you for past favors received." As for the sugar he had bought in April, he was, he said, still holding it against a rise. Albert Strauss and Jaretzki were satisfied Manuel had crushed his critic. "I think your letter," Strauss wrote, "completely disposed of the wild and unbalanced charges."

But as America went to war, there was widespread maneuvering in the market, and the sugar world gambled as troop transports set sail. Rionda wrote his old partner: "[F]or the past three weeks we have been working very hard to make prices decline. . . . [T]oday we offered sugars at ⅛ cents below what we knew we could sell them for . . . exerting all our influence toward bringing about lower prices." His explanation was pious. "We are doing this, firstly, because high prices make everything go higher in Cuba and as there are no more than about 20,000 tons of sugar unsold, it is better to sell these sugars gradually at a lower price, than to have labour, coal, bags & everything else go higher in price."[37]

Still, lower prices increased profits for the American refiners at Cuba's expense. Rionda was playing the refiners' game for them.

5

A Fixed Price

In May 1917, as the zafra was ending, Herbert Hoover entered Manuel Rionda's life. Since the United States had entered World War I, food prices had been rising sharply and demands growing that government protect its citizens from speculators. President Woodrow Wilson had, accordingly, summoned the Hoover, the Great Engineer, to Washington to take charge.

Hoover was forty-one, an Iowa-born Quaker who had earned a fortune in mines from Australia to Siberia and capped proof of his ability by relief work in wartime Belgium. Let patriotism, he advised Wilson, summon the country's most efficient businessmen to the capital to serve their country. Under their expert direction, fixed prices for necessary foodstuffs (continuing but not increasing prewar business profits) could be established. Wilson accordingly requested Congress to create the post of Food Administrator, giving Hoover "power to regulate distribution and consumption—import, export, price, purchase, requisition and storage."[1]

Hoover first focused his attention on wheat and corn. But housewives were putting on their aprons to preserve the harvested produce, and sugar rose from 5.89 cents a pound on June 1 to 6.52 cents on July 1 to 7.02 cents on August 1 and to 7.52 cents a week later. Thus, although half of the sugar America consumed was grown abroad, most of it in Cuba, Hoover could not omit it from his responsibilities. "Certain Cuban sugar producers (who are out of our reach)," he told Wilson, "have combined to force up the price." A sugar commission, cooperating "with the Allies and the Cuban producers," could "effect a considerable saving on the present inflated price." On August 15 (Congress having passed the Lever Food Control Act on August 10), Hoover chose George M. Rolph, general manager of the California and Hawaiian Sugar Refining Company of San Francisco, to head the Sugar Division of the U.S. Food Administration. The following day, at Rolph's bidding, futures trading on the New York Coffee and Sugar Exchange was halted for the duration. "Let me tell you, confidentially," Rionda wrote Julius Ganzoni, "that the Exchange was not closed without Mr. Rolph first asking me what I thought about it." Rionda was also consulted about the price to be set for sugar. That same August 16, "during my last trip to Washington . . . it was practically agreed between Mr. Hoover and Mr. Rolph, Mr. Hawley and myself, that the price of Cuba's shall be between 4.50 and 4.60 fob."

Since war had cut off its European beets, the United Kingdom had been competing with the United States in the open market. Hoover now moved to end the rivalry, suggesting to his opposite number, the British food controller, Lord Rhondda, that joint purchases be negotiated by a five-man commission in New York, three members appointed by the United States and two by Britain, with Cuba selling only to the commission and only at its fixed price. Czarnikow-Rionda would not object, Rionda wrote Ganzoni, although he also wrote MacDougall: "[T]his Committee will have more power than Mr. Havemeyer ever had." American refiners were reported "enthusiastic," with a "hearty willingness to follow the plans of the national body as a patriotic duty." Their leaders, to the exclusion of all other groups, were chosen to represent the United States, Hoover appointing Earl Babst, president of the American Sugar Refining Company, with Rolph and William A. Jamison of Arbuckle Brothers to the international body.[2]

The Ohio-born Babst, who had begun his career in biscuits, had been lured to the presidency of American Sugar in 1915. He had studied law at the University of Michigan, been admitted to the bar in 1894, and helped swing Michigan behind McKinley in 1896. About the time of the charge up San Juan Hill, aged twenty-eight, he had caught the attention of the attorneys of the National Biscuit Company on a "railroad smoker" en route from Chicago to New York. In crackers, as in other foods, the turn-of-the-century years were revolutionary, with the change from bulk merchandising (the cracker barrel in the general store) to packaged, trademarked brands. Long legal struggles, involving patent and trademark litigation, were necessary to clear the way through state restrictions to nationally advertised brands. While less swashbuckling than Sullivan & Cromwell's contributions to the Panama Canal, Babst's service as general counsel of National Biscuit was, as the *New York Times* would magisterially sum up, "the basis for the pure food movement." He was now busy replacing the village grocery's sugar barrel with the American Sugar's own sanitary "Domino" packages. With pince-nez glasses and hair neatly parted exactly in the middle, Babst was a businessman to Hoover's taste. If not a pioneer in the early appreciation of El Grecos and Monets, as Havemeyer had been, he worked hard to support Psi Upsilon, his college fraternity.[3]

That Hoover had appointed only the great refiners as buyers of sugar was instantly a source of suspicion. From St. Dunstan's Hill in London, the *International Sugar Journal* condescended that while "Mr. Hoover undoubtedly intended well in his choice of men," he had "given a handle to his critics . . . no direct representative of the sugar producers was given a seat on the committee." Although Hoover had defended his selections by saying "Mr. Rolph, Mr. Babst and Mr. Jamison had been chosen because . . . neither they nor their companies were interested in Cuban sugar," farm-state senators still questioned their monopoly. "'Do you call it no sacrifice,' [Hoover] asked, 'for the sugar refiners to have their refining margin reduced to the basis of prewar profits?' 'I do not,' responded Senator [James] Vardaman [of Mississippi]. 'They should not receive their normal profit. The men in the trenches do not.'" Hoover had retorted that "if you attempted to alter the economic system on that basis the world would not revolve twenty-four hours longer." The *Journal* thought the U.S. refining margin was six times that set for British refiners.

Sir Joseph White-Todd, a "retired merchant banker," and John Ramsey Drake, senior partner of J. V. Drake and Company, sugar merchants of Mincing Lane, were appointed to represent England and its allies on the International Sugar Committee. Manuel met them at the dock.[4]

Rionda was anxious Ganzoni should appreciate the deference with which he was treated. "When the Committee was formed," he wrote,

"Mr. Rolph came here to our office and told me he wanted to buy all the sugar there was left in Cuba. I told him . . . that we were then holding . . . about 150,000 bags and that I would give him an option . . . to be taken at any time at a price to be fixed by him. Mr. Rolph . . . through Mr. Babst has been distributing that sugar at 5⅞ cents cf. notwithstanding the scarcity of sugar. . . . Do you suppose that action of ours . . . will go for nothing?"

He did not expect anyone to question his statement, made with Robert Hawley's support, that a price of 4.5 or 4.6 cents per pound would be sufficient for the coming zafra. Hawley spoke for the Cuban-American's 3 million bags, while Rionda himself "represented for ourselves and our allied companies about 6 million bags and other clients of ours like the United Fruit Company and Atkins of Boston, 3,000,000 bags, a total of 12,000,000 bags or 60 percent of the crop." While he admitted Rolph and Hoover had consulted "other Cuban Committees . . . their aspirations as to price were higher always than ours." He was sure planters representing "probably 70 percent of the crop" would follow his lead. As for the remaining 30 percent, he dismissed them as small, independent growers "not versed in methods of selling," who would have to go along.[5]

But if Rionda thus assured his British associates that he spoke for Cuba, Cuba's bourgeoisie did not quietly accept his price nor their own exclusion from the bargaining. In Havana, President Menocal met in the chambers of the Banco Nacional with his fellow hacendados and, despite Rionda and Hawley's assurance that they already had the matter in hand, appointed Tarafa, José Lezama (whose four Matanzas plantations produced some 380,000 bags),[6] and Carlos Miguel de Céspedes, the Cuban ambassador in Washington, to negotiate. There was talk of a "fair price," once more defined as cost of production plus a reasonable profit.

What did it cost to produce a pound of Cuban sugar? That very question had risen during the angry exchange of letters between Rionda and Tarafa in June, when the colonel accused Manuel of rigging the market. It had been part of Tarafa's charge that in the 1916–17 zafra, 85 percent of Cuban planters had sold "a great portion of our sugars at prices below cost." "About the 11th of May," Tarafa had written "you called me to . . . your office and told me about the desirability of selling sugars of the next two crops to the British and U.S. Governments, at 4 cents fob Cuban ports, and you intimated the convenience of my consulting and preparing other sugar planters and manufacturers of sugar to take up this idea."

Tarafa had consulted with others on his return to Cuba and reported that sugars in the preceding zafra had cost over 4 cents per pound "without including anything for depreciation or amortization and figuring only 6 percent interest on capital invested" and that the next crop would cost at least 5 cents. Cost of production in his own *Central Cuba* had been 4.96 cents a pound and in his *Nueva Paz*, 5.13 cents.

Rionda reminded Tarafa that at the last stockholders' meeting of the Central Cuba and Flora Sugar Companies, Tarafa had given the 1916 cost of production at 3.735 cents per pound for *Central Cuba* and 3.731 cents for *Flora*. They could not have increased so materially unless Tarafa had factored in interest on the heavily bonded debt, amortization of the bonds, and, further, 10 percent on preferred and common shares. "[I]t is natural that the total of such charges would be so great as to make almost impossible for anyone to expect to realize a profit above cost so figured."[7]

Yet Rionda realized the need to repay (with interest) capital advanced. Hoover, he wrote MacDougall, "is continuously appealing to producers and manufacturers to be patriotic and turn over their product at as low a price as they possibly can, without realizing that the companies to whom they appeal are not owned by their officers but by the stockholders." The Food Administration, he went on, should not force prices "lower than the law of supply and demand should warrant."

> It is not that we producers do not want to sell the sugar at a low price but that our Cost of Production has diminished our profits. For instance, in 1911, when sugar prices were pretty low, Tuinucú made 1 cent [profit] per pound. We don't want to make any more now, in fact would be satisfied with less, but while at that time we could produce at 1½ and 1¾ cents per pound, now the actual cost of production of that sugar is 3.70 cents f.o.b. . . . Labor is now costing us $2.50 and $3 a day when formerly it cost us $1 a day.

Menocal's Cuban committee took over negotiations. The suggested price of 4.5 cents a pound FOB, it warned, would "only assure a fair return to those great companies established in the Eastern part of Cuba," and it demanded 4.75 to 5 cents.[8]

By this time, the situation in Cuba had been complicated by new labor protests. The 1918 zafra must begin in some two months, and throughout the island mechanics were in demand to install the new machines that had been ordered (many of which, due to wartime shipping difficulties, were late arriving) and to bring the older ones to peak efficiency. For a generation, secret reveries of unionization and overtime pay had been spreading among Cuba's workers. Now, strikes broke out, spearheaded by the mechanics. The center of rebellion was the older mills, with the first strike at Nicolás Castaño's *San Agustín*. It had burned the preceding May, and Castaño was in a hurry to rebuild. Manuel's old friend was eighty-one now, a profane survivor of a long struggle up from grinding Spanish poverty and a realist. Almost immediately, despite a telegram from Manuel from New York urging him not to, he granted the strikers key demands for an eight-hour workday with extra pay for overtime.

By October, there were strikes in twenty-two Santa Clara centrals—then, spreading eastward, in thirty-four, then in some fifty in all, halting progress even at Cuba Cane's *Stewart* and *Jagueyal*, forcing some gains and fortifying the Cubans' demand for a higher price by underlining rising labor costs.[9]

The official Cuban Commission met with the International Sugar Committee on November 8. It now consisted of Hannibal de Mesa, Ernesto Longa, Miguel Mendoza, and Tarafa. De Mesa, who had close ties to General Gómez and to Ferrera, owned shares in three new mills capable of producing some 400,000 bags and thus represented the owners of what were now considered medium-sized operations who were investing heavily in improvements and expansion. Miguel Mendoza had formerly owned the *Sta. Gertrudis*, which he had sold for $2.7 million to the Cuba Cane Sugar Company. With associates and family members, he was using some of his windfall to erect the *Cunagua*, which in 1918 would emerge as one of the island's giants, a source of pride to Cubans as uniquely Hispanic. As for Ernesto Longa, he had sold his *Mercedita* in 1900 to Cuban-American, becoming its administrator and, like Menocal, a Cuban-American director.

For Rionda, the Cuban Commission represented a loss of face. He had assured London of his own influence, and it could not have been easy for him, given their current bitterness toward each other, to see Tarafa thus officially in charge. He reported to Mincing Lane that the commission was political and unimportant. "The largest interests," he wrote Ganzoni, "such as the Cuban American Sugar Company and the Cuba Cane Sugar Corporation are not represented." But, although he put the best face on it, he had to admit that he was at a disadvantage. "I can gather information only from hearsay.... It is not our fault that we were not represented. We always thought the American-Cuban companies should act independently as of course being American we have certain duties to the United States Government that the Cubans do not have."

"I was under the impression," Ganzoni replied, "that you were sitting around the Green Table for the producers.... The price of 4.50 or 4.60 to us here ... seems very generous to the planters, and they in our opinion may thank Providence for being treated with so much generosity." But the Cubans, from Menocal down, stood firm for at least 4.75 cents.[10]

If he was not a member of the official bargaining committee, Rionda was still significant. On November 20, after a dinner in New York where Babst and Rolph brought Hawley and Rionda together with de Céspedes and the British members of the International Committee, Rionda wrote Higinio lofty words. If the Cubans had heard the war discussed as he had, "they would ... willingly contribute their sugars at the prices offered, and in that way do their bit towards the desire of the whole world that the free and independent people shall continue." There were hints in his letter, too, that individual Cuban mill owners were taking advantage of the impasse in negotiations to further their private interests. Higinio must, Rionda instructed, "explain to everyone that under no circumstances are we going to work sugar in any other way than as the International Committee desires, that neither Bea, Castaño, Pelayo, Gutiérrez or anyone else is going to have any advantage and supply their sugars under different conditions, different shipments of different prices.... If the Committee decides to buy the whole crop ... everyone must abide by that arrangement."[11]

By November 30, Rionda, Hawley, and de Céspedes were playing an acknowledged role in the bargaining, demanding 4.6 cents per pound plus freight. Rionda instructed Miguel Arango to tell Menocal that the president must stress that the products Cuba purchased from the United States had risen in price 100 to 200 percent and Menocal must threaten that unless a contract was executed at 4.6 cents per pound, all "negotiations should cease and the government, to safeguard the Cuban sugar industry from the effects of having only one buyer for the United States and Allied countries, will find it essential to promptly issue a government decree requiring a license from any and all shipments leaving any ports of Cuba for any foreign country."

While this drastic proposal may have been only a threat, it is revealing that Rionda went so far as to suggest so stern a measure. Only after Christmas was he able to report to London: "We have had three weeks and more negotiations with the Intl. S C of which as you probably know, finally Mr. Hawley and myself form part.... You may consider the price of 4.60 cents fob too high, but... I doubt very much if there is more than 1 cents profit and that is hardly 20 percent and the sugar business is one that carries many risks with it!"[12] Since the average annual price paid for raw sugar in New York, before duty, had risen to 4.781 cents per pound in 1916 and to 5.223 cents in 1917, with occasional highs of over 6 cents,[13] a future fixed price of 4.60 cents per pound could not have seemed a victory to Cuba's hacendados, who begrudged the fact they were unequally matched against the united British Empire and United States, on whom they were dependent for rice, wheat, oil, coal, and capital.

It is impossible to tell just how adequate the fixed price actually was. It is generally assumed that most centrals more than covered their costs and also that the larger, more modern units did better than the smaller. But what also seems certain is that, if it had not been for Hoover's mastery, if the free market had worked it out through supply and demand, all Cubans would have received more. Quite possibly U.S. consumers, given wartime prosperity, could have afforded an additional penny a pound.

Could Rionda himself have done better for the island? Many Cubans believed he had been too anxious to please the North Americans, especially since his own mills were among the most efficient. Established in his mansion high above the Hudson River, visiting the island only during the zafra when he was fortified by dignitaries and private Pullman cars, he seemed increasingly an outsider. However much he had ingratiated himself with Babst and Hoover, Rionda's reputation was not enhanced on the island.

Nor, meanwhile, could Manuel be proud of Cuba Cane's progress. His involvement in the negotiations had distracted him from its problems, and his correspondence is full of expressions of how hard-pressed he felt, with too many irons in the fire. His Second Annual Report for Cuba Cane was not completed until mid-December and commenced apologetically. Cuba Cane was not delivering the quick profits promised by Wall Street. Rionda had tried to damp down these predictions at the beginning and had personally made few promises of immediate riches. He had noted that heavy rains might harm the next crop. "Unfortunately," the Second Annual Report had to state, "that was the case, the richness in the cane having decreased, resulting in an average yield less than in the previous year by 0.55 pounds of sugar per 100 pounds of cane ground." This, in total, added up to a loss of 54 million pounds of sugar. Since the colonos were paid on the basis of the number of pounds of raw cane they delivered to the mill, without regard for its saccharine content, "the entire loss fell on the Company."

"Second," he went on, there had been the 1917 insurrection in Cuba. There had been no damage to the company's properties as fighting forces had mobilized, but much cane had been burned. Burned cane was partially salvageable if ground promptly, but only partially. All four plantations in the East had been disrupted. And winding up the explanations of Cuba Cane's lack of progress: "Third—Higher rates of wages, and war insurance, also the higher price for coal, bags and all other commodities."

The annual report totaled up the figures. The operating profit for the year had been $11 million, down almost $3 million from the year before. Deductions for "Interest and Exchange" were up from $91,386 to $244,043, reflecting considerable short-term borrowing. "Reserve for Taxes, Etc." had quadrupled because of wartime income and excess profits taxes. "Reserve for Depreciation" had been increased from $1,250,000 to $1,750,000 to take higher prices into account. "Net Profit" was thus reduced from $12,179,013 in the first year to $7,315,017 in the second, while production had dropped 362,994 bags, although the approximately $1.7 million spent in "renewals and repairs" had put the mills "in much better operating condition," and "large improvements in machinery" had been made, "especially in the four eastern plantations."

Out of the $7 million profits for the year, almost $5.5 million had been reinvested. The *Stewart* purchase, however excellent, had blocked dividends on the common stock. Now, another huge investment in machinery, buildings, and lands had made dividends impossible for a second year. That an experimental station had been established to improve cane seed was not really enough consolation for the common stockholders. The war—and wartime demand—would not last forever, now that the Yanks were landing in France.

The Second Annual Report did what an annual report was supposed to do, presenting aggregate figures, traditionally audited. Annual reports were not expected to give precise details about what rate of interest was paid on how many short-term loans and about how efficiently administration was managed. Run-of-the-mill stockholders did not generally expect to be so informed, although, of course, they could come to the corporation's annual meeting and ask questions if they chose. Lurking doubts were traditionally up to executive committees and boards of directors. Here was more candor.

Ganzoni's son was back at the front. Lagemann's two sons were in American uniform. With their sons and clerks in the trenches, brokers and investors prayed for victory as 1918 dawned. But they were also concerned about their postwar prospects. When the war ended—the conventional wisdom hoped for 1919—Rionda expected it would take several seasons for European beets to come back on the market. Still, peace would rearrange everything.

In Cuba, oxcarts discharged the bounty of the 1918 zafra at the mills, and once more Manuel went down to *Tuinucú* with Harriet, remaining a few days in Havana to discuss a projected bankers' syndicate. Soaring quantities of sugar had made financing the harvest more expensive, especially since Hooverian efficiency, given the scarcity of shipping, had decreed that deliveries of the Cuban sugar be paced evenly over twelve months, shifting the expense for warehousing and insurance from New York to Cuba. Also, since the colonos needed to pay their workers in cash every two weeks but would not be paid for their warehoused sugar until it was sold, there would be an added need to borrow.[14]

Czarnikow-Rionda could well afford to make advances to the clan's own mills, but while Rionda did not need to borrow from the syndicate on Cuba Cane's behalf, since Frederick Strauss had reported that the Guaranty Trust would look after it, constant short-term loans were still necessary. Manuel was seriously annoyed when the Guaranty, having already advanced Cuba Cane $11 million, suddenly demanded warehouse receipts against future loans. This was a mere technicality, Strauss explained. No doubt had entered the mind of any one "as to the moral or financial standing of the Cuba Cane Company and its officers." It was merely that Sabin had delegated some of his responsibility to younger vice presidents who "have occasionally been too technical."

Regardless of any short-term funding problems, Rionda conceived still more improvements in the corporation's mills and wrote Frederick Strauss about the projects. "I am glad," the banker replied, "that Stewart will at last get into its stride." But he went on rather sternly to counsel economy, reminding Manuel that "the difficulty in getting the machinery in time, the transportation . . . and the labor to secure its erection . . . all point to conservatism." "Sugar," Manuel sternly replied, "is needed by us and our allies." In Cuba Cane's third year, he would spend over $10 million more on capital improvements.[15]

If sugar was so vital, it was only fair that its price should be adequate, but as the weeks passed, colonos became increasingly restless, questioning aloud whether new sowings would pay at the price they were receiving with labor so high that the cost of planting was double what it had been. A great many, Rionda informed Ganzoni in May, were selling out their colonías, not wanting to jeopardize profits already realized, wondering aloud how much could be sold two years in the future, when the world would be at peace again. In June, the harvest over, the colonos began to organize meetings throughout the island.

In Washington, meanwhile, the beet men were urging a higher tariff. Manuel wrote Miguel Arango to "impress" that danger upon President Menocal. "Once the duty on sugar is increased, it will never be decreased," he warned, and added another threat—"the possibility of [U.S.] taxes being imposed on profits as high as 80 percent." Hitherto, he wrote, he had stopped "two or three of our corporations" from changing their nationality

> but if it comes to a point where a man like Gómez-Mena, for instance, selling sugars at the same price as, say, "Julia" as he is not under the obligation to pay 80 percent of his net profits into the U.S. Treasury while "Julia" is, it would not take very long before Gómez-Mena could afford to take all the cane away from "Julia." Such a situation would force an American corporation owning property in Cuba to convert its holdings into a Cuban corporation.

For an American corporation to take such a step would be considered unpatriotic but it would be unavoidable if such a high tax rate on Profits is imposed.

Next year's price? "[W]ere it not for the difficulties already stated..., I would immediately advocate asking for . . . 5.50 cents f.o.b. But what advantage would there be in obtaining [it], if we do not know what the taxes on profits will be."[16]

Planting, its timetable set by the summer rains, could not be delayed. In July, Menocal, averring that it would be impossible to persuade the colonos to increase their plantings unless a satisfactory price was guaranteed them, named de Céspedes, Hawley, and Rionda to bargain for Cuba. They met with the International Commission on July 12, asking 5.6 cents per pound, an increase of 1 cent. The commission offered them 5.25 cents.

In the grocery stores, supplies were running low, and, conservation campaigns having floundered, Hoover informed Wilson that "the great sugar eaters are those of the least moral resistance in the community." The Sugar Division of the U.S. Food Administration was replaced by the Sugar Equalization Board, an incorporated body, funded with $5 million from a special presidential war chest. Hoover was made its chair, Rolph its president. George Zabriskie (formerly of the Produce Exchange and of the Pillsbury Baking Company) became sugar administrator. The board would now buy all sugar, foreign and domestic, pool it, and sell it at its average cost. "The object," Hoover explained, "is to absorb the high peaks of cost in [domestic beet] sugar . . . and to make a small margin on the low cost of certain foreign sugars . . . any profit will be equalized to the consumer." It was an approach based on Hoover's conviction that the cost of production in Cuba had not increased as much as in the United States and that while some advance would be necessary to "maintain a stimulated production," a half a cent a pound over supposed costs should "give ample satisfaction to the Cuban people."[17]

Bargaining dragged on through August—Rionda repeating that rising costs justified an increase of 1 cent per pound and pointing out that the mainland beet men were demanding even higher increases. "What I can never get through my mind and I told Mr. Hoover," Rionda commented, "is why everyone should try to reduce the price for Cuba. . . .

[T]he retailer without any capital, without any risk of fires, drought, floods, cyclones, etc. is deriving a greater profit than the man who produces the article from the ground." Finally, on August 6, a price of 5.5 cents per pound for Cuban sugar for the entire crop year 1919 was agreed to—closer to Cuba's original bargaining proposal than to the 5.25 cents of the original counteroffer but still an increase of only 0.9 cent per pound, compared to 1.275-cent increases for Hawaii and Puerto Rico and 1.7 cents for domestic beet sugar. Bargaining about details and consultations with the British representatives delayed final ratification until October 24, 1918.[18]

It was, by then, obvious that the fighting would soon cease. Business letters were lightened by hope. "Indeed it is a great joy," Ganzoni wrote on November 9, "to look, so to say, Peace in the face, having it within grasp and to hope to be free from this murderous massacring, this daily butchery." But two paragraphs later, with his Swiss thoroughness, he settled down to business considerations. When convoys would no longer be necessary, a boat could make four voyages instead of the three possible under Admiralty restrictions. He wrote of White Javas and of Mauritius, of "prices paid cif Port Said." Two days later, the Armistice was signed in Europe.[19]

On January 6, 1919, as the first full year of peace began, Sir Robert Park Lyle sent a New Year's greeting to his old friend the banished Lagemann, confiding that he believed the United States had taken over the whole Cuban crop "at an absurdly high price." "I suppose our friend Rionda," he added, "and other producers are all in a great good humor."[20]

On the contrary. The shadows were lengthening over what was to have been Manuel's crowning achievement. Cuba Cane's Third Annual Report could not be a good one. To be sure, it registered gains in efficiency. The general managers were getting their teams in place. After long delays, many new machines had finally been installed, sucrose percentage had risen, while "[l]osses in milling, molasses, mud cake and undetermined" had dropped. Production, however, had been disappointing due to drought in the west and late delivery of machinery. In the First Annual Report, Manuel had confidently predicted future yields. He had been too optimistic, and instead of the "4,400,000 to 4,600,000 bags" he had predicted for 1918, there had been only 3,261,621 bags. A 2.748-cents-per-pound cost of production, FOB factory, in 1917 had soared to 1918's

3.998 cents. Interest payments for short-term loans were almost $700,000—up more than $400,000. Thus operating profits were down about $4 million from the year before, net profits about $3 million. When dividends of $3.5 million on the preferred stock were deducted, the surplus account stood at only $14,292,949, an increase of only about $500,000.

Not emphasized in the report were the "Capital Expenditures." With $1,835,050 spent on the western plantations and $8,246,314 on the eastern, the year's total investment was two and a half times the year's net profit. Zeal to bring all the complex operations that comprised the corporation's holdings to their maximum had once more killed off dividends for the common stockholders.

The report was not good. But what was most deeply troubling was the contrast with other Rionda ventures. When the figures for Cuba Cane were compared with those of their own estates or with *Manatí*'s, Manuel could only be embarrassed. The Cuba Cane estates had paid markedly more for the cane they bought from their colonos—$8.21 per bag on average, for example, compared to $5.62 at *Francisco*. This could be explained by the fact that the *Francisco* colonos were paid only 5 percent whereas the Cuba Cane colonos averaged 6.254 percent, which in turn could be explained by the fact that many of the latter's mills were in the West, where there was active competition among mills for cane. Yet it also had to be explained by the fact that *Francisco*'s yield was 13.1 percent compared to the Cuba Cane average of 11.41 percent. The total cost C&F per bag was $14.30 for Cuba Cane, $11.39 for *Francisco*. Operating profits were $2.05 per bag for Cuba Cane, $4.82 per bag for *Francisco*. *Francisco* had the best average among the Rionda ventures, but even *Tuinucú*, the plantation with the lowest, had an operating profit of $3.70 per bag—180 percent of Cuba Cane's $2.05.

Rionda, "locked up" in Havana by a railway strike in February 1919, wrote in some confusion to Bernardo and Manolo. "To say it's disappointing is not strong enough, and does not convey my feelings," he noted. "It is not as though it was due to different management or personnel. Those who managed our places are now responsible for the others; so it can not be management!! What is it then?"

Bernardo, in New York and thus face-to-face with the board members and bankers, was also puzzled. If *Manatí, Elía, Tacajó,* and *Francisco* in the East had made an average profit of $4.52 per bag, he asked, "why cannot Stewart, Morón, Lugareño, Jagueyal make the same?" If the Riondas' *Tuinucú, Washington,* and *San Vincente* in the West had profited $3.11 a bag, why should not the Cuba Cane estates "in that same section" at least equal them? "We have taken our best people," Bernardo wrote, "and given them to the Cuba Cane; Leandro in particular, who was so successful at 'Francisco,' and J. B. Rionda of 'Tuinucú.'"

Cuba Cane's annual stockholders meeting was held on January 13. Bernardo, attending in his uncle's absence, wrote that it had been peaceful. "No questions of importance," he reported, "were asked." Cuba Cane stock had gone, that morning, as low as 74½ for preferred and 24½ for common but then had risen after the meeting to close at 76 and 25⅜, respectively.

This was not enough to cheer up Rionda. True, Cuba Cane's stockholders had not proved publicly hostile, but a few had buttonholed directors on the way out. Moreover, upon hearing the report that the company would have to borrow still another $4.5 million against sugars, the directors, in a special closed-door meeting following the general session, had not only asked questions but delivered ultimatums. A Mr. Stanley of the Guaranty Trust Bank had earlier discussed with Bernardo the possibility of a note issue. Now, wrote Bernardo, he "very emphatically stated that the contemplated issue cannot be sold and that a mortgage on the property must be granted. . . . I cannot grasp "why a result showing $1,200,000 less would so materially affect a Note Issue of a corporation that has $75,000,000 of property with a future in prospect such as you show so clearly in your report." Both a note issue and a mortgage would bring in desperately needed cash. But issuing more notes would illustrate continued popular trust in the corporation, while a mortgage would not only mean a loss of face but would also reduce the security pledged to the preferred stockholders.[21]

Subsequently, Bernardo had to report that "Sabin, Jaretzki, Strauss, naturally Conway and Phillips" all insisted on a mortgage, as did two bankers from Seligmans, two from the Guaranty Trust, and Jaretzki of Sullivan & Cromwell, who was emerging as the villain in family correspondence. Since two-thirds of the shareholders had to agree to a mortgage, a special meeting was set for February 11, and proxies were readied. "Mr. Jaretzki is writing you fully," Bernardo continued. Then, despite instructions from the Sullivan & Cromwell lawyer, Bernardo broke the worst of the bad news, that Cuba Cane's board no longer trusted Rionda. "[Jaretzki] has asked me particularly not to write you about the Resolution that was adopted that will read something like this: No capital expenditures to be made nor extraordinary expenses incurred for repairs, renewals, replacements or maintenance without the approval of the Board, excepting in emergencies."

The only silver lining Bernardo could apparently think of was Frederick Strauss. "Mr. Strauss," Bernardo concluded, "has proven to be everything that we always thought—a very good friend." Strauss (whose own reputation was equally on the line, after all) was stalwart. On February 6, Rionda wrote to thank him for his "very kind and considerate letters" of January 6, 16, 17, 21, and 26.[22]

The seriousness of the situation was underlined when Leandro was sent to Manhattan at the end of January 1919, despite the fact that the zafra was at its height, while his uncle remained in Cuba. Manuel was thus shielded from the worst, although the recurrent illnesses of his adored wife, now in her late seventies, compounded all his other troubles.

On January 28, 1919, Frederick Strauss and Jaretzki met with Bernardo, Leandro, and Manolo. According to Manolo, Leandro was able to answer them satisfactorily, predicting "a very prosperous year to offset the bad impression created by our last report." A threat, however, hung over the meeting. "Mr. [Henry] Evans, the President of the Continental Insurance Co.," Manolo had to continue, "has made some rather severe statements against the Company and ourselves. He has 18,000 shares preferred and controls 7,000 more. He has asked for information as to the relations of [Czarnikow-Rionda] and [Cuba Cane Sugar Corporation], why they sell the sugars, what profits [Czarnikow-Rionda and Cuban Trading] make through [Cuba Cane] and what are the salaries of [Cuba Cane's] officers." But Bernardo assured Manuel that any "disagreeable consequences" would "only be temporary. . . . We regret it, beyond expression for your sake! We are younger and can recover more readily from the abuse." Whatever anyone said, "the management of the property has been of the highest order. . . . The financial end is up to the others and that is the only thing that is being handled badly—it is up to the others to explain the financial matters and not us."

At the next directors meeting, the hostile Evans was elected a director. A cable from Manuel was also read, welcoming a "proposed independent expert examination" as long as it was by competent, practical, and experienced men.

In his letter, Bernardo mentioned the National City Bank, where he had been summoned by Frank Vanderlip, its ambitious president. Vanderlip thought "the Cuba Cane had been very badly handled financially—that originally they should have capitalized the 'Steward.'" National City, he continued, had never refused to advance the Riondas money. "He said we could have any moneys that we wanted which is very gratifying." Then Bernardo had to add a postscript: "Jaretzki has just called up and . . . wants the figure year by year of the commissions earned on sugar. . . . we figure roughly the total is $1,300,000 for the three years." He was close. On February 14, in a "Private and Confidential" memo, he informed Frederick Strauss and Jaretzki that the total commissions that Cuba Cane had paid to Czarnikow-Rionda over three years had totaled $1,324,000.[23]

Rionda, accepting the independent investigation, had specified it should examine management's past decisions concerning "machinery, fields . . . and choosing large cane zone for the far future." But the restless shareholders and the bankers were interested in its immediate financial prospects. Unquestionably, at the minimum, the bookkeeping had been carelessly managed. Rionda now realized he would pay a penalty for that. He wrote Cuba Cane's treasurer: "We must systemize our offices. Get more help. . . . I will gladly pay out of my pocket $10,000.00 per year—even more." He must, he went on, receive monthly balances for each of the plantations, including cost and profit sheets and totals of monthly capital expenditures. "You being so busy, it was cruel to ask you for that heretofore. Now I say: get men, pay them well and let us be happy!" On the same day, he wrote Frederick Strauss, apologizing for not having answered his letters. "The reason for my silence was that I had nothing to say." He added: "I ceased thinking of myself long ago. All my thoughts were of you and the other friends who have stood so loyally by me!"

"My great faith in Cuba Cane has not diminished," he wrote, "but I am not going to prophesy any longer. Let the future speak for itself. . . . As to myself, I am satisfied that I have done all I could for the Company. . . .

I want the Company's success as much as I wish anything in this world and if to obtain it I must accept conditions I am ready to do so."[24]

In February 1919, the *Louisiana Planter* reported that, as peace settled in, the United States had adequate supplies of sugar for the first time in two years. Retail grocers, feeling "assured," were buying only "from week to week." Among those in the Cuban sugar business, there was now a certain unease. Cuba was guaranteed sale of its full crop for this year, but one year would pass quickly. Shipping was once more available from Mauritius, Java, and Hawaii, while Cuba's capacity had been doubled to 4 million tons a year for which a market must be secured. An enormous crop, the *Planter*'s correspondent reflected, "not apparently due so much to the creation of new central factories as it has been to the enormous increase in the output of the old ones, by the extension of their cane fields and the improvement in their equipment, and the percentage of yield by more scientific elaboration." There was also, he mentioned, a current "alarm . . . over the idiosyncrasies of the 'Cuba Cane Corporation.' This company, instead of dividing among its stockholders a profit of four or five million dollars, is creating an indebtedness of twenty million. This is not consoling."

It was not consoling to Rionda. Evans's charges were making it difficult to raise funds, and on Wall Street Bernardo felt excluded by the financiers and lawyers. The plan to issue mortgage bonds was abandoned for the present. It was understood, the *Louisiana Planter* commented, that only one bank had even bid on the prospective issue, and at a very low price. Three days later, the preferred stock fell to 73. A Mr. Sutro, dropping by, explained to Bernardo that this was because some of the preferred stockholders feared for their dividends. "Of course this is only Wall Street gossip for the purpose of manipulation." When Sutro then suggested their "forming a pool with him" to buy the stock at the lower price and make "a very large profit," Bernardo responded indignantly. "I told him," he proudly related, "that we would not, we never had and never would go into such a thing, that our business was to handle the company for the benefit of the stockholders and that we hoped they would make all the money. That we had absolute faith in the Company, which is shown by the fact that we still hold every share of stock we had at the time of the underwriting."[25]

Perhaps a prestigious outsider would reassure the financial community. At their March 7 meeting, Cuba Cane's board employed General George Washington Goethals to investigate Evans's charges against the corporation. Only three members, Horace Havemeyer, James N. Jarvie, and Stephen B. Fleming, asked to be recorded as opposing the investigation. The others, including Bernardo himself, did not object. Manuel, by cable, commented a day or two later that the investigation "cannot but be beneficial in its effect and convincing to everyone of our good faith throughout in all the affairs of the Company."[26]

Goethals was a neat man with a trim mustache and a bulldog gaze. After working his way through the College of the City of New York in the 1870s, he had gone on to West Point to become an army engineer. From this serviceable if undramatic destiny, he had been rescued in 1907 when President Roosevelt appointed him chair and chief engineer of the Isthmian Canal Commission to carry through "the greatest engineering work in recorded history" in completing the Panama Canal. He had lately served as acting quartermaster general of the U.S. Army in the war and had returned to private life only very recently to establish a private consulting engineering firm. The Cuba Cane investigation was among his first contracts. He had never, apparently, unless incidentally, seen a sugar plantation.[27]

John D. Ryan of the National City Bank had pointed out that deficiency in the discussion before the vote, saying that the general's opinion, since he "had no knowledge of the sugar business ... would not be of much value." "Then," Braga wrote, "Mr. Jaretzki explained that General Goethals would employ men well versed in the sugar business." Jarvie, who did know something of the cycle of plantation life, and Horace Havemeyer, who had just returned from an inspection trip of the Cuban properties, were concerned the investigation would complicate the zafra, already complicated enough by three railroad strikes, a stevedores' strike, and the influenza epidemic. But Jaretzki brushed this aside with the remark that he "understood that all General Goethals desires at the present time is to see the wheels turning so as to get an idea of the running of a sugar plantation and later on, if necessary, further details of manufacturing can be gone into."[28]

In addition to employing Goethals, the board took another step at its meeting on March 7 that would have decisive repercussions. It added to the board Charles Hayden of the Boston investment banking firm of

Hayden, Stone and Company, which had just become a "very large stockholder."

What would be remembered about Charles Hayden was that he was impatient, "a fast worker," in the parlance of the 1920s, "moving on the jump, talking in quick, clipped sentences and making decisions in a flash." He was a bow-tie man, the son of a prosperous Massachusetts leather merchant, properly descended from a Mayflower passenger. Graduating from the Massachusetts Institute of Technology in 1890 in engineering, he had toured Europe and then entered banking for a year as a $3-a-week clerk, before, in 1892, at twenty-two, cofounding the Boston investment firm with a Harvard friend. Almost instantly phenomenally successful, they had opened a New York office in 1908 and in 1915 had been chief promoters of Atkins's Punta Alegre. Hayden sat on the boards of a number of extremely diverse companies. Without family except for his younger brother, Josiah, he played bridge, belonged to prestigious golf and yachting clubs, made large charitable contributions, and headed impressive fund drives. "Time," he is remembered as saying, "is money for a business man." Manuel wrote Frederick Strauss that he was glad to have Hayden on the Cuba Cane board. "I shall meet many new faces," he went bravely on, "when I attend the first meeting after my return to New York."[29]

It proved difficult for the general to hire experts on plantations with everyone busy with the harvest, working around the clock. Only a Mr. Goodrich from tiny *Santa Cecilia*, which made 75,000 bags a crop, could finally be recruited and that only on the day before Goethals's departure, so the general had no time to check on his qualifications. Goethals had, however, gathered a staff of engineers and some twenty accountants and clerks—perhaps more to the point for what the investors really had in mind if not what the Riondas hoped for. Manuel and his nephews never doubted they were building up a superb kingdom of mills, good cane lands, and excellent new machinery. They knew, however, that they were on shaky ground with the casual record keeping. "You must always bear in mind," Manuel apologized to Strauss, "that we are not in the United States but in Cuba, where you can not obtain as efficient service for office work." The truth was, actually, that the finer points of accounting had had a low, if any priority.[30]

Goethals, surrounded by his entourage, arrived in Cuba at the end of

March. He requested that Arango, Leandro, and Bernardo accompany him on his inspection tour. Manuel, because of Harriet's illness, would remain at *Tuinucú*, where the party would stay later on their circuit. The pace and pattern of the expedition were set with a visit to *La Julia*. The visitors were shown through its sugar house by the mill engineer, who explained the machinery, and then repaired to the dwelling house for luncheon. "All the books that we had brought along," Bernardo reported, were looked into very carefully, and "some of the contents interested them a great deal, such as an itemized description to the Machinery, and the inventory. . . . They asked several questions about the average distance for hauling by carts, average length of haul by public and private railroads, and the rates of freight we paid on the cane." After lunch, Goethals spoke with Bernardo in the office. "He said that already yesterday he had changed his mind regarding the manner of his investigation. He said that Mr. Jaretzki had spoken to him about keeping the expense down as much as possible. . . . I told him that it was in our opinion imperative, in view of the publicity given to it, that a thorough, minute and complete investigation should be made, no matter how long it might take." Soon, it began to rain, and Goethals, accountants in tow, returned to Havana.

On April 4, at 8 A.M., they again set out, visiting *Jobo* briefly, spending an hour at *Conchita*, the jewel in Cuba Cane's western crown, and "less than half an hour" at *Feliz*. A stop at *San Ignacio* was spoiled by a cane field fire, since the party spent their time watching the flames. "[I]t is very unfortunate," Bernardo concluded, "that we are dealing with people who do not know the business."

Inspection of the eastern plantations between April 5 and 9 proved to be at least as hurried. Yet while Goethals was at *Tuinucú*, the Riondas struck boldly. In his fragmentary reminiscences, Bernardo gave one account of the matter. He had, he wrote, told the general that "the only way they could get at the facts would be by examining the books of Cuban Trading Company, Czarnikow-Rionda Company, Mr. Rionda's and my own."

> I gave a full report of what went on to Uncle, who was then at Tuinucú as Auntie had had her first nervous breakdown, and was quite sick. We had a train and four or five private cars and traveled to Tuinucú. There Uncle met us, and after the usual introductions,

and an extraordinarily fine dinner, Goethals, McGuire and myself went to a room alone, where Uncle gave them letters authorizing the investigation of the books of the different companies mentioned above, as well as his own private books.[31]

The family's honor had been questioned. At what had been the peak of Manuel's prestige, he had been charged with dishonestly swelling his private fortune. His nephews were hardworking men of ability. Bernardo and Manolo in New York had mastered the intricacies of the world's sugar trade. In Cuba, Leandro, Pepe, and Salvador furthered the most advanced technology. But it was implied their positions were owed only to nepotism. Goethals himself was not ignorant of the insult his inspection represented. "He was very talkative today," Bernardo wrote Manuel after they had left *Tuinucú*. "He . . . said that when [the investigation of the Panama Canal] had commenced he felt that if he had met the man who started it he would have killed him."

All the account books were opened at 9 A.M. on April 10, when Goethals and his key assistants arrived at the offices of the Cuban Trading Company in the Banco Nacional building and commanded a private room to question Cuba Cane's department heads. While many questions were asked, after the interrogation Goethals remarked to Bernardo "that, so far as he is concerned, he is now through at this end; that his plans have again changed, and that he will not go into it more thoroughly." Bernardo went on: "[T]he General stated that what he now wants to investigate is the New York end, that is, the Bankers, which in his opinion is where the mistake all the way through has been made. Upon this point, naturally, I made no comment."

On April 12, after less than two weeks in Cuba, Goethals and his staff sailed back to New York. Inspection of the mills, which Rionda had counted on to impress any sugar expert, had certainly been perfunctory. "It is unfortunate," Manuel wrote, "that we have to go through this humiliation and do not get the thorough examination I wanted." The general, however, left a number of his accountants behind, with more en route to reinforce them, to comb through the account books.

Meanwhile, in New York, the members of Cuba Cane's board of directors were becoming uneasy at what they had unleashed. The Riondas would be difficult to replace. Perhaps, also, word was circulating that Goethals was questioning the financing practices of the corporation.

Bernardo had reported him remarking "that the financing of the Company has been done very badly. . . . The error [was] in increasing the plantations without providing capital" which "he cannot explain considering the very fine Board that we have in New York." "I did not want," Bernardo continued, "to shove the responsibility to the financial part, being an officer of the Company . . . as I do not believe in criticizing something that we ourselves did not call the attention in 1915 to the other Directors." The directors, too, as Goethals fired his questions, shared the knowledge that Rionda's own profits, no matter how great over three years, had certainly not exceeded what the investment bankers had gleaned in three months from the first floating of Cuba Cane's stock without ever leaving Wall Street or seeing a single cane stalk.[32]

Confident that the investigating commission's report would exonerate him, Manuel rode a high horse. He announced he would not yet return to New York. Now that the zafra was winding down with a record-breaking crop, he informed the financiers that he would take Harriet and Aunt Isidora to rest at the Greenbrier Hotel in White Sulphur Springs, West Virginia, where he would compose a statement to be read to a special meeting of the full board, which he demanded should be called in May. He hinted that, since he was not appreciated, he would resign.[33]

Meanwhile, while the Goethals investigation was being acted out, a subplot, connected with the financing of Cuba Cane, had been unfolding, deepening his resentment. Loans to Cuba Cane had always been arranged through the Guaranty Trust Company, which had also always been the only bank in which it had carried an account, Guaranty charging the high rate of 6.5 percent against sugar already bagged and in the company warehouses. It now requested that independent warehouse receipts confirming the sugar be deposited with the Mercantile Bank in Havana, Cuba Cane paying Mercantile a $5,000 fee for holding them. Manuel was furious. Not only should the company be able to borrow "at the lowest possible rate" but "under no circumstances should we lower our own self-respect any further." "Es hora," he wrote, "que enseña los dientes." The time had come to show their teeth. In the end, the matter was smoothed over, Eugene Stetson agreeing that Guaranty Trust would accept Cuba Cane's word. But in the end, also, Cuba Cane went on paying 6.5 percent to Guaranty.

They should, after all, go slow about changing bankers, Manuel wrote, calming down. They were going to need to borrow perhaps as much as $35 million. After all, Sabin and Seligman "fueron los padres de la Criatura y nunca dejaron de alimentarla, y por tales motivos no debemos meternos a buscar nodrizas" (were Cuba Cane's parents and had never failed to feed it, and therefore the Riondas should not seek wet nurses). Meanwhile, trading in Cuba Cane stock had been active, with 15,000 shares changing hands on one day and 20,000 on another as prices advanced. Manolo believed this was partly because Hayden "was very well satisfied with the condition of the Company; as you know, his house is a large operator." Also, he suspected, advanced information might have leaked from Cuba that the Goethals report would exonerate the company. Manolo's analysis of a list of major stockholders showed they had made few changes in their holdings during the investigation. Even Mrs. Henry Evans, who had sold 3,000 shares, had replaced most of them.[34]

Meanwhile, Charles Hayden was attending his first board meeting, asking questions in an expert manner. "He brought out the point," Manolo wrote, "that in the Cash Statement the Colonos' Account should be placed as a Resource and that if this were done the Company would appear to-day practically without Liabilities." As the meeting was breaking up, he had asked "whether any arrangements had been made with the General in regards the charge for this inspection and I told him that nothing appeared on our records. . . . I can only say to you gentlemen, confidentially [Hayden then commented] that he knows how to charge."[35]

A Fixed Price   127

6

Tail of the Lion

By the end of April 1919, Manuel's thirty-one-page statement, "To the Cuba Cane Sugar Corporation," was being typed in his Wall Street offices. It was a glowing self-tribute, warmed by the belief that Goethals's report would completely exonerate him before his detractors. He had kept silent previously, he wrote, because "it was my duty to keep on making sugar." Now, with 90 percent of the crop in, he could spare time to comment.

In so doing, he identified himself with the island. A man of two countries, he had, from his Maine school days, served a dual allegiance. He was proud of his Spanish birth, but he had left the peninsula at sixteen, and his success had been in linking the island's cane fields with the sources of the northern capital they had required. Convinced of the venality of Cuban politicians, he had frequently criticized those who spoke his native tongue, for years priding himself on his acceptance by Manhattan's men of affairs. Now, stung by their criticism, he wrote of himself as Cuban.

He began by recalling how the Cuban plantations had recovered after 1898 from the ruins of war. No aid had come from the United States. Only Rionda himself, through his London connections, had arranged advances to the planters who had themselves plowed their profits back into their estates. "They did not create new bonds," he wrote, "nor did they issue more capital stock—they merely kept using over and over again their yearly Earnings. . . . To you bankers, this may sound amusing." Only Czarnikow-Rionda had stood behind them. Because of ties then established, his company now sold "nearly half" of Cuba's crop.

He went on to point out the disadvantages under which Cuban planters labored. Lack of adequate capital resources had forced the weaker among them to "sell at whatever they could get" as soon as their cane was ground. Thus prices had been driven down for everyone. "The organization of the Cuba Cane Sugar Plantation was not the work of promoters' premeditated plan to . . . make money . . . but was the result of the . . . difficulties that the Cuban planters encountered in obtaining the world parity for their sugar. . . . Here at last we had a chance to reduce the number of sellers and stop the competition that existed." This unselfish goal, he added with unabashed confidence in his own paternalism, had been "the first and only consideration as far as Czarnikow-Rionda Company and myself were concerned because, while the combining of several plantations was a good investment for the capitalist, it would be the means of bringing about what we were all wishing, namely, more unity amongst the Cuban planters."[1] Neither he nor his associates had "joined in the plan of organizing your company with any intention of making money thereby by manipulating the stock or in any other way."

He recalled that $1.5 million had been offered him for his initial work and that he had refused it, taking instead 30,000 shares of common stock. Of these shares, he had distributed 17,382 among those who had helped form the company. He had kept the remainder. "The stock went as high as 70 and back to 20 but not a share did I sell." The Riondas had been satisfied, he wrote, with the commissions they would receive "on the sales of sugar, purchases of bags, coal, machinery and supplies," which had been guaranteed in writing and approved by the board of directors and which, in the case of fourteen out of the seventeen centrals, merely continued prior arrangements. The able managers he had chosen had received only very modest salaries, Miguel Arango and Leandro, $25,000 a year each; José B. Rionda, $20,000; and Manuel himself, only $15,000.

It was true that drought, low sucrose yields, and the 1917 revolt had checked profits, as had the late delivery of new machinery, the lack of

Fig. 5. Czarnikow-Rionda headquarters building

shipping, strikes, and the influenza epidemic, when *Jagueyal*'s second engineer had died and many others had been too sick to work. But these had been temporary impediments.

Today, the investors, in asking why the Cuba Cane mills did not match the profits of his *Francisco* and *Manatí*, overlooked their early years of struggle. Cuba Cane, like all the other companies, would "come out strong." The board members had only to visit the cane fields to appreciate their value.

Malicious rumors, he wrote, had been spread last January about the corporation and about himself, and no one had come forward to defend Czarnikow-Rionda. Yet because of Czarnikow-Rionda, Cuba Cane had benefited from a prewar freight contract that had saved it in its first two years 40 to 50 cents per bag in shipping costs. This benefit alone had surpassed the total commissions paid Czarnikow-Rionda over three years. Also, the Cuban Trading Company had provided bags, coal, and oil for less than Cuba Cane's competitors had paid, and it had advanced $450,000 of its own money to the corporation's colonos, as well as renting it seventy freight cars and six locomotives at a reduced rate. *Tuinucú* had even let *Stewart* use two locomotives free of charge, "sacrificing itself in making less sugar daily for lack of locomotives." Through thirty pages of such detail, he waxed self-righteous. "What has been most surprising to me of this whole matter is how any fair minded business man could have given credence to the malicious reports. . . . It is hard to realize how a good name that has been established for many years, could so easily be torn to shreds by false and malicious reports." He came, then, with grave Spanish pride, to his conclusion: "In view of all the facts and in view of all the incidents that have transpired, I beg to hand you my resignation as President and Director of your Company." Serious or not, threat or plan or bluff, there it was.[2]

To his nephews, he could report that, since they had come to White Sulfur Springs, his wife had eaten both fish and solid food without nausea. She had been able, he wrote Salvador one April night, to walk with him for a four-mile stroll on the hotel grounds. "La encuentro alegre" (I find her happy), he wrote, and he had gone off that spring afternoon for a horseback ride. Four days later, Bernardo wired him that the closing quotations on Cuba Cane's stock were up to 84½ for the preferred and 36½ for the common. Marchena "had sold all his preferred and common at 78 and 28. . . . It must make him feel sick to see what a fool he has made of himself, but he deserved it." And in another letter: "The stock continues to go up. Everybody has faith in it."

Others in Manuel's circle also reassured him. "I'm certain that every member of the Board," Manolo wrote, "will realize the great injustice that has been done to you. Mr. Strauss . . . said that he was very sorry that you evidently were under the impression that you did not have the full confidence of the Board . . . [saying] 'I wish you could hear the way these men have talked to me . . . , speaking most highly of your Uncle and reiterating time and time again that they have absolute confidence in him.'"

Manuel wrote to Frederick Strauss, "You must give me credit for having been very patient during the past four or five months but I can not settle down to work again without first having a thorough cleaning out. . . . Nothing that we could talk of at the proposed interview . . . would make me change my mind." On May 11, he brought Harriet home to Alpine.[3]

Goethals's accountants worked through June. If the inspection of the centrals had been uninformed, Cuba Cane's books—and those of the Cuban Trading Company and of Czarnikow-Rionda—were meticulously examined. Manuel went over the completed report privately with the general on July 8, and Goethals presented it to the board of directors at a two-hour meeting on July 16. Running thirty-four pages, with three reports on land titles and mill operation, it began with a brisk endorsement of the Riondas' personal honesty. They had received no commission on Cuba Cane's purchases of mills, nor had those mills been significantly in debt to them. Their purchases of machinery and supplies had been at slightly lower costs than they charged others, and Czarnikow-Rionda had sold the sugar for slightly higher prices than they had sold the product of their own mills.

But Goethals then went on in a less complimentary way to consider the properties, operating efficiency, and rates of profit. A number of detailed criticisms filled the pages—for example, that the *Lugareño* had not been provided with adequate cane lands; that when *Socorro* had been purchased, its best cane lands had not been included; that *Lugareño*'s narrow gauge railway tracks had not been replaced with standard gauge; that there were possible defects in a number of land titles; that "wrong" methods had been used in calculating depreciation; and that although

Stewart had been appraised for $4.3 million, its purchase price had been $8.4 million. Goethals granted that Cuba Cane's seventeen centrals averaged 11.41 percent recovery of sucrose from its cane compared to the island's 10.86 percent average. But while "excellent" in seven mills and "good" in three, the percentage was only "fair" in three of the mills and "poor" in *Socorro*. Cuba Cane's rate of extraction averaged 82.5 percent, significantly lower than the Cuban-American Sugar Company's 84.3 percent. The report pointed out without comment beyond a curt "steadily improving," that overall Cuba Cane's yield had risen from 11.25 percent in 1916 to 11.41 percent in 1918 and that its losses in manufacturing had dropped from 3.07 percent to 2.36 percent.

Other tables measured how well each mill had been able to meet the goal of operating around the clock. When there was not enough cane to cut or enough men to cut it or enough railroad cars to bring it in, when there was "stoppage due to rain, holidays, no cane, machinery breakdowns, dull boiling house, low steam pressure," the elaborate integrative process had to grind to an expensive halt. Cuba Cane's percentage of "lost time" was 29.40 percent of total crop time, "comparing favorably as a whole" with the Cuban-American's 36.94 percent. Goethals noted, however, that there had been 40 percent lost time at the *Stewart* and more than 61 percent at *Lugareño*.

As for the corporation's "earning capacity," while Manuel had invoked the acres of cane, as well as growing and renewable wealth, Goethals pointed out that profits on the total capital employed had dropped from 19.7 percent in 1916 to 14.3 percent in 1917 to 7.7 percent in 1918, from $12,307,00 to $8,991,000, to $5,301,000. While the "excessive" extra $4 million that had been paid for *Stewart* over its appraised value had presumably been "figured . . . upon the prospective earning capacity of the plant," only in 1916 had earnings reached 15 percent of invested capital (after depreciation but before U.S. taxes), dropping to 14 percent in 1917 and then to 9 percent in 1918.

Unstressed was the fact that government price had not kept pace with higher wartime costs, although Goethals mentioned that machinery, freight, labor, and fuel were "almost double . . . in 1918 over what they had been in 1916" while the price was "not quite 15 percent more in 1918 than in 1916." Wage rates for unskilled labor in wartime had gone up 80 percent, for skilled labor 40 percent. "Fuel oil and coal, which cost approximately $250,000 in 1916, cost $870,000 in 1918," although partly because more had been consumed. Real estate taxes, which had been less than $100,000 in 1916, had risen to over $200,000 in 1918. In 1918, Cuba had levied a new war tax on sugar and molasses of more than $400,000.

In 1918, maintenance costs (factory, railroad) were "at least two and one-half times" what they had been in 1916. In part, this was because there were now more miles of railroad to maintain and also because "the nature of the business" was one calling "for extensive repairs"—machines being relentlessly driven nonstop around the clock. On the other hand, Goethals pointed out that maintenance expenditures had been approximately $1.26 a bag instead of the 40 cents, which "engineers familiar with conditions in Cuba" considered fair. Previous owners therefore must have skimped on upkeep. The "inference" seemed warranted, he went on, "that many of the mills were not in the best of mechanical condition when acquired by the Corporation . . . and that large expenditures [had] been necessary for renewals which, while extensive, could not be properly be capitalized."

The Riondas had been honest; the company's efficiency overall was as good as or better than that of most Cuban mills. Rising costs, most (if not all) because of the war, combined with the low fixed price for sugar, explained falling profits. It seemed far from a bad record. Yet Goethals was unflinching in his criticism. An army engineer, he was accustomed to explicit chains of command. He was not in his present business to make allowances. The Rionda management had fallen short, and the corporation's offices had muddled. "There is a Department of Railroads and Lands, yet extensions are made to the railroads and the head of such matters in Havana has no record of them. . . . An Engineering Department exists," the general wrote, "but if any records are kept of the costs of any of the construction work, they could not be produced. . . . [T]hey have not been segregated and made use of." Although Cuba Cane had been in operation for three years, "ample time to have an effective organization in charge," such an organization did not exist. There had been "an absence of coordination. . . . Instead of the various mills forming parts of a united whole, there are 17 independent centrals." In 1918, the Cuba Cane Corporation had spent over $500,000 on its own Havana office and an additional $100,000 on a New York office. Yet the purchasing and selling functions of the corporation had been exercised not by its own numerous employees but by Czarnikow-Rionda and the Cuban Trading Company, which had been paid additional sums for their services. There had been "duplication of work, delay and inefficiency, to say nothing of unnecessary expense incident to the increased personnel."

On page 30, the report again spoke kindly of Manuel but in the context of his deficiencies. If the "insinuations and charges" made against him were "without foundation," they had been understandable. The predictions of great profits had not been realized. Rionda, "a man of the highest integrity and also a man of vision," had foreseen in the Cuba Cane Sugar Corporation the realization of one of his life-long dreams. But he had "secured for another company in which he is largely interested an advantageous selling contract from the Corporation he was instrumental in creating. . . . It matters little to the gossipers that the contracts . . . , the selection of the officials and the purchases of land, were matters which received the consideration of the Board of Directors . . . . a Board of Directors offers no such shining mark as an individual." Rionda's nephews were honest, but, while they had proved they could handle individual mills, after three years they had not shown the ability to coordinate seventeen mills in one extensive undertaking.

At best, the general concluded, the old man had not been to blame. The inefficiencies revealed by the report grew from his lack of understanding large organization techniques. Rionda had "seemed to realize the defect and stated that he found himself in an entirely new environment, that he was not an operator or manager of a manufacturing industry, but a merchant." Thus the patronizing thrust of a managerial revolution.[4]

Manuel sent a subdued account of the report to Victor Zevallos and Higinio Fanjul. He wrote that he was glad "that as far as the vital questions of integrity and honesty are concerned, his findings demonstrate that without question that there was absolutely no ground whatever for the misstatements that have been circulated . . . while it hurts to hear some things."

Within the next ten days, he revised his "To the Cuba Cane Sugar Corporation" in the light of the final report. Most revisions were merely in phraseology, although he could now point out that while the previous December the corporation's short-term liabilities had reached $24 million, they had been reduced to less than $1.5 million, and that advances against the dead season just past and the harvesting and marketing had also been cleared off the books. His defense was amplified later in an eighteen-page statement to Charles Hayden. Both rebuttals were laced with hostile references to the lack of knowledge on the part of Goethals's team and the brevity of their inspections. "In matters concerning Machinery and Field Work, it was solely theoretical and academic, not practical," he wrote. Goethals had made no allusion to the clan's colossal accomplishments in securing good cane land, in installing machinery, and constructing railroads in the midst of a world war—in doing what Hoover had so urgently pleaded be done at all costs, providing the "food to win the war."

Much of Goethals's attack had focused on a series of details, and Rionda examined these disparate changes individually. Soon *Lugareño* would have more than adequate cane land when the Northern Railroad was opened and the corporation had accepted from Manuel options he had secured on Río Máximo and Redención lands. Additional lands to supply the *Socorro* had not been included in its purchase since they would have been unnecessary had it not been for the recent "borer" infestation. *Lugareño*'s railroad tracks had been left as narrow gauge because a major change was "not advisable" in wartime. As for the questions of proper title to the lands, the eight cases examined had a combined acreage less than 5 percent of Cuba Cane's total holdings and were too small to justify the importance given to them in the report, especially since the report admitted they were "more of form than substance."

Some inadequate yields or profits that Goethals had seized upon and labeled "poor" were, Rionda pointed out, already things of the past. *Lugareño* had had gross operating profits in the current year close to $850,000 against the prior year's loss of $80,000, and its yield was up 1 percent over the year before, placing it in the "excellent" rather than "fair" category. *Morón*'s profits were three times those of 1918 and *Stewart*'s nearly double.

As to the charge that the mills he had purchased had been in poor condition, Manuel included their production records for the six years prior to their purchase. In each case, they had risen. "No sugar plantation," Manuel wrote, "can increase its production if its mechanical efficiency is allowed to deteriorate."

A separate letter defending Czarnikow-Rionda and the Cuban Trading Company's relations with Cuba Cane showed special bitterness concerning Goethals's failure to evaluate Czarnikow-Rionda's freight contract concession. Since Goethals had been given full access to all the books, why had he not verified the figure and stated it "as a fact instead of a claim. . . . The auditors appointed . . . were only too ready to go into the minutest fractions whenever anything which to them appeared unfavorable was concerned, but they did not follow the same policy in presenting facts that would do justice to Czarnikow-Rionda Company." Czarnikow's own auditors had confirmed, Manuel wrote, that Cuba Cane had been saved "in freight rates, purchase of sugar bags and otherwise . . . close to $2,600,000."[5]

Underlying Goethals's and Rionda's counterexchanges lay implicit basic convictions. They differed fundamentally about whether the western mills should be written off in favor of the eastern and about the desirability of the colono system.

In Goethals's ranking of Cuba Cane's thirteen mills in the west, he had rated six as "excellent," five as "good," and only one as "fair" and one as "poor" in terms of "performance." Of the four eastern mills, only one ranked as "excellent," one "good," and two merely "fair." Yet when their respective rates of profit had been analyzed, even though the corporation had spent more than two and a half times as much on the eastern mills, the eastern mills were still more profitable than the western. This difference could be attributed to the fact that the eastern cane was cheaper because the colonos were paid a lower rate and also because there was a higher percentage of administration cane.

Under the colono system, the mills paid the colonos an amount of sugar equal to an agreed-upon percentage of the weight of their raw cane. Since in the settled West several mills often competed for a single colono's sugar and since the colonos were generally the descendants of independent landowners experienced in bargaining, the western colonos had been able to win higher percentages than the eastern colonos, who were often demobilized guerrilla fighters who had accepted not the 6 or 6.5 percent usual in the western provinces but as low as 5 percent.

Even at the lower percentage, General Goethals had concluded that it would be advantageous for the mills to own and exploit their own land. The colono, paid by weight alone, had no incentive to be concerned with

Tail of the Lion 137

the richness of sucrose in his cane. The corporation, on the contrary, would seek out "the most scientific and efficient methods." With administration cane, there would be no need for advances to colonos and no bad loans to be written off, and delivery timetables could be better synchronized.

Rionda sympathized with many of these criticisms. Very possibly he had himself educated Goethals about the weaknesses in the system. He had also already recommended moving the machinery from several of the less profitable western mills to the eastern ones. But Manuel, like the Cuban-American Sugar Company's Hawley, questioned the advantages of administration cane. The colonos, he argued, by contracting for and supervising the field labor, spared the corporation managers responsibility and took care of the agricultural end even when the price of sugar dropped so low that there was little profit. They worked in bad times as well as in prosperous ones, while the managers whom the mills would have to hire to replace them were hard to find and required adequate salaries. When hard times came, Manuel wrote, foreseeing a travail still to be endured, producers in other countries went under. "The Cuban producer survived."

Just as he defended the colono system, Rionda, although he knew sugar was produced more cheaply in the corporation's eastern mills, was not willing to write off the western units. The Cuba Cane mills, he pointed out, were not competing with each other. "Their real competition," he wrote, drawing on his merchant expertise, "is with other sugar producing countries of the world." Eastern Cuba produced only about 10 percent of the world's sugar in normal times and thus would "never regulate prices." It was not a question of how cheaply the corporation in isolation from the world market could produce its sugar but of how well it competed with sugar from other countries, just as it was not a question whether one steel factory could produce steel cheaper than another factory but whether the two could successfully compete with other steel factories. As long as the western mills were competitive with those in other countries, they would hold their edge. When a depression had occurred in the past, the producers in other countries had gone under while the Cubans had survived. "It was another instance of the survival of the fittest. While it is true that Cuba fared badly, other sugar producing countries fared worse.... Cuba is the cheapest sugar producing country in the world."⁶

Goethals had spoken on behalf of an imminent managerial revolution in which scale necessitated professionalism beyond the abilities of old-fashioned sugar barons. Before him shone the archetype of a corporate structure without waste or duplication. Rionda, on the contrary, watched the market, not granting that although an overall average production cost might be competitive, a manager could not be excused from monitoring all its component items.

Goethals's report, despite prior rumors, paid almost no attention to the corporation's financing or to its constant need for short-term loans. Bernardo quoted Goethals as saying "that what he now wants to investigate is the New York end, that is, the Bankers, which in his opinion is where the mistake all the way through has been made." And Goethals (according to Manuel) had agreed privately on July 8 that the constant need to borrow was the corporation's Achilles' heel. "The [financial situation was touched upon]," Manuel had reported, "and [Goethals] said that it was very bad for a Company that had to carry such an immense quantity of sugar, to be forced to [borrow money against it and have so little—if any—working capital].... Even the bankers concede this." Yet Goethals had not pursued the matter. He had not been employed to critique the North American financial system or to muse whether the current practices of capitalism were imprisoning the island in a deepening dependency. At no point did he mention the failure of Cuba Cane's board of directors to capitalize the *Stewart* purchase, although if an additional bond issue had been floated at the time, millions could have been subsequently saved in interest on floating loans—interest that went to the banks of certain board members. The decision process—the apparent ease with which the purchase of the *Stewart* had slid through the Executive Committee and the board—went unstudied.⁷

On the other hand, unstudied also, save for a passing reference to the $500,000 spent on a Havana office that had performed few services, was the expense of placating Cuban politicians. North Americans generally believed that Cuba's political classes trafficked in *botellas*, the plums that rewarded connections. Behind the Goethals investigation may have been a growing suspicion on Wall Street that Manuel was subsidizing parasites at the expense of the productive Yankees, milking a cash cow, shrugging the botellas off too philosophically as a necessary cost of doing business abroad.

Goethals's final conclusion scarcely veiled a racial insult. "Changes in the management are recommended, although it is admitted that this is no easy task because of the location of the properties, the absence of suitable habitation at many of them, the lack of any social environment, and the peculiar temperament of the people." Rionda could not but have resented such sneers. Goethals had paid no tribute to the men and women who had fought Cuba's way out of devastation and supplied two continents with sugar through four years of world war.

Rionda, meanwhile, was also deep in high-level discussions elsewhere. The war had been over for eight months, and the wartime authority granted Hoover's Sugar Control Board would soon expire. Pent-up demand for sweets after long rationing, not only in America but also in Europe, indicated that as soon as the uncontrolled 1920 crop was harvested, there would be wild bargaining and high prices, the refineries no longer assured their raw materials at a fixed price.

Robert B. Hawley, the Tennessean Texan who had revolutionized the scale of Cuban mills when he launched *Chaparra*, wrote his associate in that venture, General, now President Menocal, on July 3, 1919. He did not express concern for the Post-Hawley interests with which he was connected as president of their Cuban-American Sugar Company. "The outlook is prophetic for higher prices," he wrote instead. "[T]he *market*, with all its possibilities, would be controlled by speculative influences, while the *producer* and *consumer* alike would be the victims of its manipulations." He suggested that since the United States would no longer be in charge, Menocal should take the initiative in "enlist[ing] every Hacendado and Colono" to "leave the Island's product under the single . . . control of the agencies designated for the purpose." Manuel forwarded a copy of the letter to Zevallos, indicating he found the suggestion "very good."

Thus on July 15, the day before the Goethals report was presented to Cuba Cane's board, Rionda met with Hawley and Tarafa. The three men conceived a bold plan to replace U.S. government controls with a private Cuban selling agency that would "stabilize the market, fixing the price, at intervals, according to the world's needs and supplies." In this way, the producers could "receive for themselves the full benefit of whatever may rightly develop to their own advantage, every producer sharing alike."[8]

Rionda wrote Zevallos that the new selling agency would be composed of Hawley, Tarafa, and Manuel himself, plus Ambassador de Céspedes. "[T]he support of the Cuban government and the sanction or acquiescence of Washington" would be necessary, but it would not be good policy to consult Washington in advance, lest its politicians should not approve. And it would be better to act as though the plan had originated with the Cuban planters en masse rather than in their own small circle. Hawley, Rionda wrote, believed that by "agreeing to pay 8 percent on the money borrowed and 1 percent commission to the syndicate underwriter . . . the bankers would see no danger but quite a profit in the transaction." Of this, however, Rionda was skeptical.[9]

The proposal must have been in his thoughts as Cuba Cane's board of directors voted to refer Goethals's report to a seven-man committee, with Charles Hayden as chair. Henry Evans, pressed to serve on it, instead resigned from the board, announcing that he and his wife had disposed of all their stock. Goethals submitted a final bill for $191,289, of which $100,000 represented his fee; $16,819, traveling expenses; and $74,470, fees paid to accountants and experts. The New York Times and the Associated Press duly summarized the general's findings. The Louisiana Planter republished the Associated Press account and commented in a brief editorial that "no evidence of serious wrong-doing" had been discovered and that "the chief trouble with this immense sugar producing concern, which is by far the largest in the world, appears to have been the lack of operating capital." "Had I ever surmised what would take place," Manuel commented in a letter to John F. Craig in Philadelphia, "I tell you that Company would never have had birth."[10]

On the day after Goethals had called Manuel on the carpet, Hawley, Tarafa, Manuel, and Manolo, with James Howell Post and Thomas Howell, met secretly for dinner with Theodore F. Whitmarsh and George A. Zabriskie, the top officials of the U.S. Equalization Board. Whitmarsh reported he had cabled Hoover at Versailles two weeks earlier that the Cuban contingent would want to sell their sugar through one source. "[Hoover] saw the practicality of such an arrangement and even the necessity of it." Hoover would recommend it to President Wilson, proposing that the administration, possibly through the Department of Commerce, exert "some supervision in order to prevent undue speculation and consequent high prices, thus protecting the consumer." Zabriskie and Whitmarsh agreed to assure Wilson that the Cuban government wished to do nothing "contrary to the views of the American Government."

"I was very much pleased with the interview," Rionda wrote, "as it shows that our plan merits their personal approval and their recommendation to the government should be of value." Nothing was said as to price, although Rionda favored a renewal of the previous year's contract "with the only modification of 1 cent increase in price and that we would not have to pay 38½ cents freight but a price more in accordance with the present conditions." Manuel was writing in strict confidence, he reminded Higinio and Victor Zevallos. They should say nothing except to Arango and then only on condition Arango say nothing of it to Menocal "unless the latter is well informed which I presume he will be, through [Hawley]."[11] Menocal, presumably so informed, acted quickly. Twelve days later, Hawley and Rionda, writing formally to the Equalization Board, "speaking by authority for the Cuban Government" officially tendered Cuba's entire 1919–20 crop to the American government.

Hawley drafted the official letter. The former Republican congressman from Galveston was seventy now, and flourishes of old-fashioned Southern oratory underlined his warning. Only Cuba had sufficient sugar to meet world needs, but it would not take advantage of "this 'coign of vantage.'" Instead, "the Island Republic, its Hacendados and farmers and manufacturers of sugar, tender through its own Government, providing it meets with the consent and cooperation of the American Government, the entire wealth of her production." But there was a warning: "If . . . the opportunity to serve—not the American people alone but the Universal Welfare—is . . . not availed of, there is not a community anywhere in America or Europe or Asia that will not feel the consequence of our failure."

The weeks passed and no reply came from Versailles. By September 22, Hawley and Rionda gave up hope that the United States would take responsibility. They had apparently also given up on action by the Cuban government, for they concluded that "the logic of the situation" had not prevailed, and Cuba must return to "the natural law of supply and demand." Hawley again penned the letter to Washington: "[W]e reluctantly accept the situation now existing."[12]

But if neither government would take responsibility, Manuel was willing to try another gambit. Hitherto, he had held aloof from the various steps toward joint action that had been taken over the past nine years by Cuba's sugar producers, but he now put his support behind a new Asociación de Hacendados y Colonos de Cuba (Cuban Association of Hacendados and Colonos), with Arango as president and Higinio as treasurer. More, he convinced Cuba Cane's board of directors that the company should join in the venture along with Czarnikow-Rionda's other clients, with the Cuban American Sugar Company, and with Rionda's own mills. By October, the *Louisiana Planter* could estimate that the association represented more than 50 percent of Cuba's total production, although the majority of the hacendados in the western provinces and the other great American companies, such as Punta Alegre and United Fruit, did not join. Tarafa also kept his distance. "I was rather surprised of it," he wrote Hawley, "because as you know between your Company and my interests we have been keeping up the Liga Agraria y Fabricantes de Azúcar, and this new association . . . believes in 8 or 10 cents for sugar and free market for sugar and in my opinion is too radical to last. Mr. Arango spoke to me and asked me to join but I shall not do so. I don't believe in their ways."[13]

The Goethals episode officially ended in October when Cuba Cane's directors' special committee endorsed the ten points in the report's "Summary and Conclusions." Reiterating that Rionda's original "transaction" had "called for no criticism" although the mills had been "originally in rather poor condition," the report granted that they now compared "favorably" with their competitors and that their efficiency was "steadily improving." But, for the Riondas, the message was grim. "The decrease in profits," Goethals had concluded, "has been largely due to the failure of the Corporation in the past to take advantage of the opportunities for economy afforded by centralized management." "The wisdom of the Corporation's selling contract is questioned," the report continued, and it recommended "that the Corporation establish its own purchasing department. Changes in the management are recommended."

George Braga provided a final footnote in his memoirs. "In mid-1920," he wrote, Cuba Cane's board of directors had presented his great-uncle with a silver punch bowl duly engraved "To Manuel Rionda in recognition of his valuable services . . . with esteem and affection." "He graciously accepted it," George commented, "but later in the privacy of his home, he said he would like to drown the directors in it, one by one."[14]

For Rionda, more than a loss of face was involved. He had urged the formation of Cuba Cane not only because of the prestige it would bring him, not only because structural pressures were making both horizontal and vertical integration desirable, but also because he suspected that Czarnikow-Rionda might soon lose its key position as Cuba's broker. The war had tipped the balance toward the great American companies, most of them clustered in Camagüey and Oriente, and by 1919 Cuba Cane, Cuban-American, the United Fruit Company, and Atkins's Punta Alegre Company commanded the economy's heights. Whereas in 1913 only five mills had produced more than 300,000 bags apiece (topped by Hawley's *Chaparra* at 475,362), in the 1919 zafra there were nineteen, thirteen of them belonging to North American companies, Hawley's *Delicias* leading at 701,768. These mills would not need Czarnikow-Rionda's services as middleman.

In the Fourth Annual Report of the Cuba Cane Sugar Corporation, dated November 14, 1919, Manuel chronicled the accomplishments of the company under his stewardship. Although the Third Annual Report had been only eight pages long, now Rionda's "Letter to the Stockholders" alone was twenty-one, and an additional twelve pages of statistics were affixed.

There was much to which he could point with pride. At the beginning, Rionda had predicted that Cuba Cane would produce 14 percent of Cuba's sugar. In its fourth year, it had produced 15.59 percent. He had also predicted it would make 10 percent a year on its $50 million capital. Now its Annual Financial Statement reported that 1919's operating profits had been $11 million, up almost $3 million from the year before. The net profits were over $7 million, and $2.5 million could be added to the Surplus Account. In four years, the preferred stockholders had received $14 million in dividends, or 28 percent of their original nominal investment. Production had risen 300 percent in the corporation's four eastern centrals, and its *Morón* was third (524,937 bags) and its *Stewart* sixth (508,500) in production in all of Cuba. Only Cuban-American's *Delicias* (with 701,768 bags) soared very far above them, its *Chaparra* (551,000) scarcely surpassing *Morón*. Rionda also predicted that demand and high prices would continue. Somewhere down the road, he wrote, Russia would "largely increase" its production, and the United States would grow more beets. But there would remain for Cuba "the fertility of the soil and the suitability of the climate . . . two advantages which Cuba enjoys in a greater degree than any other sugar producing country."[15]

That spring, Walter E. Ogilvie joined the corporation. He, rather than Manuel, would implement Goethals's "large organization techniques" and institute the general's recommended "refinements of management." Manuel took credit for him publicly, professing he had had his eye on Ogilvie since 1917 and that the declining importance of the British-owned United Railways, with which Ogilvie had been long connected, had now finally enabled him to persuade the younger man to join him. Ogilvie arrived in Havana in December and toured the mills, paying his de rigueur visit to *Tuinucú*. "Everyone here," Manuel wrote, "seems to have been more than charmed with you and your family." This courtliness, too, was de rigueur. Manuel instructed his New York nephews to install Ogilvie in the third floor front room of 110 Wall Street with "the best connection possible with my office."

Yet despite ever-rising sugar prices that spring, sales of Cuba Cane's new bonds were discouraging. With the Goethals inquiry concluded, $25 million in ten-year 7 percent convertible debenture bonds, maturing in 1930, had finally been authorized as of January 1, 1920. But the present stockholders, on being offered first chance to subscribe, took up only some $3 million, while Babst refused a purchase on behalf of the American Sugar Refining Company, pleading the prejudice that still persisted against the former Sugar Trust. "[I]f he owned 1,000 shares," he told Manuel, "he would be accused of controlling the whole Company."[16]

At the end of January, Hayden enlisted the high-pressure sales techniques that would so enliven the stock market in the 1920s, joining Strauss in a strong pitch to some two hundred syndicate members and bond salesmen at a "pep rally." Strauss predicted that the corporation's profits would be $30 million in the coming year, while Hayden foresaw that "within a very short time" Cuba Cane stock would be selling at 70 and that the bondholder "could convert them into stock and pay taxes only on the profit between the stock at 60 and its actual value at time of conversion." The brokers, Hayden added, might think 2 percent a small commission but, since the bonds could be so easily sold, "there would not be much work involved and, furthermore, it was the duty of every broker to his clients, to call to their attention such a profitable investment."[17]

Although he wrote Strauss commending his effort, Rionda grumbled to Manolo and Bernardo that a prediction of $30 million profit was "too sanguine." The brokers' exhortations underlined that the corporation's overriding goal must henceforth be to show immediate profits rather than to go on building up the mills, the bond issue having plainly stipulated that none of the new money was to be used "for extension or betterments." This was humiliating, and Manuel was also annoyed that Strauss, in the course of his remarks, had felt it necessary to repeat Goethals's endorsement of Rionda's honesty. By March, since the dragging sale had still not raised enough to cover current operating expenses, Cuba Cane had to borrow another $10 million against sugar. The loan was through the Guaranty, which once more distributed it widely across the entire country, charging an additional percentage for obtaining it.[18]

Manuel took steps to settle his personal relations with Cuba Cane and in so doing both provided for the firm's extensive expansion eastward and transferred large sums to himself and to his close associates. Despite the bond issue's stipulated moratorium on further expansion, he made sure that the corporation took over—and paid for—options that he had personally obtained to acquire properties totaling 47,860 acres and to lease (with option to purchase) another 83,267 acres along the route of Tarafa's Cuban Northern Railroad. Rionda also arranged, in May 1920 for Cuba Cane to purchase, for $3.5 million, the central *Violeta*, a new plantation that had been developed by Hannibal Mesa, Regino Truffin, and Miguel Arango. With a number of innovations ("the first new seventeen-role tandem"), it had a capacity of 200,000 bags. Ownership of the new acquisitions was, with Sullivan & Cromwell's expertise, vested in a subsidiary, the Eastern Cuba Sugar Corporation, incorporated in Cuba on October 1, 1920, all of its stock owned by Cuba Cane.

As the 1920 zafra got under way, Manuel came down once more to manage the campaign in the Riondas' own mills. There, in the plantation office, with the pounding of machines, the tramping of ox teams, and the cries of their drivers as background, he studied reports from London and Amsterdam, from New York and Washington, and, together with his nephews, pondered the clan's future.

In their own mills, under the guidance of the Rionda y de la Torriente heirs and despite the diversion of attention to Cuba Cane, years of hard work were reaping their rewards. Output had risen from 687,890 bags in 1914 to 1,114,430 in 1919. Dividends, almost all to family members, had been proportionate. *Tuinucú* in 1916 had issued a 50 percent stock dividend on its preferred and a 100 percent stock dividend on its common, the two being thereafter merged into a common capital stock that paid 10 percent cash dividends in 1917 and 1918 and 27.5 percent in 1919 and 1920. *Francisco* had paid a stock dividend of 233.3 percent in 1915. Even in 1917, when the revolution had thrown it into danger and chaos, 10 percent cash dividends had been paid. In 1916, 1918, and 1919 there had been 20 percent, and in 1920 there would be 30 percent in cash dividends. *Manatí* had regularly paid 10 percent annually in dividends on its common stock, and *Washington*, long a burden, was at last sold in February for, reputedly, $2 million.[19]

As for Czarnikow-Rionda, which with its subsidiary, the Cuban Trading Company, had also profited spectacularly, time was growing near for the expiration of the five-year agreement that Manuel had entered into with Lagemann in May 1915. At that time, in return for a badly needed advance of $200,000 from the London partner, Rionda had agreed Lagemann should receive one-fifth of the firm's common stock. Since the common stock had voting rights, the transaction had threatened Manuel's sole control of the firm. He now was able to take advantage of the contract's expiration to exchange Lagemann's common (increased by 460 percent stock dividends over the five-year period) for $1,232,000 in newly issued first preferred (nonvoting), which should pay 10 percent annually. Although Lagemann had (on paper) profited fivefold, the matter was not settled without bitterness on both sides. "I felt all my life's work destroyed," Lagemann wrote, as he bid farewell to New York and moved on to spend his remaining years on the Continent, contemplating the Alps from the verandas of Swiss spas and writing long letters about the changes in the international world of sugar. Manuel was more concise. "I did not want him having such a large share of our profits," he wrote Westrik.[20]

Thus far, the Riondas had done well. But Cuba Cane was slipping from their grasp, and in this year that would go into history as the Dance of the Millions, they faced the growing independence of the Cuban planters and a vertical integration by U.S. East Coast refineries.

As Rionda and Hawley had predicted in July 1919, prices for Cuba's 1920 crop rose to dizzying heights, not only because of pent-up demand but also because low rainfall indicated a small harvest. As soon as he had realized there would be no government controls, Rionda had contracted for future delivery of much of the sugar he controlled at 6.5 cents a pound—1 cent a pound more than the previous year—to the American Sugar Refining Company. He had thus, before a single stalk of cane was cut, already locked in a tidy profit. He had similarly served Babst well, since by mid-January Truffin was complaining when 10,000 bags of his sugar were sold at only 11.5 cents. Inquiries from overseas spurred a general optimism. "We have a bid today from London," Bernardo wrote, "for 5,000 tons Mar/Apr. shipment to Egypt . . . we have a bid for 6,000 tons from a Chinese firm."

By March 27, sugar was selling for 12 cents a pound, 13 cents a pound by April 1. This was wildly profitable, but Manuel's clients ignored his advice to take quick advantage of such a bonanza, holding out more and more fearlessly for better offers.

The ready availability of credit reenforced their independence. Bank deposits had soared with wartime prosperity, as had the banks' openhandedness. The Banco Internacional, founded in December 1917 by a group of local clerks, had rapidly scattered 105 branches throughout the island; the more respectable Banco Nacional had expanded to 112 branches, even as it loaned millions to Pote López Rodríguez with which to buy up a majority of its own shares. New Cuban branches of the New York banks also lent unquestioningly against warehoused sugar. Freed by new laws from old prohibitions against overseas branches and shaped by the journalistic bravado of its current president, Frank A. Vanderlip, the National City Bank courted opportunities in the palmy island so close to the Florida Keys, rapidly dotting the entire terrain with its offices, twenty-two more of them opening in 1919 alone. Few North American bankers were facile in Spanish or could be spared from the banking boom at home, and young Cubans, only intermittently supervised, were recruited. When local funds ran low, they were permitted to tap New York for large advances. Only slightly less flamboyantly than National City, Guaranty Trust, Chase National, and the Royal Bank of Canada likewise expanded.[21]

Meanwhile, a trend toward vertical integration on the part of the East Coast refineries was under way, with North American interests energetically buying up Cuban mills. The key purchase had been the American Sugar Refineries' acquisition of the newly launched *Cunagua* for $14 million in November 1919 from Miguel Mendoza, Truffin, and Arango. "There is no doubt," Manolo wrote, "that [Babst's] plans are very vast and that he is a great organizer and knows how to keep his organization together." Built near *Morón* in the area opened by Tarafa's Northern Railroad, *Cunagua* was completely electrified and double tandem, with two club houses (one for its "colored" employees) and with billiard tables, two schools, and a baseball as well as a pelota field. Its first real zafra in 1919 had brought in 452,000 bags and put it eighth in production in all of Cuba. With the current 1920 crop, it would be third, with 553,121. Babst planned to erect a second mill, twice as large, beside it, and it was rumored he desired to control the Northern Railroad as well.

Other American refiners were likewise expanding into Cuban cane fields. Howell and Post's National Sugar Refining Company was "strengthening its position through the new Cuba–Santo Domingo Sugar Development Syndicate." Hires Root Beer was purchasing *Dos Rosas*; Loft Candy bought Central *Dulce Nombre*. All these mills had been Rionda clients. Even more seriously, the Warner Refinery had acquired a controlling interest in the Gómez Mena family's *Gómez Mena* and *Amistad*, with their combined capacity of 625,000 bags, for which Rionda had hitherto been broker.[22]

Manuel still did not think such acquisitions would endanger Czarnikow-Rionda's business. Babst's anticipated production at *Cunagua* would, he pointed out to Manolo and Bernardo, supply "at the maximum 20 percent of [American Sugar's] monthly requirements." Howell and Post's National Sugar Refining Company had for years drawn on their Cuban-American and Guantanamo Sugar Companies, "but have we ever seen that make matters worse for the Cuban Producer?" Rather, new

American acquisitions in Cuba could well "be leading into free Cuban sugars for the United States and 1 cent duty for refined. Also making our government keep an eye on the Cuban administration, somewhat as it is doing in Santo Domingo . . . thus helping us rather than otherwise."

The New York nephews did not agree, nor did Higinio Fanjul. Their commission business, Bernardo wrote, was probably doomed. Manuel had estimated that, in addition to the Cuba Cane plantations, they would have 6 million bags of sugar to sell from other sources, perhaps if they tried their hardest 10 million. That was far too high an estimate, Bernardo thought. Except for their own estates, which were they sure of? Only Pelayo's and those bound to the Castaño interests (interchangeably now, in family correspondence, referred to as the Gutiérrez holdings, since Carlos Felipe Gutiérrez—Viriato's brother—had married one of Castaño's four daughters and was taking charge). Nor were these guaranteed in the future. "As to Gutiérrez, Pelayo, Violeta and Caracas, it is only a question of time when someone will buy them all out."

Actually, it was a question of very little time. While the Guitiérrez-Castaño holdings remained in the hands of those merging families, *Caracas* was bought by the Atkins interests by March. Mesa, Truffin, and Arango would sell their *Violeta* to Cuba Cane that May. Pelayo's *Rosario*, with its extensive private railroad, would be sold to the Hershey Company in June.[23]

If vertical integration's time had come for the North American refineries, perhaps it had also arrived for the Cuban mills. The nephews believed it had. "[T]he time," Manolo wrote, "is now very close at hand when we producers of raw sugar must gradually go into the production of granulated sugar either at our own plantations or by becoming interested in refineries in other parts of the world."

He was whistling tunes already in the wind. The survivors among Manuel's Spanish-born contemporaries were retiring that giddy spring. On the island, their sons, sons-in-law, and nephews were taking over. Most were island-born of Cuban mothers, brought up to the mills' roar and educated in the law or engineering. They had just experienced a four-year boom, and, with old debts repaid and new wartime profits to invest, they were not only diversifying into Havana real estate and U.S. securities. For the first time in the history of an independent Cuba, they had generous credit facilities available to them. Although the promise of the Underwood Tariff to institute free sugar had been broken, many still saw no good reason why Cuba should not refine its own. The product of their mills, they were informed, if treated by a new, relatively easy "boneblack" process, would be white enough (even if technically speaking not "refined") to be sold directly to retail grocers, and a group, led apparently by Mesa, was anxious to move forward. The Cuban producer, Mesa wrote to President Menocal, already had "his furnaces and boilers, evaporators, vacuum pans and centrifugals . . . he only needs the addition of boneblack filters to make complete refineries of his raw sugar factories. . . . Almost any Cuban factory could be arranged to work one of these processes and at but little expense." In New York, Arthur H. Lamborn of Lamborn & Company, Inc., a rival broker, put forth feelers, asking Manolo and Bernardo to inform their uncle that he would be very glad to put $1 million into a Cuban refinery started by the Rionda group and "guarantee to raise another $10,000,000 if necessary." Mesa made a similar proposition on behalf of himself and his "partner General Gómez." "La garantía de Mesa no sirve para nada," Manuel replied, vetoing the idea for the clan. Bernardo and Manolo then proposed that the Riondas acquire the McCahan refinery in Philadelphia. Manuel objected that the United States already had an abundance of refining capacity. Besides, to buy McCahan they would have to borrow from $5 million to $6 million. "That means that we must apply to Wall Street. I am sick of Infante [the Cuba Cane Sugar Corporation] and we rush into another baby."[24]

Ideally, Bernardo replied, he would prefer a refinery in Cuba, but to refine there would leave them at the far from tender mercy of the U.S. Congress, which could, at any time, impose a higher import tax. They should write off the brokerage business and first be bankers; second, producers; and third, refiners. Manolo wrote Victor Zevallos on the same day. Oil, steel, and copper, Manolo observed, were "evolving" vertically. Sugar must follow.

While this debate proceeded, Manuel and the Rionda y de la Torriente nephews decided to go ahead on their own in an expansion of *Francisco* and *Elía*. "[I]t is very gratifying," Bernardo wrote Manuel, "to see that out of their own resources they can assume an expenditure of an increase aggregating $3,000,000 to $3,500,000. I say this because I consider it far preferable to make the increase out of the companies' own resources rather than resort to Wall Street and have a repetition of the turmoil with which we had to contend with Infante." They must not be the tail of the dog again. He wrote: "I advocate giving up [Cuba Cane]."[25]

In the Easter season, the zafra well along, prices still rising in a dizzy crescendo, Manuel moved north once more. By mid-May, he and Harriet were back at Río Vista, whence he could be smoothly chauffeured to 110 Wall Street. He would be in his offices there almost every day through the coming hot summer. On May 14, a jump of 1.5 cents in the price of sugar occurred between one sale and the next to 22.57 cents per pound. By May 19, the price was 22.575 cents. Those hacendados who still had any sugar held it tightly, waiting for the market to go higher, while after evaluating matters from Wall Street, Manuel decided to be guided by his nephews' advice. On June 24, 1920, he cabled Zevallos that the decision to buy the W. J. McCahan Sugar and Molasses Refining Company, Philadelphia, had been made. They had paid $5 million for it, the McCahans retaining a 30 percent interest. The basic argument was the irreversible decline of the brokerage business. "[B]y sales of Cuban sugar properties to American corporations this year, we lost clients representing close to 2,000,000 bags amongst which are Gómez-Mena, Pelayo, Zorilla and others." Nearly 70 percent of Cuban sugar production now belonged to American corporations. Soon, it might well be 90 percent. Then where would their commission business be? "[I]n the long run we would find ourselves thrown aside completely." He wrote Nieberg in London a month later that while at first sight a Cuban refinery might have been preferable, it was canceled out by the prospect of a future U.S. tariff if U.S. interests "saw any danger of Cuba becoming a great competitor as she, undoubtedly, would become eventually. . . . [W]e can work cheaper, we can combine the profits of the raw material with the refined and we can pay higher wages in the United States and thus overcome some of the labour difficulties . . . skilled labour is not procurable in Cuba."

Meanwhile, the rise in the price of sugar began to slow and in late May to drop. By July, it had fallen from 22.5 cents to 17.25 cents per pound. Rionda had predicted the decline. Cuban producers, by hoarding their remaining supplies to force the market up still more, had attracted to the United States sugars from Java and the Philippines, from Formosa and Mauritius. Czarnikow-Rionda itself had profited from sources other than Caribbean.[26] Blame those, Manuel wrote, who had filled the growers with false illusions. They should have realized that Cuba was not the entire world when it came to producing sugar. An unnamed "official of one of the large sugar companies" in Cuba was quoted on the front page of *Facts about Sugar* as saying: "It stands to reason that if a sugar mill costs twice as much as formerly the price of sugar must be proportionately higher." From a merchant's point of view, that was nonsense. "It is not a question of what it costs to produce sugar, but a question of what other countries are willing to sell at." Cuba, he went on, produced only a quarter of the world's sugar and so was vulnerable.

He himself, he wrote Urquiza, had been selling his holdings at 12.5 cents for the past six weeks, at which price he had made "bastante dinero" (money enough). He pushed his clients to sell whatever they had left at once. By the beginning of August, when sugar sold for 15 cents a pound, he could write Laborde at Biarritz that "of our friends," only Laurentino García with 60,000 bags and Falla Gutiérrez with 40,000 still held out for another price rise—plus Laborde himself, who held 25,000 bags and was not answering Rionda's advisory cables. LaBorde surrendered, but by October, when sugar sold for 7 cents a pound, the other stubborn clients, plus Antonio Pérez of *Céspedes*, still held theirs, and the situation was much worse.[27] "The inexorable working of economic law," observed the *Louisiana Planter*'s New York correspondent, "has overtaken the speculator and the hoarder." Manuel wrote Laborde that perhaps some 2 million bags of sugar remained in Cuba. They could have been sold for $65 to $70 a bag; now they were scarcely worth $25, a difference of some $80 million. This great discrepancy, he commented, fell only on perhaps twenty hacendados and probably on only fifty or sixty colonos.[28]

Still, they would not be the only ones to suffer. In scarcely three months, the 1921 harvest would begin to reach the market and find it saturated. Even if only a few men were to blame, so large a carryover would ruin sales. The banks that had with uncritical zeal loaned heavily against warehoused and now unsalable sugar began in panic to refuse the usual seasonal advances to carry the 1921 zafra. In September, Higinio cabled that several colonos had to stop cultivation. Manuel, he advised, should use his influence in Washington to persuade the Federal Reserve Bank to come to the rescue. The American cotton and wheat interests had already tried that, Manuel replied, and had already failed.

Sugar was not the only agricultural product in trouble. "[T]he Reserve Bank objects on the ground that it is not their duty to help enhance the value of any commodity particularly during these times when prices are already high enough."

The Cuban Association of Hacendados and Colonos, stirring itself, talked (once more) of creating a special bank to make loans, with each planter subscribing $6 a bag. That, Manuel thought, was "descabelladas" (empty-headed). How could the Cuba Cane Sugar Company, which made 4 million bags a year, be called upon to subscribe $24 million for a bank? Why, he wrote, should Cuba Cane, which had sold its own sugars at a fair price, subscribe so large a sum to rescue those who had been too greedy to sell when they could? In the second place, Cuba Cane did not have that much money.[29]

In the Cuban Trading Company, Fanjul was taking the helm. Writing to him, Rionda tried to be cheering. Things had been far worse—he recalled 1901 and 1905. The next crop might have to be sold as low as 5 or 6 cents per pound, but "those prices used to be considered very good." Some colonos would have to be carried, but on the whole the country was all right. He was more grave with Laborde. It was impossible, he admitted, to be in business and feel content when one saw others losing great amounts of money. However much thou and I, he wrote his old friend, gain in what remains of our lives, we'll leave more money than we had when we came into the world.

That was October 5. The next day in Havana, anxious lines formed at teller windows, and the panic engulfed the banking establishments. On October 11, President Menocal proclaimed a temporary banking moratorium, and W. A. Merchant of the Banco Nacional was hastily dispatched to New York to see if a syndicate of Wall Street's bankers and sugar merchants could not arrange through the Cuban Trading Company to buy Cuba's sugar so the planters could repay their loans. Bernardo opposed any involvement by Czarnikow-Rionda. "Our year is finished and I do not care about entering into any more complications." Yet clearly something must be done. Last year's unsold sugar must not in desperation be thrown helter-skelter on the market. While the existing banking moratorium might help temporarily, simply ameliorating the financial crisis would leave the sugar crisis unsolved.[30]

In Washington, the many millions of dollars that American citizens had invested in Cuba were taken into account, and a conference was arranged among the New York bankers and refiners and the representatives of the U.S. State and Commerce Departments and the Federal Reserve Board. President Menocal requested that Rionda and Hawley once more join Ambassador de Céspedes to represent the hacendados. After the meeting and lunch at the Cuban embassy, de Céspedes cabled Rionda's and Hawley's bidding to Havana. "[W]e think it is absolutely safe for the Cuban Government to assume the responsibility of guaranteeing a minimum price of seven cents f.o.b. Cuba. . . . Operating . . . through a single agency will enable you to secure for the remnant of the Cuban crop the fullest price that can be obtained."

It was vital that unsold supplies be disposed of gradually before the 1921 zafra reached the market in January. "The Banks . . . should put all the sugars they hold into the pool and then get someone to act for them as brokers," Manuel wrote Higinio. "I am not hankering for the job but, seeing as we are best qualified, I would have no objection to our firm acting." But he did not wish to offer their services at once, after the way the planters had ignored his advice to sell. "Our Companies have money in the bank," he commented. "What we ought to do is . . . keep our plantations going and keep free of any alliance. . . . The Cubans thought they could get along without us. . . . They have been wanting to follow the advice of such men as numbers 8 and 9 and they now have the results."[31]

October closed with sugar at 8.03 cents a pound. "[T]he sugar market is a stagnant and lifeless affair," wrote the *Louisiana Planter*, headlining the story "Philosophy the Only Comforter Remaining." "No flurry of demand rustles the dead calm of the market." It was "inconceivable," Rionda mused in a letter to Frank Tiarks, that Cuba should be bankrupt when it had sold sugar that year for "probably $800,000,000" and was within six weeks of a new crop that, even at only 7 cents, would give another $600 million. The moratorium "will . . . check the many mushrooms that sprang up during the prosperous times; it will cause the disappearance of many people who started in the business thinking they . . . could manage affairs far better than their peers, and we will enter again upon a happy existence, with conditions normal." Cuba had gotten along with sugar at 2 cents a pound. Why should 5 or 6 cents sugar now be fatal? "Of course labor will have to come down but that can be easily arranged as the Cuban laborer did not acquire any extravagant habits

Tail of the Lion 155

during the prosperous times; once the chief commodities such as flour, rice, provisions, etc. go down in price, the cost of living will do likewise and our laborers will adjust themselves to new conditions readily." He was only partly correct, for while H. O. Neville's "Letter from Cuba" in *Facts about Sugar* bore the good news that "field hands . . . formerly difficult to obtain for $3 and $4 a day, can now be hired for $1.50 and $2," because of the shortage of currency "the prices of nearly every commodity have risen."[32]

While gloom depressed the headlines, Rionda had the satisfaction of reporting to Cuba Cane's stockholders in its Fifth Annual Report that Cuba Cane had come through the storm. Thanks to a wise selling policy (his), the company had escaped the disaster. Total sugar sales, including molasses, were $126,323,157. Sugar had brought an average of 10.2 cents per pound, almost twice the government price of the year before, and total operating profits, which had been $11,069,881 in 1919, were, for 1920, up 101 percent to $22,249,020. While 1919 had ended with the corporation's Surplus Account at $16,712,304, it had now risen to $23,473,102. If one added the $10 million that had been set aside for depreciation, $67 per share on the common stock had accumulated out of earnings, while Cuba Cane's properties and plants were valued at almost $80 million.

Less cheering statistics, while included, were not commented upon. Production had, because of the drought, dropped from 4,319,189 bags to 3,763,915. Thus, while price had risen 91.6 percent, total income was up only 54.9 percent. Meanwhile, the cost of production per pound had risen 85 percent from 4.6 cents to 8.5 cents. Thoughtful stockholders might have been puzzled why, if production costs had risen almost as much as had the price received and if quantity had gone down, operating profits had more than doubled. They would have found an explanation had they noticed that, while the 1919 report had made a deduction of over $6 million for marine freight, an FOB figure had been substituted for 1920. Had the earlier report not subtracted $6,056,108 for freight, the operating profits for 1919 would have been not $11,069,881 but $17,125,989, and the increase would have been not 101 percent but 29.9 percent.[33]

Also, since the sale of the new bonds had lagged, interest paid on short-term loans had more than quadrupled. By the issuance of $25 million in the ten-year 7 percent convertible debenture bonds, dated January 1, 1920, Cuba Cane had added $1.75 million to the $3.5 million it already owed annually in dividends. It had also committed itself to repay $25 million on January 1, 1930. (But 1930 was a long way in the future. Surely all would be prosperous by then.)

As for the $67 per share on common stock, it might have accumulated, but no common stockholder had received a penny. This stood in contrast to the fate of those who held stock in other sugar companies. Atkins's Punta Alegre, incorporated four months earlier than Cuba Cane, had paid 10 percent since October 1919. The annual report did not comment on the matter of dividends, nor did it mention how far short profits had fallen from the $30 million Hayden had promised at his "pep rally" for bond salesmen.

Rionda summarized the fortunes of that variable year in his "Letter to the Stockholders" and also in a final section entitled "Review of the Sugar Situation." "The proportion of the Cuban crop sold at the highest prices was relatively small," he noted. "The peak having been reached during the months of May and June when there was very little cane being ground, neither the colonos nor the plantation owners participated to any great extent in the high prices." And he went on to point out the moral, blaming the U.S. government for ending government regulation and also those Cubans who had in May hoarded their sugar and then, in June and July, when sugar "was pouring into the United States from other countries," had "tried to force their holdings upon a market already satisfied."

The careful reader might here have hesitated once more. In two years of wartime price controls, all of Cuba's sugar had been sold at a fixed price—4.6 cents a pound for the first year, 5.5 cents for the second. Most Cuban producers believed these prices were too low, given the steep rise in costs. But Hawley and Rionda, at war's end, had offered Cuba's production to Washington for a third year for 6.5 cents. Of this they were now boasting, pointing out that had Washington accepted their advice, the Dance—and the Crash—would have been averted. However, had the whole Cuban sugar crop been sold at their proposed 6.5 cents a pound, no one's sugar would have earned more than $21 a bag. Instead, bags sold at the top of the market brought $73. Few had been sold on that day, but still the year's average had been almost $37 a bag. For a very modest central producing 100,000 bags, the difference between $21 and $37 would have been $1.6 million. Unregulated except by market forces, the price per pound had risen high enough for the smaller hacendados to do well if they had sold by midsummer (as the majority had done, according to Rionda). Had Cuba, despite market chaos, not come out ahead?

On the other hand, had a reasonable contract been agreed upon, all the sugar would have been sold. The refiners would not have turned to other foreign suppliers, setting a dangerous precedent. Cuba's warehouses would be empty and the banks content, with their advances repaid, and the 1921 zafra could bring a good return. Instead, some 200,000 tons from Cuba's 1920 harvest remained on a glutted market.

In his official letter to Cuba Cane's stockholders, Manuel was properly optimistic. With prices low and European beet production not yet recovered, matters would right themselves. "As in the past," he assured them, "Cuba will continue to be the cheapest sugar production country in the world . . . and the probabilities are that the Island will be able to extricate itself from the present financial situation within the next few months."

On November 5, when he presented this report to the board, in advance of its issuance at the annual meeting of stockholders, Rionda reached another milestone. "I stand here," he wrote Miguel Arango, "with my overcoat already on, about to leave for the Board of Directors meeting of Cuba Cane to resign my presidency."

I have found no written comment to indicate whether this resignation might have been deemed advisable by the corporation's directors at the time of the Goethals report and been courteously delayed as a face-saving device or whether it was his own free choice. Still the corporation's largest single common shareholder, he now became chair of its Executive Committee, replacing Frederick Strauss, who became chair of the board, while Ogilvie became president. Rionda's exclusive selling contract for Cuba Cane still had over five years to run, and thus he continued to have on his own shoulders the all-important problem of bridging the chasm between the mills and the purchasers of their sugar. He presumably saw resolving the problem, however difficult, as more satisfactory than management.[34]

7

The Steel Gray Battleship

Usually Rionda was in *Tuinucú* by Christmas. In 1921, he was busy with bankers, and when he sailed into Havana harbor on January 19, conditions had become so threatening that the U.S. battleship *Minnesota* lay there at anchor. From its steel gray decks, General Enoch Crowder, Woodrow Wilson's emissary, could survey the harbor's arc, the modern office buildings and banks now defended by the moratorium, and could ponder the millions owed his country. Beyond his immediate vision, but taken into account, were the cane fields. Ominously, no smoke came from many smokestacks, although it was past time to be bringing in a crop. Only 124 centrals were grinding, compared to 197 a year earlier. The plans made scarcely a year before to erect Cuban refineries had already crumbled. Across the bay from Havana at Regla, the half-constructed factory of the Compañía Nacional de Refinerías loomed up abandoned, its superintendent having returned to New York.

Manuel was struck by the men waiting for him at the pier. Laurentino García, principal owner of *Progreso*, had not met him for years. Now there he was, owing almost a total of $2 million to the Banco Nacional, the National City Bank, Gómez Mena, and Czarnikow-Rionda, to beg another $100,000 against *Progreso*'s sugar. After a lecture, Manuel agreed. But the next night, seeing conditions "chaotic" and everywhere "complete discouragement," he halted further advances.

Laurentino's plight illustrated what many hacendados were facing. His *Progreso* yielded some 100,000 bags a harvest. True, against Manuel's advice, he had delayed too long in selling his last crop. He had borrowed too much, and the banks had loaned it too easily. But the *Progreso* was a viable concern. If no one advanced him (and all the men like him) the money necessary to make the harvest, Laurentino (and all of them) would earn nothing to redeem the machines they had ordered or to pay their colonos, nor would there be work for the cane cutters, already dangerously restive. Rionda had planned to go directly to *Tuinucú*, but just before he was to take his train, Farnham, vice president of the National City Bank, who had also come to Cuba in person, called upon him. "We agreed," Manuel related later, "that emergency assistance from the Cuban government was imperative." He remained in Havana.[1]

Even as retribution was shaking down Cuba's sugar economy, spreading from the speculators and the high-flyers to take its toll on average men, so in the offices of the National City Bank in New York retrenchment was settling in. Its own debt to the Federal Reserve Bank was now some three times its required reserve, and the Federal Reserve's examiners would soon be questioning the soundness of hundreds of National City's loans. In the heyday of the boom, 80 percent of the bank's entire capital had been loaned against Cuban sugar. Even if the bank foreclosed on all its collateral, that collateral could be sold for only a fraction of what had been advanced against it. For the Royal Bank of Canada, Chase National, and the Guaranty Trust, the situation was almost as serious. For Cuba's Banco Español and Banco Internacional, perhaps even for the Banco Nacional, the case was hopeless.[2]

Hawley, too, was in Havana. His Cuban-American Sugar Company, like the Rionda mills, could finance its own harvests, but both Hawley and Rionda knew they would not be able to withstand the low prices that wholesale dumping of Cuba's glut would entail. On February 3, they met in conference with Menocal in the presidential palace. Later the same night, Cuba's hacendados assembled to discuss the situation, while on the New York market, the price of sugar dropped to 4.64 cents a pound.

The next day Rionda was transported across the harbor to meet with General Crowder. "[H]e and I alone," Manuel wrote, "in the 'Minnesota.'" There Rionda proposed a plan of action, a five-page "rough draft" that he sent to Menocal, Crowder, and Cosme de la Torriente, Leandro's and Pepe's cousin, who had reemerged as Menocal's secretary of state for foreign affairs. Cosme had done well. His Havana law practice had become prestigious, and while he had been periodically a senator and active in Conservative Party politics, he seemed above their murkier depths, a civilized man, admirably to North American taste. He would be remembered by his young kinswoman Lola de la Torriente, from her childhood, as a Sunday visitor dressed in "dril blanco y sombrero de jipi" but also as a rich relative who was "discreto, cultísimo, amable, agíl y muy político."[3]

In his proposal, Manuel suggested a quid pro quo. The mill owners, instead of dumping their unsold sugar on the market (which would make the banks' collateral sugar worthless) would entrust its sale to "a Committee composed of representatives of the principal producers," thus guaranteeing its more orderly disposal. In return, the bankers would supply the money to make the next harvest.

To the general, the plan seemed a possible solution, dampening the threat of revolution by putting men to work. Therefore, with Crowder's blessing, on February 11, 1921, a Cuban presidential decree created the Comisión Financiera de Azúcar (Sugar Finance Commission), to become effective when "75 percent of Cuban planters" agreed. "Cuban planters" were defined as owners of plantations in Cuba. Seventy-five percent referred to total sugar production. Since the 66 American mills produced about 48 percent of the sugar and the 126 Cuban mills some 52 percent, neither the Cuban nor the American interests alone, even if they agreed among themselves, could set the commission in operation. The plan would mean that Cuba's hacendados would be bound once more to the dictates of a government agency, but at least it would be their own government's.

Menocal appointed seven members to the commission. Two (Rionda and Hawley) would "represent the large producers"; two (Tarafa and Manuel Aspuru), "the other producers"; two (Porfirio Franca of the National City Bank and Frank J. Beatty of the Royal Bank of Canada), the bankers; and one (the Cuban secretary of agriculture, General Sanchez Agramonte), "the public interests." No one represented the smaller mill owners or the colonos, nor were Tarafa and Aspuru really average representatives of even the medium-sized hacendados. Aspuru had inherited the *Toledo* (1920 output, 353,653 bags), had bought the *Providencia* (165,007 bags in 1920), and at the height of the Dance had invested in *El Pilar*, a project chiefly Menocal's in which Sánchez Agramonte was also involved.[4] A highly political seven men from among Cuba's most wealthy would "take charge" of all Cuba's sugar, "distributing pro rata among the producers the sales and the price."

It was February 21 before the required 75 percent support brought the agency into existence. Although Hawley and Rionda publicly pledged that they would sell the sugar produced by their own mills equally with the rest, it took a leap of faith for Cubans to trust them, since no one saw Menocal or his appointees as incorruptible. Nicolás Castaño, now eighty-five, was reluctant to surrender his independence. Better than most, he could get along without loans. But grudgingly, in the end, he enrolled his mills. "To please you, I have agreed," he wrote Manuel. "Ahí vá pues, mi aceptación y cooperación." But I would prefer to be free, he wrote, to sell when I needed money or when I thought I must. Let us not speak of your friends, it is for you that I have accepted. Manuel replied that in this life "tenemos que poner el hombro" (all of us must put our shoulders to the wheel). But he included an admonition: "Had you not accepted, you would have found many difficulties in getting permission to ship your sugar."[5]

So the men who produced the sugar and the bankers agreed eventually, uneasily. The refiners had not been consulted. They, too, had been hurt by the dislocations of the Dance of the Millions, with its skyrocketing prices for their raw material. The American Sugar Refining Company's net income had dropped from a $9.5 million profit in 1919 to a deficit of over $3 million in 1920. Other refineries had suffered proportionately, just as they, too, were investing millions to acquire their own mills. For them to now agree to purchase from a pooled island production at prices enabling smaller, more inefficient centrals to survive made no economic sense.

Rionda cabled Bernardo and Manolo to persuade the refiners to cooperate. Only Hawley's Post/Howells connections were sympathetic. At most, the refineries would agree to purchase through the commission *after* they had exhausted their own production. Sales by the commission, Rionda had promised, would be allotted "pro rata" among all the mills. But in fact, it was not politically possible to keep the American refineries from drawing first upon their own. "We all know," Rionda wrote later, "that General Crowder would never have agreed to the organization of the Committee if those operations were to be denied." The United Fruit Company's Revere Sugar Refinery in Boston would thus draw 1 million bags from its *Boston* and *Preston* mills before it purchased from the commission. American Sugar would have 1 million bags from its *Cunagua* and *Jaronú*. The Warner Sugar Refinery would count on some 900,000.

Nor was this all. The commission conceded as well that sales pledged prior to its creation would be honored. Among such contracts was one for 2,050,000 bags made by the so-called Caledonia group of fourteen centrales, which included the interests of Edwin F. Atkins and his Boston associates. Nor were Hawley and Rionda themselves innocent. Cuban-American had already sold 56 percent of its production. Manuel, in the summer of 1920, had pledged some 400,000 bags of the 1921 harvest and in January, a suspiciously short interval before he confronted Crowder, contracted for another 900,000. Thus he had arranged to dispose of a respectable share of Cuba Cane's sugar before launching the commission. About 66 percent of *Manatí*'s sugar had also been sold in advance, as had about 59 percent of the sugar made by the Riondas' own factories. Hawley and Rionda between them would entrust only slightly more than half of what they handled to the Sugar Finance Commission, which they themselves managed. All in all, 8,834,522 bags were exempted from the commission's control. The modest Cuban mills must wait until after the major foreign interests were served.

For a brief interval, nevertheless, results seemed promising, and the commission made sales in February at 5 cents a pound. By March, however, although it gradually reduced its asking price, sales stalled, and Rionda scrawled discouraged letters to New York. Instead of buying Cuban sugar through the commission, now that there was abundant shipping, the refineries increasingly purchased duty-free sugar from Puerto Rico, Hawaii, and the Philippines. Suspicions grew among the hacendados that the refineries were boycotting the commission to teach Cuba a lesson, punishing it for holding for a better price. "It will be found that for week after week and for month after month," the *Louisiana Planter* wrote in its lead editorial, "the American refiner would not buy sugar from the Cuban Commission. . . . They may claim that it is no boycott but it would be difficult to explain."[6] But the harsh economic fact was that the colonial sugar, untaxed, could be obtained for less. In Cuba, men blamed the commission. If they had not surrendered their freedom of action, they reflected, even if they sold at only 3 cents, they would at least have some cash coming in. Now, they had nothing.

A three-way correspondence between Rionda, Castaño, and Laureano Falla Gutiérrez illustrated the growing dissatisfaction. By March, Castaño was in rebellion. "Soy un practicón" (I am a man with common sense), he wrote. The commission must give up trying to force high prices. Cuba, politically, commercially, agriculturally depends on the good will ("benignidad") of the United States, and its demands are counterproductive, ridiculous. "Hay que vender y embarcar, o ir al abismo" (We must sell and ship, or we go down). There was no longer room in his warehouses, he noted, for his unsold sugar.

Discouraged, Manuel struggled in a six-page reply to put the best face on matters. The commission, he argued, had saved the situation by obtaining credit to make the zafra. If it had not been created, the refineries would have obtained their sugar from their own plantations anyway. Nor was the commission to blame that there was no longer a European demand.

"Amigo Don Nicolás," Manuel wrote, you are right to say that it is better to be free, but we are living in abnormal times: "y a grandes malos, grandes remedios," the stern Spanish proverb, for harsh ills, harsh cures.

"Comprendo y acepto," Castaño replied. "I understand and accept that something had to be done, but in practice very little has been sold and shipped, there is no money. Our relations with the American refiners and consumers must be cordial. Cut the price from 5 cents to $4\frac{7}{8}$ or $4\frac{3}{4}$ or 4, but sell and ship, because it is a life-and-death question. I must have a ship—*San Agustín* has no place to put more sugar and must stop grinding, *Dos Amigos* has room for only 2,000 or 3,000 bags." Without credit from North America, Manuel replied, Cuba could not have made its crop at all, and many smaller planters would have already gone down to ruin.

Laureano Falla Gutiérrez took up the argument in the April week when the Banco Nacional finally closed its doors for good and Pote killed himself, the same week that Alfredo Zayas's election to the presidency was finally acknowledged. Laureano, like Castaño, was of peninsular origins. Born in a little village in Santander, Spain, he also had come to Cienfuegos as a boy, begun humbly as a clerk, and struggled up from nothing to become among the richest of the islanders. Unlike Manuel, he had not limited himself to sugar but had ventured shrewdly out to invest in a number of other fields—in fishing, in paper, and notably, together with Gerardo Machado and Orestes Ferrera, in the Cuban Electric Company. His investments in centrals had spread out as well, and his holdings now included the *Andreita, Patria, Manuelita, Adelaida,* and *Cieneguita* mills. He and Castaño had bought shares in each other's ventures, and a daughter of each had married an influential Gutiérrez Valladron brother. But there was a difference between Castaño and Falla Gutiérrez—Laureano was twenty-one years younger.

As Laureano saw it, the fatal flaw in establishing the commission had been exempting the plantations belonging to the U.S. refineries. Collective defense was good, but not if some were privileged. Unlike Castaño, who saw safety only in the island's subservience to its major customer, Laureano was suggesting Cuba take full control of the island's crop.[7]

Meanwhile, Walter Ogilvie had taken over Cuba Cane. His letters back to New York were short-tempered. He was finding considerable reason to agree with Goethals's criticisms of the company's inefficiency. Convinced that its managers "had no idea of the necessity for economy" he had set out "to impress them with the seriousness of the situation . . . and examine in detail every item of the proposed expenditure," as well as to "take a strong stand regarding the amounts to be advanced to Colonos." In doing so, he had capsized in a sea of detail. "I have only one man to work with," he wrote Henry Kroyer, the corporation's secretary-treasurer, "notwithstanding the number of high salaried employees that we do have in this office. When you realize that it is the first time in the history of the Company that any of the officials have made a thorough analysis of all expenditures, you can get some idea of the amount of work involved."

Rionda, himself stretched hard, was cavalier about "Infante's" problems. "I have been so busy," he finally wrote, "that I have hardly had time to think. It was owing to this that I cabled you that I had had no time to talk with Mr. Strauss." It was not an ideal response from the chair of Cuba Cane's Executive Committee.

Ogilvie replied effusively. "[N]o one appreciates more than I do, the enormous volume of work which you have undertaken this winter. . . . No one who is not thoroughly familiar with you and your life can understand how much you are continually sacrificing to help others." He girded his criticism of the Cuban operation in tactful phrases. "If Cuba Cane had been run along the lines of the Rionda Estates and not created this enormous organization, we would have been very much better off. . . . We have too many men, too many Departments, and no coordination, and the vital part of the business, the mills, in my opinion have been neglected to build up the big organization in Havana." Rionda was mollified but pessimistic. As for advances to colonos, he replied, "[M]y advice is that we should only advance what is absolutely necessary for weeding, absolutely nothing for fomento, and if some [fields] have to be abandoned in the West, better do so."

As for cutting back in the Havana office, however, the matter was not so simple. Ogilvie's letter had ignored the fact that some of the responsibility borne by its Havana functionaries had been not necessarily in fulfilling the functions for which they were ostensibly paid but rather for possibly useful tasks elsewhere. There were certain adjustments possible if politicians were approached correctly. A letter from Ogilvie to Kroyer less than a week later illustrates this. "Mr. Truffin," he wrote, "notified Mr. Manuel Rionda that he was about to take up the question of the adjustment of Manatí taxes with the Secretary of the Treasury, and Mr. Rionda suggested that at the same time if he could render any service in the matter of Cuba Cane, to do so. The result of Mr. Truffin's effort is embodied in the enclosed copy . . . and I hope that this will form a basis for settlement of our other tax adjustments."[8]

"[W]e must get into the inner circle of the new [president]," Manuel wrote more informally to Zevallos, as Zayas assumed office, "through [Truffin], [Arango] and the others." Also, he added, Albert Strauss, Sabin, Seligmans, and the Guaranty Trust, seeing notice of a possible Cuban government loan, had asked that in case any bonds were sold, the loan should come through the Guaranty. "You will remember," Manuel wrote, "that I was the originator of that bond issue and naturally, if anything is to be done, I don't want our friends to be frozen out."

Through the summer, the commission stood firm in setting prices, and, with only fleeting exceptions, the American refiners, also standing firm, bought their sugar elsewhere. "We will have many dead, but some will survive," Manuel wrote Falla Gutiérrez. "If, with sugar controlled, we must struggle so much, God knows what would have happened without control." "What must be done," Castaño wrote, "is to come to an understanding with the American refiners. We must work and put aside our dreams ["dejarnos de lirismos"]."

Rionda sent instructions, as the 1921 zafra came to an end, to discharge all the workers in their own plantations. "Let the weeds overrun the fields," he wrote Oliver Doty at *Tuinucú*. "[W]e are producing an article that the world won't take ... there are 2,400,000 tons ... that is not wanted anywhere. The more fields abandoned the better." Let the cane land be put to better use. There was no reason why Cuba should continue to import pork, lard, and other provisions. The Finance Commission should recommend that Cubans produce their own food. "One travels all over the island and never sees a vegetable, eggs, butter or even milk—everyone uses condensed milk."[9]

General Crowder's insistence on exempting the mills owned by the American refineries from the commission's control, a boycott on Cuban sugar by the refineries, delayed approval of a loan to the Cuban government—these were bad enough. But a worse disaster blanketed all the mills in Cuba in May 1921 when the U.S. Congress passed the Emergency Tariff, raising the duty on Cuban sugar from 1.0048 cents to 1.60 cents per pound. Only eight years earlier, the Underwood-Simmons Tariff had promised Cuba equality. Instead, the Emergency Tariff underwrote U.S. beet sugar and Philippine, Puerto Rican, and Hawaiian cane.

Many in sugar circles blamed the new tariff on the Sugar Finance Commission, seeing the tariff as retaliation. "The situation grows worse daily," Falla Gutiérrez wrote. "Now some of the hacendados and almost all the colonos can pay neither their business expenses nor their employees and day laborers, and the laborers go around with chits and IOUs in their pocket, but cannot eat. . . . Cuba thinks little. It does not hold with what it has [No tiene tenacidad]."

Manuel hammered at costs in his own mills. Laborers' wages must come down—it was not possible to pay $2 a day. "Your salary," he wrote Oliver Doty, "Leandro's and Pepe's and Aunt Isidora's must also be reduced—there is nothing to be gained by shutting our eyes and continuing to pay those figures."

"Mi estimado amigo," he wrote Falla Gutiérrez, "the situation is not improving, but growing worse. There will still be great surpluses in December, and I see no way but for the Cuban Government to order the purchase of from 800,000 to 1 million tons on its own account, paying the hacendados in Cuban bonds. . . . I am glad you can go to Spain to rest.

I would do the same, but I have taken on a task—perhaps too great a one for me—and my Spanish nature does not permit me to leave the ship in a storm."

Laureano reported he had paid a farewell call on Castaño before sailing. The man was sick, he wrote. He did not have the serenity to face the situation—not for lack of funds but because of his age.

"Mi estimado amigo," Manuel wrote Castaño, "I am sorry I have delayed so long in answering your letters. . . . The Cuban government must take command. This situation is not for us merchants, but for the governments.

"This government does not pay attention. . . . They lament, they tear their hair, they blame the whole world, but they do nothing. . . . I hope that when they see thousands of men without work, they will awaken and do what I suggest, or any other thing—instead of continuing with their arms crossed, waiting for help to come from the heavens."

American refineries, he pointed out, were buying only from day to day. His nephew, Manuel Enrique, had just gone to London, hoping for more business overseas, but the coal strike there had shut down the English refineries. "Se hace todo cuanto se puede, amigo Don Nicolás." Everything that can be done is being done.[10]

Whatever Rionda had done for Cuba Cane, it had not been enough. The corporation's preferred dividend, due July 1, had to be suspended, and the preferred's price on the Stock Exchange dropped ten points to 40. The July 1 payment of interest due on its bonds was arranged with difficulty. At the end of July, Cuba Cane had to extend for ninety days acceptances totaling $18 million, which were to have matured in August.[11]

Through June and into July, traditionally high consumption months, the Sugar Finance Commission made almost no sales. "Collective efforts have been worth nothing, nor private ones to avoid disaster," Castaño wrote. "The perspective is only of horror, of ruin." Rionda could only resort to the traditional Spanish proverbs. No evil lasts forever, he replied. "Dios aprieta pero no ahoga" (God crushes down, but does not annihilate). In less than six months, he promised, the problem would be resolved. Supplies of duty-free Puerto Rican sugar must be almost exhausted. There was a drought in Europe, so beets there would suffer and European demand rise. Before Falla Gutiérrez had sailed for Spain,

Rionda reported, he had asked Czarnikow-Rionda for a loan of $1 million against 200,000 bags of his sugar, which had been granted. "We want to treat you," Manuel continued, "at least as well as Laureano." Perhaps they could also arrange that Castaño's sugar be shipped before that of other friends or before *Tuinucú*'s.[12]

Meanwhile, on July 21 an even higher tariff passed the U.S. House of Representatives and sailed on into the Senate, where it was referred to the Agriculture Committee, ominously chaired by Senator Reed Smoot of beet-sugar Utah. Smoot, a Mormon elder, took the high ground in the Senate. "It is all very well," he wrote a Rionda publicist, "to take care of your sugar brothers, but in doing so . . . rather would I take care of the man who is paying American labor at least $3 and above per day. If there is any humanity and moral right involved in this it would be to pay a living wage to the Cuban laborer." The countercharge that many beet-growers in the Southwest were relying on immigrant Mexican child labor apparently did not interest him.[13]

At last, at the end of July the Finance Commission finally sold about 100,000 tons of sugar out of Cuba's total production of 3,934,297 tons. Briefly, Manuel hoped things would improve. Every quarter of a cent rise in the price at which Cuba Cane's unsold production could be disposed of would, he wrote Albert Strauss, equal $2.25 million. Yet the price now dropped to 3 cents per pound. If the commission had not existed, he wrote in its defense, "the large Cuban producing companies would have been able to turn out their usual yields and would have made a great deal of money . . . but other planters and thousands of small cane growers would have been ruined." The next year the world would be back to normal.[14]

In July 1921, the National City Bank sent an emissary to Cuba. The bank was reshaping itself, pulling back from the edge of the abyss where its overseas adventures had positioned it. Since May, after the Federal Reserve Bank's examiners had called it on the carpet and found it shaky, a new president had been put in charge. A midwesterner and forty-three-year-old champion securities salesman, Charles E. Mitchell was a "tall, handsome, genial man," none the less shrewd for all his geniality. Confronting the bank's overseas disasters, he dismissed the executive in charge of its foreign branches, as well as the vice president heading its Latin American sector, and as promptly dispatched an old Ohio contact,

Gordon S. Rentschler, to Cuba to investigate possible alternatives. The bank was spending large sums to store mortgaged sugar and preserve mortgaged mills (some only half finished), while new machinery rusted away in shipping crates. Would it be throwing good money after bad to try to salvage anything? If the bank's sugar loans had to be written off, its capital would be correspondingly reduced, lowering its legal lending limit.[15]

Although born on a farm in 1885, the also genial Rentschler was son and heir to the president of Hoover, Owens and Rentschler, an Ohio company that made sugar machinery, among other machine tools. He had, after Princeton, rapidly worked his way up from puddler in a family foundry and had sold the company's products in Cuba, thus becoming familiar with the island's potentialities. When the sugar market collapsed in 1921, he had gone to Cuba, toured the plantations, and sought financial aid from the National City for his stranded customers.[16]

How many Cuban estates owed National City how much is not readily apparent. Later, the number "100" was to be mentioned, a suspiciously rounded figure and a sizable proportion of the total 192 mills in existence. Albert Thompson, who represented the Fulton Machine Works in Havana, hazarded a hypothesis of an initial 50, but contemporaries, even Rionda, could only guess. Nor was guessing made easier by the fact that hacendados had borrowed from a mix of lenders.[17]

At the end of 1921, Rentschler reported back to Mitchell "that, with efficient management, [the properties] should generate the revenues needed to repay the bank's loans and to yield a reasonable return on the additional funds." Built into this assumption was the hypothesis that the price of sugar would rise.[18]

Cuba Cane meanwhile struggled on, resorting to high interest short-term loans. In September, $10 million was needed for the coming harvest "and to complete the 'Violeta' mill extension." It therefore became necessary for the directors to ask holders of its debentures to subordinate them in return for an extra 1 percent in future interest. Only the new loan, a circular threatened, could save it from receivership, as some 2,170,000 bags remained unsold out of its 3.9 million bag production. Thus the corporation's sixth fiscal year ended in desperation.[19]

Only Truffin's connections in political circles helped somewhat. He wrote that he had engaged a new bookkeeper for *Manatí* "who told me how to obtain from the Secretary of the Treasury a reasonable assessment of the tax on the *profits* not only of Manatí but also of Cuba Cane—whereby we have saved $84,151.84 for Manatí and $555,555.57 for Cuba Cane." As for the "Balances" before the Treasury Department, "I believe that by giving some gratuity, say 10 percent, we might be able to have returned to us about $100,000 for Manatí and about $590,000 for Cuba Cane." Manuel had suggested eliminating *Manatí*'s Havana office. "Under the circumstances," Truffin concluded, "I beg to ask whether at the present moment it would be wise to dispense with the services of a man who has saved us a large amount of money and who may save us many more.... I believe that a gratuity of $5/6,000 to be contributed by Cuba Cane and Manatí would leave the Government employees satisfied and well disposed towards us.... As to my salary, it is at the disposal of the Company, although I believe the work that I am doing is worth it."

Manuel replied that he was expecting to meet with Eduardo de Ulzurrún, and they would discuss "the question of the Havana office and the last part of your letter, the subject of what our friends think, should not be mentioned officially." He thanked Truffin for also getting the payment of taxes due on *Elía* and *Tacajo* postponed.[20]

At the end of December 1921, over 1 million tons of Cuban sugar were still unsold, and the market was down to 2⅛ cents a pound. The refineries had bought elsewhere, allegedly to teach Cuba a lesson. The banks were ready to press on. No one except Rionda and his immediate circle came to the Sugar Finance Commission's defense. Rionda himself, writing Tiarks in London, expressed his desire to have the attempt over with. "[W]e endeavored to help all Cubans alike, but we have met with so many obstacles particularly from the political factions ... since the [Commission] started I have dedicated nearly all my time to it, with no recompense but with a great deal of trouble and worriment."[21]

Four days later, he was deprived of the man who had shared that struggle, when Robert Hawley was found dead in his Gramercy Square bedroom. Since 1898, when Hawley had crossed the Gulf from New Orleans and taken the lead in building Cuba into a modern sugar empire, through the boom days when an unlimited market existed for them both, the two men had been close friends. Manuel believed that his death had been brought on by overwork in the service of the ungrateful and expressed relief when on December 21, 1921, President Zayas dissolved the Sugar Finance Commission.

The hacendados had already begun the 1922 zafra. Prior restrictions did not apply to the new crop, and as soon as sugar was available in early December, they promptly sold it for ⅜ cents a pound less than the Sugar Finance Commission was asking for the previous year's holdover. When the commission's demise dumped the still unsold portion of 1921's crop back on their hands, they settled for whatever it would bring, "breaking the market" to below 2 cents a pound in a bargain clearance.[22]

In December 1921, at the depth of this carnage, Herbert Hoover summoned Manuel to Washington. Hoover had become secretary of commerce in President Warren Harding's administration and was eager to oversee the expansion of world trade, which the postwar economic supremacy of the United States seemed to him to mandate. Sugar was an important segment of American foreign commerce and, although Senator Smoot's Agriculture Committee was conducting hearings on Capitol Hill to demolish it by a still higher tariff, Hoover had no intention of leaving its fate up to purely domestic interests. He may have felt no personal responsibility for the disasters that were buffeting Cuba, but before the crash it had been one of America's best customers for both agricultural products and manufactured goods.

The beet-sugar interests Smoot represented had grown powerful, and much of their growth had been in response to Hoover's crusade to feed a world at war. Although in 1899 they had harvested beets from less than one tenth of 1 percent of the land then farmed, now scattered local ventures had coalesced into the Amalgamated Sugar, the Great Western, the Holly Sugar Corporation, and the Utah-Idaho Sugar Company. The value of their crop had grown from $30 million in 1914 to reach almost $100 million by 1920. Like the cane interests, they had then suffered greatly from the postwar drop in prices, the $100 million falling to $40 million in two years.[23]

At one end of Pennsylvania Avenue, spokesmen for western beets defended their vegetable. At the other, facing Hoover, Rionda found himself at a loss for any solution to Cuba's suffering. A higher U.S. tariff would cost the island its competitive advantage. He had hoped, he told Hoover, that "the United States might buy the Cuban surplus." Hoover was against this. "I did not know of anything else to suggest excepting a restriction of the Cuban crop," Manuel reported.

At a private conference with the beet men, which Hoover arranged for the next morning, the remolacheros proposed to Rionda that Cuba should cut its production to 2 million tons. They "believe they have the Cubans by the throat," Rionda reported, "they are very hoggish." But what could he do? That afternoon he went back to Hoover with a draft proposal accepting the curtailment on Cuba's behalf.

Hoover, Manuel reported, "immediately . . . jumped upon" such a proposal. He would, he said (apparently without irony), never permit Cuba to be dictated to, since to so limit production might lead to high prices for American consumers. He promised to confer with the Federal Reserve Bank and then with the Guaranty Trust, the National City, J. P. Morgan and Company, the Bankers Trust, and the First National of Boston about financing for the immanent harvest. If a year earlier banks had been eager to salvage their warehoused collateral, now that the market would soon be cleared of that accumulation, they wanted to garner as much as possible against the sums they had invested in the mills. That would mean taking complete advantage of their economies of scale—full steam ahead.

Rionda then took the train back to New York. Whether Rionda knew it or not, Hoover had already been in conference with Dwight Morrow of the Morgan bank and had that same day, December 11, received from Morrow a memorandum that "stated the bankers' opposition to either production or marketing restrictions." The House of Morgan was about to advance the Cuban government $5 million and was considering a further $50 million loan. An island with a high percentage of idle *macheteros* would be in no position to meet future interest payments.[24]

On January 9, 1922, President Ogilvie issued the Cuba Cane Corporation's Sixth Annual Report. Although the firm's cost of production had dropped almost 50 percent, primarily because its colonos had received so much less, Cuba Cane showed an operating loss for the fiscal year of almost $6 million, its perfected management techniques useless against the forces of the market. Its sugar had sold at an estimated average of 3.891 cents a pound, scarcely a third of the previous year's 10.345 cents, and even that figure was optimistically based on the assumption that the approximately 1.1 million bags still unsold could be disposed of at 2.5 cents a pound. The average was as high as it was only because Manuel had contracted ahead to sell 400,000 bags in the summer of 1920 and another 900,000 bags in January 1921 at an average of 7.66 cents per pound.

Rionda's "Review of the Sugar Situation" appeared on the final two and a half pages. It analyzed the political factors that had buffeted the corporation, blaming the "ruinous . . . increase in the duty on Cuban sugar . . . imposed by the U.S. Emergency Tariff Act . . . a severe blow at a moment of the greatest adversity."[25]

In the spring of 1922, Manuel's heart was elsewhere. Harriet's illness was becoming more grave, and they did not go to Cuba. Instead, in mid-March, there was a visit to the Greenbrier Hotel at White Sulphur Springs. At first, Manuel wrote that "Auntie" slept better and was well enough for a walk on the hotel grounds. But such hopeful signs were ephemeral. They returned to Alpine on April 6, and Manuel ceased going into the office. On May 17, Harriet died after a fatal stroke. He had loved her, and if in her pictures she seems ordinary enough, whether in carefully posed salon portraits or in snapshots amid Royal palms, a full-bosomed, corseted matron dressed for a starring role in an old-fashioned Victor Herbert operetta, he mourned her passionately.

There was a six-day wake, a high mass in Our Lady of Lourdes church in Manhattan, and a rather perilous Hudson ferry crossing back to Río Vista, the bronze casket roped to the deck lest it slide overboard into the river. A marble mausoleum was begun on the estate. Manuel, "shattered," would not go to 110 Wall Street again for eight months.

Nor was this the only family bereavement that year. In September, Maude Atkinson de Braga, Bernardo's wife, succumbed to cancer at forty-five. Manuel wrote her son, George, who was nineteen: "[R]eturn of love is the only happiness in this world. That is the only thing I have now—love that comes in these days from those whom we, in our earlier days, loved and took care of. Take plenty of exercise, be out in the open, look forwards, not backwards. This is your Spring—do not turn it into Winter. There is time enough for that."

With Harriet's death, the nephews came closer to autonomy in the places Manuel had schemed for them, dividing among them the parts of the Rionda empire. In New York's cavernous world, Manolo, his brother Joaquín's son by the daughter of the Sephardic merchant Benjamins, and Bernardo, his sister Bibiana's son by a Spanish mule-driver, took charge. Bernardo drank more heavily with Maude's death. Yet neither tragedy, whiskey, nor matrimony—he was to remarry within a year—seemed to inhibit his keen market sense. He was big, gruff, and bearlike, but the slighter Manolo balanced him with suaveness. In Cuba, Francisco's sons, Rionda y de la Torrientes, were supervising the cane, the mills and fields. Intermediary in Havana, sister Maria's son, Higinio Fanjul Rionda in the Cuba Trading Company, traded in contacts, business contracts, and political influence.

Manuel had schooled them all, had seen that the New York nephews visited the plantations yearly, as he had called the Cuban nephews to the New Jersey palisades in the hot summers, uniting them around Harriet and himself at Río Vista and at *Tuinucú*. To be sure, Bernardo and Manolo had married New York women, while the Cuban nephews had wed Cubans. Bernardo and Maude's children, George and Ronnie—Manolo and Ellen were childless—were as North American as their names, while the young Cuban Riondas and Fanjuls were Hispanic. But all were bilingual and bicultural citizens of the blending world of global investment. Manuel had done and was doing all an uncle could.

Family unity was much on his mind that year of mourning. At all costs, he wrote, they must stay "siempre unidos.... [T]odos los Riondas deben de trabajar juntos, ya sea en los ingenios, o en las casas comerciales de Nueva York y la Havana, o en la Refinería" [Always united. All the Riondas must work together, whether in the mills or in the commercial houses in New York and Havana, or in the Refinery]. And they must preserve the family name, the family honor. When his nephew Salvador, who was serving an unsuccessful apprenticeship in the Cuban Trading Company, suggested joining Mendoza y Cía on the stock exchange instead, Manuel was angry. Mendoza's, he wrote, was only a gambling house.

"In 1896," he wrote, "I tried something similar and swore never again would I be a stock-broker, knowing how difficult it is to trade in margins. The Cuban Trading Company and Czarnikow-Rionda will never play the stock market with other peoples' money although the men who do so may become millionaires." "What Bernardo does," he commented, "is to buy and sell future sugar on the Exchange, but that involves no speculation."

"Que es muy bonita" (it is very pretty for you to say), he wrote Salvador, "'all the risks are for the clients' accounts,'" but when a client loses, he goes away discontented and attacks ("echa pestes") his agent. "Thus it does not please me after I have placed our name at the height where it now is.... Always remember, that it is not a question of money, but of name." He went on, however (apparently without irony), to assure poor Salvador that merely because he was not in favor of Salvador's plan, his nephew should not hesitate in the future to state his opinions frankly.[26]

He was almost completely detached from the Cuba Cane Sugar Company. Ogilvie had been in New York for two weeks in June, he told Eduardo de Ulzurrún, but they had not spoken together. He did not propose to deal with business except with his nephews and saw no need for Eduardo to send him copies of *Manatí*'s reports. But this very letter was four pages long, touching on many details regarding rolling stock, cane cars, new installations, and the renovation of colonías. He wanted from *Manatí*, he wrote, 500,000 bags by the end of July. Two weeks later, there was a six-hour visit from Frederick Strauss to discuss the "colonitos" and whether to buy a Dorr clarifier for *Manatí*. For the edification of Higinio and in the interest of extending Czarnikow-Rionda's surviving commission business, he made long lists of all Cuba's plantations, like a general surveying the terrain of battles to come, naming twenty-six "plantations we should try to get as clients" to add to the thirty-four that Czarnikow-Rionda still represented.[27]

When Victor Zevallos retired from the Cuban Trading Company that year, his place was filled by Aurelio Portuondo Barceló y de Régil. Aurelio's family ties were good—there had long been Portuondos and de Régils in Santiago de Cuba, and a Portuondo had been a general in the Spanish-Cuban-American War and chair of the Executive Committee of the First Cuban Assembly. Aurelio was active in hacendado circles. He had been one of the investors in 1920 in the Cía Azucarera Andorra, in which Truffin and Arango were also interested, and president for a time of the Association of Cuban Hacendados. Zayas had added him to the ill-fated Sugar Finance Commission in 1921 to represent the smaller cane growers. A tall man with a long, sagging, rather equine face, he had access to Zayas in the presidential palace, while in Washington he had learned to lobby in congressional corridors and was already active in the hopeless attempt to defeat a higher U.S. tariff.

Despite that coming blow, by June 1922 sugar prices were finally rising, if rather shakily, with the final sacrifice of the stored surplus, the clearing of the "invisibles" from grocery shelves, and increased demand as the overall economy recovered. For the next two and a half years, prices would tend upward. After February, the price never fell below 4 cents a pound in 1923 and by November was consistently in the 6-cent range. In 1924, the price would open at $5^3/_{16}$ cents.

At the end of 1922, as the 1923 zafra approached, Manuel's life began to resume its former rhythms. If he never ceased to mourn his wife's death, commemorating its anniversary, expecting annual expressions of grief from their families, he took up his old patterns with some pleasure. In late November, he sailed south on the S.S. *Murargo*. Writing Tiarks in London an invitation to join him at *Tuinucú*, he showed his anticipation. "The island has greater possibilities than ever," he wrote. "The only trouble is that there are too many new men in the game, but they will soon find their road to the old standbyers!" Albert Strauss, Hayden, and Jaretzki came to the Manhattan pier to see him off, and even Ogilvie (who did not come) sent a basket of fruit to his cabin.

Rionda's letterbooks show little correspondence with his successor as Cuba Cane's president. As soon as he arrived in Havana, he saw to it that Regino Truffin resigned as the corporation's vice president and that Higinio, Leandro, Pepe, Truffin, and Arango surrendered their powers of attorney. Ogilvie, actually, had requested the resignations, and an official letter of revocation had been dispatched, prompting Truffin to remark that it would have been "más delicado" if he had been given time to resign. Crosby, he reported, had replied that it was "a mere question of form and so the thing stood." Manuel was still a director, but he was no longer listed as chairman of the Executive Committee; he no longer asked to see the "usual data" and only to "be kept informed of the principal items." Czarnikow-Rionda still sold the corporation's sugar, the Strauss brothers occasionally wrote him about its financing, and he advised Hayden when Hayden requested. But on December 31, he was reduced to asking Truffin to tell him who the new directors of Cuba Cane's Eastern Cuba subsidiary were.

Now he focused on improvements to the family plantations. "Cuba is prospering," he wrote Leandro, "and inside of five years we will have another crazy little time like 1920." There must be no competition for the acreage surrounding their factories. "We have too much at stake to allow a Falla or somebody else to come in and spoil our picture." He went back, too, to an earlier theme, the need to care for the land. Everyone must fertilize, husband, replow, replant. "*Nature* must be helped. . . . Heretofore Cubans in the East have been getting all from *Nature* without giving her anything in return."

He pointed out to *Manatí*'s directors the desirability of renting its land to small colonos. The East had been sparsely settled, and labor had to be brought in from Haiti and Jamaica. Now drought in western Cuba was leading to in-migration. "These small farmers are men of experience . . . good assets to sugar companies like ours. Having their own oxen, large families and taking charge of only 5/6 cabs, they are able to take good care of their fields and are always on the spot in case of *fires*. . . . [W]e can not see any better opportunity than now that these long-tried, hard-working men are leaving their old homes." He had, he wrote, accepted twelve or fifteen, although so far he had to admit that in the aggregate they would work only from seventy to ninety caballerías. As for *Francisco*, in a flurry of capital letters he advised Leandro that Czarnikow-Rionda was behind him financially. Loans should be entirely within the family. "Make business a pleasure not a burden. I had to push forward; you boys do not have to do as I did. Then, live happily."

"Put in the finishing touches," he wrote, "clear your Bateys of old scraps, beautify around the Bateys, and let the increase in capacity *go*, so as to be easy financially and the management be a pleasure rather than a tiresome task."[28]

In these few years, the Riondas' own estates plus *Manatí* and *Tacajo*, which they managed, were third in production among the groups of mills on the island. Cuba Cane was first, accounting for 13.02 percent of the island's total production in 1923, with Cuban-American at 7.21 percent. But the Riondas were very close behind, with 6.33 percent in 1923. Only in 1924 would they fall by a hair to fifth place, to 5.46 percent, behind Punta Alegre's 5.62 percent and the General Sugar Company's 5.47 percent.[29]

The General Sugar Company was a new grouping, the result of Rentschler's advice to the National City Bank in 1921 that some of its indebted mills would be worth the foreclosures. In 1924, eleven mills (out of the fifty or hundred rumored in 1921) were being organized into subsidiaries of the bank's own subsidiary, the National City Company. Rentschler was in charge of National City's Management Corporation, seconded by Colonel E. A. Deeds and G. H. Houston, two "industrial advisers." Six of General Sugar's mills were in the East along the line of the Cuba Railway. One was in Piñar del Rio, two in Santa Clara, two in Matanzas—as spread out as Cuba Cane's own. Seven were new.[30]

Optimistic predictions seemed justified, and for a few years there was, for Manuel, almost an Indian summer interlude, to remind him of the turn-of-the-century days when men, cleaning up the rubble war had left, developed the island's wealth and thus grew rich from it, when there was a market in the United States for all the cane that they could grow.

Edwin Farnsworth Atkins, Manuel's contemporary and opposite, also believed himself entering a cheerful old age. The various Atkins operations were doing well. "I was now," he wrote as he penned his memoirs, "free to spend my time in Cuba and to have my children and grandchildren with me," while Mrs. Atkins could devote herself to "good works among the Soledad people."

This idyll was shattered. While Atkins's *Sixty Years in Cuba* does not include the story, at the beginning of January 1923, the regular daily flight of the Aeromarine Airlines from Key West to Havana crashed into the sea, and Edwin Atkins Jr., his two children—Edwin III, aged five, and David, aged three—and the boys' governess were among those lost in the twenty-foot waves. For a century, creaking sailing ships out of Massachusetts had borne four generations of Atkinses through Atlantic storms to Cuban harbors. Now, Robert Atkins watched the salvage operations, hoping uselessly that the bodies of his brother and nephews would be recovered from the shark-filled depths.[31]

Manuel held aloof from the daily operations of his gigantic infant and was held aloof by it. With improving conditions and under Ogilvie's control, Cuba Cane's next three annual reports showed operating profits. The $6 million loss in 1921 was replaced by 1922's $3.5 million profit, which then quadrupled so that $12.5 million was netted in 1923. As more and more of Cuba Cane's sugar was being produced in the East, the smaller percentages paid the colonos there for their raw cane led to significant savings.

Yet despite the three years' profits, its obligations still weighed the company down. There were depreciation allowances, taxes, write-offs for obsolescence, and the inherited arcane legal jungle of subordinated debentures and indentures to be slashed through, slowing the pace of recovery. Assets carried on the books must be written down. In 1924, $1.5 million was charged to dismantling and obsolescence, and valuation dropped to $80,576,977. Another $3,033,101 was deducted from surplus reserves to bring colono advances down to "sound value."

The company had not been able to make its quarterly payments to preferred stockholders since April 1921. Thirteen unpaid quarters had accumulated, adding up to a debt of $13,125,000. Since no dividends could be paid on the common stock until the preferred had been paid up in full and had accumulated a reserve to guarantee payment for two future years, the situation for the common stockholders was hopeless.[32]

Yet a rising tide is said to raise all ships, and for most of those concerned with sugar, the higher prices brought hope and optimism. But they were not shared by Cuba's railroads, as a growing number of trucks rolled along improved highways and as the sugar companies planned to develop their own ports. The situation was particularly unpropitious for Colonel Tarafa's heavily indebted Northern, which had carried in supplies and machines to build the new factories along its route, notably the American Sugar Refining Company's *Cunagua* and *Jaronú*, and had planned on also carrying out all they would produce to the Northern's terminal, his Puerto Tarafa. The colonel, a practiced guerrilla tactician, therefore moved in the summer of 1923 to wrest a political rescue from the Cuban Congress. In August, he had a bill introduced to close the island's private ports. There was a patriotic twist. Profits from carrying freight subsidized the public railroads' passenger services.

Rionda at first assumed the law would apply merely to *Cunagua* and *Jaronú* and was rash enough, when he first heard of it, to express some sympathy for Tarafa. Tiarks had been visiting, and he had mentioned to the Englishman, while the two were taking a walk before breakfast, that Tarafa might have some right to prevent those two plantations from opening new ports. The realization, however, that all private ports, even those as long established as *Manatí*'s and *Francisco*'s, would be included, made him realize the need of all participants in the sugar economy to support allocative efficiency. The bill's passage, he estimated, would cost *Francisco* $72,000 a year and *Manatí* $102,000. When contributions for a $50,000 war chest to lobby in the Cuban legislature against the "Tarafa

Bill" were solicited, the Rionda plantations subscribed $6,000, matching Cuba Cane's, Punta Alegre's, and the American Sugar Refining Company's contributions, the large Cuban interests joining with those of Wall Street. If the law threatened to pass, Manuel wrote, they must "see some one in authority in Washington." Once more, he looked to the northern eagle to swoop down and rescue the island from its local patriotic-sounding but noneconomic impulses.

He cabled Portuondo arguments to use in Cuba. Should the Tarafa Bill become law,

> Cuba's great advantages of being long and narrow and having plenty of ports will be lost. Java uses all her ports, so does Porto Rico. . . . Why should Francisco, Cape Cruz or anyone else ship sugar 100 miles off when they have a port 10 miles from the factory. . . . Why should the [Cuban] Government . . . kill Cubans' great advantages of producing cheap sugar? To benefit the Cuban roads? Who own the Cuban roads, anyhow? Foreigners, not Cubans. It is my desire that you inform Higinio's friend, Juan Cabrera, of everything in the matter so that he may know how to defend the point in the Lower House.

Washington proved cooperative. Sullivan & Cromwell lawyers and Elihu Root were called in and deals were suggested, so that when the Tarafa Bill passed by an overwhelming vote in September, it had been amended to mollify most interests, including Rionda's own, although the American Sugar Refining Company's *Cunagua* and *Jaronú* were denied their subports and forced to ship all the way to Puerto Tarafa. The Tarafa Law also (which had no doubt been the wily colonel's chief purpose from the beginning) provided for the amalgamation of Tarafa's Northern with the financially sounder Cuba Railroad. Tarafa became a director of both roads, profiting financially and freeing himself from regular administrative tasks, which had never been his forte.[33]

Various implications lingered. The American companies had not been able to secure all they wished, nor had their partial victory come too easily. Cuban nationalism was gaining ground. But the larger sugar companies, Cuban and North American alike, had cooperated, despite any linguistic and ethnic divisions. Their interests would merge in defense of profits and economic rationality.

8

Visible Hands

In 1923, Cuban sugar brought 5.25 cents a pound on average, but the industry's Indian Summer was already ending, and the next year, as production increased all around the globe, the price dipped to 4 cents. In December, Manuel wrote from *Francisco*: "Do nothing from now on but tighten up the loose ends and put money in the bank. No more lands, no more leases, no more machinery." In Cuba Cane's annual report for 1924, he predicted that "with world conditions rapidly on the mend . . . [i]t may well be that the promise of increase for the coming year will not prove in excess of world requirements."[1] But "it well may be" was too tentative for comfort.

In the United States and Cuba, 1924 was a presidential election year. Given the generally satisfactory state of the economy in the northern republic, Calvin Coolidge's reelection went smoothly. A monosyllabic Vermonter, he served business interests respectably. In Cuba, it became smooth-shaven Gerardo Machado's turn. Although he had the classic caudillo résumé—he had fought in the War for Independence and owned a sugar central, the tiny *Carmita*—his chief connections were with utilities. As Gómez's minister of the interior, he had handled light and power concessions and had been rewarded by a vice presidency in the Cuban Electric Company. His ample campaign funds were allegedly from Henry Catlin, president of the Electric Bond and Share Company of New York.[2]

Sugar barons were no longer Cuba's only capitalists, and only about half of the U.S. billion-dollar investment in Cuba was now in sugar. A new Cuban bourgeoisie, however limited and dependent, was taking shape. For many years (Rionda being the exception), men like the Gómez Menas and the Mendozas had seized more varied opportunities for investment and diversified into Havana real estate and banking. There were more and larger factories. Ford, Coca-Cola, Armour, and other companies were establishing branch plants and training local managers. Machado appealed to entrepreneurial ambitions, campaigning on a program of public works and schools, honest and efficient government, politely but consistently suggesting repeal of the Platt Amendment. Easily elected, he traveled north in May, addressed Chambers of Commerce, and was Coolidge's guest of honor at the White House. A luncheon was arranged for him at the Bankers' Club in New York by Earl Babst of the American Sugar Refining Company, with "refiners, producers, merchants and brokers" in attendance.

After-dinner speeches were cordial. Babst paid tribute to Cuba's wartime production. Through "the diplomatic mission of de Céspedes, Mendoza, Longa, Tarafa and de Mesa, ably assisted by Rionda and Hawley," the island had joined the United States on "the common ground of a common patriotic purpose." But its sugar, as a contribution to the war effort, had been sold, he admitted, "below [its] economic value and world parity," and as soon as the war ended, it was his "humiliation to acknowledge" that U.S. government policy had "led directly" to "unnecessary disaster . . . hardest on Cuba where it was least deserved." He recommended that Cuba now "develop foreign markets" and build "automobile roads in all directions" so that, by greater self-sufficiency, it might reduce the cost of living and be the better equipped for world competition "on a low cost basis." Machado, replying, assured the guests that he would promptly introduce antistrike legislation and that the Cuban army was "in admirable shape to guarantee the protection of property and the prevalence of peace."[3] It was a script to Manuel Rionda's taste.

U.S. influence in Cuba was being shifted from the State Department to businessmen. General Crowder disembarked, was promoted to ambassador, and no longer sent moral directives to the presidential palace. Instead, after office hours, he would stop at the Havana-Biltmore for a dry martini and join the Steinhart family for dinner at the country club. The House of Morgan's $50 million loan had purchased high-level cooperation, and quid pro quos could be negotiated in boardrooms.

Yet despite diversification of investments, however promising manufacturing might seem, most of Cuba's foreign exchange was still earned by one export. Sugar was supposed to pay for promised public works. And sugar's price, as Machado settled in, continued to drop, so that in 1925 its average would no longer be 4.20 cents but 2.57 cents a pound and a bag no longer brought $13.65 but only $8.35. For even a modest mill producing 100,000 bags, that was a drop in income of more than $500,000. In the Rionda mills, despite rising production, *Francisco*'s operating profits went from $2,348,993 in 1924 (674,000 bags) to $1,401,268 in 1925 (880,000 bags). *Manatí*'s fell from $1,818,120 (541,000 bags) to $354,228 (618,000 bags).

Rionda watched the statistics, noted the yield of Java's new miracle cane, and checked on the weather in Czechoslovakia and the Colorado beet fields. In 1925, world production went up, not by the 2 million tons Cuba Cane's 1924 annual report had predicted but by 3.4 million tons. True, most was consumed, so there would be no great surplus carried over. But by the time Cuba Cane's 1925 annual report went to the printer, the price was down to $1^{15}/_{16}$ cents per pound.

Cuba Cane's total production had risen over 20 percent, to 4,471,357 bags. Rionda had managed to sell them for an average 2.515 cents per pound. Yet each pound, despite the managerial refinements of Ogilvie's presidency, had cost 2.363 cents to produce. When taxes and the interest on bonds and bank loans had been paid, depreciation taken into account, and $300,000 necessarily applied to redeeming sinking fund bonds, only $2,486,907 could be carried to surplus. The corporation's operating profits dropped from $12.5 million in 1924 to $5 million in 1925. Other companies did as badly, or worse—the Cuban-American Sugar Company's net earnings declining from $8.5 million to less than $3 million.

Cuba Cane's 1925 annual report urged orthodox trust in the invisible hand. At current prices, farmers around the globe would cut back until "eventually" there would be "a favorable reaction in prices." But how long was "eventually"? In the United States, beet farmers had few options. Prices of other agricultural commodities had also dropped, and instead of cutting back, farmers could only grow more to compensate, racing bank foreclosures. The classic presumption that dropping prices led to a fall in production did not seem to apply. Also, the invisible hand was powerless against rising tariff barriers. Eighty percent of the world's sugar production, according to the distinguished Dutch scientist H. C. Prinsen Geerligs, was already protected by tariffs.[4]

In the fall of 1925, as preparations were made for the 1926 harvest, Cuba's colonos lost patience waiting for the economic laws to run their course and met to confront their grievances. In December, a number threatened not to begin the zafra unless they were promised a larger return. Joint action began in Camagüey and spread throughout the island. Manuel watched with anger, recalling in Czarnikow-Rionda's weekly *Sugar Review* that in the old days colonos had not organized for collective action but had come individually and respectfully to the mill offices.[5]

The colonos' strike spread, bringing even *Francisco* and *Tuinucú* to a halt and shutting down Cuba Cane's plantations, along with many others. It was obviously a time for strong official action, and local men with the right political connections became more important to North American investors. On December 3, Rionda, with Portuondo and Fanjul, met with Machado. The president, Manuel reported to New York, was most affectionate ("cariñoso"). Two days later, Machado issued a decree, which Manuel promptly cabled to Charles Hayden, ordering that the colonos' strike end within five days.

But although Machado thus ordered the colonos to begin the zafra, he dared not appear to his own compatriots as a mere tool of the Americans. Labor organizers could be forcibly deported as Spanish anarchists or as agitators sent by a Moscow International, but the colonos were constituents, with respected and politically active leaders. Solutions, Machado announced, must be found for their problems, which would be submitted to a Comisión de Inteligencia.

The commission met at the presidential palace on December 7, with eighteen representatives of the colonos, ten of the hacendados, and four of the government. Speeches stressed cooperation. But this lip service to harmony, Rionda believed, could not last. "The seed of disagreement has been planted," he warned in a fourteen-page memo.

He was especially disheartened that the colonos at *Francisco* had joined the strike. It seemed "as though it does not pay to be kind," he wrote. He (who had always favored the colono system) now recommended that from 10 to 15 percent of *Francisco*'s fields be taken for administration cane. It might be more expensive for the company, but it would discourage the colonos from taking future action. "Whenever it is shown that a Colono mixes in politics, lives outside of his colonía, keeps extravagant establishments, lives beyond his means or is likely to be a disturbing element," every effort should be made to get rid of him. The colonos must recognize the contracts they had made, for "[i]f contracts are not respected, Civilization fails." But he privately admitted that things were not well for them. "The colono has only himself. The companies divide the losses among their stockholders." If they came individually, rather than as threatening members of a united "agricultural bloc," something could be done for them. *Francisco* might pay 15 cents each toward the jute bags the colonos used or might lower interest rates to 7 percent. In January 1926, when *Francisco*'s colonos lagged behind other plantations, being reluctant to pay their field hands more than 60 cents per 100 arrobas for cutting and lifting on the good fields or 70 cents on bad, he proposed the company pay for an increase of 10 cents per 100 arrobas. It might, he thought, cost $50,000 or $60,000, but it would enable the mill to grind more cane "and show a good disposition to meet the reasonable demands of our colonos."[6] Yet throughout the island, colonos continued to organize although even if they won a larger slice of the Cuban pie, that would not solve the problem of low prices and overproduction, for the problem was of world dimensions.

By January 1926, a bumper crop seemed inevitable. From one end of Cuba to the other, production records were toppling, as prices fell below the cost of production. There was, Rionda wrote in April, nothing else to be done but to cease waiting on an invisible hand and cut the harvest 10 percent. Since Cuba was the world's largest producer "and consequently the greatest one to blame for the increased production," it must be the one to act, even if unilaterally, and "this not being speedily possible by natural laws it had to be done by act of the government." On April 26, 1926, the Cuban Congress passed the Verdeja Act, authorizing the president to limit the crop to 90 percent of the previous year's 5,189,346 tons. Mills had three days to lurch to a premature halt and the colonos to discharge their workers, leaving many caballerías of cane uncut. This sacrifice notwithstanding, the price dropped from 2.24 cents to 2.22 cents a pound. Apologists could only argue that, without curtailment, it would have gone still lower, and "while it is a negative benefit the law has at least prevented matters from becoming any worse."[7]

Edwin Atkins was no longer there to take charge. The Bostonian, who had heard the plantation songs of slave-born African women, had died in May, a month after his surviving son had resigned the presidency of the Punta Alegre Sugar Company. Edwin Atkins's role was now assumed by men from a more impersonal world. E. Atkins and Company passed into the hands of Frank Lowry, Eugene V. R. Thayer, and Horace Havemeyer and became E. Lowry and Company, while William C. Douglas, representing the "Pittsburgh interests," became Punta Alegre's president.[8] The transition was symbolic of the passing from an intimate world of individual founders. Increases in scale brought in professional managers.

Regino Truffin, too, died that summer. He had long been president of *Manatí*, and its board of directors requested that Manuel succeed him. There were many reasons, Manuel replied, "why I should decline the honor, the principal one being my age, and this reason being insurmountable, I do not consider it necessary to state any other." The presidency then remained unfilled for five years, when Manuel, at seventy-seven, finally accepted the post. In the meantime, he signed the letters to the stockholders as "vice president." *Manatí* was barely scraping by, running a deficit in 1926 and ceasing to pay interest on its preferred stock. Payment on the common had been discontinued the previous September.[9]

Other sugar companies were as badly off, many worse. There were almost no dividends for anyone. On top of a coming prolonged dead season, a lean *pascuas de Navidad* was in store for the cane cutters, for in early September Machado delayed until January the start of the 1927 zafra.

End-of-year prices then rose to 2⅞ cents per pound. But European demand languished, and a hoped-for sale to China fell through. Manolo asked Portuondo to inform Machado that only the president himself could save the situation, while simultaneously Manuel once more closed ranks with Tarafa. Since Tarafa's Northern line had merged into the Consolidated Railroads, the colonel had been celebrating in Paris. Returning via New York, he passed a day "very agreeably" at Río Vista, taking with him a copy of a letter to the Havana newspaper *El Sol*, which had alleged that pressure to set limits to the next crop was a Rionda clan device to enable them to manipulate the sugar market.

Only through a restriction of the harvest, Tarafa's letter argued, could the colonos receive a good price. Therefore, he had been astonished at the paper's criticism. It was, he wrote, "lamentable" that there should be "demonstrations so full of irresponsibility and of ignorance . . . whether through bad faith or envy."

"What I imagine," he asserted, was that Rionda "feels alarm, justifiably so, for the immediate future of the industry and—whether or not liking a policy of restriction—has seen, as anyone who really knows the world sugar problem must, that Cuba has no other path." He concluded: "Without restriction, the day is not distant when all properties in Cuba, including urban real estate, will be worth only half what they are today."[10] He thus spoke for those who, having already sunk their money into lands, mills, docks, and railroads, would now shore up their investments.

Cuba Cane fell deeper into deficit financing. After taxes and interest, there had been a net loss of $232,080 for the year 1926.

On December 17, Higinio Fanjul cabled New York. Was the rumor true that Ogilvie was resigning? Manolo cabled back that it was. He did not know who would replace him, but Hayden would be acting head at least until his annual visit to Cuba. "Mr. Ogilvie," Bernardo summed up, years later, "was a very honest man, but he did not at all understand our business. He came to us during the dance of the millions, and tried to reorganize the whole firm. He had all kinds of departments and bosses, but when the crash came, all these were wiped out and we returned to the usual modest ways of doing business."[11] The inadequacies in this summary illustrate how little he had learned about the necessity for efficient corporate organization.

Since the Goethals debacle, the Riondas had taken no part in Cuba Cane's management but had concentrated on their own plantations, on the McCahan refinery, and on Czarnikow-Rionda's remaining clients. While innumerable hitherto independent sugar properties had been swept into the possession of the northern banks, the Castaño, the Falla Gutiérrez, the Tarafa, and other operations had survived, and the Gómez

Mena brothers had returned. The brothers had sold their *Amistad* and their superb *Gómez Mena* to the Warner Sugar Refinery in February 1920 when prices had been at their height. When the banks that had backed the Warner's expansion had cut their losses, the mills had in 1924 again become the brothers' property in their newly incorporated Nueva Compañía Gómez Mena.[12]

Toward his former "Infante" Manuel now paraded a lofty detachment, writing, when Strauss suggested Rentschler as Ogilvie's replacement, "that I did not believe that R. would ever accept a position of such a character and of such small importance, judging from the way he lives in New York—with a magnificent house on Fifth Avenue."[13] But during the 1927 harvest, Manuel dispatched Manolo to Cuba in his stead and regularly, if without enthusiasm, began to attend Cuba Cane's Executive Committee meetings once more, telling Charles Hayden that "he was going to attend . . . until he was kicked out."

Whatever influence remained to him, he would exert to win Cuba Cane's support for restricted production. There was more sugar than the market could absorb. Theoretically, the low prices that had resulted should drive the smaller, higher-cost mills out of business, bringing supply and demand into balance. Yet under the most ruthless scenario, this could not happen overnight or even in one or two years, and in the meantime even Punta Alegre, General Sugar, Cuba Cane, Cuban-American, and the others were losing more money than they could afford to borrow. Only, he argued, if the next harvest or two were limited could the cash hemorrhage could be stanched. Machado had already delayed commencement of the 1927 harvest, but merely limiting the duration of the zafra would not accomplish the desired aim. Cane left to ripen for another month would be richer in sugar content, actually increasing production, while the colonos would meanwhile be driven deeper into debt since they would have no money coming in.[14]

In the first week of December, Machado took the drastic step of ordering that 1927's crop be limited to the 4.5 million tons for which a market was thought to exist. "[Machado] told me confidentially," Manolo reported, "he has absolute support from Washington in everything he has done and is doing," and the price of sugar temporarily rose to 3.375 cents per pound.[15]

To impose cuts, quotas had to be set. Each mill, Machado ordered, would be permitted to produce 92.25 percent of what it had bagged in 1925, except—a sweeping touch—for "special circumstances." He resurrected an existing mechanism to determine the "circumstances," the previously appointed Sugar Finance Commission, all of its members Cuban. But weeks passed without their agreeing among themselves. With the delay, investors grew uneasy, then desperate, so that in late February Charles Hayden and representatives of the Cuba Cane's bankers descended on Havana. Arriving simultaneously also were Dwight Morrow of J. P. Morgan and Rentschler of the National City Bank and its General Sugar Management Company. Of the major sugar producers, only Cuban-American and United Fruit were not represented when these magnates met at dinner in Havana on February 21. Manolo was present for the Riondas and was probably the host, for there are references to "Manuel's dinner." Among them, the heavy-chinned and worried dinner guests represented some 15 million bags, Manolo reported. They represented, too—he did not need to say it—the capital on which the island depended, and they were prepared to make extensive concessions. They agreed (as they had not in 1921) to accept quotas. This time, they would not demand that the mills that were subsidiaries of their refineries should be exempt from the common limitation. They also agreed that no company would further increase its mill capacity or clear new fields. But they insisted they must know without further delay what their quotas would be, and therefore, apparently trusting he would prove sympathetic to their interests, they agreed to petition Machado to bypass his wrangling commission. Higinio was appointed to draft the petition asking Cuba's president to assume sole power over the quotas, but the next day the swashbuckling corporation lawyer Thomas L. Chadbourne became alarmed that the U.S. sugar companies might be accused of violating the Sherman Antitrust Act and therefore rewrote Higinio's effort to guard against that possibility.[16]

Chadbourne was himself an investor in sugar as well as the head of a noted law firm that represented some 150 prominent corporations. In his midfifties, six foot seven inches in height, and nicknamed "the Viking," he had by his own offhand account met "Charlie" Hayden in Havana two years earlier while on a yachting cruise and had then purchased from Hayden a controlling interest in the central *España* (a heavily indebted venture that had been Pote's) for $1.75 million. A little later, he had joined with his brother, Waldemar, whose wife was Cuban, in acquiring the *Trinidad* for $350,000. In 1927, the two mills had produced a total of 500,000 bags.[17]

On February 23, the day following the petition, Machado set the allotments for each mill by proclamation. "Ya eso está del otro lado!" Rionda wrote. But it was not behind them, for instead of rigidly adhering to the 92.25 percent formula he had set, Machado's quotas varied. The American Sugar Refining Company received 98.2 percent of its preceding year's production, with *Manatí* (97 percent) and Cuban-American (95.3 percent) close behind. Yet the National City Bank's General Sugar Management Corporation received only 85.3 percent, its Cuban-Dominican Sugar Company only 81.3 percent. Cuba Cane's western plantations, most disastrously of all, were granted only 69.5 percent, its eastern plantations only 84 percent. Much, obviously, must have already happened behind the scenes. The American investors would not have turned details over to Machado without expecting their interests to be protected. Deals presumably had been cut and now were being betrayed.

Antonio Mendoza of the sprawling Mendoza family had lobbied for the American Sugar Refining Company. He had built *Cunagua* and *Jaronú* and was now their manager. "[E]vidently satisfied," Manolo had reported, "that he can exercise his personal influence with the Authorities, [he] had the audacity of claiming not less than 1.2 million bags of 340 lbs. for 'Cunagua' and 'Jaronú,' and an increase over last crop's figures for 'Senado' of 34,000 bags." A 340-pound bag would be, of course, 15 pounds heavier than the usual average.

Eduardo de Ulzurrún had likewise fought for *Manatí*. "He has had conferences with the President as well as with Barceló, Governor of Oriente," Manolo wrote, "and with Zayas Bazán, Secretary of the Interior. Yesterday evening, General Molinet called at don Eduardo's house to offer him 650,000 bags." "I think," he added, that

> the Executive Committee should know that if 'Manatí' secures for itself an amount in excess of the original allotment made by the Commission of 608,000 bags, such additional output is due en-

tirely to his efforts and to the personal influence that he has been able to exercise with the high authorities.... One of his arguments, for instance, was that in giving 'Delicias' more than 'Manatí,' the Government was favoring those who have, up to the present time, always opposed the Liberal party, whereas 'Manatí' had always been loyal to the extent that at one time even the life of the Manager was at stake.

But Manuel had opposed de Ulzurrún's request for even more. "I cannot at the same time," he wrote piously, "oppose injustice and favoritism and on the other hand claim larger quantities for any of our plantations.... To do so would be to place me in a position which my dignity does not permit."[18] The four Rionda family plantations had been granted 90.4 percent, 1.85 percent less than the 92.25 percent formula. This amounted to a loss of 22,156 bags, representing a potential loss of $252,135 if the price rose to 3.5 cents per pound.

The gross unfairness of Machado's allotments did not go unremarked on Wall Street. In Cuba Cane Executive Committee meetings, Manuel confronted resentment. He stood his ground, counseling the board to accept their treatment. The price of sugar had risen "and . . . if perchance [their protest] found its way to the press . . . it would disturb once more the confidence of the markets." The most important thing was price, not quantity. Rionda was, by these arguments, able to tone down a remonstrance, thus "making it appear that we were relying on Mr. Machado's integrity." But there was anger. Stetson of the Guaranty Trust "did not think the Company should stand idle . . . but, on the contrary, make some very strong protest, even thru Washington. This I told him would have a tremendous bad effect on the market . . . but Mr. S., like a good Southerner, kept on saying that such an injustice could not be tolerated." There was talk of Machado's corruption. Stetson reported that, when he had dined with George E. Keiser, Hawley's successor as president of Cuban-American, Keiser had "smiled at the treatment his own company had received."

"Someone stated," Manuel continued, "that it was rumored that the reason why some Companies received such good treatment was due to their having paid somebody $1 to $1.50 a bag." Manuel had denied this: "I said that I did not believe there was anything of that kind and that I did not know of anybody having paid anything. . . . It is unfortunate, however, that Cunagua and Jaronú and Cuban-American had such a good treatment accorded to them, while others received a bad deal. I am sorry for [Machado's] reputation. In the course of discussion I said that if they had had employed Mr. Vázquez Bello before, they probably would have had better treatment."[19]

There was sufficient indignation within the board to lead to a conclusion that John Foster Dulles, currently head of Sullivan & Cromwell, "should be given full particulars." On March 11, Dulles came to lunch with Manuel. "[I]f the restrictions had not taken place," Manuel told him, almost all of the companies "would have gone into the hands of the receivers." The restriction would assure sugar would sell at 3 cents or even 3.25 cents a pound, "and while I admitted that Cuba Cane, for instance, was penalized to the tune of 325/350,000 bags and in this it lost $3 a bag or $1,000,000, I was quite sure that, on the other hand, the restriction put the Company in much better financial condition."

A footnote is found in a cable from Manolo to his uncle, reporting that a meeting had been held in Havana at the request of Ambassador Crowder, who had asked American companies to send representatives and who stated Machado would listen to their arguments against unfair quotas. "Nothing whatever," however, had been accomplished, as Crowder spent all morning shut away in a private conference with Machado, while Cuba Cane's Gerard Smith and Punta Alegre's Douglas assured him that they had only attended as a courtesy to the ambassador.[20] The great North American companies, partly because of Rionda's urging, thus held their fire. For them to attempt to drive the Cuban mills out of business by cutthroat competition would unleash national and class hatreds on an island where bombs were already exploding.

At this juncture, action by the North American Atlantic coast refineries suggested an alternate approach. They, too, had once more overexpanded and were now being forced to grant concessions to their customers on an old-fashioned pre–Sugar Trust scale that made nominal prices meaningless. Forty years earlier, when there had been similar excess capacity, the senior Havemeyer had talked their predecessors into voluntarily joining to rationalize their industry, to the advantage of all participants. Now Havemeyer's successor was thinking along similar lines. Earl Babst, the neat man who had pioneered the packaging of crackers before advancing to a world perspective, had spent three months in the fall of 1926 circling the globe, visiting Germany and central Europe, where cartels were the accepted pattern. He had been, he was now reporting back, impressed by "the results obtained by cooperation." In Java, the Philippines, and Hawaii, too, he had found their sugar producers "as closely organized."[21]

Other refiners and their bankers listened with interest. Rionda reported that Rentschler had told him at lunch that Spreckels of the Federal Sugar Refining Company had invited Post of the National Sugar Refinery, Lowry, Babst, and representatives of the United Fruit Company to a luncheon "to see if some arrangement can be made whereby the refiners stop . . . making special discounts or rebates on the freights." The Riondas' McCahan refinery, Manuel agreed, "had lost about $50,000 up to now. The only way to make it up is by cooperation during the rest of the year."

Would not an approach along the same line also rationalize the Cuban cane fields? Attorney Chadbourne, at the end of March, had talked to Manuel about "a large merging corporation with all the American sugar companies in Cuba or the majority of them." In April, Rionda suggested to Hayden that Cuba Cane should join with Punta Alegre and, if possible, with Antilla. "By merging in this manner all the different interests would disappear and there would be a lesser number of men, and, consequently, a better way of coming to some arrangement in the operations as well as in the disposal of the sugar." The American companies could make their own internal arrangements, thus economizing on bribes to Machado's henchmen.[22]

Meanwhile, the quotas Machado had decreed were not drastic enough to bring lasting positive results. The year's highest price, $3^7/_{16}$ cents per pound was on January 4. But reversing the usual seasonal pattern, it then declined, to a July low of $2^{11}/_{16}$ cents. Cuba had cut production unilaterally by almost 500,000 tons, yet the world's other producers were simultaneously increasing their outputs, nullifying any benefit to Cuba from its self-sacrifice.[23] Given the tons of sugar unsold in Cuban warehouses, there was agreement both in New York and Havana that quotas would be necessary again the next year—only, hopefully, fairer ones. Rionda suggested that Hayden write Machado personally, reminding him of "the disappointment you had in the treatment received by Cuba Cane" and hoping that in 1928 "that injustice will be corrected."

"I am sure such a letter from you," he concluded, "will do more good than any appeal to the Secretary of State in Washington." Hayden's resulting communication was put into stately Spanish by the Riondas and stressed "el alto espíritu de justicia que resplandece en todos los actos de Ud. como gobernante" (the high spirit of justice which shines through all your acts as governor). Rionda also wrote Machado a week later. Cuba Cane, he claimed, deserved "aid and sympathy, since we must not forget that its incorporation signaled a new stage in Cuba's sugar industry." "It had been the first," he wrote, with an odd disregard for the facts,

> to bring foreign money into Cuba for the sugar industry. Until then, ingenios and colonos had lived poorly [lánguidamente], their lands without value and with planting and improvements scarcely imagined on the scale which Cuba Cane initiated. The Company contributed notably to the development and prosperity of extensive zones, hitherto unused, and distributed resources to numberless colonos, many of whom had been able to make and keep sizable fortunes.

He reminded Machado that the corporation's common shareholders had received no returns at all and the preferred shareholders none for years.[24]

With the businessmen of his own island as well as those of the United States pressing him to protect their interests, Machado turned to Rionda and Tarafa to draft a Cuban Sugar Restriction Law, which the Cuban Congress passed on October 3, 1927, at a night session. Also known as the Tarafa Law, it would apply to the next six crops and authorized the president to appoint a permanent, five-member Cuban Sugar Defense Committee to advise him, its members serving at his sole discretion. It also established the Cuba Sugar Export Corporation, with an authorized 25,000 shares to be distributed among the owners and lessees of the mills in proportion to the number of bags each manufactured, with these owners passing on a proportionate number of shares to their colonos. The Export Corporation (whose officers and members would be elected by its shareholders) would have no jurisdiction over sales to the United States, but it alone would be authorized to sell or otherwise dispose of all the sugar the United States did not purchase.[25]

Colonel Tarafa was made chair of the Defense Committee, with Jacinto Pedroso, General Eugenio Molinet, Dr. Viriato Gutiérrez, and Aurelio Portuondo as the other members. All were from the interwoven Cuban hacendado aristocracy, mill owners themselves and active in Machado politics. Pedroso, of an old merchant banking family, had recently participated in Menocal's *Santa Marta* venture. Molinet, close friend of Menocal and his replacement as administrator of Cuban-American's *Chaparra*, was, Manuel had assured Portuondo, "un buen amigo" who would be "siempre... fiel" to the Rionda interests. Gutiérrez was Laureano Falla Gutiérrez's son-in-law, while Portuondo was Higinio Fanjul's associate in the Cuban Trading Company. Rionda had written Hayden he would try "to have Mr. Portuondo, whom you know and who is very close to President Machado in everything pertaining to sugar, be one of the five members of the Commission. Mr. Portuondo can be more useful to us in everything concerning sugar than any other man I know—be he lawyer, merchant or even Banker."[26]

Tarafa promptly took to the road, mounted on a high horse of enthusiasm at the prospects of his power, dashing off long letters to Rionda from all over Cuba about his conferences with local officials. He rounded up predictions for the future crop, stared out of train windows to evaluate the cane fields as they passed, lunched at the presidential palace, and headed to Santo Domingo to discuss possible crop limitations there as well, his enthusiasm not checked but extended and encouraged by Machado.[27]

Cuba's next step, Tarafa decided, must be to think in worldwide terms, to recognize that Cuban restrictions on its own crops alone were insufficient to check a surplus that was engulfing them all. In Java, in one year, production had risen more than 630,000 tons. European beet estimates indicated "additional plantings of 500,000 tons." English beet sugar had risen over 100,000 tons in a year "due to the protection and bounty of 5.83 cents per pound" recently granted English farmers by the statesmen of empire. Philippine production was up some 126,000 tons. There was revolution in China and financial crisis in Japan to cut Asian demand, so the export of Cuban sugar to the East, 200,000 tons in 1926, dropped to 90,000 tons, while more Java stocks sailed west of the Suez Canal in search of an alternate market. Only bad weather conditions had checked further Hawaiian and Puerto Rican production. Cuba, the colonel believed, must take the lead in stabilizing conditions by convincing other countries to support worldwide restrictions on production and export. In October, Machado authorized him "to enter into negotiations with the sugar producers in Germany, Poland, Czechoslovakia and Holland (the latter country in connection with the Javas)." Tarafa packed his bags for Paris.[28]

As he was packing and just before Cuba's selling corporation came legally into existence, Czarnikow-Rionda's competitor, Galbán, Lobo y Cía, sold 150,000 tons of leftover Cuban sugar to Tate and Lyle in England. The Lobo firm, with its office on narrow San Ignacio Street in old Havana, had long been a thorn in Manuel's side. Heriberto Lobo, a refugee from a turn-of-the-century Venezuelan revolution, had taken over from Luis Galbán and been recently joined by his son, Julio Lobo Olavarría, born in 1898, who had just graduated from Louisiana State as a sugar engineer and who, aged twenty-one, took over the firm's sugar trading. Julio was tough, a gambler in the market to equal Bernardo Braga.

The sale to Tate and Lyle was a $6 million deal, reputedly the world's biggest private sugar transaction to date. For the Riondas, it came as a thunderclap. Manuel told Horatio Rubens that he had had offers of 12/3 shillings from London, which he had declined "believing it impossible to sell anything until the Export Company had been organized." In the sugar trade there was some consternation at the low price. But while a mere 11s. 7½d. CIF per pound (equivalent to 2.34 cents FOB) was, in Willett and Gray's word, "puzzling" (a full 12 shillings might have been expected), there was a general feeling it was healthier for the market to have Cuba's leftover supply thus finally disposed of and only "an amount now available barely sufficient for United States' wants" left on hand.

Czarnikow-Rionda had lost a handsome commission and been humiliated in the eyes of the trade. Further, according to Manuel, Tarafa had told Manolo "that he did not want to inform me of the sale because in Cuba it was presumed that we were short on the Exchange" and that Manuel "not having been a success in the Sugar Finance Committee should not be given a chance of selling for the Export Corporation." When Tarafa stopped over in New York on his way to Europe, there was, once again, a violent break between the two men. "I told him," Rionda noted, that "although he was 55 and I 74, never again would he betray me ["nunca más me sería infiel"]."²⁹

To make matters worse, the founding meeting of the Sugar Export Corporation, held on Wall Street as soon as Tarafa reached New York, chose the colonel to be its president, ignoring Manuel's wishes. Manuel had instructed Manolo to inform Albert Strauss and Charles Hayden of his disapproval, but neither Strauss nor Hayden had been "available," nor had Manolo been able to communicate his uncle's wishes to Cuban-American, General Sugar, Cuban-Dominican, or Punta Alegre.³⁰

But when Tarafa returned to Manhattan from his Paris conference at the end of December—having received promises from the mighty representatives of the other sugar-exporting countries of a further meeting the next year along with fulsome, if not concrete, letters from such associations as the Vereenigde Javasuiker Producten and the Hungarian Sugar Manufacturers—Rionda, surrendering, sent his limousine and chauffeur to the Ritz-Carlton to fetch him to a luncheon in his honor at the Downtown Club, at which eleven great banks and sugar companies were represented. Tarafa, Manuel said in introducing him to the assemblage, had gone into the lion's den and done in Europe what no other man could have. Later, in a private meeting in Manuel's office, Tarafa had tears in his eyes when he denied he had ever been unfaithful to Manuel. Matters were too desperate for them to hold grudges against each other.

At the Downtown Club luncheon, the National City Bank and its General Sugar Company had been conspicuously unrepresented. Instead, Tarafa reported, Charles Mitchell and Rentschler had met with him alone for three hours the night before. They did not, they told him, agree with restricting Cuban production, blamed his earlier Tarafa Law for denying their mills their own ports, and asked him, as they had earlier asked Rionda himself, to ensure them a larger quota. This, Tarafa said, had greatly disheartened ("descorazonado") him, because it showed that they thought only of their own personal interests and favored the "survival of the fittest" in order to destroy ("matar") the hacendados in the western provinces to benefit their eastern mills.³¹

In 1927, Czarnikow-Rionda once more succeeded in selling Cuba Cane's sugar at a slightly better price than the island average. The corporation's operating profit for the year reached $5,275,599, more than twice what it had been the year before, and its indebtedness was reduced by more than $500,000 to $519,100. The colonos were also able to pay off $1,778,710 of their debts. Despite the unfair quota it had received, the overall decrease in Cuban production had brought benefits for the company.

Nevertheless, Cuba Cane's annual report admitted that 1927 had been "difficult." Because of crop limitations, less than two-thirds of its cane had been cut. Unit costs had thus increased, leaving it an operating profit of only a third of a cent per pound, while at the end of the fiscal year it still held a stock of unsold sugar worth (hopefully) $2,779,626.

The Riondas had played a conciliating role with both sides, stressing to men of two countries the usefulness of their mutual cooperation. Yet they were still suspect to both sides. The North Americans remembered Manuel's touchy Old World pride, his rival mills, his sympathy for his Spanish-speaking compatriots. The Cubans knew that the Riondas spent most of their time on Manhattan and (logically enough) still blamed Manuel for having accepted too low a price for their sugar during World War I. They also knew the clan had turned dazzling middleman's profits during the good years. They remembered Manuel's responsibility for 1921's Sugar Finance Commission maneuver that had granted such special advantage to the U.S. refineries. Thus neither Wall Street nor the hacendados were convinced of the clan's disinterestedness. Besides, Manuel was growing older, Bernardo was more and more consumed by his skillful but hairbreadth operations in the futures market, Manolo was competent but overshadowed by his uncle, and Higinio was only beginning to emerge as a force in his own right.

For one more year, Machado held to a policy of limited production. This time the cut islandwide was 11.3 percent, considerably more than 1927's 7.5 percent and also compounded by the fact that it was calculated on a base of 1927's reduced output.

Once again there were deviations from the average. Westernmost Piñar del Rio, with only ten small mills, was cut 24.2 percent, while in the East, where the giant operations clustered, Camagüey was cut only 7.6 percent and Oriente 10.6 percent. On the island as a whole, the sixty-one small mills producing fewer than 100,000 bags suffered most, cut on average 18.5 percent; the eighty-eight medium-sized mills (between 100,000 and 300,000) were cut 12.8 percent; the twenty-seven giants (over 300,000) only 7 percent. But if the smaller hacendados thought that they had been targeted to placate the northern capitalists, neither were those capitalists themselves satisfied. The American Sugar Refining Company's *Cunagua* and *Jaronú* averaged a 2.4 percent *increase* over the preceding year, while the Hershey Company, which in 1927 had been generously handled, was now cut 16.7 percent. Cuba Cane this time was favored over Cuban-American, while both (cut 6.6 and 9.9 percent, respectively) were under the stipulated average. As for the Hispanic bourgeoisie, the Gutiérrez-Castaño interests suffered a 12.2 percent reduction. The Rionda mills (except for *Manatí*, for which de Ulzurrún again bargained) were down 12.7 percent; Tarafa's *Cuba* was down 17.5 percent. The three Gómez Mena mills were cut 24 percent. In the face of so much apparent favoritism, with only fractional improvements in price, no one was surprised when Machado told the Cuban legislature in April that "the time has come when other means must be employed."[32]

Reluctantly, still arguing that only a cut in production would save the situation, Manuel consoled himself that 1929 would be merely a year's hiatus and that no planter could in 1929 harvest much more than 10 percent above the previous year, since almost nothing had been done in Cuba to care for the fields. But he believed more than one year without limits would be a disaster. In earlier days, secure in his personal influence, he had written scornfully that only the "lame ducks" need work together. "Would it not be better," he wrote Leandro, "for all Cuban planters to come together and agree on a program of plantings for 1929/30 than for each one . . . to go by himself, battling along and increasing his plantings."[33]

August was a month of defeats for Rionda. Czarnikow-Rionda's rival Galbán, Lobo for the second time ignored the Export Corporation and sold a consignment of sugar directly for overseas delivery. "There came vividly to my mind," Manuel wrote Portuondo, "the first blows that finally threw down that Sugar Finance Committee that we administered with so much ardor, enthusiasm, liberality and honesty in the memorable year 1921. Now I hear the bells tolling the burial of the Export Corporation unless General Machado works more energetically than his predecessor. . . . Now they know in London . . . they need not respect the Export Corporation. Now its reputation is lost. . . . Poor Cuba, poor hacendados. This old man sees only *egoismos, chismes, desengaños* [egotism, misrepresentations, reproaches]." Gloomily, he continued, "We had best stay home and attend to our own affairs. A river in flood profits the fishermen. None know better how to fish than MR, MER and BBR. If we now trust ourselves into Machado's hands, may God save us."[34]

In August, his influence in Cuba Cane was still further diminished. Since Ogilvie's resignation, Charles Hayden had been acting head. A hasty man with a multiplicity of other interests—mines in South Africa, for instance—he had been willing, in the abbreviated intervals when he concentrated on sugar, to listen to Rionda in matters pertaining to Cuba's politics and policies. But now a new, full-time (and authoritative) president took control of Cuba Cane.

John Roy Simpson was fifty-two. Born in Ohio in 1876 into a Presbyterian clergyman's family, he had worked his way up through various miscellaneous companies, Western Electric in Chicago and St. Louis, then Filene's department store in Boston. In 1917, he had gone off to the war in U.S. Army Ordnance. Returning a colonel, he had been a vice president in the Consolidated Oil Corporation for nine years. He was thus presumably effective in a business setting, almost any business setting, and not handicapped as Rionda was by a lifetime's devotion to one product. His picture shows him thin-lipped, with a starched collar and spectacles. Almost at once, he brushed aside Manuel and Manuel's belief in limiting production, informing Hayden that he had discussed a new Cuban policy with Rentschler of the National City Bank, Douglas of Punta Alegre, and Noble of the Royal Bank of Canada. Under Rentschler's lead, they were petitioning Machado that the sugar industry "be set free to rehabilitate itself along economic lines, and that the government adopt and strictly adhere to a policy of non-interference." He continued: "Because of my unfamiliarity with the Cuban political situation and my present lack of any acquaintance with President Machado ["My present lack"; he did not, apparently, intend that to go long unremedied] I do not consider myself in position to express any intelligent opinion as to the time at which this memorandum should be presented to him or the method of presenting it." In timing, in method, he would take direction. Not, it would seem, in content. He went briskly on. "As I am leaving for Cuba tomorrow, I shall have no opportunity to talk with you about the matter . . . therefore, I am sending the memorandum to you with the definite recommendation that I be authorized to sign it on behalf of the Cuba Cane Sugar Corporation provided Messrs. Rentschler, Douglas and Noble take similar action." If, he added, Hayden thought it necessary to consult Cuba Cane's Executive Committee, Rentschler would discuss the matter with Stetson. "I am very much interested," he concluded, "in this first attempt of the big companies to present a united front on matters of important policy."[35]

Rionda, according to his own account, did not see Rentschler's petition until almost two weeks after Simpson had reported the project under way. All that he could do then was to refuse to sign, which he did in a letter dated August 16. Conceding the end of crop limitation was politically inevitable, he strongly objected to the North American proposal to liquidate the Cuban Export Corporation as well. All the American industries, he pointed out, including U.S. Steel and the copper companies, wanted export committees to sell their surplus production to foreign countries. But when Cuba set up a mechanism so that everyone, "large and small, Cuban and American," furnished "his rightful share," the American companies wished to abolish it.

Throughout Manuel's letter was anger that he had not been consulted or even informed. The companies' ultimatum had been shown him only because the Riondas had happened to hear of it at a meeting about something else. "I regret," he concluded, "that I did not have an opportunity to present my views on this matter at an earlier stage and before the conclusions of those who signed the letter to General Machado had hardened to the extent to which they now seem to have done."[36]

The Cuban sugar magnates, strained and disagreeing, consulted among themselves. From the presidential palace, where he now served as Machado's confidential secretary, Viriato Gutiérrez sent Manuel a five-page communication that he had received from José Gómez Mena as well as an anonymous nine-page comment upon it. He requested Manuel's opinion "as to what should be the modus operandi which, without going contrary to the immutable laws of commerce, would justify the continuation of the Export Corporation." The problem, he noted, was whether to continue the Export Corporation only for sales outside the United States or whether to extend its authority to include all sales to the States as well.

Gómez Mena wrote that he was ready to give up on the quotas. They had been, he wrote, "absolutely necessary as long as it was a question of saving the interests of the smaller mills established for generations." He himself had been "one of the first in favor." But restrictions had not brought higher prices, and "we cannot produce cheaply without turning out large quantities of sugar per mill." The smaller producers would have to be abandoned to their fate and the stronger survivors do joint battle against the North American refineries. Prices had not advanced, he commented, largely because the refineries owned mills of their own. "The refiners do not need to buy sugar because it is being constantly furnished to them." All sales, including those to the United States (even those by U.S. companies to their own refineries), must be "controlled by one single seller."

The author of Viriato's other enclosure (who may well have been Viriato himself) was less courageous. The United States was Cuba's best customer. Cuba must not "wage an open war on the American refiners" but "comply with [their] wishes."

Rionda's comments ran to thirty-four pages. Soon, Cuba would have some 5 million tons to sell. The United States could not "consume more than 3 million tons," leaving therefore a "colossal" 2 million tons that must be sold elsewhere. Cuba's unilateral cuts, he argued, were not to blame for the rise in production worldwide. Hawaii, Java, and the Philippines had found a better variety of cane. The Puerto Ricans had eradicated the mosaic disease. U.S. beet producers had enjoyed good weather. England had granted "an enormous subsidy" to its domestic beet growers, "costing Cuba an outlet there for possibly 250,000 tons, but that had been an effort to solve her unemployment problem, not a reaction to Cuban policy."

The real problem had been the U.S. tariff. "Instead of trying to better our situation in the United States, making them cut the tariff to what it was when the Reciprocity Treaty was made, we . . . complain that world crops have increased and that the refiner is strangling us." They must "approach Washington." But to deny North American companies the right to export to their own refineries "should not even be thought of." It would place Cuba "in conflict" with the United States. Washington would never accept Gómez Mena's "single seller." "These gentlemen—

although they are ready to consider methods of that kind when it comes to their own product—are not willing to compromise with countries that want to impose them."

Why had Cuba "marched with gigantic strides towards the production of 6,000,000 tons" when the United States had offered a "market for only half that quantity[?] . . . We made clothes without anticipating who was going to wear them. Nobody is a greater sinner in that respect than the author of these lines."

In the United States, he observed, there was talk of the Republicans creating "an organization for the purpose of buying the crops of American farmers and selling these commodities or rather the over-production, to foreign countries. . . . There are others who claim that the Treasury Department of the United States should buy over-production, store it and keep it in store until there is a good market for it." If, in the United States itself, there was talk of forming such companies, "why should we in Cuba destroy what we have built up?"

Bitterly, he turned to another theme. "[L]et us produce as much as the Good Lord will permit us, and let everyone save himself who can." There seemed nothing to do but to give up on the smaller Cuban producers. The major Cuban mills were helpless if the weakest ones spoiled their market.

His letter had reached its twenty-ninth page. Each point had been stressed more than once. He began to subside into a tired realism. "Turn where we may, our only salvation lies in lowering the cost of production. To do this we must learn from our neighbors in Porto Rico, Hawaii and especially in Java, by planting better cane, producing more cane per caballería, not planting lands which are not good for cane and stop the use of fertilizer that costs more than the cane." And again, "Let us discard the theory that sugar should be worth 3 cents. . . . Let us prepare with better cultivation and better cane to produce sugar at 2 cents." A long, repetitious letter.[37]

Tarafa weighed in as well, still standing foursquare behind his crusade, cabling that Cubans must make "the inevitable reduction . . . in a methodic manner." Otherwise, it would come, willy-nilly, "in a violent and ruinous form. . . . The good or harm of no restriction which means life for the strong and the fall of the weak we shall see once restriction is abandoned." The Export Corporation must be preserved "as the most efficacious organism for the defense of Cuban sugars in the world market." Rionda and Tarafa won at least a partial victory, since Machado, although surrendering to his own bourgeoisie as well as to pressure from New York by removing all restrictions on production, allowed the Export Corporation to remain in existence, if dormant.[38]

Meanwhile, other trouble was brewing. While the mill owners argued, their colonos again grew restive. A year earlier, thirty-two colonos from Cuba Cane's Eastern Cuba subsidiary had appealed to Gerard Smith, describing their "desperate situation." The eastern mills, they complained, favoring administration cane, had ground only between 28 and 50 percent of what they had grown, although production had theoretically been limited by less than 10 percent. Furthermore, the corporation was attempting "to collect the full amount of the large rentals collected by it . . . on land the cane from which has not been ground."

Smith sent their letter on to Hayden, who passed it on to Rionda. It was the kind of annoyance where the New Yorkers still sought Rionda's advice. He agreed it would set a dangerous precedent for the colonos to learn that their communication was being passed on to Cuba Cane's top people, for then "you would be flooded with similar ones." But the colonos' complaint must be acknowledged. They do not seem "either purposely or through ignorance . . . to grasp that our Company . . . was unjustly treated. . . . But in reality I do not think we should collect rents on lands the cane of which was not cut."[39]

The colono situation festered. Almost a year later, Manuel wrote a memorandum to Manolo concerning Pedro Pelegrin, Cuba Cane's largest colono in the east. He had, despite his contracts with Eastern Cuba, sold some of his cane to the American Sugar Refining Company's adjacent *Cunagua* and *Jaronú*.

> Gerard himself admits that Pelegrin only ground 64 percent of his cane in 1926/1927 and 40 percent last year. Therefore, Pelegrin's situation must be desperate. Of course, Pelegrin has no right to sell his cane, but, on the other hand, it must be awfully tantalizing to any one who has cane, to see it left standing in the fields . . . and yet have a man next door ready to buy it. . . .

> I don't like Gerard's idea that we were neither morally nor legally responsible. . . . It is unfortunate that [Pelegrin] has consulted Ferrara.

Manuel's attention now focused on Washington and the tariff. Cuba should approach the "beet people" in the States to see if they could not make common cause against the free entry of Philippine sugar as soon as the 1928 U.S. elections were held.[40]

9

Receivership and Reorganization

In Cuba, after three years of quotas, the 1929 harvest was unrestricted. In the mills, the machines, their promised economies finally tested, thundered day and night. Yet bankers, hacendados, and colonos alike watched the laden carts with apprehension. How low must the price go to attract buyers for it all?

An "exclusive selling agency" to handle future sales of sugar outside the United States was proposed to a special meeting of hacendados in Havana, but it was voted down three to one, with its defeat attributed to "the Cuban native mill owners." A voluntary Joint Foreign Sales Syndicate for "cooperative selling in Europe" was then organized in New York by the U.S. companies. Manuel remained discreetly in the background, cabling Portuondo, "we never wish to appear as leaders in any movement," but he was put in charge, supervised by a committee composed of Charles Hayden, Eugene Thayer of Punta Alegre, and E. A. Deeds of the National City Bank. He received a reward of sorts, since he was also entrusted with selling the General Sugar Company's production, which, with its 0.5 percent commission, should yield Czarnikow-Rionda almost $80,000.[1]

Few Cuban growers agreed to participate in the New York syndicate. When Gómez Mena in April did decide to do so, Manuel wired his joy that "el elemento americano y el cubano" might no longer be completely isolated from each other, but his hope was not fulfilled while Galbán, Lobo was rumored to be making a rival Cuban "pool" to compete abroad. By April, Manuel had successfully disposed of some 600,000 tons overseas out of the 850,000 tons entrusted to the syndicate. This was helpful but not sufficient.[2]

In March, President Hoover had been sworn into office. While prosperity was soaring in America's factories and financial markets, the good times of the 1920s had never reached the agricultural South and West, and Hoover could not ignore their poverty. Even as Cuba's unlimited zafra raced to its conclusion, a proposal to increase the duty on sugar, this time from 1.76 cents to 2.40 cents a pound, easily passed the House of Representatives and was sent on to the Senate, where lobbyists from the American Farm Bureau Federation and the Grange waited in the corridors.

Cuba's only hope seemed an appeal to agriculture's self-interest. Manuel remembered how, in 1921, Hoover, then secretary of commerce, had arranged for him to meet with the remolacheros. The beet men had at that time proposed that Cuba cut production to 2 million tons, in return for which they agreed they would cease their current campaign for a higher tariff. Manuel had been ready to surrender. It had been Hoover who, after a discussion with the New York bankers, had dismissed the possibility, recognizing that the banks needed to safeguard their heavy advances against sugar. Now, eight years later, the banks had realized or written off their loans, and Rionda had a new, stronger argument. Neither domestic beet nor Cuban production had risen appreciably since the war, but America's dependent islands had more than doubled their output (from 1,100,834 to 2,453,409 short tons). Thus he could point out that they, not Cuba, were to blame for falling prices.[3] Since sugar from Puerto Rico, Hawaii, and the Philippines entered duty free, a higher tariff would do nothing to check the flood of imports from those islands. Manuel suggested that Cuba should agree to limit its exports to the United States if Senator Smoot and the domestic beet and cane forces would turn their attention to their real competition in their own colonies.

But the Cuban Trading Company and the Riondas, Manuel wrote, should not elaborate any such proposal as their own. It must seem to come from the hacendados themselves. When Higinio called upon Machado, he should do so in company with other important planters, especially some from Santa Clara.

Although various illnesses often kept him away from his office, Rionda went on that summer attending meetings of the Cuba Cane Executive Committee. The committee was changing, those who had founded the company in 1916 dropping away. Alfred Jaretzki, the wily strategist of Sullivan & Cromwell whom Rionda blamed for the Goethals imbroglio, had died in 1925, although the law firm now employed his son, Alfred Jr. Albert Strauss, long Rionda's best ally, became too ill to attend meetings and died in March, while his brother Frederick's mustache was turning white and Earle Bailie, a younger Seligman partner, was being groomed to replace him. The ever-bullish but loyal James Jarvie, although he faithfully attended, was obviously failing. Walter Ogilvie, who would serve as a director of ITT until 1954 and live to be ninety-two, had withdrawn from his directorship in January 1929 because of "some organic heart trouble," arranging that, because of all the stock he owned, his son, George, should replace him on the board. Eugene Stetson of Guaranty Trust and Charles Hayden remained as the key men, with John Simpson as president very much in charge. Hayden presided over executive meetings, and Rionda reported himself as speaking up only when his opinion was sought.[4]

In Cuba itself, the distance between the Riondas and the management of Cuba Cane is reflected in a long report from Manolo from an inspection tour through Cuba. The tour (which had included a visit to the deathbed of Falla Gutiérrez), had begun with a stop at Tarafa's *Central Cuba*, which greatly impressed Manolo. Practically all Tarafa's cane fields were "absolutely free of all grass, which seems to be the result of years of very careful cultivation," there were experiment stations testing cane varieties, a good irrigation system was being extended, and the sugar house was "probably the most modern one in Cuba." Tarafa was in the midst of a drawn-out controversy between his Consolidated Railroads and Cuba Cane over whether Cuba Cane's private rail line could cross Consolidated's main line at Quesada and whether the corporation's use of the Palo Alto port to ship the sugars of *Morón*, *Violeta*, and *Velasco* violated the Tarafa Law. While Manolo was apparently unconvinced by Tarafa's arguments, writing that "throughout this tirade . . . Aurelio and I merely listened," he relayed them to Simpson, with whom he had a friendly conversation at *Mercedes*, Simpson passing on the information that the investment banking firm of Brown Brothers had, in the last few months, accumulated some 40,000 shares of Cuba Cane preferred stock. Manolo promised that Portuondo would inform Simpson whatever "information or gossip" he might hear relative to the corporation, and Simpson, in turn, "said that from several sources in Cuba he had learned that our firm was giving out very bearish information as to the market . . . ; that he felt that owing to his friendship towards us it was his duty to give me this information." Simpson's warning against pessimism could not have deterred the Riondas, for when Manuel and Manolo lunched with Charles Hayden on Manolo's return north, Manuel warned the banker that the market would probably drop to 1.7 cents per pound.

Yet if the Riondas were pessimistic, costs of production were falling. The island, Bernardo wrote London, had "her back to the wall," but Cuba would "show the world that she can not be pushed out of the earth, even by her father-in-law, the U.S.A." and Manuel tried to cheer his correspondents by recounting savings in fields and mills: "[J]ust now we do it by sacrificing the colonos and the common laborer, and also throwing away the amounts the colonos owe us. But we are bettering our cane seed, introducing new methods of cultivation, etc., all of which in the long run will make the colonos able to sell their cane at present prices and make money. This may take place in the course of 5/6 years . . . ! [Cuba] will give a very good account of herself in spite of tariffs and petty jealousies."

Yet the day was less than a year in the future when Cuba Cane must pay $25 million to redeem the bonds that would fall due on January 1, 1930. At the February 18 luncheon, Hayden proposed to Manuel and Manolo that the corporation repay the bondholders by selling off the six more profitable eastern mills. This would leave Cuba Cane's stockholders with only the five older western mills, but they would no longer be weighed down by debt.

Rionda thought the plan would not leave the stockholders with much, but "certainly Eastern Cuba will then be very excellent properties with 3 million bags and only $8.5 million in bonds." Two days later, he gave Frederick Strauss an order to buy "up to $100,000 on [Cuba Cane bonds], anywhere between 71/75 9-good until canceled."[5] But refinancing dragged, and by early May, when Cuba Cane's current balance was down from $9,630,000 the previous year to only $6,284,000 and when sugar was at 1⅞ cents a pound, Hayden gave up on his plan as "impossible to carry out," for it had been premised on sugar selling at 2¼ cents." He commented: "Mr. Hayden said that one thing was to finance such industries as railroads in the United States when real earning power could be shown, and another to deal with bond holders in an industry which is not showing any profits whatsoever.... In the course of his remarks he mentioned that he personally had 25,000 shares of the preferred stock... for which he had paid $54 a share."

Rionda complained that, to Hayden, the manipulations of refinancing seemed a kind of game. The financier was playing, he wrote a little later, "the DEVIL on a subject so much to our heart, to such an extent that he absolutely seemed to have no consideration." He was "like a boy going to a base-ball game, without realizing how others feel."

Cuba Cane was not the only sugar company in trouble. Hayden thought that Punta Alegre was in many ways worse off, while *Manatí* badly needed short-term loans, and Manuel lashed out against "the torture of getting money from banks under present circumstances."[6]

Unquestionably, something had to be done. Tarafa was appointed Machado's "confidential delegate" in Washington to confer with President Hoover, Senator Smoot, and representatives of the domestic sugar industry, with Machado's promise that if the Senate voted a "reasonable" 2.5 cent duty that also provided a 30 percent preferential (thus setting the actual duty Cuba would pay at 1.75 cents), Machado would decree a "Single Seller," which, by limiting sales, would protect the North American domestic beet and cane interests from Cuban competition. Machado also promised that if other countries cooperated internationally, he would sternly limit the entire 1930 Cuban crop. Tarafa's task was to convince the U.S. domestic industry and also the rest of the world that Cuban sugar "would work with them in dividing the market." In this cause, he visited as far afield as Denver and Kansas City. Deeds, who had his own lobbyists in Washington and knew that limiting General Sugar's production would cost the National City Bank heavily, was displeased at Tarafa's mission. Rionda, not wishing to be caught in the crossfire, used the Washington heat as an excuse not to come to the Capitol to meet the colonel. In his New York office, however, he brought together Petrikin and W. D. Lippitt of the Great Western Sugar Company with Deeds and Simpson, and was informed when Petrikin and Lippitt, on their way back to Denver, consulted with General Crowder in Chicago where Crowder, upon his retirement as ambassador, had established a law office. With only "life savings of $16,000" and an army pension of $6,000 a year, Crowder was receiving a $12,000 annual retainer from "Cuban Planters' companies which included Gómez Mena and Tarafa interests," with lesser retainer fees from Cuban-Dominican, Lowry and Company, Cuba Cane, and United Fruit.[7]

Meanwhile, Machado appointed Viriato Gutiérrez, now a senator, as Cuba's representative to an international sugar conference to be held at Geneva on June 21. By the recent death of his father-in-law, Viriato represented six viable mills, four of them in Santa Clara, two in Camagüey. Collectively, they had produced 1,057,068 bags in 1929, a number comparable to the United Fruit Company's 1,801,276 or the American Sugar Refining Company's 1,346,496. A lawyer by profession, he was part of a politically active clan that included David Suero, Falla Gutiérrez's other son-in-law; Laureano's nephew Ricardo Cervera Falla; and Laureano's brother, Juan. Castaño's other daughters had also brought Rogelio Díaz Pardo (a member of the Cuban legislature) and Albert Betancourt into his immediate circle. In addition, there was Domingo Nazabal, Castaño's nephew.

When the midsummer congressional recess began in the United States with nothing accomplished, Tarafa, too, left for Switzerland. Gutiérrez was not enthusiastic over his arrival, while the Europeans were confused as to which of the pair spoke for Cuba. Despite both men, nothing concrete came of the international meeting, and Java's producers remained aloof and (although they were Dutch) were reported as inscrutable.[8]

Meanwhile, the colonos of Cuba Cane had formed an association of their own. At its late May meeting, many complained that the National City Bank's Havana branch had denied them financing, although they had strictly observed all their past obligations. Manuel sadly commented that, given the present situation, the banks could scarcely be blamed for not wishing to lose more money.[9]

By July 1, Hayden arranged for the Guaranty and Chase banks to put up half of the $2.5 million Cuba Cane required to meet interest due on its bonds, with Hayden, Stone and Company; Jarvie; Seligmans; and Czarnikow-Rionda dividing the balance.

Jarvie, who was seventy-five, came around a few days later to say goodbye to Manuel. He was leaving for England on a golfing trip, sailing (he was long a widower) with his three nephews. Manuel thought "the old man was sorry to go away and leave me alone in the battle," and they talked a while, agreeing "we should not hang up our fate with the refiners." A week later news came that Jarvie had died at sea. His nephew, Harry Worcester, who was in charge of the United Fruit Company's sugar operations, was, at Manuel's suggestion, chosen to replace him on the Cuba Cane board. "Ya, soy el único que queda de los antiguos," Manuel wrote. Now I am the only one who remains of the old men.[10]

On June 19, the Cuba Cane executive discussed where to borrow the $6.3 million that would be needed by September 1 to carry the plantations through the dead season. Net earnings for fiscal year 1929 would be only about $3 million, whereas annual interest charges on the present funded debt alone were about $2.6 million and annual depreciation approximately $1.75 million. In addition, unpaid dividend accumulations on the preferred stock amounted to $28,850,000. Reorganization could no longer be postponed, and committees were organized to represent the corporation's creditors and its debenture holders while Hayden headed the Reorganization Committee. On July 25, he announced a revised plan of reorganization. Stock and debenture holders were requested to give their approval by depositing their holdings by August 20.

Under the proposed plan, a new company would extend the maturing debt and reduce compulsory fixed-interest charges. It would also raise $4.5 million in cash through capital stock offered first to the present stockholders, while the bondholders would receive new bonds plus stock. The Eastern Cuba Sugar Corporation would remain a fully owned subsidiary. The voting power of the former common stockholders would thus be considerably diluted and that of the preferred stockholders proportionately increased.

But could the new stock be sold? In late July 1929, when Hayden announced the plan, the great bull market was soaring ever higher, yet optimism on Wall Street did not extend to Cuba Cane, whose common stock had fallen from $20 per share in 1923 to a current $3 and whose preferred stock dropped from $71.37 to $11 per share. Nevertheless, for those who did stick it out, the new company would be free of some of the old debt, and the sums owed by the colonos and the value of the aging machines discounted to more realistic levels.[11]

The sheer quantity of sugar Cuba produced that unchecked 1929 harvest was frightening. On the one hand, it showed the fertility of the fields, the strength of the workers, and the capacity of the voracious machines.

Yet economies of scale did not balance a glut on the market. The total value of the 1929 crop would go up, but barely. In 1928, with the crop limited to 4 million tons, an average of 2.18 cents per pound had brought in $197,733,841. In unlimited 1929, over 5 million tons would fetch 1.72 cents a pound on average, totaling $198,661,078. A rise of, to be precise, 27.6 percent in production would yield scarcely 0.5 percent more in income, while a larger harvest had meant more expense and hence the need for even greater advances to meet payrolls, shipping costs, warehousing costs, and all the rest. As the zafra ended, the belief was confirmed that a revived export agency, or a single seller, or both, or something, or anything must be tried once more.[12]

Machado was facing rising nationalistic political rhetoric and moved to counter it. On July 20, 1929, banner headlines on the *Diario de la Marina*'s front page proclaimed his Executive Decree 1224, approving Tarafa's proposal for the immediate creation of a single seller to be known as the Cuban Cooperative Export Agency. A large picture of Machado and a smaller one of Tarafa showed the two leaders, smooth-shaven, with fleshy, worried faces, curiously alike except for Machado's heavy spectacles and the downward thrust of Tarafa's lips. Limiting the amount of sugar Cuba exported, Tarafa's statement explained, was the only way to convince the American beetgrowers and the Louisiana cane farmers that Cuba would not threaten them. The way to world cooperation would be smoothed. "More Work and Better Pay for Sugar Workers" ran a subhead. The sugar problem, it promised, would not be solved at the expense of the workers.

In inner circle correspondence, Manuel expressed concern about various concrete details of the new agency's organization. He inquired of Higinio why the Pennsylvanian Milton Hershey (who had acquired three mills in Havana Province to sweeten his famous chocolate bars) should have been suggested as a vice president and not Portuondo. There seemed a predisposition, he cabled Aurelio, to eliminate mercantile groups, especially Czarnikow-Rionda, when their expertise would be most valuable. When Simpson proposed Salvador Rionda as a director, his uncle opposed it, rejecting any family participation. He would relent shortly, writing he might consider the appointment if it could be seen as suggested by Machado himself, not by the North American Simpson.

Manuel carefully checked the agency's rules. Contracts already made posed countless problems, as they had in 1920. The United Fruit's *Preston* and *Boston* mills had signed a ten-year contract to sell their sugar to United Fruit's Revere Refinery in Boston, while the American Sugar Refining Company had done likewise with its *Jaronú* and *Cunagua*. If these must be accepted as by-products of vertical expansion, they would still skim off a portion of the American market. American Sugar's five U.S. refineries processed 1,250,000 long tons of raw sugar annually, while its two Cuban plantations produced fewer than 200,000 tons, but even this reduced the amount American Sugar needed to buy from others by 15.5 percent.

On July 26, Machado signed the decree officially empowering the Cooperative Export Agency to take over on September 1 all unsold sugar and to control all future sugar sales. Contracts for sugar produced in the 1929 harvest (although not in subsequent harvests) could, however, be made until August 29. Machado appointed the Export Agency's Executive Committee, comprised of Viriato Gutiérrez and José Gómez Mena to represent the Cubans, with F. Gerard Smith of Cuba Cane, M. L. Leonard of Punta Alegre, and W. H. Armsby of the Cuban-Dominican Sugar Company for the American companies. With two Cubans and three North Americans, rivalries soon surfaced. Rionda cabled neutrality on whether to support Gutiérrez or Tarafa as the agency's head. Privately, he complained that since he had told Tarafa the Riondas did not want to be represented, Tarafa had evaded him until Rionda had concluded that the colonel believed he did not need them and was entirely in the hands of the U.S. companies. When word came (interestingly enough, via Simpson) in October that Tarafa and General Molinet had resigned, Rionda wrote Portuondo he had decided that nobody could occupy the post of head of the new Cuban agency as well as Gutiérrez.

The U.S. companies, Rionda believed, had split into two groups, a National City Bank group led by Deeds of General Sugar and Armsby of Cuban-Dominican and a second group headed by Douglas of Punta Alegre and perhaps Elmo Miller of Antilla. He suspected that Cuba Cane's Simpson and Smith were uncertain which group to join. If there were this dissension among the Americans, he concluded, what must it be among the Cubans. He was glad he had decided to stay out of it. To Eduardo de Ulzurrún, in Navarro, Spain, he commented that Eduardo should be happy he was not in Cuba. There were so many skips and jumps ("brincos y saltos") with "la Cooperativa" that it was impossible to form an idea of what was going on.[13]

As the August 20 deadline for the deposit of Cuba Cane's securities neared, prospects were gloomy. If the reorganization were not approved, Hayden warned that a receivership would be inevitable, with long and costly proceedings in both Cuban and U.S. courts and all stockholder equities totally extinguished. The nondepositing security holders would have the right to demand the property be sold to the highest bidder and to receive from the proceeds their full share of their investments before the depositing security holders received anything at all. A voting trust was formed to hold the stock of the new company, with George W. Davison, president of the Hanover Bank and Trust Company, and Irénée Du Pont of E. I. du Pont de Nemours and Company joining Hayden, George Roosevelt, and Frederick Strauss as members. But although by October 1 more than 84 percent of Cuba Cane's bondholders and more than 80 percent of the stockholders had come aboard, this was insufficient, and federal judge Thomas D. Thatcher appointed John Simpson as receiver, with the Irving Trust Bank and Elihu Root Jr. as coreceivers.[14]

It seemed, at least, that this would be a "friendly" receivership. But when Manuel had written after Jarvie's death that he was now the only survivor of his generation of sugar men, he had been wrong. On October 29, 1929, as prices of the Stock Exchange finally crashed and crowds vengefully gathered at the corner of Wall and Broad Streets in the hopes of observing brokers plunging out of windows, the attorney for a group of stockholders who held 700 preferred shares argued what would be known as the "Doscher complaint." Doscher bore a name once famous in sugar circles. His father, emigrating from Germany in 1848, had founded a Brooklyn refinery and John, aged eighteen, had become its assistant manager in 1883. It had been sold to Havemeyer in 1891.

John, like Manuel, remembered the swashbuckling traditions of the Sugar Trust. Unlike Manuel, since the subsequent Doscher money had been turned in Brooklyn real estate, his memories had not been chastened by current sugar history. It was humbug, Doscher thought, to blame prices and events. Instead, the Riondas must have colluded with the bankers to defraud investors like himself.[15]

"I do not know who could be so evil," Rionda commented, "as to wish to ruin the market in an industry in which not only his own life but also those of all his family members are involved." He, Hayden, and Simpson filed affidavits in their own defense. Since much of the Doscher complaint attacked the selling of futures on the New York Coffee and Sugar Exchange, several paragraphs defended that practice. The futures exchange involved "no speculation" but represented "a business of arbitrage known all over the world not only in . . . sugar but also every other commodity which is dealt with on exchanges." Later affidavits repeated defenses from the Goethals investigation, thus freshly recalled to men's memories, and legal formalities ground on while Cuba Cane borrowed another $3 million at 6 percent to tide it through.[16]

On his return from Europe, on December 24, Judge Thatcher handed down a decision accepting the reorganization plan as "essentially fair." The decision contained, however, a humiliating penultimate paragraph. While stating much of the Doscher charge "in criticism and condemnation of past transactions was entirely irrelevant," it ruled that "in view of these contentions there will be exempted from the assets to be acquired by the new company . . . all claims, demands, and causes of action against any officer or director of the defendant corporation, Manuel Rionda, the Czarnikow-Rionda Company, any relative of Manuel Rionda and any corporation in which Czarnikow-Rionda Company or Manuel Rionda, or any relative of his, is or has been interested." The insult stung, and the matter probably helped keep any Rionda from being openly active in the Export Agency, which may even have been its secret purpose. Thatcher then adjourned the case until the new year without setting a date for the obligatory decree of sale of the Cuba Cane properties. Since a fixed number of days notice had to be given, the sale could not occur until at least February 1930.[17]

As for the U.S. tariff, throughout the fall there were Senate hearings, clouds of witnesses, and lobbyists hovering in Washington. But as the depression everywhere deepened, there had been no resolution.

Manuel had worked to convince President Machado of the necessity for a Cooperative Export Agency and as 1930 began proudly cabled Fanjul that sugar brought 0.25 cent more per pound than it would fetch without it. But on January 2, the agency (of which Viriato Gutiérrez had been put in charge) sold 350,000 bags of sugar directly to Babst's American Sugar Refining Company without going through Czarnikow-Rionda or any other broker. The sale was made, Manuel fumed, behind "everyone's" back and on a half holiday, and for at least 10 cents a bag less than sugar was worth. It proved, Rionda believed, that one "could not trust in Babst or in anyone" and that Gutiérrez "does not know how to reciprocate all our attentions." When Gutiérrez arrived in New York a few days later, Rionda reported that he was "not very cordial" and that Julio Lobo had also been at the station to meet his train. Two weeks later, he advised Portuondo that the Export Agency would destroy itself if it continued doing favors for the American Sugar Refining Company, United Fruit, and Cuban-American.

Czarnikow-Rionda, he decided, was handling the warehousing of Cuba Cane's sugar for too low a percentage. "We must not go on permitting them to exploit our company," he wrote. "We must free ourselves from this ungrateful daughter who fills my old age with vinegar." He added a little later, "[I]n the future, we want to eliminate direct relations between [Cuba Cane] and [Czarnikow-Rionda] and between [Cuba Cane] and the [Cuban Trading Company]."[18]

But soon there would not be a Cuba Cane. The date fixed for the auction of its assets was February 7, its minimum price set at $6 million, with the buyer assuming the Eastern Cuba Sugar Company's bonded indebtedness. Hayden suggested that six firms ("like J & W Seligman, Czarnikow-Rionda and some bankers") should each put in $100,000 and form a syndicate to buy the properties. Distancing his firm from these financial maneuverings, Manuel turned his back on Wall Street and went to Cuba for the 1930 zafra, notifying the corporation before he left that neither he nor any Rionda would serve on the board of the new company. He left Manolo to report on the last days of Cuba Cane.

Cuba Cane's Executive Committee met on the day before the final sale. It was agreed the Equitable Trust would advance $3 million to acquire the corporation; Central Hanover, $2 million; and probably the Chemical Bank, $1 million. The balance—$12 million to $14 million would be necessary to keep operations going—would be divided between Chase and Guaranty. "After the meeting was adjourned," Manolo wrote, "Bailie came over and told me that he was very much surprised and sorry of our attitude in not wishing to continue on the Board, adding that without the presence of [don Manuel] the meetings would not seem the same." He had then walked back to the office with Colonel Simpson, "who . . . expressed some surprise that you had not discussed the matter with him before taking that action." Mild expressions of regret, more sentimental than substantive.

On February 7, 1930, Cuba Cane's assets, which had been valued on the corporation's books at $64 million, were sold at public auction and, no one else wanting them, bid in by the Reorganization Committee for $6 million. A new company was incorporated in Delaware on the same day as "successor in re-organization" and named the Cuban Cane Products Company. It formally acquired its predecessor's properties on February 16 and valued them at $20 million.

Hayden became chair of the new company, as he had been of the old. Simpson continued as president, with the board of directors composed exclusively of representatives of the New York banks. On February 11, Simpson notified the Riondas that Cuban Cane Products was moving out of the Rionda building into the Brown Brothers building at 63 Wall Street, paying three months' rent in lieu of notice. The Rionda building, he remarked, was too cold.[19]

The Rionda clan did become major shareholders of Cuban Cane Products. Manuel personally exchanged 155 preferred and 12,618 common shares in Cuba Cane Sugar (plus $20,082.50 in additional cash) for 2,755 new shares. In January 1930, there had been in Czarnikow-Rionda's vaults 46,613 common shares of Cuba Cane Sugar and 18,448 preferred, roughly 70 percent of them the property of the firm, some 20 percent belonging to the Cuban Trading Company, and the balance to a few individuals. For these, they received 36,994 new shares of Cuban Cane Products, although only after investing $208,275 more. These shares, less than 4 percent of the approximately 1 million shares actually outstanding of the 3.5 million shares that had been authorized, made them, with Hayden, the principal shareholders of Cuban Cane Products.[20]

There was a final meeting of the old Executive Committee on the morning of February 13. Only Simpson, Barr, Frederick Strauss, and Manuel, back from Cuba, were present. Simpson, as was traditional, gave the day's cash position, with debts up $350,000 from a year before and with 539,000 bags of sugar unsold. "The main object of the meeting," Manuel wrote, "was to determine the valuation of the PLANT in the Balance Sheet of the new company, and after a great deal of discussion it was decided to make it $35 million." Strauss had thought that the valuation should be much higher, for otherwise "it would be practically admitting that the old Company had been carrying the PLANT in their books at too high a figure," while the Committee for the Debenture Holders wanted a low valuation to be put on the plant "in order to avoid having large amounts charged off in the future for DEPRECIATION, thereby decreasing the EARNINGS of the Company and automatically reducing the rate of interest on the debentures. Col. Simpson seemed to be in favor of having a low valuation, saying that we could not say that the properties were worth more than what we said when we recommended to Judge Thatcher that the valuation should be made low." There was a discussion of whether Cuba should set future crop restrictions, Barr of Chase National apparently favoring them, Simpson violently opposed, Rionda diplomatically evasive.

Manuel, like the other members of the Reorganization Committee, received $10,000 for his services. A letter six weeks later from Manolo in Havana to his uncle reflected the current coolness when he reported several "casual conversations" with Gerard Smith. "He has not told me any of the important things that constantly are being communicated to us by [Stetson]—this friend goes out of his way to keep us posted—and even Pepe Gómez Mena is helpful at times. Such is life, those who are under no obligation treat us better than the ones who owe their position to our kindness."[21]

But more than mere ingratitude threatened. Czarnikow-Rionda's sales were languishing. An attempt in February to sell 100,000 tons to the Canadian refiners—Rionda even went to Montreal himself, despite the bitter cold—failed because of the latter's purchases from the British West Indies. A secret deal with W. J. Rook in London to sell 100,000 tons of Cuban sugar to the Russians was spoiled by being leaked to Lobo. Tate and Lyle, "despite all the attentions Lyle has received from Higinio," were negotiating with the rival brokerage firm of Farr and Company. This, to Manuel, was an especial blow, not only because he thought the low prices tendered were "disastrous" but because Farr and Company "had no right to receive [such consideration] because it was not interested in Cuba and was only a middleman [corredor] whose only object was to get their commissions."[22]

Although Machado had delayed commencement of the zafra until January 15, Cuba had begun 1930 with 341,000 tons of its previous crop still unsold and with warehouses in the United States still piled with an additional 596,865 tons. The U.S. market was being "saturated" with duty-free sugar from Puerto Rico and the Philippines. With no money coming in and unable to borrow against their own sugar since they had no right to sell it themselves, Cuban planters and mill owners organized against the Cooperative Export Agency, while labor unrest led Machado to issue a decree to ban all labor, political, and public meetings and parades.

Manuel wrote to Manolo that they might as well accept an end to government control. They both knew, he wrote, that Cuba had been far more harmed by 1929's unchecked production than by the restrictions of previous years, but they "must leave that to history." Other countries, he wrote, had governments who protect them and local markets. "Poor Cuba has nothing but her workers who suffer as many blows as come without any murmur." But the Riondas must fight on. "As for [Gómez Mena], you must convince him that to speak of giving up is for boys, not for hombres de negocios who were born to struggle as their fathers did before them." Manuel's moods constantly shifted, and he was often ill. While he prophesized doom if crops were not limited, he also often expressed relief at the thought of washing his hands of restrictions. The Cooperative Export Agency's dissolution would be terrible, he wrote, but given its lack of confidence in his firm, he would be happy when it ceased to exist. The agency, he thought, had sold little and let various possible sales escape. They would do better independently. His nephews agreed. "It is a great misfortune," Manolo wrote, "that the producers and the industry at large should be at the mercy of men who are entirely ignorant of commercial dealings, but after all we must continue to play with them and be nothing more than school masters."[23]

If there was apprehension about falling profits among United States investors, the Cuban bourgeoisie were beginning to fear for their very lives and were ready to surrender. Viriato Gutiérrez came to the office of the Cuban Trading Company to warn that political unrest was rising. "When we asked him," Manolo reported, "whether he realized where the market would go if everyone was allowed to sell independently, he replied . . . that if a plantation was forced to sell even at 1 cent a pound, it could not blame anyone but itself, and that those who were in a position to hold their sugars would benefit by the misfortunes of others." Manolo himself had an appointment with Machado for the next day, but he doubted that he would be able to convince the president to hold firm. Instead, Manolo was inclined "to recommend [to the New York headquarters] that [Czarnikow-Rionda] begin to discount the strong possibility of [the agency's] dissolution by selling ahead on the exchange a fair percentage of their production."

Traditionally, the planters and mill owners of Santa Clara took the lead in the search for solutions to sugar's problems. Midway down the island, in the shadow of the Sierra de Escambray, the province held the largest number of mills, some fifty, only a handful producing more than 200,000 bags, none producing as many as 300,000, although family control of groups of mills, as in the case of the Gutiérrez network, raised the collective stake of a few considerably. Quotas in 1928 had cut Santa Clara's larger mills by an average of some 11 percent, its smaller mills by more than 18 percent.

On March 17, the Santa Clara Association sponsored a central meeting in Havana where the strongest attack on the Export Agency came from the Riondas' rival, Julio Lobo. At first Manuel saw it as a division along national lines. There was no doubt, he thought, that there were "two elements in Cuba—native and American. . . . [T]here can be no coming together [mezcla] of the two."

Yet many in both groups were at least in agreement on the desirability of abandoning government controls. On April 1, the Cooperative Export Agency survived a meeting of its stockholders by so slim a majority (12,918 shares to 11,139) that Rionda decided to cable Machado his congratulations for a "triumpfo moral" and to suggest, in a well-turned euphuism, that he "should take advantage of the present moment to harmonize differences"—in other words, that he should give up on restrictions on production. To Portuondo, he cabled that he believed Machado and Gutiérrez should avoid the defeat that would surely come if the agency's opponents convoked a second meeting. Rather than local men, he specified Gerard Smith of Cuban Cane Products and M. J. Leonard of Punta Alegre as the ringleaders.[24]

On April 14, the agency was dissolved by unanimous vote, leaving 3.7 million tons of sugar still unsold. The price dropped to 1⅝ cents per pound. Manuel did not comment until the end of April, writing Portuondo then that he had been ill for six weeks "whether from old age, exhaustion or other analogous causes." It was becoming more and more obvious that efforts to strike a bargain with the U.S. beet and cane interests were doomed to failure. To Doty, Rionda commented that "the only ray of hope I see is that at the next Presidential election the Democrats may win."[25] But that election was more than two years away. For the next thirty-five months, the Great Engineer was securely in the White House. In the meantime, Senator Smoot shepherded the Hawley-Smoot Tariff through Congress.

In mid-April, Simpson proposed that Czarnikow-Rionda should act as selling agent for the new Cuban Cane Products for a gross commission of only one-tenth of 1 percent. Rionda's reply, sent to Hayden, went through three drafts. In them, indignation was phrased with grave Spanish courtesy. "Analyzing this proposed arrangement purely from the point of view of substantial stockholders in your Company," he wrote, in the longer of the canceled versions, "we deem it our duty to call to your attention that for a Company producing in the neighborhood of 3 million bags of sugar with a gross value of about $20 million, the payment . . . of about $20,000 . . . from which must be deducted the usual overhead expenses, such as clerical hire, cabling, office rent, the maintenance of the proper Statistical Department, etc. . . . is not adequate . . . to render the services which you should have." If Cuban Cane Products, "thru careful and efficient salesmanship" should sell its sugar for one-tenth of 1 cent more a pound, it could add $1 million to operating profits. "The merchandising of the product is the most important factor in the success of a sugar producer." In the third draft, because of his firm's "desire as substantial stockholders . . . to see that the Company obtains this service at the lowest rate consistent with the service performed" he agreed to accept a commission of 0.25 percent.[26]

The Hawley-Smoot Tariff went into effect on June 18, raising the duty on raw sugar from 2.20 cents to 2.50 cents a pound, which meant that Cuba's sugar, even with its 20 percent preferential, must pay a full 2 cents per pound, although its price in New York remained unchanged. The campaign to weld a compromise with U.S. beet and cane producers had failed.

What course of action was left? For more than a quarter of a century, since he had joined C. Czarnikow, Ltd., Manuel's work had taught him how international a business sugar was, and he could now only fall back upon the hope of mutually agreed upon worldwide curtailment of production. It was a slim hope, but the Brussels Agreement (until it expired amid the chaos of World War I) had seemed to him proof that men of different nations could be brought to a consensus by intersecting self-interests. A new international pact would this time have to stretch far beyond Europe to the Indian Ocean and the South China Seas, but if producers in Java, the Philippines, and Czechoslovakia would agree to limit their production, they might collectively escape the disaster that was pressing in on them all. The Riondas had backed Tarafa when the colonel had sailed on his forays to Geneva in January 1929 and to Brussels in June 1929. Manuel had seen Viriato Gutiérrez off to Geneva in May 1930 as the effort continued, and the two conferred in New York now in early July, on Viriato's return.

The alignment of forces had changed for Manuel. In the early 1900s, when the island's hacendados had been struggling to rebuild their ruined holdings, they had turned to him to arrange desperately needed loans. Equally, North American investors, wise in corporate law but uninformed about the viability of plantations, had called upon him for advice. Most notably in the formation of Cuba Cane, he had given Wall Street lessons in the intricacies of all of sugar's phases, from production to marketing. He had represented, translated, and advised for both groups, playing the traditional merchant's role of intermediary. But now the hacendados' heirs were bilingual, and North American investors had hired professional managers to displace his nephews. Second-generation hacendados like Viriato Gutiérrez aspired to represent themselves. Nor was their president, Gerardo Machado, a mere pawn of the United States, as his predecessors had been when the Platt Amendment had first defined the rules. Machado had put through tariffs that had challenged U.S. manufactured imports; he had built roads across the island for its infrastructure; and, with Cuba's new capital building squatted like a giant toad athwart Havana's avenues, top heavy with the bronze and Italian marble that had enriched a generation of politician-contractors, the *New York Times* had not exaggerated in nicknaming him the Mussolini of the Caribbean.

On Falla Gutiérrez's passing, the ambitious Viriato and old Manuel had inherited each other and a range of common problems. In Manuel's office that July after Cuba Cane's demise, they discussed whether Viriato should buy a seat on the Exchange. Manuel wrote Aurelio that he had convinced Viriato that it would be better for him to stick to business proper rather than go "bailando en comités villaclareños, americanos o de otra nacionalidad" (dancing in Santa Claran, American or other committees). They eventually agreed ("decidimos") against the Exchange seat since "it would call attention to him and cause unfavorable comment for Viriato in his own career."

They also discussed what Viriato had learned abroad. Viriato laid on Manuel's desk a "stabilization" proposal by the prestigious authority Dr. H. C. Prinsen Geerligs, with whom he had become acquainted in Geneva. Prinsen Geerligs was a heavy-set Dutch scientist with thick spectacles, a drooping, white walrus mustache, and the dejected expression of a man who now saw the crop to which he had devoted his life going for naught. Born in Haarlem in the Netherlands in 1864, he had, after acquiring a degree in chemistry, gone out to the Dutch colony of Java in 1891. Twenty-seven when he arrived in that remote paradise to work miracles in its research laboratory, he was fifty when he returned home, if "not quite the father of the Java sugar industry . . . the teacher who set it on its way." He had gone on to fill out a "career of forty active years . . . as a scientist, as a statistician, and as a consultant on . . . practically every phase of the industry." Viriato had carefully studied Prinsen Geerlig's "Project of Reconstruction of the Brussels Convention of 1902" on shipboard. It might, he now flatteringly wrote its author, be "the solution" to all the current disasters of overproduction, and he drafted a seventeen-page memorandum expanding on it which, when Manuel's own secretary had put it into English and seen it properly typed, he now forwarded to the Netherlands from New York's Plaza Hotel.[27]

A few days after Viriato continued south on his journey home, a delegation from Havana found its way north. Four months earlier, the Export Agency had been extinguished, in large part because of the influence of Santa Clarans. Now a group referred to in the press as the Santa Clara Commission arrived at Manuel's office. It comprised, however, only two mill owners from the province, José M. López (president of the *Santa Lutgarda*, 1929 production 171,877 bags) and Marcelino García (of *San Isidro* and *Mabay*, 1929 production 182,535 and 119,042 bags, respectively), plus Percy Staples of the Hershey mills and Julio Lobo. Although they had come in hopes of selling 100,000 tons of sugar to the Soviet Union, they had also a wider goal. Thomas L. Chadbourne, senior partner of the corporate law firm Chadbourne, Stanchfield and Levy (and also a principal owner of the *España*, 1929 production 467,644 bags), was being considered to take charge of a rescue mission for their joint commodity. On July 16, Manuel hosted them at a luncheon. "They told me," Manuel wrote Portuondo, "that they have appointed [Chadbourne] Chairman of the Committee composed of Deeds, Simpson, Douglas and Bartlett, and given him full powers from that Committee as well as from the Santa Clara Association of Planters." Manuel remarked that while he would have preferred Charles Evans Hughes as "Cuban Head of Sugar," he agreed that "Chadbourne would be the next best man if he wanted the job. . . . no one could get in touch with the Banks as well as Mr. Chadbourne." Besides, Manuel hoped the corporation lawyer would not want "any remuneration as he would make money by buying stocks and bonds of the sugar companies."

Thus a group ostensibly speaking for the presumably nationalist Santa Clara mills selected someone from Wall Street to lead them. It was, after all, desirable that the New York banks play a role in an operation that to succeed would have to bring not only U.S. beet interests but also the hacendados of Puerto Rico, Hawaii, and the Philippines as well as the European and Javanese producers to heel in negotiations. Tarafa and Gutiérrez alone, representing only Cuba, had held few bargaining chips abroad. But National City, J. P. Morgan, and Chase were backed by the authority of millions in floated bonds worldwide. If German beets as well as Colorado's and California's must be dragged to the bargaining table, the banks could help a great deal in the dragging, although Java, the competitor to be most feared, was less vulnerable because of the independent wealth of the Netherlands. Rionda reminded his luncheon guests that to bring Java into an agreement, Cuba should not promise too quickly to curtail its production but rather hold over the archipelago the threat of unchecked competition.

Manuel himself invoked the rising Cuban nationalism, although he did not frame his distinction on national lines but on the natural division between owners of property and hired managers.

> I brought out the fact that some of the American representatives by reason of not having any stock in any Sugar Company—being merely employees—are not so interested in the problems of our industry as we whose fortune is involved, and that I could not listen

> to people who do not have any money in Cuba on matters bearing on the solution of our problems as much as I would listen to others whose whole life depends on the sugar industry. Of course, my foregoing remarks were aimed at [Farr] . . . as well as to [Simpson].
> . . .
> I wanted them to see the difference between us and . . . [Farr] and also the difference between Lito López and [Simpson].

López, he suspected, was learning from his visit to New York with the delegation. And Manuel concluded, "[W]e did well giving them a luncheon."

The next day, Manuel lunched alone with Chadbourne at the Recess Club. Manuel again belittled the current president of Cuban Cane, remarking, "[S]uch men as [Simpson] should not have much to say, because while I had nothing against him, still, after all he was nothing else but an employee."

> After lunch we went into the parlor. He said that he could speak plainer there than in the dining room. He told me that he had already approached Mr. Mitchell, Mr. Wiggin, Mr. Hayden, The Royal Bank of Canada and the First National Bank of Boston, suggesting to them that their Chairmen . . . should be announced as the bankers who were in charge of stabilizing the Cuban Sugar situation. Chadbourne claimed that the fact of having the co-operation of such men would be a notice to the world that the Cuban affairs were being managed by very large bankers and would consequently have more weight in the outside world. . . . It would be a sort of warning to all countries.

They went on to the matter of "remuneration." Chadbourne, Manuel thought (to his disappointment), "seemed to like the idea of a retainer. . . . I mentioned that there was a great deal of money to be made in buying securities—for instance, Manatí common stock selling around $2. He agreed on that, but I think he expects more: We must sound him further on this point."[28]

These seem to have been the preliminary skirmishes in what was first known as the Chadbourne-Gutiérrez Plan and later, less politely and less accurately, as the Chadbourne Plan. Over the next few months, there were complex negotiations with domestic and colonial U.S. interests, with Cuba again promising to limit its own exports in return for a promise on the part of the remolacheros and of the Hawaiian and Philippine companies not to expand further. Out of fear of Sherman Antitrust legislation, U.S. companies could not formally join to curtail production, but a "gentleman's agreement" was arranged.[29]

Meanwhile, adding tension to the discussions, workers were setting cane fields afire in Cuba and students were holding angry rallies. *Manatí*'s colonos, too, were militant. Salvador, as the mill's administrator relaying their demands, bore the weight of his uncle's fury.

"If your colonos are down-hearted so am I and everybody else that has money in the sugar industry," Manuel wrote. They were better off than the shareholders and bondholders because they did not have to go "literally on their knees" begging for capital. "If they were threatening to form an Association, let them! I'm looking our for the interests of the stockholders. . . . Let them associate if they want to." He concluded, ominously, "Give me the names of the colonos that do."

A month later, he was told only 2, out of approximately 150, had dared open defiance. He was glad of that, he wrote, but it would not have mattered if it had been 100. "What in thunder can they do!" None could free themselves from the present misery. "If they can do better, let them go to it."

In October, Salvador informed his uncle that the colonos, denied further financing by the banks, had sent a delegation to confront him with their suffering. Manuel still did not sympathize. While he was working, he wrote, "not for ourselves, since our shares are worth nothing, but for the good of the colonos . . . there comes a cable signed 'Zayas, President, Association of Colonos, Manatí' saying they are impatient. What can I reply? With prices so low, the Company is *pasando una borrasca* [going through a tempest]. The true owners of Manatí are its mortgage holders. No more can be done." All that held him, he went on, was his "many friends—employees and colonos. . . . If not for them, this old man would have told thee to surrender the field and go back to Elía. Read Zayas this letter—I won't deign to reply to him." As for a delegation of colonos going to Havana to see President Machado, "let them." *Manatí* had a contract with the colonos and was fulfilling it, and Rionda did not believe that even the president of the republic could change contracts, especially when the trouble came from *la situación angustiosísima* of the entire sugar industry.

A letter went to de Ulzurrún in Spain. The dreary process of reorganization that Rionda had gone through with Cuba Cane was now under way with *Manatí*. Approximately $5 million in bonds were outstanding, while its preferred shares (which had paid no interest since 1926) were selling at $10 a share and its common (which had paid none since 1925) at $5 a share. How could the colonos expect concessions and gifts? They were *"borricos"* (asses)! He had, he concluded, bought another $50,000 in bonds for Eduardo's account.

What harm could the colonos do to *Manatí*, he asked Salvador. If the bondholders hang it, it doesn't matter if the colonos shoot it. But to Portuondo he wrote: if Cuba doesn't sell all its sugar in the next zafra, there won't be one stone left on top of another.

By the end of December, *Manatí*'s Association of Colonos had fifty-four members, 32 percent of the total. If they didn't want to harvest their cane, Manuel wrote, bring in cane to grind from *Elía*. In the midst of all the danger of bankruptcy, the colonos had been demanding "villas y castillos" (estates and castles).[30]

Throughout 1930's continued crises, Cuban Cane Products appeared periodically on Manuel's agenda. In 1930, it turned out 3,251,362 bags. Its sugar cost it 1.6 cents a pound to produce, (of which the colonos received 0.6 cents) and sold for 1.3 cents per pound. As a result, the new company began life with a net loss for its first year of $3,111,775 compared to a 1928 profit by its predecessor of $214,269 and a 1929 loss of $805,832.

In mid-November, Charles Hayden called Manuel and Manolo at 11 A.M. and invited them to lunch. The banks, Hayden explained after they had been served, were "insisting on having a lien on the sugars," and Wilbur Cummings, a senior partner of Sullivan & Cromwell who had inherited Alfred Jaretzki Sr.'s prestige, had suggested the Cuban Trading Company and Czarnikow-Rionda serve as trustees.

"Seeing the great opportunity that [Hayden] gave me to express my feeling," Manuel wrote, "I told him that the Banks were perfectly justified in claiming control of the sugars. . . . [W]e had no objections to [the Cuba Trading Company] and C-R Co. being the *trustees* . . . but that . . .

some time ago *we had made up our minds not to continue being the sellers for Infante next year*, because we did not think they had treated us very well in many ways, especially in reducing the commission."

"I told him," Manuel continued, "that I did not want to dwell on old affairs, preferring to throw a blanket over the whole past." As the luncheon wound down, they talked of Chadbourne's mission to Europe, and Rionda, out of his old dislike, was delighted to hear that, while Simpson had been eager to accompany Chadbourne, Hayden had refused to let him.

Rionda's current code word for Chadbourne was Chaco. It followed the general letter scheme for his current codes but meant "shako" in Spanish, invoking the pompous plumed headdress worn by Hungarian military officers. "I also availed myself of the opportunity to tell him that I wanted him to inform Chaco that while I did not think he had treated me very kindly, yet I did not have any resentment against him." Hayden had replied by saying *"that he and ourselves being the largest stockholders of the company should work for its welfare."*[31]

Manuel transmitted instructions to Portuondo and his nephews. "We called Mr. Cummings on the telephone and told him we were willing to serve as *trustees*. . . . We shall not make any heavy charge but merely cover expenses. This arrangement will bring us back all the *warehouses* of *Cuba Cane*. . . . I am sure that will please Higinio." Then he continued in Spanish: "For some time, I have been wishing to let Infante's people know we did not wish their selling business—and I could not have had a better occasion than that today."

Ten days later, he wrote Portuondo that while he hoped they could be paid 0.75 cent per bag for the warehousing, the contract would simply read "the actual cost." They were not seeking profit as much as to show that "they need us, they who wanted to throw us aside." Cuban Cane employees were not to be hired for the warehouses. "We'll be able to put in our own employees—not those that *Nuevofeo y su compañero* [Simpson and his associate] indicate."

It was not flattering to think that the New York bankers and operators were turning back to him because they could hire his services more cheaply than they could arrange details for themselves. But it was something.

In mid-November, Tarafa was more pessimistic than Rionda had ever seen him. Rionda wrote Rook that "only he [Tarafa], ourselves and a few others, he says, will be able to stand the law of the survival of the fittest!"

Rionda himself had lost confidence even in that Darwinian axiom. In his "Review of the Sugar Situation" in *Manatí*'s 1930 annual report, he concluded that "the law of the survival of the fittest does not work in sugar or if it does, it operates so slowly that no one can survive." To Mincing Lane, he went further, commenting, "We hear a lot from economists about allowing the law of the survival of the fittest to prevail, but these gentlemen—although highly educated—look upon economic problems from a theoretical point of view. None of them have a dollar invested in the industry." There was no doubt, he went on, "that sooner or later if things are allowed to go on without governmental interference or cooperation amongst producers, the time will come when production will materially decrease, with the corresponding effect on prices; but during the period of readjustment practically all investors in sugar securities and individual owners of sugar plantations will have lost all their equity, and bondholders and creditors will take over the properties, and a new element will derive the benefit of the misfortune of others. This does not seem human!"[32]

10

Empty Saddlebags

There was no decrease in world overproduction in 1930, but since the North American interests were honoring the gentleman's agreement not to expand, Machado saw that Cuba kept its word by appointing a new Export Committee to keep Cuban exports from flooding the market and by demanding a law for the stabilization of sugar from his Congress. The law empowered the president to determine crop size and authorized a foreign loan to purchase almost 1.5 million bags of sugar at $4 per bag. This brought some relief to the hacendados, but much of the loan ("the bulk," according to the U.S. Foreign Policy Association) went to the North American mills.[1]

Gutiérrez and Chadbourne, joined by Gómez Mena and José M. López, now proceeded to Europe, sailing first to Amsterdam, then Brussels. Henry Luce's glossy *Fortune* magazine would glamorize the mission as an individual triumph for Chadbourne, described as tall, convincing, and blue-eyed beneath crystal chandeliers. Meanwhile, Rionda and his clan, in their everyday offices, worked for it at home, no easy task since Machado's constituents suspected that any concessions would be at their expense. Behind the scenes, Manuel doggedly carried on Tarafa's work when Tarafa himself gave up, puzzling over details, convincing Machado that only the bankers' worldwide agreement could stabilize the hungry, angry island. His support for the fine-sounding arrangement did nothing to enhance his standing among the island's hacendados, even if Wall Street appreciated his services.

Chadbourne had carried with him to Europe a seventeen-page detailed outline from Manuel of the goals and tactics of the mission. Make no threats, Manuel advised the lawyer. Put all the cards on the table. "Cuba's position is strong—in fact, stronger than ever before." If everything desired could not be obtained, all parties should at least pressure their own governments to reduce "duties, bounties, excise taxes and export bounties." When, at last, in February 1931 a private cable was sent Czarnikow-Rionda confirming that the "Javan Government" would "implant" the agreement, he wrote Chadbourne another outline, this one eleven pages long, proposing the organization to put into place.

"What is really aimed at," he wrote, "is the creation of what might very appropriately be called a league of nations on sugar affairs." There should be an International Sugar Council, the parties having votes in proportion to production. It should appoint an Executive Committee, which should appoint a general manager, some prestigious man without previous ties to any particular nation's sugar to bias him. There should also be a Committee on Statistics and a Commercial Advisory Committee "composed of men with commercial minds, familiar with merchandising methods," to "study market conditions throughout the world," as well as a Committee on Arbitration, a Legal Committee, a Committee on Research to find uses for sugar's by-products, and a Committee to Increase Consumption. He suggested thirteen prominent men to be involved—Dr. Hartmann of Czechoslovakia ("director of largest group and son-in-law of Vice President Czecho Bank Controlling majority of Industry"), Dr. Rabettge of Germany, Mr. Bennink of Java ("Sugar Director of Handelsvereening, Amsterdam"), Dr. Zazdzynski of Poland, Dr. Aozel of Hungary, and so on. But perhaps out of the knowledge that his own prestige was now so low that he was not even in the running, he spelled out that neither he nor his associates desired "any prominent or active part."

In May, the pact was finally signed in Brussels. That so utopian a project had been agreed upon, at least on paper, by so many diverse interests was proof of just how deep the worldwide depression cut. Only desperation had made it possible, fear that economies in ruins were again unleashing the dogs of war. But like the Brussels Convention of 1902, its crafting had required patient effort. Chadbourne's salesmanship had played to the footlights, but backstage there had also been Prinsen

Geerligs with his respected technological expertise; a covey of international bankers tired of making loans on a crop for which there was no market; Tarafa to involve a dictator; and Rionda to puzzle out what kind of enabling rules might be contrived.

An impressive office was duly established for the International Sugar Council in the Hague, and a distinguished former oil executive was named to head it up. Although born in Cincinnati in 1863, Francis Edward Powell had been dispatched to Europe in 1901 on behalf of Standard Oil and had remained in London in its service ever since, acquiring the Edwardian gloss, growing a suave mustache, and raising hogs on his estate in Surrey.[2]

Well and good, although expensive. But the market did not improve enough to make the International Sugar Council seem worthwhile, and support crumbled almost immediately. As 1932 began, both Java and Cuba were threatening to secede, while Cuba's 1931 exports had fallen some 700,000 tons short of expectations. "Who will be left to tell the tale," Manuel wrote, "is hard to predict!" He arranged for Portuondo to lobby Machado to restrict the Cuban harvest to 2.35 million tons, but it was March 25, 1932, before Machado finally overcame his apprehension of the reaction among his desperate constituents and issued a decree limiting the crop to 2.7 million tons.

Manuel calculated various elaborate hypotheses about what would result if Cuban production was or was not cut. If *Manatí*, for example, was permitted to produce only 300,000 bags and sugar brought 1 cent a pound, it might realize a $575,000 operating profit. If its quota was 340,000 bags sold at 0.75 cent per pound, it might realize $366,000. If there were no restrictions and its full 600,000 bags sold at 0.75 cent, it might profit $610,000. The first, he thought, would "relieve pain" but not cure the patient. The second was worse than the third because prices would fall as low. He wrote that he was inclined to favor the first because it did not "put so many of the small planters out of business," but Bernardo and Manolo preferred the last in the hopes of ruining foreign competition once and for all.[3]

If 600,000 bags could be made at *Manatí*, he wrote Salvador the next day, the cane cutters would at least have work for three or four months, and thus they could be paid less per day. No one was more sorry for them than Manuel himself, "but what else can I do! God knows I want to save the properties and do for the laborers all a human being can do." But if wages did not drop, many American companies would not grind at all. "Their banks are tired of throwing good money after bad."

As it turned out, *Manatí*'s production that year would actually be 410,627 bags. It would receive an average of 0.984 cent per pound and show an operating loss of $463,374 and a net loss of $1,348,435. The net loss included interest payments, "write-off of lands," and loss on sale of Cuba stabilization bonds due in 1940.

Increasingly discouraged, Manuel did not go in to his office for three months. In February, the Irving Trust Company was appointed receiver in equity of *Manatí*. Only in April did he stiffen. All Cubans were in the same boat, he wrote Salvador. They must buckle up and face the music. Cuba must wash its hands of international limitations and produce all it could. This year, no one could convince him to go along with restrictions. The banks supported them, he wrote, because they hoped to sell off the bags already in their warehouses. Cuba must look after its own interests and make the next harvest a "zafra libre." Let the sun sink where it would, and if they were going to sink, let all other countries sink with them. Cuba could make sugar cheaper than anyone, and national quotas benefited only its enemies.[4]

In early April, Manolo reported to Higinio rumors that General Sugar's mills and those of Punta Alegre and Cuban-Dominican would not grind for the 1933 zafra, that their banks were saying openly that they would not advance anyone a single cent ("ni un centavo a nadie"). Only the smallest mills, Manolo predicted, those administered by Cubans, would hold on somehow—those under American management would fail. Manolo had no information about Cuban Cane Products and rarely saw its officers. Only 6,143 bags of the 1,799,851 it had produced had been sold through Czarnikow-Rionda. The banks had kept its mills grinding by advancing still more millions to add to those already written off, but accumulated debts now totaled more than $9.5 million.

It was the Guaranty Trust Company that first lost heart. On April 15, 1932, Manuel, Manolo, and Bernardo were invited to luncheon with Eugene Stetson and John J. Sample, Guaranty's vice president in charge of loans on such staple commodities as sugar, coffee, cotton, and grain. The Riondas assumed the discussion would be about the market and were surprised when Stetson began by bringing up five other topics that actually concerned management—rents overdue from colonos and possible evictions of tenants, "preservation of the properties," food for workers, possible sale of some properties, and taxes.

Manuel replied in sequence. Any evictions, he told the bankers, must be considered individually. "Of course, where the whole life of a plantation was dependent on the cane from leased lands," the procedure would have to be different than in the East, where there was administration cane. As for "preservation," if the mills shut down, men must be kept on in the workers' barracks (the batey) "to protect the same in case of fire, riots or other similar developments" since Manuel thought that "if any such unfortunate happenings should take place, the ex-employees living at the Batey would naturally be of assistance to the Company—because, after all, they had a home there and hence would act as the negroes used to in the old times." As to whether to continue the "cocinas económicas" (the feeding of the workers), since Gerard Smith claimed to feed a worker for 3 cents a day and since only $33,000 had therefore been appropriated, the matter was "of small importance." The next two topics were also passed over quickly. The sale of *San Ignacio* and *Araujo* had already been discussed. The 21-cents-a-bag tax levied by the Cuban government would, of course, have to be paid.

Then came a sixth question, the one that mattered. Did the Riondas think Cuban Cane Products would be better off in the hands of a receiver? Manuel asked for time to think it over. "In reality," he wrote, speaking of himself in the third person, "what M.R. sought was to evade the issue, because he did not want to advise one way or another on such a vital question."

The next turn apparently came as a surprise. The banks were considering, Stetson told him, "the idea of appointing a Rionda *receiver*." This time, Manuel's answer was immediate: "under no circumstances would a Rionda ever accept such a position, because we are Cubans, we may go back to Cuba, and we do not want to have the onus of such a position." Any receiver would be there to recover the banks' advances by cutting expenses still further. More colonos would have to be ruined, more employees discharged, hungry field hands and their malnourished children starved. "Our impression is," Manuel decided, "that the object of the meeting was to talk about a Rionda taking charge. . . . No tenía otra finalidad que echarnos el muerto!" [Its only purpose was to throw us to the wolves!]

For his Havana nephews and to Portuondo, he analyzed the situation. "We all feel that ultimately the Company will go into the hands of a *receiver*, simply because in that way the *banks* would be in a better position . . . , but none of us Riondas want to appear that we were recommending it. . . . *Que lo hagan si quieren, pero no con nuestra aprobación!"* [Let them do so if they wish, but not with our blessing!][5]

The banks by now held first mortgages amounting to $4.75 million on the properties of the Eastern Cuba Sugar Corporation as well as on those of Cuban Cane Products. Six days later, on April 21, 1932, on petition of Victor C. Mendoza and Company, the U.S. District Court in Wilmington, Delaware, appointed Charles B. Evans of Wilmington, George Roosevelt of New York, and Charles Hayden as receivers. Cuban Cane Products had been in existence two years and two months.

Should the properties now be sacrificed for whatever they might bring, or should there be an attempt to preserve them in case the market improved? The banks agreed to give Hayden an option to see what he could arrange, the Guaranty Trust Company acting as trustee on their behalf. Sample, Guaranty's vice president, would deal with the immediate situation.

If he had refused to take charge of his expiring offspring, Manuel was willing to study Cuban Cane Products's proposed budget, and throughout May he conferred with Sample, pointing out the economies Cuban Cane Products must make. The company had $45,000 in its proposed budget, for example, for electricity and pumping water, which could be reduced to, say, $20,000. He advised Sample not to discuss with "#120" how to accomplish these economies, warning him that "#120" was, like all the Rionda administrators, opposed to any economy. Sample must simply order him to conform to the budget. The only thing, he wrote, in which he did not recommend "grandes économías" was in the cultivation of the cane. The two men also discussed cutting the staff in the Havana office as General Goethals had once proposed. Sample spoke "of the possible extravagance of #120 in attentions to some great friends [*obsequio a algunos amigotes*] that he had in the Machado administration." Here, Manuel assured him that "the Company's cost of production compared favorably with our own, and that everything considered the administration was not bad. . . . I told him that the way Cuban Cane had sold its sugar was what had caused the hard times they were going through." But they could hire Cuban administrators for smaller salaries than the Americans were receiving, and even if they were not as efficient, under present circumstances "they were better—because cheaper."

The banker then suggested that some of the stored sugar held at the centrals might be shipped to warehouses at the ports, so that it could be better protected. Rionda agreed. It was an indication both suspected that violence might soon erupt.

He thought, Manuel summed up, that the purpose of Sample's trip was to make as many drastic economies as possible—giving the least possible amount of money to sustain the small colonías and discharging as many employees as possible. Any sums advanced for the dead season would be insignificant. Nor would Cuban Cane "take care of" all the centrals. Perhaps they would not even grind since they had 450,000 bags still unsold and Czarnikow-Rionda had had to sell 10,000 tons for them yesterday for Europe for only 0.65 cent FOB.

Manolo wrote Higinio, sending him a copy of the agreement the lawyers had drawn up. It provided that the Cuban Trading Company should act as agents of the trustees, taking charge of shipping all Cuban Cane's sugar for a quarter of a cent per bag. Manolo warned his cousin that he must be careful to recover any costs incurred promptly since it might be difficult to collect later. The Riondas were getting a few crumbs—but only crumbs. The Cuban Trading Company would play only a local, modest role in Cuban Cane Products' languishing affairs, with the price of sugar so low it would make little difference. Manuel and his nephews, struggling desperately to save their own plantations, had little time to mourn what the bankers were doing to their former offspring nor, given their own troubles, feel with any smugness that they might have done better.

Watching the Wall Street men, the clan had at least learned how to finesse bankruptcies. Manuel applied the art to *Céspedes*, feeling responsible for its late owner's surviving family as well as wishing to recover the loans he had made it. To reduce the danger of an unsympathetic creditor requesting an outsider as judicial administrator, submitting them to the "inconveniences" of attachments of property, he wrote Higinio that they must themselves start foreclosure proceedings quickly through a friendly trustee. Once an administrator they nominated had been appointed, they would have time to reorganize since no auction of its property would take place except at that trustee's request.

Higinio was in full charge in Havana, Portuondo having gone on to Ostend for still another wrangle with Java over proposed world quotas. Ostend ended in stalemate, and the Cuban Sugar Institute, Viriato Gutiérrez at its head, broke with Chadbourne and withdrew from the Chadbourne Plan, while Java's masters were desperate from their own losses. Rionda stated that he didn't know whether to be glad or sorry over the failure. Its proposed quotas had been, he thought, not worth the trouble.[6]

Tarafa arrived in New York in early July to, Rionda wrote, "put Senator Smoot wise." In the debates over crop restrictions, the colonel had recently kept in close touch with Rionda, writing with the utmost tact and diplomacy. He was sorry that after so many years when Rionda had followed a "constructive policy," aiding Cuba with his good counsel, he should now give up and oppose any limitation of the crop. But he did not blame Rionda. When one considered the various absurdities of Cuban policy over the preceding five years, why should not Rionda and everyone else who knew the situation believe the only solution must be "natural restriction," survival of the strongest? Yet he still hoped that Rionda would play a conciliatory and constructive role.

On July 21, Manuel wrote Higinio, the colonel came to ask if he had changed his mind about accepting the Ostend proposals. Rionda tried to evade answering, since Tarafa himself said that he had come as "an ambassador from the [National City Bank] to investigate our attitude." "We limited ourselves," he reported, to saying that the Riondas would "adapt themselves to whatever the majority accepted" even though, for their own plantations, the best thing would be to be rid of all regulations. There was apparently a reference to Hayden, for, according to Manolo later, Tarafa spoke of a proposition Hayden had made him, which he would not accept because—again that favorite Spanish saying—it would make him the tail of the lion, and he preferred to be the head of the mouse.[7]

Two days later, Manuel dictated a note to Tarafa, suggesting they save $750 by not renewing a $100,000 insurance policy on *San Vincente*, a small, unlucky central in whose fortunes both men had been involved for more than twenty years, signing it "your affectionate friend." Before it was mailed, news came of Tarafa's death. He sent it on later to Tarafa's office, labeling it "My final letter to this friend. q.e.p.d." (may he rest in peace)—the classic, businesslike, realistic Spanish abbreviation.

Tarafa had died very suddenly of a stroke, while reading in bed in his room at the Carleton House. Newspapers honored his memory with long obituaries, retelling the legends of the young patriot who had fought in the Cuban jungles for independence and who had built a sugar empire and 500 miles of railroad line to open Cuba's north. "Feudal Lord at Home, Noted for Obscure Philanthropy" read a *Herald-Tribune* subhead, the recipient having been a Miami taxi driver to whom he reportedly had given a fleet of cabs, while the *Times* set "Ally of American Capitalists" followed by "Paternal Interest in Workers" in boldface.

In Cuba, there were front-page portraits smudged in printer's ink, the colonel as 1920s businessman—clean shaven; with a starched, white collar; and with the plump, rather cherubic face sagging a little, looking somehow rather puzzled. Higinio and Pepe Rionda were listed among those who came to the Havana wharf to receive his bronze casket, draped with the Cuban flag and with cloth of gold and lilies. The next day, they formed part of the long procession that, with honor guards and military band, accompanied the casket to the Colón Cemetery. The *Mercurio* reprinted many messages of condolence, expressions of grief from Budapest and from Milan as well as from Prague, which cabled that "the Czechoslovakia Sugar Industry deplores with you the decease of the eminent man who was the first to proclaim the necessity of international cooperation of the sugar exporting countries, thus ensuring his everlasting memory throughout the world sugar industry."

My friend's death, Manuel wrote Higinio, I really feel. "Whatever happened [*En medio de todo*], the Colonel was always our client." He had died, Manuel added, owing Czarnikow-Rionda $33,200 on the *Central Cuba* and $119,920 on the *San Vincente*. His son, Miguel, seemed "un buen muchacho" but without experience. Tarafa was survived by his widow, Maria Luisa Govin, and by two sons and three daughters, one the wife of Oscar B. Cintas, who was shortly to become Machado's ambassador to the United States. One of his grandsons would be taken prisoner in 1961 at the Bay of Pigs.[8]

In the market, all continued badly, although Rionda was cheered by hopes for Franklin Roosevelt's election and worked smoothly with *Manatí*'s friendly receivers. To Salvatore, he went on counseling economy. He should not hire more office employees but let the present staff work nights. In his youth, he recalled, "we worked until 10 or 11." Manolo was also firm with Higinio. The Cuban Trading Company's total expenses must "be limited to $50,000, including salaries and all other expenses and not counting on any additional salaries from the New York end." He would like to come to Cuba, "yet conditions just now don't justify spending money on trips unless they are inevitable." He wrote fewer letters that fall, although Manolo reported to London that "he still rides on horseback and can tire out any of his nephews."

As for Cuban Cane Products, the clan believed its "desintegración" was coming. Manuel analyzed its 1933 budget for the Guaranty Trust and, reprising Goethals's role, reported that office expenses could be cut by about $159,000 out of $600,000. Railroad freight rates must be reduced. Oxen must be used whenever possible, and wage scales lowered once more. And Manuel, who had not believed in refining on the island, added that "by selling locally to Cuban refiners, the Company could save the marine freight, the bag, warehousing and some other items that may aggregate net 25 cents per bag on say 400,000 bags or a saving of $100,000."[9]

Higinio did, however, perform a signal service for Cuban Cane in February when some of the major European investors in Consolidated Railroads visited Havana. He asked them for at least "an emergency provisional reduction" of freight rates, pointing out that if plantations did not grind, the railroads would "die of consumption, as they would have no freight to carry." The next day, with Pepe, he went to see Gutiérrez to arrange an interview with Machado for the British bankers. Higinio then spoke of the railroad rates weighing hard on *Céspedes*, and Viriato proposed they have *Céspedes*'s cane ground at his *Adelaida*, "and he would then give us the sugar at Puerto Tarafa with one year's free storage" for $2.00 a bag, and if that should violate the government's rules "he could get around this somehow." It was an hour's interview, most cordial. But an interview with Machado was impossible, for the president "had overexercised himself the day before walking" and this brought on an attack "of his old trouble (inflammation of the prostate) with fever and he was feeling very depressed."

Clearly, Higinio wished to show the Guaranty Trust the value of his connections, for Sample was included at a luncheon that he hosted the next day at his home, Linda Vista, for the European bankers and Viriato. It went smoothly. Higinio pointed out "that if there were less political speeches, less meetings and more seating around a table of the prominent men that had the say, to figure out in dollars and cents what was to be done, it would be better." But he repeated his warnings: if railroad rates were not cut, many plantations could not grind, "and a state of anarchy would ensue."

Violence, although it may not have been mentioned further, was on the minds of everyone present. Viriato had arrived "well guarded in his armored car." The revolution that would topple Machado was already under way. Students were rioting, even as the men sat around Higinio's table, and rumblings in the bateys were an undercurrent to every consultation.

Higinio, Sample may have concluded, would be a useful man for the Guaranty. Manuel's days were numbered, and his major theme seemed always the value of his own skill in the selling of sugar. Higinio was on the spot, vigorous and with powerful connections.

A few days later, Stetson came to Havana to reinforce Sample. Stetson was ready, Higinio reported, to confess that Guaranty's management of Cuban Cane Products "had failed and was beaten." Cuban Cane owed some $4.75 million, and Guaranty was "not willing to go on sinking more money." They had already written off $800,000, and he would write off the remaining $450,000 "that he was ready and willing to do it now, admit he was licked, and call it 'quits,' and that this would not break the Guaranty. But that he hated to abandon a thing he had so long been connected with . . . , that he always wanted to go through to the end in anything which he undertook." Therefore, before he left, he had called a meeting in New York, and the bankers had agreed to put up another $900,000. But "he thought the days of the sugar industry in Cuba . . . were practically over and that he did not see how an enterprise like [Cuban Cane Products] could be managed by a lot of American Bankers, seated around a table in New York, and with different opinions and opposing points of view. That he thought all plantations should finally revert to the Cubans." For the present, "for the sake of the people in the plantations," he was willing to go ahead with the harvest if Consolidated Railroads would make some concession in the freight. But before doing any of these things, he wanted to see what was Higinio's opinion as how to proceed.

Higinio, after an exchange of compliments, then spoke his own mind: "That, although he was not connected any longer with the Cuban Cane, it had been very sad for him to see the Cuban Cane loose prestige and go down every day, as he had been one of its promoters and always had a soft spot in his heart for its welfare. That Stetson and the Senior should never had drifted apart in the management of the Company. That Charlie Hayden, without having the right men in charge, meddled in a dictatorial way into everything and added to the confusion." Nevertheless, Cuban Cane had valuable properties and, he thought, "with a good management could be pulled out of the hole ... their ... expenses here in Havana and also in the plantations, as compared to ours, were exceedingly high and extravagant." He believed that the controversy with the railroad should never have happened and that Gerard Smith had angered Machado "by agreeing with him ... to vote for the Single Seller, and then, on the following day, reversing his opinion and voting against it—that this Machado had never forgiven him."

Higinio then offered Stetson Viriato's cooperation ("the man who had closest access to Machado's ear and the one who had the greatest influence with him"). "Then Stetson said item number *one* in his program consisted in turning the affairs and management of the Cuban Cane to some one group, influential and well connected in the island, and that he thought no better one for this than the Riondas. . . . That they [the Guaranty] probably would foreclose their properties and turn the management over to us."

Family ties held, and Higinio remarked "that if Stetson wanted to have this thing done, he should get a hold of the Senior and Braga and get them enthused at the idea. Stetson asked Higinio if he thought it advisable to tell Viriato anything about the probable turning over of the Cuban Cane to the Riondas, and Higinio said he did not think it advisable."

The final matter to be discussed concerned insurance. For seventeen years, Cuba Cane had been insured with the Compañia de Seguros Cuba, controlled 25 percent by Viriato, 25 percent by Machado, and the remainder by the Falla Gutiérrez and Castaño estates. Recently, however, "a friend of Charlie Hayden" had appeared and closed a policy with another company.

Higinio explained that at the meeting with Viriato this morning, the latter asked who was the Guaranty, and J. B. Rionda told him they were backed up by Morgan.... That Viriato had said if they did not get their policy, they would allow the Compañia de Seguros "Cuba" to go bankrupt, in which case the plantations of the Cuban Cane, in spite of any foreclosure or reorganizations, would still be liable for this pension fund to injured and dead employees, which amounts to a large sum.... Stetson then said: "Tell Viriato that this is fixed for him." Whereupon we parted to meet tonight at 9 P.M. at Viriato's house.

That evening, Stetson repeated to Viriato that it had not been decided whether the Cuban Cane mills would grind that harvest but "that he was a friend of Cuba and realized that if the Company did not grind a lot of suffering would result to the people around the plantations, and that although the Guaranty was not a philanthropic institution, he morally considered himself bound to do something for this people." But first, the controversy with the railroad must be settled. Since only Machado could tell Consolidated to reduce its freights, Stetson "was willing to leave the matter entirely in the President's hands and abide by Viriato's decision as an arbitrator."[10]

Another memorandum summarized Viriato's two-hour interview with Machado the following morning. The president was "very well disposed to help." He confirmed his annoyance with Gerard Smith and promised to intercede with Consolidated about the freight rates. "[Viriato] mentioned the fact that very likely there would be a change in the Cuban Cane, and that another group, probably the [Riondas] would take charge. Machado was delighted at this, for he had always held a high regard for the [Riondas]."

Once more, Viriato brought up the insurance and again asked Higinio, "[W]ho is the Guaranty?" "Higinio replied they are as good as the National City—and [Viriato] commented: 'Well, I don't think much of them.' Then, again, J.B.R. said the Guaranty was backed by Morgan and that he ought to remember Stetson told him the night before that Mr. Lamont, Morgan's right hand man, was President of their Executive Committee. Thereupon [Viriato] decided to have $150,000 deposited with the Guaranty." It would be later decided that since Sample and Stetson "did not wish the thing to appear as a trade . . . they may deposit the funds with the First National Bank of Boston or some other Bank."

They then went on to lunch at the Florida Restaurant, where they found Stetson, Sample, Lawrence Crosby of Sullivan & Cromwell, and F. Gerard Smith. Shortly, Higinio, Pepe, and Stetson withdrew to a smaller table, and Stetson was told of Machado's promise to have the freight rates cut but that "[Machado] does not approve of [Smith], as he had been making criticisms of his administration and playing politics." Stetson remarked that Smith's contract would not be renewed but that since the harvest was beginning, he should stay on another two months until it was completed.[11]

The next day, the *New York Times* and other papers would carry fresh reports of planned coups against Machado. More students were killed, and more bombs exploded. On February 11, there were reports of raids on the plantations and of the burning of sugar mills. The 1933 revolution had begun. There was a final comment when Stetson, on the way to his plane to return to Miami and an unrelated crisis, called Higinio to say good-bye. He told him that

> Franklin Roosevelt had coined a new phrase "a new deal" and that this was what was happening with Cuba Cane now. . . . That on the 6th March he would make a deal with us as to the turning over of the properties, that a few hundred thousand dollars more or less would not matter. Higinio said he felt so keen about it that although he knew a judicial administration was disagreeable to the Senior, he even would like to take charge of affairs right away, at which Stetson said: "I would be delighted at this." . . . Higinio also told him Portuondo might be able to help in persuading Senior and Braga to go along with this new deal.

Manuel, meanwhile, had fallen ill again. "I am trying to do some work," he wrote, "but although the spirit is willing, the flesh is weak—and I find it hard for me to be anything like I was. Any little thing upsets me." He concluded—the letter was to Oliver Doty, his niece's husband

and manager of *Tuinucú*—"I leave Leandro and Bernardo to attend to the other matters mentioned in your letters Nos. 67 and 68. I can not."

Manolo corresponded with Havana and kept Manuel informed, as well as reminding Higinio that Stetson had already told Manuel he hoped to have Cuban Cane Products return to Rionda management, the clan receiving "a substantial stock interest in the Company . . . in consideration." To Manuel, this had been "very gratifying . . . and I feel that it may happen within the next year or two, provided, of course, that the bankers agree to give the [Riondas] a free hand in the management and to supply the necessary working capital, and to have nothing to do with the sales of the sugars."

In a month, Roosevelt would succeed Hoover. Manolo was optimistic. "There is no doubt that the Democrats have some ideas as to settling the international debts. This must be based upon some reciprocal trade agreement between nations, all of which will tend to stimulate commerce and permit idle factories to operate, thus diminishing unemployment . . . confidence will be restored."[12]

Higinio wrote Governor Herbert Lehman of New York. Charged with entertaining visiting celebrities—he had recently, despite the penury of the times, been allotted $500 by his uncle for that purpose—Higinio numbered Lehman among his contacts. He hoped, he wrote, that the governor would convey to the incoming American president the grimness of Cuba's situation.

It was a five-page, single-spaced letter, beginning with a defense of Machado, who, he argued, could go down in history as one of Cuba's greatest men were sugar only at 2.5 cents per pound. Machado had "done more for his country than any previous President. . . . He has made tremendous efforts to protect the American capital invested in this country by maintaining himself in constant personal contact with Bankers and planters, whose advice he has always followed." It was the low price of sugar, not the president, that threatened Cuban stability.

What good, Higinio asked, had a higher U.S. tariff on sugar done the American consumer? The American people were paying yearly over $200 million more for their sugar than necessary, while the beet growers "for whom that protection was intended, have scarcely increased their production" and only the U.S. insular possessions had benefited. "[T]he enormous cash investments made by Americans in Cuba have practically disappeared," while exports from the United States to Cuba had fallen from $500 million in 1920 to less than $30 million in 1931. Soon Cuba would be unable to pay its foreign obligations.

What then? American intervention? "What would it accomplish with sugar prices at these low levels? . . . [T]he only [way] of helping the unemployed of both countries, is by having the courage to go to the root of the trouble and knock down the tariff barriers that make commerce between two neighbor countries an absolutely hopeless proposition." The Hawley-Smoot Tariff had forced Cuba to manufacture "many things which we used to buy from you," lowering "the standard of living of our working classes . . . to the point of starvation. . . . Many of the poor people on the plantations have nothing to wear excepting used yute bags. They go barefooted. . . . Millions of American dollars were invested here in sugar mills at Hoover's request. . . . What revenue are American investors receiving now for their millions of sugar bonds? How many factories in the industrial districts of your country have closed down or are working part time only for lack of orders from Cuba?"

Communism had been unheard of, he wrote. But if conditions did not improve soon, not "Machado nor a thousand Machado's will be able to restrain the starving masses from robbing, plundering and killing." While the American press exaggerated atrocities, reform could not come without an end to the desperation. "One of the most conspicuous opposing Factions is the A.B.C., composed of students (some of them members of our best families); the majority of the University professors, young lawyers, doctors, and small merchants. They . . . stand for something new, pure, without contamination whatsoever." He was not unsympathetic toward pure government. But "Cuba must first evolve a balanced system of supply for its economic needs. Then will it be possible to prepare, in a gradual way, the conscience of the new generation for a truly democratic government." Instead, the ABC Party had adopted terrorist methods. Vázquez Bello, president of the Senate, had been shot and killed only a few blocks from Higinio's house. The government had therefore adopted "strong, repressive measures. It is a fight to the finish in which many precious, innocent lives have been needlessly sacrificed. The saddest part of it all is that each day that goes by conditions get worse, business is at a standstill ... and in all the Cuban homes, where a relative ease and happiness was a general rule, now constantly hovers the fear of death and imprisonment."

The solution, he repeated, must be economic. If the Roosevelt administration would "be willing to lower the duty on sugar, either by modifying the existing tariff or revising our Reciprocity Treaty," if it would "exert its best influence with the banks" to grant Cuba a moratorium, there would be "an immediate, almost magical effect in restoring the country to a normal footing." If not, the United States would see "at their very doors a catastrophe whose deplorable effects it would not be difficult to foretell."

"I am not a Cuban," he wrote at the end, "I am a Spaniard, but I have spent practically all my life here, where I have my home and four boys."[13] Alfonso, his eldest son, was twenty-four; Charles, twenty-two; Rafael, nineteen; and Harry, eighteen. Increasingly, Higinio made Alfonso his lieutenant, having him sit in on the late meetings and drive him through the threatening Havana streets.

In February, around "red" Manzanillo in southwestern Oriente, strikes spread out along the railroad lines, reaching the General Sugar Company's *Mabay* and Cuban-American's *Niquero*, moving north in March to *Tacajo* and to the United Fruit Company's *Boston* and *Preston*. Rebellion seemed to flash wherever there was a nucleus ready to take action. There were almost daily reports of cane fields burned, and on March 11, the "head of Machado's strong-arm squad" was assassinated.

With the sporadic strikes, the violence, and the uncertainty, the 1933 harvest produced even less than the 2 million tons to which it had been restricted. Selling on average for 0.97 cent per pound, it grossed the island only $43 million. For *Francisco* and *Tuinucú*, the decline was steeper —down 28 percent, only slighter better than Cuban Cane Products's 30 percent decline. Cuban-American's production dropped 34 percent, *Manatí*'s, 38 percent. There were in these figures no salvation for bankers any more than for the colonos and cane cutters.

In Washington in March, Roosevelt took his inaugural oath, looking out from the Capitol steps on a country one-third of whose own citizens were ill-fed and ill-housed. Facing a thousand problems, he had begun to collect information about Cuba, dispatching two of his advisory intellectuals, Charles W. Taussig and Adolf A. Berle Jr., to "make a fresh study" of the island. Taussig, then thirty-seven, had inherited his family's American Molasses Company. Berle, thirty-eight, more conventionally among Roosevelt's Brain Trust, was a professor of corporate law at Columbia. They had already reported back to Roosevelt at Warm Springs, Georgia, with a confidential account of both the corruption of Machado's politics and "American exploitation." Taussig and Berle believed the American companies "overcapitalized and overbuilt." When the sugar collapse came, they reported, most of the companies had been "thrown into the hands of banks in New York which tried to oversee the business from that distance . . . maintaining their hold over President Machado by the threat of military and fiscal intervention by the United States."

Roosevelt presumably took this under advisement. His own family, the world against which he was to some degree in mischievous rebellion, had once been involved in the sugar trade. In May, Roosevelt sent Sumner Welles to Cuba, and in September, Berle would join him.[14]

As the dead season of 1933 settled down, the already daily violence throughout Cuba escalated. On August 1, Havana bus drivers triggered a general strike and brought the island to a standstill. A week into it, as it held and built, the Guaranty Trust moved once more to salvage its Cuban Cane liabilities before a deluge of class struggle should submerge its assets altogether. On August 8, 1933, in New York, Stetson, reinforced by two high bank officials, invited Rionda, reinforced by Aurelio Portuondo and Manolo, to another luncheon. Five days earlier, Manuel had celebrated his seventy-ninth birthday. "[F]ew can go much over three score and ten," he had replied to a letter of congratulations. "I have had my full share!" To Rentschler he had written: "Yes . . . I am still in the ring!"

Manuel reported to Bernardo on the luncheon. After some generalities, Stetson spoke, following up on his conversation of the preceding February with Higinio "about the reorganization of Cuban Cane and our taking charge of its management . . . the idea being that the Banks collect all their advances plus interest, but make no profit whatever—thus avoiding complications because of some of the Cuban Cane directors being also directors of the Creditor Banks." Some $5.5 million, Stetson thought, would be owed the banks, and he proposed to recover it by selling 1 million shares at $10 par each, with many Cubans purchasing them at that low price. Rionda brushed this aside—there was no money in Cuba to purchase anything. Stetson then went on to report that Robert

Atkins (now employed by a Stock Exchange firm) might bring "the Dupont group" in. Manuel faced this maneuver coolly. "I told him," he reported to Bernardo, "that I would not be surprised to see [the Duponts] go in on that basis, because the valuation of $10 million for plantations with a capacity of 3.5 million bags, even if only making 1.5 million bags, meant $7 per bag—and this was ridiculously low!"

This was not, as Manuel reminded Braga, what Stetson had proposed to Higinio in Havana. His proposal then had indicated the banks "were to attend to the financing and we, to the management." He then added another of his favorite Spanish proverbs. "Para ese viaje," he wrote, "no se necesitan alforjas!" For a trip like this, we do not need saddlebags. They would not be going far. As for the future, the second foreclosure auction of Cuban Cane Products was scheduled to take place on September 20, the third and final one, for which Hayden was biding his time, about December 10. "The banks," he pointed out, "do not want to go into the grinding season."

How could they under the militant circumstances? On August 12 (the general strike having reinforced the students and professors), Machado fled the presidential palace, taking a plane from Havana to some unknown destination. In his flight, Rionda privately played a part. As much as is said, he wrote Bernardo, about all the money Machado is supposed to have escaped with, Manuel had received instructions from the Cuban Trading Company to draw against an account held by the Montañez heirs, handing on $85,000 to the Royal Bank of Canada to put at Machado's disposal. This had been given to the toppled dictator only moments before his flight. Where are those millions it was said Machado had somewhere? Manuel asked. "Así," he concluded, "se escribe la historia." So they write history.[15]

A part of the Riondas' strength had been their ability to serve as go-betweens for American investors wishing access to the palace. In helping pay off Machado, they were reimbursing past services. Replacing him, with the blessing of Roosevelt's emissary Welles and with the Riondas' cousin Cosme de la Torriente prominent among those consulted, a provisional president was duly installed. Manuel wrote a letter of congratulations to Carlos Manuel de Céspedes, the polite son of the hero patriot. He had, he wrote, great satisfaction in seeing his distinguished old friend at the head of "our beloved Cuba" and desired his success in working for the country and "for all of us who depend on sugar." To Alfred Thompson, he commented that he was still a great believer that Cuba would come into its own—"or at least part of her own." The Democratic administration in Washington would see justice done. He kept believing, he wrote Bernardo, that finally all would be resolved by Roosevelt, that the president would be careful Cuba "no se le caiga en el mandil" (does not fall into the net).

Although the field and mill workers on the plantations shared a mounting militancy with of the rest of Cuba's working class, for the three weeks that de Céspedes remained in office it apparently seemed to property-owning Cubans that the center might hold, and they made claims of their own. On August 23, the Asociación de Colonos y Agricultures de Cuba wrote the American and Canadian banks. The letter was signed by Walfredo Rodríguez Blanca, the association's president and a director of the Céspedes Sugar Company. It blamed the bankers themselves for having stimulated Cuba's fatal overproduction, "indiscriminately" acquiring plantations at "preposterous prices" and loaning money too easily. They had then imposed "artificial measures" upon Cuban sugar and stubbornly adhered to them "long after results" had proved them "utterly erroneous and harmful."

In another memorandum, this one to President de Céspedes, the colonos pleaded that the corporation controlling all sales of their sugar should be replaced by one composed of equal numbers of mill owners and cane planters, which body would itself choose a Cuban citizen to replace Chadbourne as its president. The present corporation, Rodríquez pointed out, was composed of eleven men. Only one of them was a colono and he a handpicked dependent of Cuban Cane, although there were some 3,600 Cuban colonos who owned almost half the island's sugar. The other ten were mill owners, six from the great American corporations. The four Cubans (Gómez Mena, Cervera Falla, and two other hacendados) were all from Santa Clara Province, and Machado "en un rasgo de servilismo" (with a servile flourish of his pen) had appointed Chadbourne as their president. The laws that defined their power, the charge continued, had been drawn up in a New York office, badly translated into Spanish, and rubber-stamped by the Cuban Congress on orders not to change a single letter. The budget allotted for the corporation had been far more lavish than that of any local business, so that it had stood as "a shining lighthouse of luxury over the shadows of the general misery."

A day later, Manuel wrote Bernardo that everyone was sure that Cuban sugar would be given a quota in the U.S. market of at least 1.7 million tons, perhaps 2 million, and that Cuba's preferential would be increased from 25 percent to at least 40 percent. Czarnikow-Rionda, Manuel wrote, had already begun gambling in the futures exchange that the price of sugar would rise. Also, Manolo had been summoned to Rentschler's office, where Rentschler had been amiable, almost affectionate, and had spoken of how cheaply Cuban Cane Products and various other companies could be acquired, saying there was much money to be made by buying ingenios.[16]

But this general hopefulness was confined to the bourgeois levels of society. For the Cuban hacendados, control of their own production would be a sufficient reward if Roosevelt provided them a lower tariff and a more generous preferential. For the Cuban workers, however, that was not enough, nor did it mean anything to the army ranks. The soldiers now joined the rebellion, and on September 4 their united power brought in the dean of Havana's Medical School, Grau San Martín, as provisional head of a five-member coalition of students and other radicals. The *New York Times* printed a smudged picture that was not reassuring—Grau and three of his "junta," intellectual, almost mournful, dark-eyed men in crumpled white suits, with Colonel Fulgencio Batista y Zaldívar a little apart, gaunt, watching them.

The sugar workers now occupied the bateys and mill offices; Atkins's *Soledad*; the *Caracas*, which the princes of Terry had built; the *Gómez Mena*; and the United Fruit's *Preston* and *Boston*—spreading out until almost every mill in Cuba had been occupied, 120 by one estimate, the Cuban Cane mills and the Riondas' mills among them. Unions came forward, demanding an eight-hour day and more pay. Joint Committees of Action were formed. Rionda wives and adolescent offspring were commanded to the States for safety. Salvador remained at *Manatí* and Oliver Doty at *Tuinucú* whence Aunt Isidora, who was eighty-seven, and Aunt Conchita, who was seventy-eight, refused to budge despite their kinfolk's pleas. Higinio bore the brunt of the crisis in Havana, he and Pepe Rionda spokesmen for all the Rionda interests in the embattled island. Higinio's family could not leave, his wife in the hospital recovering from an operation, his sons going with him daily to visit her despite the armed groups roaming Havana's streets. Portuondo was in Washington, acting spokesman for Cuba's bourgeoisie. Higinio helped Portuondo's family escape and watched, helplessly, as Portuondo's house was sacked by a mob. At the mills, the workers, impatient with the compromising ways of conventional bargaining and spurred by starvation, elected committees and demanded that their pay be doubled. "[A]ll the properties," Manuel wrote Bernardo on September 9, "are in the hands of the laborers."

Bernardo was in London, where he had gone in the hopes of arranging some abatement of the claims of Czarnikow-Rionda's London partners. He had found it hard going, and Manuel was "disturbed" that he had been unable to arrange for either the cancellation of unpaid accrued dividends or a reduction of the future dividend rate. It was impossible, he wrote, for London not to realize that Czarnikow-Rionda had been paying "dividends 8 percent larger than we should have . . . they have had the benefits of all our relations in Cuba (for instance, the great control we had in 1920, that of the Single Seller in 1921); in fact, whenever we were 'on the saddle,' they had the benefit of it) and that they did not lose one penny whereas we holders of common shares lost nearly all its value." Manuel had not liked Bernardo's suggestion that all contacts with London be severed, "but once again I see my mistake. I am too old-fashioned, exceedingly fond of old relations and perhaps too soft-hearted. . . . If humanity is going to be so groping for money and there is no consideration but money, then I would much rather prefer to get out of business." Before the letter was mailed, he received a cable from Bernardo that London had "signed on [Bernardo's] terms."

From Cuba, reports detailed fire and bloodshed. With the army officers besieged in the Hotel Nacional, the government could do nothing to repress the workers' anger. Cuban Cane's administrators abandoned their ground. In the Rionda mills, more than 300 men tried to force their managers to sign statements agreeing to their demands.[17]

Pepe wrote Manolo: "In Francisco, Elía, Tuinucú and Céspedes, as in all the other fincas in Cuba, including Cunagua and Jaronú, all work is paralyzed and inactivity in the bateys and colonías absolute. . . . The last motorcar had left yesterday with Mr. McNulty. . . . The workers stand is threatening and we foresee, if things continue in this way, true anarchy because when men lack food and any way to buy it, what can hold them back from looting?" The Rural Guard, he reported, was useless. The Strike Committees at the mills discharged the office workers, refusing to let them do their jobs. The corporation's inspector was denied entrance to the batey, the strikers announcing that the property now belonged to the workers. Even should the United States intervene, the seeds of Communism had been sown. He, too, used a Spanish proverb. "Que hay que arar con esos bueyes." These are the oxen we must plow with. There was no use protesting to a government that could give no guarantees. Pepe, Salvatore, and Higinio, who had signed no agreements thus far, now decided to offer wages of 60 cents a day, recognition of the union, and the eight-hour day, with some allowance for food. That might avert violence and the destruction of property. The *Times* reported a day later that 1,200 Americans were in "potential danger." In some places, the term "Soviet" seemed appropriate.

Although Silvestre, their half-brother, had been ordered to rescue them, Aunts Isidora and Conchita still refused to leave their "beloved Tuinucú," Isidora insisting she would rather die than abandon it. Within the clan, she was famous for her charities to the workers on the home plantation, which had earned her a family reputation as a lay saint. Tales had long circulated about the processions of humble supplicants who came every morning to her rooms for her alms and blessings. Now, Higinio wrote indignantly, not a single man had risen to her defense from among those whom she had protected ever since they had been born.

I have refused to believe, Higinio wrote Portuondo, "that the radical movements could come to ingenios like Tuinucú and Francisco, but we live and learn. Now I no longer trust even my own employees. This wave of communism, which was not checked in time, will overthrow this government, and all that follows it!"

"Today," he reported, "Manatí was surrounded by 1,500 men. Communications are cut. . . . We are sending you copies of the workers' demands. . . . What is essential is to send out some money, for unhappily the principal cause of all these evils is hunger—and none are more to blame for that than Hoover and Smoot." He understood, he added, that at least the insurance company had gotten Portuondo's car back from the "ABC Radical."

Although his uncle insisted that he, as well as his family, should come north as soon as his wife was able to travel, Higinio refused to leave Havana. There was no other remedy, he wrote, than to stand and face the tempest. If the strikers would not let the administrators leave the mills, then they must "agotar hasta el último esfuerzo" (use the last ounce of force).

Do not think we are afraid, he wrote two days later, of Pepe, himself, Silvestre, and those administrators who still remained at their posts. Those who lose their heads now are disgraced. We must inform the strikers that we will not honor any agreements signed under compulsion and that all work will be stopped until they modify their demands. If the zafra cannot be made, it will be the responsibility of the strikers themselves. The Gómez Menas, he observed, had used that threat at their *Mercedita*, and the more sensible elements among their workers were using all their influence to arrange an accord.[18]

As the time approached when the harvest would have to begin, if it were to take place at all, strikers and investors alike had to think through the consequences if it did not. The cane was ready for cutting, and the zafra could not be delayed beyond mid-January. The workers had seized the mills' company stores, but now those shelves were empty. If the macheteros held the cane fields, they could slash down the crops and drive the plodding oxcarts to the mills. The millhands and engineers might have the solidarity and expertise to keep the machines operating, but they would need replacement parts, fuel, and credit to pay for transporting the sugar to the ports. In addition, the overseas sales must be bargained. It was one thing to burn a cane field or occupy a mill office. It was another to deliver a harvest. The more pragmatic among the workers argued it among themselves. Get it out of your head, Higinio wrote Portuondo, that the zafra cannot be made. The difficulties will be enormous, but they can be overcome. If we succumb to the pessimism which reigns everywhere, we will end up in a Madhouse.

Grau, speaking in English, broadcast an appeal to the United States, attacking the great sugar companies.

> Certain financial interests are . . . sworn enemies of our people and they are still conspiring our destruction. . . . You know these American interests . . . and your depression has been their masterpiece. . . .

> We can no longer tolerate puppet governments born of monopolies and concessions, converting Cuba into a sweatshop for a privileged few.... Our success will mean a new Cuba, born to new ideals and a new order of things....
>
> We are called ... radicals because we are closely following in the tracks of your own National Recovery Act; we are called Communists because we endeavor to return the buying power of the Cuban people.

The broadcast might have been more reassuring if had not been shared with Colonel Batista and with a representative of the Students Directorate. "The students of Cuba," maintained the latter, "are the vanguard of the revolutionary movement that aspires ... to conquer economic and political freedom, together with our inalienable right to self-determination." No representative of the labor unions or the colonos had been invited to speak.

Practical considerations gained strength both in the bateys and in the head offices, for if the workers needed the administrators and brokers, the zafra could not proceed without laborers. The settlement reached at the Hershey sugar mill illustrated the compromises that were painfully negotiated. Hershey agreed to an eight-hour day, which created a third shift and thus gave employment to many additional people, while the employees accepted a 10 percent pay cut in return and were denied the right to have a "walking delegate" in the mill.

The stress of the revolution took its toll on the Rionda clan. "I fear," Higinio wrote Portuondo in late October, "that with Rionda denned up ["en la Cueva," literally "in the cave"], Braga too busy in the market, Leandro hors-de-combat, Oliver Doty more or less the same and Crawley too timid, you will have to take charge of our mills there. Pepe is here doing all he can." In New York, November 15 was "a day of mourning" for the Riondas, as interest on *Francisco*'s bonds fell due without funds to pay it. Therefore, this last receivership could no longer be evaded. The lawyers advised that they must request it quickly before some outsider acted. "You can imagine," Aurelio wrote, "how it is for all of us, and especially for Rionda, for whom it is a very strong blow."[19]

Around the zafra, other questions hung fire. Roosevelt had denied recognition to Grau's government, and with the violence and talk of confiscation, no more loans came from the U.S. banks, nor did New Deal proposals to guarantee Cuba a larger share of the United States market move forward. Roosevelt's secretary of agriculture, Henry Wallace, believing in central planning to check gluts, feared Grau would not accept the limitation on Cuban production proposed by the International Sugar Council, while on the island the *Times*'s correspondent noted in her diary, "Nothing to write about except shooting and bombings." Welles returned north and was replaced by Jefferson Caffery as Roosevelt's personal representative. Only Batista's greater control over the army ranks gave some promise of future order.

Higinio reported that the members of the acting government's inner circle were in disarray. Many rumors were circulating, he wrote Portuondo, about solutions for the political problem. For him, he went on, the preceding week and the beginning of this one had been terrible because of the intransigence of *Francisco*'s workers, who had sent a delegation to present their complaints to the secretary of labor. Higinio had decided, after several members of Grau's administration had given him differing opinions, to placate the union. He tried to avoid trouble, he wrote, by appearing "unas veces suave y otras enérgico" (sometimes conciliatory, sometimes firm). But he told the delegation that he had not called in the army only because he did not want to repeat the sad events at *Senado*, where various workers had been killed. "I repeat," he concluded, "that the zafra will be made, with or without the Grau government. I understand your pessimism, but *Por Dios, chico*, don't lose your equanimity!"

He wrote to Manolo a week later: "Last night I jumped out of my bed three times hearing bombs and gun shots, and today, Sunday, am in the office. I struggled six hours yesterday negotiating with the workers at Elía and they know that if they do not work, the Army will move in."

But did they know that? The Grau government seized the *Delicias* and *Chaparra* mills from the Cuban-American Sugar Company when the company ordered the mills closed in the face of the workers' unrest. In rapid-fire succession, Grau piled up a series of measures to ensure the future welfare of Cuba's laboring classes. A decree fixed the minimum wage for cutting and hauling the 1934 sugar crop at 50 cents per hundred arrobas (it had gone as low as 20 cents in some places), while another promised to divide government lands and tracts confiscated from

Machado's henchmen among the poor, who were to receive thirty-three acres, a yoke of oxen, a milch cow, some seed, and scientific advice. The Nationalization of Labor Law was proclaimed, providing that at least half of all workers hired must be Cuban-born. On December 12, Grau also removed Chadbourne as president of the National Sugar Exporting Corporation. Then he accepted the International Sugar Council's proposed limitation of Cuba's 1934 crop to 2,315,459 tons and ordered the mills to start grinding on January 15.

Would they? "It is highly doubtful at present," reported J. D. Phillips in the *New York Times*. "However, the foreclosure sale of eleven of these mills set for Jan. 17 will not take place, it was learned today."

The eleven mills were those of Cuban Cane Products. Under Cuba's existing law, a bankrupt property must be put up for sale three times at public auction. The first two times a minimum price was set by the court. If that price was not met, it would go to the highest bidder at the third auction. Charles Hayden had depended on this procedure to secure control at a bargain price. The debenture holders' protective committees would bid on the corporation's assets for a song and own them henceforth free and clear, unencumbered by continued interest payments on previous advances, the slate wiped clean.

"The mortgage holders," the *Times* continued, "have held up the auctions, apparently due to the provisions of a recent decree signed by the President, giving the government the right to bid at the sale of properties and giving it preferential rights to take over the properties under the terms of the highest bidder. [This decree would become known as the Right of Tanteo.] The present state of the Cuban Treasury precludes the possibility of the government's paying for any properties thus acquired except in Treasury certificates or long-term bonds."[20] In selling the eleven mills at a bargain basement price, the Wall Street men had not planned to sell them to the Grau government or to exchange them for Cuban paper of doubtful worth.

11

From the Wolf, a Pelt

On January 15, 1934, Grau, denied recognition by the United States, resigned his office. The date itself was significant, commented the *New York Times* correspondent, since it was the day that the Cubans "had set as the deadline on which the political situation had to be settled if Cuba was to be able to make a sugar crop this winter." The presidency passed to Carlos Mendieta, a respectable statesman, and on January 23, after Roosevelt's emissary Jefferson Caffery had assured the U.S. State Department that Colonel Batista would keep order, recognition was granted. The zafra could now proceed.[1]

On the day that Roosevelt recognized the legitimacy of the new government, Cuban Cane's lawyers, accompanied by Sample, descended on Havana. The third and final sale of Cuban Cane Products's properties was now set for January 30. The man they must see, Caffery informed them, was Cosme de la Torriente, Cuba's new secretary of state, and accordingly, they immediately requested Higinio to arrange an interview. Higinio did so and checked over a memorandum they had prepared, deleting two paragraphs in which the banks confirmed that they did not want to continue in the sugar business and that if the bondholders did not redeem the Cuban Cane Products properties, they intended to sell them to the highest bidder. On the same day, after a visit to Cosme's new office, Higinio was able to telephone New York that Mendieta would name Portuondo as Cuba's Washington representative in all matters involving quotas and reciprocity. Portuondo, whom the clan had kept on their New York payroll during their darkest days, would guide Marquez

Sterling, now Mendieta's ambassador, through the morass of new sugar legislation.

Rionda, Aurelio wrote Higinio, was a changed man, as they all were, "full of hope and enthusiasm." This did not mean, he continued, that they were ignorant of the immense difficulties before them—the prospect of continuing strikes, radical discontent, and Communist bombs, for example. But, he noted, "ahora hay horizonte" (now we have a future) and men like Mendieta and Cosme–as well as Roosevelt and his advisers in Washington—were alerted to the dangers of mass starvation on their doorstep. The Platt Amendment would soon be officially laid to rest and the Hawley-Smoot Tariff's imposition on sugar abated. Bernardo was even confident the advantage given Cuba would be raised from 20 to 60 percent.[2]

Higinio believed Cuba's sugar business could best be rebuilt by Spanish-speaking men who made their home on the island, specifically the Riondas and Fanjuls, and he was convinced that now the North Americans would know they were indispensable, if only because of the Right of Tanteo, that troublesome bequest of the Grau regime.

The idea of a "right of estimate"—as the phrase is usually (and clumsily) translated—had first appeared on August 24, 1933, in the Student Directorate's "Manifesto-Program to the Cuban People." The manifesto had demanded that only Cuban citizens should be permitted to own more than 165 acres of land and that larger holdings should be progressively taxed. It had also demanded that, whenever land was sold, the state would possess the first right to buy it by matching the selling price. Seen as a way for the Cuban people to recover their own acres from foreign ownership, it would prevent an owner taking advantage of bankruptcy protection to avoid debts and taxes.

The Right of Tanteo had been given the force of law by Grau's Presidential Decree No. 102 on January 8, 1934, and his fall from power a week later had not wiped it from the law books. Should Mendieta's government choose to take up the properties for the low price at which the New York banks had planned to acquire them, it could do so legally under Cuban law and pay in Cuban paper. If a lawsuit were filed, the Cuban courts might very probably declare the decree unconstitutional, but the legal proceedings would inevitably be costly and stretch out for years.

Cosme received Higinio and the Guaranty Trust lawyers courteously, reassuring them that, although there had not yet been time to modify the decree, nevertheless the Americans could rest assured ("seguros y tranquilos") that the new government would do nothing to injure the legitimate interests of anyone wishing to do business in Cuba. He arranged an interview for them with the new secretary of justice, Roberto Méndez Peñate. But it was understood this was merely a courtesy visit, for the matter was, for all practical purposes, settled then and there in Cosme's office.

The account is in Higinio's letter to Portuondo the next day. He also touched, again reassuringly, on the threatening labor situation at *Francisco*. He would see Colonel Batista about it. The political problem, he wrote, may be resolved for the moment, but the labor problem remained and could not be resolved unless the army imposed its authority wherever the workers were not satisfied with legitimate improvements but created problems by dreaming of a social revolution.

In the midst of a hasty move from New York to Washington, excited by the knowledge he would be working very closely with Márquez Sterling and Sumner Welles, Portuondo took time to reply, warning Higinio not to be too hopeful in what he called "el embrollo de Baby." His efforts would be appreciated if Tom Garrett (the attorney for the Guaranty Trust) and Sullivan & Cromwell's Lawrence Crosby gave him proper credit. But, Aurelio warned, we cannot have many illusions, since our former experience tells us they use us when they need us and then forget we exist. Higinio's position was "fragile," and the future of his sons (as of Aurelio's sons) was "más nebuloso" (very cloudy). "I have tried to do much," Aurelio wrote, "with Cuban Cane, that is, with Hayden and Stetson, and with General Sugar, Deeds and Rentschler, but up to now, I must sadly confess, without any immediate result."

On January 30—the same day that President Mendieta signed a decree returning *Chaparra* and *Delicias* to the Cuban American Sugar Company—the Cuban Cane Products Company's assets were auctioned off as scheduled. Its eleven sugar mills and other holdings "passed into the hands of its mortgage holders," that is, the four New York banks, "to satisfy encumbrances amounting to about $4,125,000." The banks agreed, the *New York Times* reported, that the bondholders would have until May 15 "to buy in the properties from the banks at a price not to exceed that paid . . . plus interest and expenses."[3]

Thus, although they would need to subscribe additional sums, they would obtain the mills free and clear of debt for about 4 percent of their original cost and about 16.5 percent of their appraised value. Included were some 472,000 acres owned outright and leases on 298,365 additional acres, mills with an annual capacity of some 5 million bags of sugar, plus such things as machine shops, stores, workers' houses, offices, and residences for managers, superintendents, and chemists, as well as 799 miles of standard gauge and 184 miles of narrow gauge railroads.

Fanjul was then asked to assume a public role. Directly after the auction, Crosby representing the bondholders, Garrett representing Guaranty Trust, and Henry Kelley of Central Hanover came to the Cuban Trading Company's office. They were forming a new company, the Compañía Azucarera Atlántica del Golfo, which would hold all Cuban Cane's supplies, and Stetson wanted the Cuban Trading Company to be in charge. Fanjul agreeing, Atlántica was established that day, with Fanjul as president and three of the Cuban Trading Company's senior men as officers. It was capitalized for $6 million. When Fanjul inquired why the capitalization was so high—50 percent more than had been paid for all the fixed assets, including the supplies—Garrett told him they planned for the new company to take charge of all Cuban Cane's properties, becoming its successor company. A week later, a one-paragraph note from Stetson on Guaranty Trust stationery thanked "Friend Fanjul" for "the splendid manner" in which he had "assisted Mr. Sample."

On February 6, the legal papers were signed. Smith, signing on behalf of Cuban Cane Products, was, Fanjul reported, plaintive ("quejoso") that the bankers had made Fanjul president. Fanjul replied that although experience had demonstrated that bankers as a general rule did not appreciate the services they received, in this particular case Stetson himself had picked him, adding, "you know the many services we've constantly rendered almost without charge." Smith replied sarcastically that if he had met someone who had served the banks as Fanjul had just done, he would not have minded cleaning his shoes. "I imagine," Fanjul continued, "that he believes that we will have some important post in the new company." Fanjul had also heard, some days earlier, that Smith had said he was about to resign from Cuban Cane since he feared it would be investigated by the U.S. Senate.

The letter was to Aurelio. "I want you to be informed of all these matters," Higinio wrote, "in the first place because I have accepted the presidency without any consultation with Rionda—who I am sure would not have agreed." He was ready, he commented, to do everything humanly possible to "second Mr. Sample" helping "solve all the problems that arise both with the workers as well as in high official circles." He added a postscript. Perhaps Portuondo would have his letter translated and send it on to Stetson.

Aurelio was far too concerned with negotiations in Washington to be involved. Finally, Roosevelt had sent a special message to Congress asking that sugar be added to the basic commodities placed under the Agricultural Adjustment Administration's control and proposing quotas for it. Portuondo had telephoned the news to de la Torriente. Cuba, he advised, must not poison the Washington atmosphere with quibbling ("mezquindades") because the Cuban quota was set at only 1,944,000 tons instead of the 2 million tons they had hoped for. Cubans must remember the political strength that U.S. domestic beet and cane men still wielded. Only Roosevelt's ascendancy could carry the day. As for Atlántica, he did not know what Manuel thought but dismissed it as no problem since Higinio had always kept Manolo informed.[4]

Higinio was not the only nephew with hopes of recovering the clan's former power. Manolo wrote his cousin that Stetson had invited him to a dinner at the Waldorf-Astoria, sitting next to him and telling him "that at some future date he wanted to discuss with Uncle and me certain matters relative to the plantations of Cuban Cane, all of which confirms your views that he prefers to 'play ball' with us than with anyone else." He added, "I feel quite confident that . . . we will get the sale of those sugars. . . . But I had hopes that even something more would come our way—namely, the management. There is no doubt that *Baby* suffered a great deal by reason of inability to make itself *persona grata* with the local authorities—and they will never do that until they succeed in having a management that has access to public officials who will give them a helping hand in time of need."

In March, Fanjul came to New York to join Manolo in a meeting with Stetson. The New Deal was riding high in its investigations of Wall Street practices, and Stetson believed that "conditions were not favorable for [Hayden] exercising [his option to regain control because of the

Securities Act].... He then also made it very clear that the Guaranty Trust Co. will not under any circumstances make any profit thru the foreclosure of [Cuban Cane] not wanting to submit themselves to possible criticism and litigation; and that, furthermore, as he was member of the Board of Directors of [Cuban Cane] (and so was [Hayden]) and also an officer of the Guaranty at the time that the mortgage was given, that as individuals they did not want to submit themselves to the same risk." Nothing, he said, would please the bank more than to have a group headed by Manuel, perhaps jointly with Hayden, make an offer on the properties.

A week later, Hayden returned from a visit to his copper mines in South Africa and invited Manuel and Manolo to lunch. "We spoke at length," Manuel wrote, "that any new company must be Cuban and that everything relating to its administration must be decided in Cuba, where the head of the company must reside." Only "capital expenditures" should be referred to New York. It was unclear whether Hayden agreed or merely listened.

In the first week of April, Higinio, on behalf of Atlántica, added his signature to the necessary legal documents, as all of Cuban Cane's properties were transferred to it. He then—apparently so instructed—resigned as its president, Sample replacing him, although as an afterthought he was named a vice president a few days later. Mention of these developments formed a single paragraph in the letter Higinio wrote Aurelio about the negotiations for the Reciprocity Treaty. The Cuban Trading Company would be agent for the selling of Atlántica's sugar.[5]

At this point, the Right of Tanteo, which they believed had been laid to rest, came back to life. Mendieta's government moved, after all, to exercise the right to acquire Cuban Cane properties on behalf of the Cuban people. A particularly ominous shift in Mendieta's frequently changing cabinet partly explained the development. Méndez Peñate, who as secretary of justice had three months earlier assured the banks' lawyers there was absolutely no fear of such a government action, had recently denied any memory of that promise. He was "already mentally unbalanced," Higinio wrote, and shortly thereafter had killed himself. He was replaced by Carlos Saladrigas, who had been a leader of the ABC Party and author of Presidential Decree No. 102. In his prior post as secretary of the treasury, Saladrigas had ordered an investigation of the foreclosure sale.

Now, Higinio wrote, "he called in the District Attorney of the Matanzas Audencia and ordered him to establish a suit of annulment, based on supposed flaws or lack of second notice."

Cabinet shifts were symptoms of Mendieta's need to strengthen his base. His new government lived in fear, Higinio observed, "of doing anything that would spoil its members' future political chance and if to this you add a tremendous current of opinion favorable to nationalizing industry, you will readily understand how hard it will be to stop a suit that appeals very strongly to the masses, without the aid of very heavy outside influence."

Promptly, Lawrence Crosby of Sullivan & Cromwell and Henry Kelley, Central Hanover's attorney, reappeared at Higinio's offices. "They, of course," Higinio reported, "are very bitter ... and quite outspoken about the effect this would have in the U.S., probably greatly handicapping Cuba's chance for further help from Washington, and absolutely closing the doors to any further American investment in Cuba." Higinio told them that only the American ambassador could "squash" the suit, "as not only was it a political issue of the ABC, but that private interests were probably bringing pressure to bear." Even Cosme, he told them, could do nothing.

Yet Fanjul believed he himself could do something, precisely because the matter was "a political issue." That it had surfaced was, he believed, proof of his hypothesis that only those of "the same race" would be able to handle Cuba's current government correctly. Many steps, varying in expense and respectability, could be taken to persuade individual politicians to vote in helpful ways. For one, Atlántica's colonos could be mobilized against the government's suit. Large and small alike, they were still facing disaster. They were selling 64 percent less cane than they had in 1925, less than half what they had sold even in 1930. In the five western mills, production was down some 16 percent in one year. As budgets had for years been pared to the bone, their cane fields had become clogged with weeds. Replantings could not be postponed any longer. Cane was a perennial but was not immortal, and if new advances were not made promptly, Fanjul predicted Atlántica would have only enough sugar in the next harvest for 800,000 bags. But money would not be advanced with a lawsuit pending. By promising the colonos advances if they helped kill the suit, delegations could be rallied, illustrating fervent support for letting the foreclosure sale stand and reminding the president that some 10,000 workers depended on work in the cane fields to support their families, work that must be funded by northern capitalists.

Yet Atlántica's local management ignored Higinio. Why, Higinio inquired of Manolo, should he kill himself if he was to be treated with no consideration?[6]

The Central Hanover Bank's attorney had made no progress with Mendieta and might no longer be able to count on the U.S. Marines. In the U.S. embassy in Havana, Ambassador Caffery and F. Freeman Matthews, the first secretary, pondered the situation, and in Washington the State Department's legal advisers wrote ten-page summaries for Sumner Welles, cynically hypothesizing that the Right of Tanteo had been "a clever scheme for the enrichment of its proponents" whereby Cuban Cane's properties would "be sold on favorable terms to the tricksters." "There were boasts," it was reported, "that original owners who had been glad to sell at the fictitious prices of the 'Vaca gorda' or who had been content to lose properties through foreclosures of mortgages contracted on profitable terms in that period of banking optimism would reacquire their original holdings at the bargain prices of January, 1924.... The process could then be repeated at the expense of the American public." "I never heard," the analysts continued, "of a serious plan to divide the Cuba Cane's lands into small parcels for distribution to individual agriculturalists in accordance with the undefined 'agrarian reform' project of the Grau regime."

But even Sumner Welles was not forceful. "From a political standpoint," he replied, "it is obviously undesirable for this Government to press the Cuban Government at this time on this matter." There were even, he went on, "many phases of the past history of Cuba Cane in Cuba which do not incline me to the belief that this is a clear-cut case on which all right and justice is on the side of these American interests."

The bankers feared it was even possible that Roosevelt's radical Brain Trust sympathized with the idea that the Cubans should make themselves masters of their own land.[7] Yet Roosevelt, like Mendieta, could not ignore domestic politics. The Jones-Costigan Bill that would guarantee Cuba prices far higher than those in the world market for at least a specified quantity of its cane passed the U.S. Congress on April 19, but Roosevelt delayed signing it. The sugar interests of the insular possessions were still fighting to retain their privileges, and Washington's net of quotas, preferentials, and reciprocal arrangements was stretched and brittle.

In the Czarnikow-Rionda offices and at Rio Vista, Higinio's hopes as well as his fears were discounted. Manolo was matter-of-fact. Higinio had warned Cuba clearly of the dangers if Cuba did not "forego all its rights—now and forever," and thus he had done all he could. Manuel, in addition, questioned any real danger from the Right of Tanteo. All Cuba's talk of nationalizing the industry is just theoretical, he wrote. A country without money cannot nationalize anything. The government does not even have money to make the next zafra. "Therefore we consider the plan to acquire Baby's mills an absurdity. In addition to being a robbery from the bondholders, it would be a stain the country could never wipe out. . . . [I]t would be impossible to get money again in the United States or anywhere else. It would make us thieves. . . . I trust you will not go so far as to kill yourself over it." Cuba had acted unjustly in resurrecting the Right of Tanteo, Manolo observed, but the Americans had been mistaken in not putting Cubans at the head of Atlántica.

Unappreciated both by the banks and his kinsmen, Higinio pressed on. He passed on confidential information of behind-the-scenes developments that Mario Lamar, Cosme's law partner, had given him. "[E]stan moviendo sus peones," he wrote, using a chess metaphor (They are moving their pawns). Lamar had been named a member of a newly constituted fifteen-member Council of State, set up to serve until a new Constitutional Convention was called. It would be desirable if this council took up the matter of Atlántica, since its members were conservative and solvent men of property.

Two days later, a letter illustrated how Fanjul saw his role as lobbyist for the bankers as closely tied to his desired role as head of the new Compañía. "Persons of important social standing," he commented, were pressing him to arrange appointments of their friends "as managers, field inspectors, office clerk etc. as it is publicly known that I am personally attending to the disagreeable affair of the suit brought on by the Government, which is taking up practically all my time and perhaps without even the cognizance of Sample or Miller, as I hardly ever see them." The company's case could eventually be won in the Supreme Court, if it came to trial, but it would drag on for several years, causing great expense.

There were "other ways of winning" if Stetson would "[give] me absolute control and direction of the Company . . . to change the management of the Mills, allowing me to put my own men where I need them. . . . The new Company is hated, and this is common knowledge . . . but with a good management I am sure it would have more sympathy and better standing." He could visit each plantation and organize "a campaign of protest against the suit." Fanjul named influential men—the editor of the *Diario de la Marina*, Senator José Manuel Casanova, Walfredo Rodríguez Blanca—who owed him favors. Rodríguez "would be a good field inspector. . . . With a salary of $500 per month we would have a very useful man in the Company."

If he handled it through the courts, a lawyer might cost $50,000. Fanjul himself could "make it" for $20,000 or less. Perhaps Stetson was afraid he would want a large salary, but he would not even mention an amount. "The management of the Cuban Cane, together with that of our own Mills and our help to other clients, would give me a tremendous political power." As for de la Torriente, "being at the head of the Company, I could demand more from Cosme and his partners and accomplish a great deal more. . . . Can any mister so and so do this? No! Will your people ever acknowledge these facts? I doubt it."[8]

"Your people." Over the years, he had occasionally distinguished between himself and his cousins in North America. The references were becoming more frequent.

Manolo counseled Higinio to take it easy. Probably the North American bankers and investors would "continue along their present lines without following your sound advice. . . . However, all this is their affair and not ours. You have done your best." Their uncle, he reported, warned that even if Stetson should now put Higinio in charge, he would be there only temporarily, until Hayden exercised his option to retake the property. Cuban Cane's stock and bondholders, Manuel thought, believed the bankers had "left them out in the lurch" and they resented it. If any Riondas were tied too closely to the Guaranty Trust, they would share the odium that was bound to fall on it in the future. Meanwhile, Higinio was making enemies of members of the government. Finally, Manuel warned Higinio that he was risking his health, and even if he should succeed, he "would not receive any appreciation—and much less remuneration." He was sorry, he concluded, if his letter was a disappointment.

Portuondo's opinion, he added, was that the Tanteo suit was "all a bluff for political purposes." How could Cuba ever "raise the necessary money to pay up the Bankers in order to take full title to the properties[?]"

Higinio thanked Manuel and indicated that he agreed with everything Manuel had said. But Higinio continued writing almost daily. He informed New York that he had learned that the General Sugar Company had wanted its *Vertientes* and *Agramonte* mills to go to their third, final foreclosure sales but that General Sugar had suspended the process until the Cuban Cane matter was settled. Dominican-American, he thought, was doing the same with some of its mills. They should join together and appeal, while the Association of Cuban Hacendados should also make a written protest. And so on and so on.

There was, on May 19, a three-page single-spaced report on Fanjul's farewell interview with Sample on the eve of the banker's return to New York. Tears in his eyes, Sample had embraced him, saying that "he would never forget what Mr. Fanjul [had] done to help him when things looked the blackest."

On May 23, Manuel wrote his Havana nephew. Manolo tells me, he wrote, in a brief paragraph at the end of a long letter about negotiations over quotas, that you are continuing to write him reams of papers. What a pity! What a waste of time! With the horse you are riding, you won't go far. Between Higinio and his uncle, there thus yawned a difference of opinion. Higinio trusted Stetson to deliver the future leadership of Atlántica into his hands. Manuel expected, however, that the bankers would get out of the sugar business the moment they could recoup their advances. Hayden, once Cuba had calmed down, would raise the necessary sums to buy Atlántica's mills back, and Higinio would have nothing to show for his pains. If Czarnikow-Rionda could get enough money from Schroeders to buy a respectable amount of stock, Manuel thought their firm might be able to continue the warehousing and selling of future crops. That was all, and in any case with *Manatí*, *Francisco*, and all the other ventures in which they were enmeshed, they could take on no more. What was important was the new U.S. policy toward the island.[9]

But Fanjul pulled strings, lobbied, and brought in delegations of colonos from Atlántica's mills, promising them that if the Tanteo suit were dropped, he would guarantee them the advances they needed. The matter ground on through late May and June, with violence in the streets of Havana between the ABC Party's supporters and Batista's military. Only on June 25 did a final parting between Mendieta and the ABC members of his cabinet clear the path for a resolution. On that day, Mendieta met with Fanjul and decided to "take the bull by the horns." The next day, he saw a delegation of colonos and on June 28 met with Crosby and Kelley, the secretary of agriculture, and a representative of the Asociación Nacional de Colonos de Cuba.

At this point, Manuel summoned Fanjul to New York. In the week's interval, Fanjul seemed to have lost hope. "If the Riondas are not going to put in money [into Atlántica] and Hayden is going to reap the harvest, why should I spend money I don't have on the trip. Nothing is going to happen just because they see our pretty faces [Por la cara bonita de los (Riondas) nada se va a conseguir]. Crosby and Kelley are going to get the credit for everything and I am not going to boast of all that I have done."

Would it not be better, he suggested, to delay his trip until Stetson or Hayden asked him to come? He reminded his uncle that when Hayden had returned from his trip to Africa, he had invited Manuel to lunch, but once lunch was over they had not heard from him again. Higinio himself was "terrified" of the next Cuban elections. In the political infighting, the politicians would think only of their own ambitions, overlooking the fact that confidence in the economy was what was needed most. "Mendieta's situation is horrible. He cannot govern unless he makes himself into a dictator—and that is what the poor man does not wish to be."

The matter, still undecided, was supposed to come before Mendieta's new cabinet on July 20, and Fanjul continued organizing pressure on its various members. On July 23, he was finally able to telephone Manolo that the suit had been withdrawn.

From his kinfolk in New York, Higinio now received congratulations. There were letters of thanks from Tom Garrett and Stetson. The attorney's was so carefully measured that it is impossible to tell from it how much credit was being given Higinio. "I have at all times felt confident," Garrett wrote, "that you were doing all in your power. Mr. Kelly and Mr. Crosby from time to time have reported to me the cooperation and independent effort put forward by you." No question had ever arisen, Garrett stated, of the "efficiency and propriety with which the Cuban Trading Company had handled the Company's sugar." The letter closed vaguely with "hopes for further and more close association."

Stetson wrote only half a page. He had been in the hospital for two days, but he was "fully conscious of your splendid cooperation and effectiveness" and would write more fully after a few days' rest at his country place. Manolo duly reported that Stetson had told him to tell Higinio that he knew that if it had not been for Higinio's efforts, the matter would have never ended satisfactorily.[10]

Atlántica saved from confiscation, there remained the all important matter of whether Hayden or Stetson would henceforth have control of its mills. But Fanjul still had unfinished business and wrote a long memorandum to Edward G. Miller. Rumors had been circulating, he wrote, to the effect that the banks had invested over $500,000 to obtain the support of Mendieta and "some members of the Cabinet and other political elements of prestige." The rumor, of course, was "absurd and unfounded.... Needless to add that I would never have lent myself to any combination involving bribery. All the work had been done through personal friendly contracts." He enclosed a copy of a letter from the president of Atlántica to Anthony G. Mendoza, "who so admirably and disinterestedly served as intermediary between ourselves and the President."

Yet many people had helped. "Mr. Enrique Pedro, who is the Treasurer of the Republic and a very close friend to the President. Mr. Pedro should be given a colonía." Mario Menocal should become manager of one of the plantations. Pío Alonso, "a personal friend of Justo Luis del Pozo, President of Unión Nacionalista," should have a colonía, as should Adolfo Méndez Güedes. Then there was Aurelio Vigil [president of the Asociación de Colonos], "an untiring fighter," and Benigno Rodríguez and Angel Uvera, who had helped him. "I understand that these latter are interested in obtaining the concession for the gasoline transportation from the 'Motembo' Mines through the narrow gauge track of Central Alava." As for the Menese brothers: "You know that day in and day out they have gone wherever we have asked them to go. I understand that they are in negotiation with you to obtain the Colonía of Mr. Isidoro Benavides." He must also recommend the lawyers Mario Lamar and Ramon de la Cruz. "Finally, I understand that Mr. Antonio G. Mendoza intends to write you to recommend one of his nephews. . . . [I]t would be well to remember that we have a certain moral obligation with them."

He was pleased, he concluded, that the banks had approved "the budgets for new plantings and cultivation." He had promised the colonos that he would try to obtain for them "more than $2 million. . . . I not only pledged myself with the Colonos, but also with the President of the Republic and Messrs. Cosme de la Torriente, Miguel Mariano Gómes, Justo Luis del Pozo, Antonio G. Mendoza and all the other personages who helped. . . . In my interview with the President. . . . I also mentioned . . . that in re-organizing the new company, the Colonos would be benefited thereby through the readjustment of their old accounts."

His conclusion was dignified: "I do not wish to meddle in the internal affairs of the company; my task has already been accomplished upon the Government withdrawing from the law suit. It has been a very difficult and tiring battle, because of the very little sympathy that the company enjoys in Cuba, and, for this reason if for no other, it will be to the advantage of all to bear in mind the services which the persons recommended in this memorandum have been good enough to render the company so that they may all continue to cooperate and defend it hereafter."[11] The next steps would be up to the New York Riondas and to Hayden.

On August 1, 1934, Frederick J. Leary of the Central Hanover Bank invited Manuel and Manolo to his office to go over the budget proposal for the Atlántica properties. Whether the Riondas still hoped they might be called to play a major role or out of a resigned sense of duty, they went as summoned and advised him that the main thing was for the bank to provide money for new plantings, for "without cane, it would be most difficult for the Banks to get rid of the properties."

The banks had grudgingly agreed upon precisely that the day earlier, although Clarkson Potter of Guaranty Trust had cited nobler motives: "the moral obligation they felt toward the security holders. . . . The banks' implied promise to [their] own State Department to continue the property in production if the suit were withdrawn"; and "similar representations made to the Cuban Government." The bankers would advance the necessary sums but believed the sooner they could get out from under, the better.

"Leary expressed a great desire," Manolo reported, "that we should, through a group of our own, take over *Infante* . . . if we could get a group to subscribe a substantial amount, we could write our own ticket." Even Hayden might concur, although he was "inclined to want full control and say in everything in which he is interested." Meanwhile, Hayden had been given another extension—this time to September 30.[12]

Fig. 6. From left, Alfonso Fanjul Estrada, Higinio Fanjul Rionda, Bernardo Braga Rionda, Antonio Barro

August was chiefly dominated in the clan's thinking by Cuba's delays in signing the Reciprocity Treaty. Fanjul's political expertise was shifted into organizing a campaign to push for acceptance, bombarding the press with articles and putting together a delegation of some 700 to wait upon Mendieta. When the treaty was finally ratified, de la Torriente, as Cuba's secretary of state, traveled to Washington for the signing. Rionda saw that Cosme was invited to a luncheon in his honor in New York. Rionda wrote that he would pay for it, but it should seem to be given by the sugar industry and the bankers.

At the Downtown Club deep in the Wall Street canyon, Hayden sat on Manuel's left and Stetson between Cosme and Manuel. Babst, George Davison, Carl J. Schmidlapp, George Keiser of the Cuban-American Sugar Company, a vice president of the National City Bank, Harry Worcester of the United Fruit Company, and the president of the Cuba

Company were present. There was also a Sunday dinner at Río Vista for Cosme "to meet all the family."[13]

Few hints of Hayden's progress in being able to exercise his option reached the Riondas. Do not be discouraged, Manuel wrote Higinio at the end of August. "La vida es muy larga."

But Fanjul had a personal reason to be impatient. Manolo was childless. Bernardo's George and Ronnie were entering Czarnikow-Rionda. But the Cuban Trading Company was at so low an ebb that it offered few prospects for Higinio's own four sons. If they could enter into some arrangement to step into Atlántica, he wrote Portuondo, the young men would have a future. Discouraged by the way Miller was refusing even to consider employing Menocal's nephew and by Galbán, Lobo's rising fortunes, he put some of the blame close to home. It seemed, he wrote Manolo, that his uncle and New York cousins were no longer capable of managing bold operations. In answering, Manolo ignored the rebuke and signed himself "Tuyo afectísimo" (thine most affectionately).[14]

Atlántica's shares, Manuel continued to believe, were worth buying. The mills had a capacity of 5 million bags, and while the Cuban government restrictions had, in the last zafra, limited their production to a mere 1,573,374, even that low figure meant a price of only about $4 per bag. Cheap Philippine sugar was still holding the market down. But "since the present Washington Administration cannot afford to have Cuba go to smash," he was confident that the United States would take "a strong hand" in making some future arrangement.

The final disposition of Atlántica's new shares moved at a dignified legal pace. An American company, the Cuban Atlantic Sugar Company, of which the Cuban Compañía Azucarera Atlántica del Golfo became a subsidiary, was incorporated in Wilmington, Delaware, on March 1, 1935. The few remaining assets of Cuban Cane Products were auctioned off to it for $53,000 on April 19. Stock of the Eastern Cuba Sugar Corporation and the Violeta Sugar Company was acquired for $5,000 (loaned by Hayden, Stone at 6 percent interest) by the Eastern Cuba bondholders' committee.

Manuel played with a rough five-page "Plan of Campaign" by which a four-man group of "Managers and Liquidators"—in other words, the Riondas—would run the company for some 5 percent of the gross annual income. "There is no need," he wrote, "of our going into this business unless we are remunerated. We should not follow the old policy of doing work for glory . . . nothing came from that *Baby* but work, disappointments, and—worse yet—accusations, investigations and other unpleasant things."[15]

In May, when Cuban Cane's bondholders and stockholders had been given their full opportunity to protect their initial investment by gambling further funds—an opportunity that few took advantage of—matters were tidied up for a conclusion. Those who had served as receivers, the attorneys and the accountants, put in bills for their services and expenses, whittling down the estate from $342,288 to $198,065, which was not even sufficient to cover the $230,000 owed in settlement of U.S. tax claims. Nothing was left for any other obligations.[16]

The settlement did not go unremarked by the more crusading of the New Dealers. Congress had voted that the Securities and Exchange Commission should investigate various suspicious reorganization procedures, and in August the commission turned its attention to Cuban Cane. Manuel, as well as the other players, submitted to its Protective Committee Study a summary of his shareholdings. He had, he recapitulated, been given 30,000 shares of Cuba Cane common stock in 1916, of which he had kept 12,618. He had purchased 2,125 shares of preferred stock by December 23, 1920, at an average price of $58 a share, and sold 2,000 of them on December 21, 1921, for $15 a share, losing $93,489.38. He had purchased an additional 30 shares for a total of $100 in November 1922, so that he had held 155 shares of preferred stock when the Cuba Cane Sugar Company came to its end.

In return for the 12,618 shares of common stock, under the reorganization plan he had received subscription warrants permitting him to buy 2,523$^{3}/_{5}$ shares of stock in the new Cuban Atlantic for $7.50 a share, as well as the right to purchase an additional 12,618 shares for $20 a share before January 1, 1940. For his 155 preferred shares, he received the right to buy 232½ shares of Cuban Atlantic for $5 a share, with the right to purchase an additional 155 shares for $20 each.

He was apparently not investigated further when the commission moved on to public hearings. While bankers and their lawyers staunchly defended the reorganization procedures, the newspaper accounts had a sinister ring, stressing the high costs of the reorganization (estimated at $1,071,052) and the fact that the banks were to be repaid 100 percent of their loans before any other outstanding bills were considered. Damning, too, to the general reader was the information that, while the preferred and common stockholders had been offered new shares at $5 and $7.50, respectively, 183,534 shares of the new common stock were being distributed at $4.36 a share to J & W Seligman; Hayden, Stone and Company; Roosevelt and Company; and Irénée Du Pont. However nefarious this may have seemed to the uninitiated, none of it was news to the Riondas. They had been eager for the banks to keep the mills grinding over the last few years by continued loans on any terms, and as for the $4.36 price, they had tried their best to buy some for that sum themselves.

For a few days, the glare of publicity continued. Bank officials and lawyers were cross-examined, as were Stetson and Hayden. Among the evidence introduced was a record of Hayden's own transactions from 1929 to the present. Hayden had indignantly denied, explained the *New York Times*, that he had used "inside" information, "although he insisted that [reorganization] committee members should not be deprived of the right to trade in the issues of companies whose affairs were in the committee's hands." He had, he testified, personally lost more than $600,000 in his transactions in Cuba Cane stock.[17]

The matter then vanished from public scrutiny. For the Riondas, the hearings had been subordinate to their own struggle to pull their plantations out of receiverships and also less significant than the price of sugar. They were quite accustomed to the vigor with which the banks protected the rights of capital.

The New York banks became owners of the Cuban Atlantic Sugar Company in settlement of their claims for $7 million against Cuban Cane Products. "Since the inception of the original enterprise in 1915," Manuel commented, "there has been a huge loss of capital. Assets of Cuba Cane Sugar were carried in the balance sheet of 1923 . . . at about $100 million. As nearly as can be determined the properties are about the same."[18]

Sample became president of the successor company and began the year 1936 by notifying Fanjul that the Cuba Trading Company's services would no longer be needed as Cuban Atlantic's "warehouse men, custodian and otherwise." "Your company," he wrote politely, "has rendered

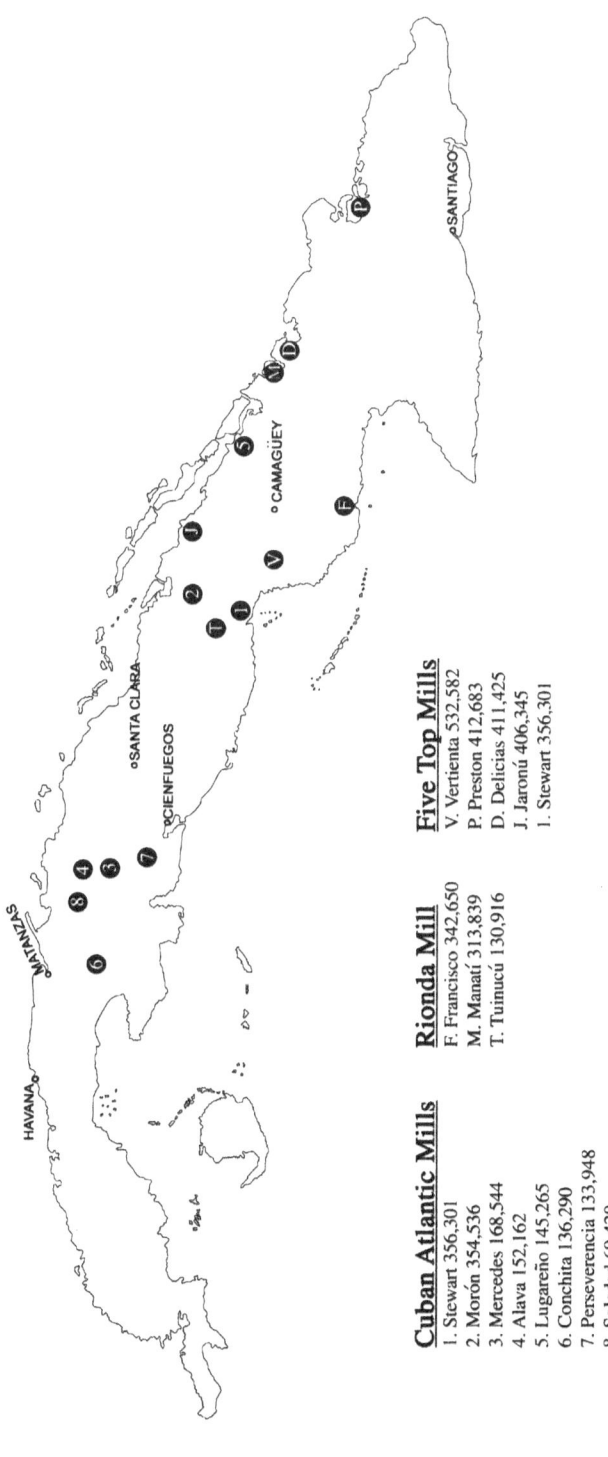

Cuban Atlantic Mills
1. Stewart 356,301
2. Morón 354,536
3. Mercedes 168,544
4. Alava 152,162
5. Lugareño 145,265
6. Conchita 136,290
7. Perseverencia 133,948
8. Soledad 69,420

Rionda Mill
F. Francisco 342,650
M. Manatí 313,839
T. Tuinucú 130,916

Five Top Mills
V. Vertienta 532,582
P. Preston 412,683
D. Delicias 411,425
J. Jaronú 406,345
I. Stewart 356,301

Map 4. Cuban mills, 1939. Production in 325-pound bags. Source: Farr & Co., Manual of Sugar Companies, 1941.

excellent service. . . . The relationship has certainly been most satisfactory in every way." Fanjul, too, replied politely. "One more link," he wrote, "that kept our Companies so close together ever since the birth of the Cuba Cane is thus broken." But he wrote full details to Stetson.

"I must confess to you," Stetson replied promptly, "that I had to find out what [your letter] was all about as I have not been keeping in touch with the Cuban Atlantic Sugar Company's affairs for quite some time." He had then, he wrote, immediately called a special meeting of Cuban Atlantic's directors and read them Fanjul's correspondence. "I reminded the Directors of your valuable assistance during the several trying periods that the old Cuba Cane and its successor went through . . . . [M]y deep sense of appreciation of our friendship, as well as your loyalty and cooperation and assistance to the Sugar Company, makes me more definitely mindful of the fact that you should not be counted 'out' or 'dropped from the team.'"

The letter pleased not only Higinio but also his uncle. To some extent, Manuel wrote, it restored his good opinion of Stetson. The family must try not to lose the bankers' friendship "and, much less, the income." Atlántica had the previous year paid them $16,000 for their stewardship, which was not inconsiderable at this low ebb of their fortunes. They should now waive $500 a month, since they would no longer have the responsibilities of inspecting the warehouses, and charge instead 1 cent per bag for attending to shipments and assorted services. This was then agreed upon, although it was scrounging for pennies. The assorted services were to include warehouses and warehouse receipts trusteeship, contracting officials, and representing the company in the Sugar Institute, plus whatever else that might come up. Higinio pointed out that at 1 cent per bag they would presumably gross no more than $14,000 in 1936, $12,000 of which would go to pay and insure the guards in the warehouses. Gómez Mena and Tarafa's heirs, who also paid only 1 cent, at least paid the guards' salaries. Sample, presumably reproved by Stetson, also wrote Higinio, apologizing at profuse length that his dismissal of the latter's services had been only because of a misunderstanding. He had not realized that, although warehouse receipts would no longer be necessary for the banks, they would, as Higinio had pointed out, be required by the Cuban Sugar Institute to ensure no mill was exceeding its quota. Higinio was also officially informed that he had been reelected a director and a vice president of Atlántica. Manuel wrote that he was happy to hear it all. "Del lobo un pelo" (From the wolf, a pelt).[19]

Some time later, Manuel reported that a group of banks—Wertheim and Company, Lehman Brothers, and Ladenburg, Thalmann and Company—were considering buying a large share in the Cuban Atlantic Sugar Company. They might wish that the Riondas join them. How much, he asked, could Higinio raise in Cuba? There was no point in their considering it, Higinio replied, unless they should have absolute control. He was convinced of the value of local management, especially when he considered the advantages obtained by the colonos in Cuba's new Ley Azucarera. "The mills the Cubans manage," he wrote, "I assure you, do not lose a single dollar." Manuel agreed. He was concise. "Ya basta," he wrote, "trabajar sin cobrar" [To hell with working if we don't get paid]. Their own affairs must come first. He went to Cuba for conferences at *Tuinucú* with Higinio, Leandro, Salvador, and Oliver Doty, inspecting the cane and mills. Coming back ill "with a little malaria," he knew that the hard times had not released their grip. "The future of sugar," he noted, "is held up by pins! All can go any time. We must not fail ourselves." The family must "follow [his] wishes without complaint."[20]

Shares in Atlántica dragged. Neither Guaranty nor "the new pretenders" were decisive, Manuel thought, and the latter were like bees who sought honey now in one flower, now in another. "No echan raices" (They did not put down roots). Civil war began in Spain that summer, and Manuel's gloom was compounded by sorrow for his homeland. To W. J. Rook, he wrote at the year's end that Spain had lent its territory for battlefields between Russia, Germany, and Italy. While he hoped Franco's troops would emerge victorious, in any case Spain would be ruined.

In October, there was a brief flurry as the Right of Tanteo was again flourished, the Cuban government threatening to take possession of the Eastern Cuba Sugar Company's *Violeta* for $1.8 million, for which the Chase National Bank was planning to auction it off. Once more attorney Crosby made his way to 106 Wall Street to report it to the Riondas before taking the plane to Havana.

He will ask your aid as soon as he arrives, Manolo informed Fanjul. "Our uncle says you are free to do whatever you wish, but that this time you should do nothing without a prior understanding that your services will be paid for. Crosby threatens the United States's ire, Cuba's loss of her tariff benefits, but Manuel feels such threats are mere 'pamplinas' [chickweeds, trivialities]." Sullivan & Cromwell, together with the great bankers, had tried playing the Washington card before when the Right of Tanteo had challenged Cuba Cane, boasting of the great influence they had on Capitol Hill, but Cuba had withdrawn its suit against Cuba Cane only because of Higinio's clever efforts. "Crosby will ask you to organize public pressure on the Cuban congress," Manolo predicted. "But in this case we owe no obligations, to the banks nor to Hayden, who has behaved equally badly toward us."

Higinio suspected at once that Manolo and Manuel were wrong. The old days were really gone. Crosby would not approach him, he wrote Manuel, unless he thinks all is lost, and things will probably not come to that extreme, for the Chase Bank has many powerful champions in Cuba. The U.S. ambassador was active and the Cuban Congress would not favor giving Cuba's president the necessary power to take the *Violeta*. In case, Higinio continued, Crosby should need to appeal for his aid, he would bear in mind that Manuel had advised him to do the New York bankers no favors. But he went on, boldly differing. "I will never forget," he wrote, "that above all what is important are the Cuban Trading Company's and the Riondas' interests. Miller and Crosby too, have treated us fairly in buying our sugar bags and in selling the Cuban Atlantic's sugar through us whenever we offered them prices as high as they could get elsewhere."

He reminded his uncle that Galbán, Lobo had been able to take away much of the clan's former business. "Their sugar sales are rising," he wrote, "while ours are falling. A César, tío Manuel, lo que es de César. Face it, Uncle Manuel, Lobo is a better merchant than we are."

Rionda's reply was gentle. "I admire," he wrote, using as always the affectionate Spanish "tú" form,

> the way in which you take these things, because you have very good reasons to say that the most important thing is to stay on good terms with Miller and Crosby . . . instead of following the path that I proposed in my letter, telling Mr. Crosby off [cantarle clarito a Mr. Crosby].

Now, as regards Lobo, I accept much of what you say. The man is continually on top of his business deals, and we, on the contrary, scatter our energies, not dedicating ourselves only to operations in the sugar trade.

He then went on to other matters. The Cuban president, perhaps because he lacked the support of his Congress, possibly because of something behind the scenes, lost interest in flourishing the Right of Tanteo, and no more was heard of the matter.

By late November, Manuel had learned that Hayden had finally acquired if not a clear majority, at least a large share of Cuban Atlantic's stock. Since Guaranty had not sold all its shares, he asked Fanjul to approach Stetson about obtaining some. In December, Manolo was instructed to send a check for $27,160 for 2,800 shares at $9.70 each, "which," Manuel added, "I consider cheap." It was an undistinguished finish to his great adventure. He ended 1936 by at least settling the *Francisco* receivership.[21]

The Roads Taken

Manuel Rionda lived until 1943, still stoically clinging to his lifelong belief that with Cuba so adapted by nature to the growing of sugar, and with the world's greatest customer only ninety miles away, market rationality would triumph over the distortions governments put in its path. Five months before his death, he wrote Higinio that he had faith in Cuba's natural advantage, in its soil and its nearness to the United States.

But as the 1930s ended, his hopes for the New Deal faded. He saw Roosevelt and his secretary of agriculture, Henry Wallace, surrendering to domestic politics. The New Deal's Jones-Costigan Act had pledged an adequate, even generous price for the sugar the United States would henceforth import from Cuba. But at the same time it had guaranteed that price, it had also set a limit on the quantity to be imported, and Cuba's share fell with each election's requirements.

In 1940, when Cuba's quota was cut by 30 percent, Rionda read with approval a letter from Higinio to the American ambassador. "The Reciprocity Treaty . . . hailed in 1934 as the corner stone of a new era in Cuban-American relations," Higinio wrote, had "failed dismally," become "simply a one-sided scheme . . . similar in its destructive effects to that of the absurd protective tariffs which a few years ago brought [Cuba] almost to the brink of social disintegration."

"I fear," Higinio warned, "that we may again witness the . . . calamities and social upheavals which attended the downfall of the Machado regime." Even five years earlier, writing a previous ambassador, he had called the U.S. quota system "un sacrificio estéril" (a sterile sacrifice).[1]

At the end of Manuel's life, war again brought prosperity to the world of sugar. World War II was at first a European war, a reprise of 1914, but with the difference that Great Britain no longer depended on German sugar supplies, having in the intervening years subsidized its own beets at home. There was thus no immediate bull market for Cuba as there had been in 1914. On the contrary, in 1940, with Atlantic shipping curtailed, the value of Cuba's crop dropped from $100 million to $98 million, although it rose in 1941 to $115 million. But in 1942, after Pearl Harbor, the United States again contracted to buy all Cuba produced.

The price for the first year was set at 2.65 cents per pound, and although Viriato Gutiérrez and many other Cuban mill owners and investors believed that, just as in the First World War, it was unfairly low, the 1942 zafra brought in over $250 million, more than doubling the income from the previous crop. *Manatí*'s operating profits rose from $63,491 in 1941 to $1,279,174 in 1942. *Francisco*'s in the same years went from $636,000 to $1,527,273. Cuban Atlantic's rose from $784,926 in 1940 to $1,533,258 in 1941 to $3,378,044 in 1942.

Rionda no longer had any privileged contact with Cuban Atlantic. Of the seventeen plantations he had originally purchased for Cuba Cane, eight remained to its successor company plus the *Violeta* and the *Velasco*, which together legally formed a separate company sharing the same directors and office. Cuban Atlantic's major investors were reported in 1941 to be the Chase National Bank (186,535 shares), the Charles Hayden Foundation (104,254 shares), and Wertheim and Company (123,400 shares). These firms were in the hands of men with whom Manuel had no particular acquaintance. Hayden had died in 1937 at the age of sixty-six in his apartment at the Hotel Savoy-Plaza in New York. He had been, at his death, a director of fifty-eight "corporations, banks, mines and railroads." He left no kin except an elderly brother, although the movements of mechanical stars perpetuated his name.

Rionda had only watched from some distance as Cuban Atlantic's lawyers and bankers went about safeguarding its assets in byzantine ways. Even starting out debt free, with obligations to former bondholders canceled, even having purchased all of Cuban Cane Products' assets (valued at $64 million) for a mere $4 million, Cuban Atlantic had barely survived its early years. It paid no dividends until 1940. Only with the war was there a 50 cents dividend in 1940, rising in 1941 to $1.50 and to $2.50 in

1942, when the stock sold at a high of 14⅝, which could bring its shareholders at long last, if they sold, a respectable profit of some 11 percent annually on their Cuban Atlantic investment, leaving out of account whatever they might have lost on the corporation's two predecessors. Rionda could, if he had sold his shares at the end of his life, have added $40,000 to his bank account. It was little enough after all the millions that had changed hands over some twenty-five years.[2]

It was better, Manuel had written long before, to be the head of a mouse than the tail of a dog. He had refused in 1903 to sell *Tuinucú* to Van Horne's Cuba Company in order "that my brother's heirs have a sure income and the young men is [sic] to be employed." His clan had thereupon built for themselves a leading place in the island's sugar economy. Although diminished by the depression, *Tuinucú*, *Francisco*, and *Manatí* had ridden out the low prices of the 1930s better than most sugar companies, Cuban or North American. In 1939, the eight mills that the *Anuario Azucarero* listed as Rionda "controlled" had a combined production of 1,128,620 bags, not too far below Atlántica's 1,452,880 and greater than Cuban-American's 1,013,273. The Rionda mills had given wide opportunities to Manuel's nephews, and he could look back with some satisfaction.[3]

If he looked ahead, however, the sky was darkening. His nephews, too, were aging. Manolo and Higinio were each sixty-six in 1943, and Bernardo was sixty-eight; even Salvador was fifty-six. Bernardo and Higinio had both experienced serious heart attacks, while Pepe, Leandro, and Salvador skirted breakdowns. Bernardo drank heavily, with Julio Lobo outsmarting him again and again in the Sugar Exchange's cutthroat operations.

Those in the clan's third generation were now of age—in addition to Riondas there were Estradas, Fernandezes, Ervesúns, Antuñas, Alonsos, Dotys, Crawleys, Fanjuls, and Bragas, named from the men his sisters and nieces had married. He found little comfort in most of them. The young men would, he feared, be careless with what had been won with such difficulty and sacrifice. When his great-nephew John Doty Jr., who had replaced his father as manager of *Tuinucú* after the latter's death in 1942, wrote that he had been impressed by a tractor he had seen on a visit to another central, Manuel replied firmly that he didn't favor any new method to cut cane. "It requires cash," he wrote, overlooking that he himself, in more prosperous days, had spent thousands of dollars bankrolling a Mr. Luce's attempt at a workable cane cutter, "and I have always been in favor of oxen. . . . They do not require gasoline and are always more reliable than tractors!" But, inevitably, the heirs would inherit power before too long. In the spring of 1943, Manuel pored over the budgets for the dead seasons, writing everyone very long letters counseling economy.

All his life he had insisted their mills produce sugar, and again sugar. But now the crop was so limited—with quotas having continued, no factory was allowed to produce more than half of what it was capable—he reluctantly agreed to their expanding into its by-products (invert molasses, industrial alcohol) and exploring new uses for bagasse. In *Francisco*'s 1942 annual report, he made excuses for—rather than welcomed—the new "various agricultural and related activities." They could be, he grudgingly conceded, secondary sources of income and "means of gainful employment" in the "plantation areas." He agreed that his grandnephew, José Andres Rionda, Pepe's son, now thirty, whom Manolo reported was "the only young blood in the family with engineering ability," could be made general manager of *Tuinucú*'s alcohol venture and that younger family members could sit on the board of this new wholly owned subsidiary. But, Manuel instructed the lawyers, they must be subject to orders from *Tuinucú* itself and from Czarnikow-Rionda, "who are the ones who are risking money." For experienced men, he wrote, they must still rely on the second generation. "While I want to use the third generation in this business, I don't want to leave the door wide open; we want to have control."[4]

As his eighty-ninth birthday came and went, he labored over *Manatí*'s and *Francisco*'s annual reports. Once he had lavished annual explanations of Cuba Cane's development on its stockholders, eager to make them see what their investments had created, realize what worldwide competition sugar must face, and understand what dangers it ran from weather, cane fires, political disturbances, and other sovereign forces. But Cuban Atlantic's reports were now produced by others and were cut and dried, taking for granted—as he had never been able to do—that investors were without interest in any growing plant, any food source of energy, that they were interested only in the company's balance sheet. Manuel's eagerness to elucidate and to justify had therefore been shifted to *Manatí*'s stockholders, although now he wrote briefly here as well. His "Letter" for *Manatí*'s annual report for 1943 went to the printers on August 24. It was published only after his death, Louis Mendoza and Company's weekly newsletter referring to it as "the posthumous work of . . . the late lamented Sugar Trader."[5]

He died, as the phrase goes, with his boots on, having gone into his office the previous day. He passed the day at his desk at his usual tasks. The last letter he dictated that afternoon was to an employee concerning the material presented to *Francisco*'s board of directors. He had, he said, been studying the minutes carefully because he had disagreed with certain appropriations. He then questioned seven specific details, the final one concerning the net increase of $5,086 for "corn, oranges, honey but particularly lumber." Copies of all his correspondence, from the beginning of his career, had been bound into 1,000-page onionskin letterbooks. This letter filled page 390 of volume 95.

The market had, at last, turned favorable. From a low of 2⅛ in 1941, *Francisco*'s stock was reaching 15¼. As he rode back to Río Vista late that afternoon with Bernardo, he predicted that he would soon have plenty of money again. Bernardo teased him, affectionately: "No, you won't," he said, "no sooner will you get the cash than you will spend it on a plantation or something else." The next morning, September 2, a month into his ninetieth year, already dressed and ready to leave, he had fallen to the floor in Río Vista's front hall.[6]

Wall Street paid him tribute, with a meeting in the boardroom of the American Sugar Refining Company. Although none of the current leaders of the Cuban Atlantic Sugar Company were listed as present, Earl Babst; William Nelson Cromwell of Sullivan & Cromwell; Ellsworth Bunker, chair of the U.S. Cane Refiners' Association; and Horace Havemeyer were among those there in his honor. Babst, in his fluent, grandiloquent prose, delivered a eulogy. "Mr. Rionda typified in an admirable way," his text ran, "the patriarchal character of the Cuban mill owner, especially of his time." "Next to his family," Babst stated, "Cuba was the romantic interest of his life." It was condescending and far from complete. The mourners then passed a resolution. "Called upon to face all the troublesome times and catastrophic perplexities arising from the War of Liberation in Cuba and later of the First World War," it recounted, "he had never lost his abiding faith. . . . In his private life, there clung to Mr.

Fig. 7. Manuel Rionda

Rionda a kindly and patriarchal interest in the members of his family and in his business associates. 'Noblesse oblige' was but second nature to him."

This was, presumably, the way it would please them to remember him. But true to the merchant's calling, he had been more realistic, harder.

He had been proud to be Spanish, but a few years before his death he had seen Spain go down in a civil war that he believed would leave the country in ruins for generations. Although he favored Franco, no one, he wrote, could win a war. He finally filed papers to become a U.S. citizen.[7]

The questions on the citizen application forms had wearied him. "I arrived in the United States in May, 1871," he filled in, not too patiently, looking back seventy-two years toward his remote boyhood. "The person in the U.S. to whom I was coming was George S. Hunt of Portland, Maine, in 1871." Are you a believer in the practice of polygamy? "No." And so on. His height was five feet six inches; his weight, 157 pounds. "The name of my wife was Harriet Clarke," he wrote. "I have no children. . . . My occupation is Merchant."

To be a merchant of so internationally traded a commodity as sugar was to be sentenced to the real world in its entirety, to be if not its citizen at least a student of and operator within it. A merchant's job was to establish contacts and weave common interests into profitable links. To sell his sugar, Manuel had cultivated men of another culture, mastering the English language, playing gracious host to American businessmen, showing them on their tropical holidays what a growing cane crop and sweating macheteros looked like, acting (as the memorial resolution was to commemorate) the "romantic" and "patriarchal" part. But no social ties had ever overridden price advantage. Those who purchased sugar and those who sold it were always antagonists.

Manuel had, all his life, met worldwide competition, from Java to the Elbe. Most of his rivals had been sheltered by special favors from their own governments—most fatally for Cuba, those competitors under the shadow of the eagle's wings: the American beet interests, Puerto Rico, the Philippines, and Hawaii. He had realized that if Cuba were to compete, efficient technologies, however expensive, were necessities, and he had embraced them. Moving beyond the broker's office, he had made his way into the private sanctums of America's bankers. Throughout his life, far from apologizing, Manuel was proud that he had raised vast amounts of capital on Wall Street. Without such backing, Cuban jungles could not have been cleared, railroad lines laid, machines installed, and, ultimately, so much sugar bagged at competitive cost. The money could have come only from Wall Street, and obtaining it had not been a crime, as he saw it, but his triumph.

In an apologia for himself, apparently for some public relations purpose a few years before his death, he had written of himself in the third person. "Who is Manuel Rionda?" "Manuel Rionda was one," he continued, shifting tenses, dictating in Spanish over the telephone from the Palisades, "who did the most to introduce American capital" into Cuba. In its war for independence, Cuba's properties, crops, and cattle had been destroyed. He had, he recounted, exaggerating, been one of the first and principal ones to interest U.S. capitalists in employing large fortunes in the industrial development of Cuban sugar. He had organized, he went on, dictating his apologia, the greatest sugar company yet known.

His obituaries and the memorial resolution in his honor by Babst, Havemeyer, and the others were also to select this for special praise. "[H]is most outstanding effort to uphold the Cuban sugar industry," the resolution concluded, had "culminated in the formation of the Cuba Cane Sugar Company in 1915."[8]

But if the formation of Cuba Cane had been Manuel's greatest service, to what had it amounted, after all? The resolution did not mention that the company had failed, that its common stockholders had lost whatever they had invested in it, and that the banks that had backed it, although they did far better, had still written off thousands of dollars in bad debts. Manuel himself, who had chosen its common stock instead of $1 million for his efforts in its formation, had, as he often remarked, tossed that stock into his wastebasket. He had organized it in a prosperous time during World War I, when all the sugar its mills could supply sold for guaranteed prices. He had put it together by buying, at the prices asked, centrals already in operation.

Had he "upheld the Cuban sugar industry," been "patriarchal" toward the majority of those engaged in the industry as well as "toward the members of his family" and "his business associates"? No. The corporation's colonos had become answerable to distant investors. When times became hard, they would suffer from the "administration cane" those investors considered more profitable. Nor had his accomplishment rewarded the Cuban cane cutters and mill workers. The corporation would bring in laborers from elsewhere in the Caribbean to push down wages. At most, it could be argued that, when the hard times came, the banks had loaned it money that they might not have loaned if they had not been already so involved. But the fate of Cuba Cane's mills was no different from those of the rest of the centrals on the island, most of which also somehow continued in operation despite foreclosures, while for its colonos, and macheteros, *carreteros*, engineers, and men on the mill floor, things were as bad as elsewhere on the island.

Nor did Rionda claim otherwise. When he prided himself on the creation of the Cuba Cane Sugar Corporation, he did not say it was a step on a march to social justice. His justification was rather that, by bringing marketing under more centralized control, a better price could be obtained because the vast disparity between the power of the few North American refiners and the many Cuban sellers would be reduced. This, he explained, would benefit every producer in Cuba.

At best, such a hypothesis was questionable. World supply, consumer demand, and government controls set the parameters of price. While within these parameters a merchant's skill might be marginally useful, any further expectations were illusory.

In World War I, Rionda would bargain, with the full authority of the Cuban government behind him, on behalf of the island. "In promoting the sale to the United States Government of the entire 1918 and 1919 raw sugar crops of Cuba," ran the memorial resolution, he had performed "the greatest merchandising transactions known at the time." The bankers who were meeting to remember him, there in the offices of the American Sugar Refining Company, could well be complacent, for he had served their interests well. He had accepted in 1917 Hoover's appeals to "patriotism," more patriotic toward Woodrow Wilson's war than toward Cuba's interests, accepting on the island's behalf a lower price than Tarafa, the Mesas, the Fallas, Castaño, and the Gutiérrezes knew to be justified, solidifying his own alliances on Wall Street.

Convincing men with capital to bankroll it, he formed the world's largest sugar corporation during days of skyrocketed demand and plunged into perfecting its operations. Ambitious, he plowed back its wartime profits into expansion at the cost of dividends, gambling that before the window of opportunity closed, it would be unshakeable. But to mesh sixteen diverse centrals into a single efficiently functioning unit, while the demands of Czarnikow-Rionda, the Cuban Trading Company, and his own family mills continued, put a burden on him with which he did not have the managerial sophistication to cope. The Goethals investigation resulted from the firm's failure to turn profits, and the report's critique of Rionda management seems justified, even if it could be argued that the fatal decision to purchase *Stewart* out of 1917's profits had been the responsibility of the bankers on Cuba Cane's board. As Louis Brandeis had predicted, they might well have had their banks in mind. With wartime profits pouring in to be reinvested and knowing that short-term loans to fund Cuba Cane's current operations would bring high interest rates, they had welcomed Manuel's expansion, without concern about what would happen when the guns were silent and the European beet fields producing once more.

General Goethals did not conclude Manuel was dishonest, although certainly, for most of their services to Cuba Cane, Czarnikow-Rionda and the Cuban Trading Company had been paid very respectable commissions. Goethals instead turned the spotlight on Rionda deficiencies in administration. The North Americans reclaimed management of their purchase, and it was under the superintendency of their chosen subordinates that the Cuba Cane Sugar Corporation went into bankruptcy. Although for some ten more years Manuel and his nephews tried to hold on to their vestiges of influence, encouraged from time to time by hopes that the board of directors would call them back to authority, they were never again given significant power. This part of the story was politely omitted from Rionda's memorials.

However wounded his pride, Manuel could not realistically afford to show anger toward the men who had backed his great venture or to write off his connections with such necessary North Americans as Alfred Jaretzki of Sullivan & Cromwell; Charles Hayden of Hayden, Stone and Company; Eugene Stetson of the Guaranty Trust; Earl Babst of the American Sugar Refining Company; and Gordon Rentschler of the National City Bank. He had no choice but to continue going into Czarnikow-Rionda's office at the foot of Wall Street to consult with them at the lunches and in the board meetings and the private conferences. Annually each zafra, from *Tuinucú*'s veranda, he must still place his cigars and his private railway Pullman car at the disposal of assorted visiting magnates, acting the gracious host.

In the 1920s, the sugar world entered a new period. The first twenty years after Spain's defeat in the Spanish-Cuban-American War, for all their ambiguities, subserviency, and corruption, had been a positive building time for Cuba. Locomotives had whistled down newly laid railroad tracks, smokestacks had risen among cane fields planted where there had been jungle, and it could be assumed that the United States would purchase all the sugar the island could produce. Now the straightforward heroics of construction were finished, and the northern market was increasingly being supplied by its own beet fields and its colonies. A glut of unsold sugar would define the future.

As the price of sugar fell in the 1920s, Rionda stressed the importance of a united front of Cuban mill owners and North American investors in Cuba. The postwar decline, he argued, must unite them against common enemies, not turn them into antagonists. The heavier lifting in opposing higher U.S. tariffs could be best done by the East Coast refiners and bankers who, as constituents and campaign contributors, could best influence the U.S. Congress. In dealing with labor, it would be better public relations if union organizers were checked by Machado and later Batista rather than by the U.S. Marines.

But this compatibility of interests could not hold after a policy of vertical integration brought the northern refiners their own cane fields and when a serious depression clamped down. Inevitably, the North American mills would receive preferences when buy orders were placed. Rionda had long taken the virtues of the free market to be self-evident. But by the mid-1920s, he was no longer so sure that the market was still free or that freewheeling competition was the best policy.

Despite his long fealty to Adam Smith, Manuel began to argue that steps must be taken to limit future production and to dispose gradually of surpluses in a controlled way that would share the sacrifice among all the mills. Here, as central government planning and controls loomed, Rionda's long friendships with the heirs of Castaño and of Falla Guitiérrez and his connections with Tarafa, the Gómez Menas, and Portuondo were a capital as important as his ties to men like Hayden and Babst. He tried to build a working alliance between his associates among the sugar elites in both countries, with the gains and setbacks that have been described.

There could be no way in which government-imposed quotas could satisfy everyone. With a government like Machado's (and more so in the future with one like Batista's), suspicions of favoritism and bribery were justified. Everyone connected with controls came to be tainted by them. With the quotas, too, divisions sharpened not only between the Cubans and Americans but between the larger and the smaller interests. If at first the larger Cuban mill owners showed some concern for their smaller cousins, that fraternalism went down under the blows of the depression of the 1930s. "Hace falta unión; hay mucha envidia!" Rionda wrote Higinio. They are not united, there is too much jealousy. Many suffered losses without any interest in working for the general welfare, and thus only a minority carried the burden. This, he wrote, must be remedied for the sake of the future. There must be a future policy.

He had seen the necessity for economies of scale and built up his own clan's mills. He had fought the union organizers and the colonos who would organize. But a lurking preference for those who spoke his own language persisted. Two weeks before his death, however unrealistically, he asserted the rights of the island where he had made his clan's fortune: "The time must come when Cuba must not show fear of bad treatment from anyone. Cuba must act as a perfectly independent entity. I cannot see why the buyer of any commodity should intimidate the seller."

If Manuel had not turned to politically imposed solutions for economic problems, what happened to him after his loss of Cuba Cane would be only a tale of ebbing influence. One might perhaps think that the financiers had used and then discarded him, when they might at least have sold him some shares in Cuba Cane's successor companies at the same reduced price at which they sold them to themselves. Or one might think Manuel should have expected it. He went where the big money was and paid a price.

He, too, was tainted by the corruption of controls. But there is more to it than that. It was a time when suffering cut so deep that it seemed only central power sufficed. From the Kremlin to the Roosevelt White House, government planning was in fashion, and in Rome, Mussolini had set an example that Machado was eager to follow. A merchant could hardly avoid knowing that the real problem was the mounting glut of sugar on the world market. This is still, more than half a century after his death, the conundrum to be solved. Therefore, even now it is informative to remember how he tried to influence governments of two countries—their financiers, refiners, mill owners, and politicians—and what came of such attempts.

Neither the Cuban ambassador to Washington, Manuel wrote Portuondo in June 1943, nor the U.S. ambassador in Cuba nor the U.S. Congress must decide sugar's fate, but "las necessidades en el mundo entero" (the needs of the whole world) should determine sugar's fate.[9]

He had become, if usually behind the scenes, a key player in international sugar politics when Cuba's unilateral sacrifice failed, backing the bolder, creative Tarafa in his Machado-supported ventures abroad and sketching out a plan for Chadbourne. The results proved hollow. Chadbourne, collecting his pay, gave up on it, although there was in 1937 a complicated International Sugar Agreement launched, if timidly, by the League of Nations. But less than a year after the agreement went into effect, Nazi troops entered Vienna, and its lofty rhetoric was put on hold for the duration, not to be resurrected until after Manuel's own death and in an even more lukewarm manner.

His peers paid his struggles for a "League of Nations of Sugar" a vague lip service in their memorial resolution. He had "rendered public service of the highest order" in "his effective efforts to ease and finally to overcome the disastrous economic conditions that ensued on the close of the War," they wrote. But his efforts had not been "effective" enough to earn him a triumphant place in history.

The secular fall of sugar prices through the 1920s, the depression of the 1930s, the resultant social and class tensions, the rivalries between nations and between nationalisms engaged him. Unlike Goethals, Manuel could not seek a microsolution by way of efficiency in a single enterprise. (He approved of efficiency in its place but knew it had its limitations.) Unlike Hayden, he did not seek merely to lock in his own personal profits by salesmanship, legal legerdemain, and diversification. He recognized instead that in the case of a tropical export crop like sugar, a market must come through a balance that must be sought on an international level. Obtaining money in Manhattan, however much, to invest in a sugar company, even in the world's greatest, had proved too local an accomplishment.

In his eighties, Rionda moved back and forth among conflicting forces. When Cuban workers and students toppled Machado in 1933 and when soon afterward Batista and his puppets, interrupted briefly by the reappearance of a chastened Grau San Martín, took charge, Higinio in the field was able to draw on his uncle's friendships, the loyalties Manuel had inherited from his older brother Francisco, as well as on the common ambitions of their business class. The heirs of the Falla Gutiérrezes and Castaños and the Gómez Menas were holding their own when Manuel died, and for the next decade they and others of their generation would exert increasing power in the cane fields and the mills as well as in Batista's councils, repurchasing the companies their grandfathers and great-uncles and fathers-in-law had founded. With more staying power (or fewer options) than the North American investors, in due time the most powerful of them would reclaim title to many of the diminished cane fields.

Perhaps Fanjul, who always remained in Cuba, who had married locally, and who was raising four sons on the island, was less suspect than Manuel had become in his mansion above the Hudson River. Fanjul survived the hard times and, like other local magnates, improved his standing. He had been slower than his uncle in surrendering hopes for taking back management of the Cuba Cane mills. It was at least in part owing to his tireless campaign—aided behind the scenes by who knows what other pressures—that Cuba Cane's mills avoided the Right of Tanteo. He contributed to that campaign partly by rallying a force of colonos—he himself had begun as a colono—illustrating to Batista one more use of the appeal to nationalism.

When Castro's forces fought their way west from Oriente to Havana, *Francisco*, *Manatí*, and *Tuinucú* were still in the family's hands. George A. Braga, Bernardo's oldest son, was the president of both *Manatí* and Czarnikow-Rionda, with George's younger brother, Bernardo Rionda Braga, president of *Francisco*, having succeeded to that post after Leandro's death in 1952. Sullivan & Cromwell was still their general counsel, and Higinio Fanjul, Alfonso Fanjul, Aurelio Portuondo, Aurelio Portuondo Jr., and Alfred Jaretzki Jr. prominent among the directors of their assorted companies, as was Pepe Rionda. Salvador was at the end a "consulting vice-president" of *Manatí*. Leandro and Manolo had been childless, and Manuel's two remaining Rionda nephews each had only one son, Salvador's boy, born in 1925, christened for his great uncle. "I hope that he will have a happier life than mine," old Manuel had wired for the young Manuel Rionda's tenth Christmas, not foreseeing that his namesake would die twenty-six years later at the Bay of Pigs.

By 1959, Ruby Phillips, the *New York Times*'s expert Cuban correspondent, estimated the Atlántica del Golfo and the Rionda group to be the two greatest landholding companies on the island, with 500,000 acres each, followed by the Cuban-American Sugar Company with 350,000 and United Fruit with 266,000.[10] Thus the Rionda holdings, when the Castro government's Agrarian Reform Law became effective, were among the most weighty in the Cuban plantation world. The new Cuban government took them over and gave them new names; *Tuinucú* became the *Melanio Hernández*, and *Manatí* was renamed *Argelia Libre*. *Francisco*, rechristened *Amancio Rodríguez*, no longer commemorated the Spanish-born harbinger of U.S. incorporation who had died in New Jersey but a proletariat hero. The U.S. companies duly filed claims with the U.S. Foreign Claims Settlement Commission in Washington, D.C., $58 million for *Francisco*, $55 million for *Manatí*, and $38 million for *Tuinucú*. Total claims for the properties Manuel had launched, those independent mills where he had been head of the mouse, totaled $171 million, compared to $90 million for the American Sugar Refining Company and $85 million for United Fruit.[11]

As the revolution settled in, the family members remaining in Cuba left the island, regrouping in Miami, Palm Beach, and Guatemala. Higinio was among the last to leave, apparently feeling as he had felt in 1933—that he should hold his ground. But he was eighty-two, and his family worried they might be forced to ransom him if he lingered. In July 1960, he and Doña Maria joined their sons in Florida. Alfonso Fanjul Estrada, their eldest, who as a young man had stood with his father through the earlier revolution, was himself now fifty-two. His marriage to Lillian Gómez-Mena had not only been a valuable alliance but had also provided four heirs, including Alfonso Jr., already twenty-four, and José, seventeen. Several handsome Fanjul homes were erected in Palm Beach, where before too long their owners would entertain dukes and duchesses, Kennedys, statesmen, and celebrities. To the east of Palm Beach, the dams built by the U.S. Army Corps of Engineers had opened a wide area adjoining the Everglades in which to plant sugarcane, and Alfonso Sr. was intrigued. "The potentials that Florida has in sugar," he wrote an English friend, "are such that we in Cuba could never have realized them until we came here and saw them and I hope to look back in the midst of our tragedy [and] say how fortunate we were to go into it."

The Cuban Atlantic Sugar Company had been joined with Hershey and had expanded and profited in the interval before the Liga Agraria expropriated its mills in the name of the Cuban people. Through the years between Manuel's death and Castro's triumph, letters and cables periodically went back and forth between Havana, New York, and London, exchanging information about a battle for control of the former Cuba Cane properties between the New York investment banking firm of Carl W. Loeb, Roades and Company, and Julio Lobo, the clan's longtime rival, who was riding high now, as high as Manuel himself had ridden forty years earlier. The two Czarnikow firms had, from outside, speculated about rivalries and about possible secret alliances between the investment firm and Lobo. "We have spoken with John Loeb," George Braga wrote London in 1956, after Loeb became chair of Atlántica's board, "and are meeting with him to discuss the sale of their next crop." But it was a passing reference, soon forgotten. In March 1958, the Cuban Atlantic was dissolved, its assets sold to the Chiriqui Sugar Mills Corporation for $24.5 million. Since Chiriqui, which was Lobo's, was a Panamanian company, no appeal could be made to the U.S. Foreign Claims Division on its behalf when the *Lugareño*, the *Morón*, and the others were rechristened the *Sierra de Cubitas*, the *Ciro Redondo*, and so on, in the wake of the revolution that Higinio had warned would come unless conditions improved for the mass of Cubans.[12]

The rights of capital (both foreign and domestic) versus the rights of working people (native-born or contract labor), the protection of the smaller mills versus the advantage of economies of scale, the justification for the colonías, the desirability (or undesirability) of cartel arrangements, "free trade" ("supply and demand," "survival of the fittest") versus state planning, the virtues of nationalism versus a globalized economic rationality—all these would have to be weighed in judging Manuel Rionda. In his time, he had to deal with all of them.

Notes

Merchant at the Crossroads

1. *Moody's* 1917, 539; *Moody's* 1912, 1347; *Moody's* 1924, 195; *New York Times* (henceforth NYT), 3/16/1916.

2. Here and for additional biographical details, see Van Ness, "Guide."

3. Manuel Rionda (henceforth MR) to Higinio Fanjul (henceforth HF), 1/22 and 1/16/1916, Record Group II, Ser. 2, Braga Brothers Collection (henceforth BBC). Unless otherwise noted, all future correspondence is from this collection and from Record Group (henceforth RG) II.

Chapter 1. Business with Aliens

1. Van Ness, "Guide"; MR to William S. Clarke, 5/10/1929, Ser. 2.

2. Bergad, 53, 171, 202; Santa Cruz y Mallen, 380.

3. Hazard, 31–47; W. Rowe, 116–18; Hatch, 4: 266–67; "Rionda Family Genealogy" in BBC; Hunt Correspondence and Fred Allen to Joaquín Rionda, 8/28/1880, both RG I, Ser. 31, BBC; Neal, 136–37; MR to J. Infante, 7/23/1900, Ser. 2.

4. Van Ness, "Guide"; Ely, "Old Cuba Trade," 456–78; Chernow, 34; Cleveland and Huertas, 17; Winkler, 39–41.

5. Van Ness, "Guide"; Farrel to Kelly, 1/19/1878, RG I, Ser. 31, BBC; Farrel obituary, *National Cyclopaedia of American Biography* (henceforth NCAB), 21: 97–98; Weigle, 179; Farrel to MR, 10/20/1882, RG I, Ser. 31, BBC.

6. Thomas, 1582; Bergad, chap. 14; Bonnet, 2651.

7. Kelly to MR, 10/7/1880, RG I, Ser. 31, BBC.

8. Van Hook, 112; Ratner, 33–35; Kelly to MR, 10/7/1880 and 1/11/1882, RG I, Ser. 31, BBC; Kelly obituaries in NCAB, 14: 242, and NYT, 10/31/1906; Van Ness, "Guide"; Kelly testimony, U.S. Senate Committee, *Cuban Sugar Sales*, 141, 150; *Moody's* 1919, 2322.

9. "Rionda Family Genealogy"; G. Braga, 17–30; Bernardo Braga Rionda (henceforth BBR), Part 1; Weigle, 190; Clarke obituary, NYT, 2/29/1922.

10. Bergad, 27, 62, 69; Atkins, 30, 67, 81; Weigle, 180–86; Atkins obituary, NCAB, 16: 52.

11. MR, "Cuban Colono System," 20–21.

12. Ratner, 36–37; Atkins, 108, 79; Thomas, 1576–77.

13. Catlin, Mullins, Weitzenhoffer, and Eichner tell the Havemeyer story; Zerbe, 351.

14. Havemeyer, 27; Zerbe, 353, table 2. The difference in price between raw and refined sugar is called "the differential." It should be noted that the tariff had dropped in 1883 from 2.7 cents per pound to 2.2 cents and was completely abolished in 1890 (Van Hook, 112).

15. Weigle, 189; MR to W. V. King, 7/20/1933, Ser. 2; U.S. Senate Committee, *Cuban Sugar Sales*, 5, 11.

16. *Moody's* 1915, 3432; Weigle, 191; Jencks, 35; Fiske obituary, *Facts about Sugar* (henceforth FAS), 5/4/1918, 356.

17. *Anuario Azucarero de Cuba* (henceforth *Anuario*), 1942, 67; FAS, 7/2/1927, 647; *Sugar*, April 1952, 37; Atkins, 144; Porter, Appendix, 88–90, 94, 131, 144.

18. Janes and Sayers, 10, 15, 28, 39, 31; Czarnikow obituaries in *London Times*, 4/9/1909, and NYT, 4/18/1909.

19. G. Braga, 48–50; BBR, Part 1, 16; MR to Lewin, 2/16/1897, Ser. 1.

20. MR to Lagemann, 9/7/1912, and MR to Westrik, 2/9/1906, both Ser. 2; MR to Czarnikow, 3/7/1897, and Czarnikow to MR, 4/9/1897, both Ser. 1.

21. Ratner, 40; U.S. Department of Agriculture (henceforth USDA), *Yearbook 1912*, 651; BBR, Part 1, 16; G. Braga, 43–44, 50, 55.

22. MR to Rabel, 9/18/1896, MR to Placé, 3/5/1898, MR to Czarnikow, 3/8/1898, MR to Allen, 2/18 and 3/24/1898, all Ser. 2.

23. MR to Rabel, 4/2/1898, MR to Pelayo, 4/20/1898, MR to Rabel, 4/20/1898, all Ser. 2 (translations are mine unless otherwise noted); MR to Francisco Rionda, 5/21 and 6/4/1898, C. Czarnikow to MR, 5/21 and 6/4/1898, all Ser. 1.

24. FR to Czarnikow, MacDougall (henceforth Cz, M), 7/8/1898, Ser. 2. (1898 translation in Letterbook); C. Czarnikow to MR, 8/31/1898, Ser. 1; MR to Westrik, 2/9/1906, Ser. 2.

25. Rionda Family Genealogy; MR to Dos Passos, 8/7/1899, Ser. 2; Manuel Enrique Rionda (henceforth MER) obituary, NYT, 2/10/1950.

Chapter 2. Head of the Mouse

1. Bonnet, 2702–3, 2709.

2. Day, 392; Bonnet, 2636–39; Deerr, 222–27; De Abad, 198–212; C. Czarnikow to MR, 8/13/1897, and MR to Allen, 2/18/1898, both Ser. 2.

3. Francisco Rionda to Cz, M, 7/8/1898, Ser. 2; Castaño obituary, *La Lucha*, 1/28/1926; Porter, Appendix, 88–90, 104.

4. MR to Clark, 5/22/1899, Ser. 2; Porter, Appendix, 231–34; Santa Cruz, 1: 375, 380; Romney in *Louisiana Planter* (henceforth LP), 12/15/1902, 316; Clark to MR, 3/25 and 4/5/1899, Ser. 1; Thompson obituary, NYT, 12/28/1937.

5. G. Braga, 22, 59–60, 62, 65; BBR, pt. 1, 21.

6. MR, "To the Cuba Cane Sugar Corporation," 2, Ser. 64 (revised version dated 7/29/1919); Minutes of Incorporation, 3/1/1899, in "Francisco, Original Minute Book"; RG IV, subgroup 1, BBC; MR to Craig, 5/15/1899, Ser. 2.

7. Clark to MR, 5/12 and 5/21/1899, Ser. 1. *San Manuel* was listed in the *Cuba Review* (henceforth CR) as Cuban-owned as late as 1913. The LP, 9/28/1907, 199, referred to *Lugareño* as owned by Melchor Bernal and "the third largest estate controlled by the Havemeyers in eastern Cuba," while the CR listed its owner, the "Sociedad Anónima Central Lugareño," as "Spanish-Cuban." The intricacies of "owning" and "controlling" are subtle. MR to H. O. Havemeyer, 5/13/1899, and MR to Craig, 4/21/1899, both Ser. 2.

8. MR to Placé, 4/18/1901, Ser. 2; Placé obituary, LP, 10/30/1915, 282; G. Braga, 74–76. Mrs. Risley's letters are in Ser. 17, BBC.

9. J. M. Clark to MR, 4/26/1899, Ser. 1; Hawley obituaries in NYT, 11/29/1921, and FAS, 12/3/1921, 443.

10. MR to Craig, 6/30/1899, Ser. 2; Benjamin Howell obituary, *Willett and Gray's* (henceforth W&G), 4/19/1900, 2; Post obituaries in NYT, 3/6/1938, and W&G, 3/10/1938, 100. Frederick H. Howell (ca. 1850–1929), Benjamin's son, became a Cuban-American director in 1907 and retired in the 1920s (F. H. Howell obituary, W&G, 3/14/1929, 153). Thomas A. Howell (1878–1930) graduated from Yale in 1900, married Emilia de Apezteguía, and became a partner of the Cuban-American Sugar Company in 1905 (Thomas Howell obituary, NYT, 4/20/1930, 8; Cuban-American Sugar Company Annual Reports).

11. *New York Journal of Commerce*, 9/24/1899, reprinted in LP, 10/7/1899, 239. It was reported that $420,000 was paid for 6,500 acres of cane fields (LP, 10/1/1899, 249). Anicete G. Menocal (1836–1908) graduated from Rensselaer Polytechnic Institute. He was the chief engineer of U.S. government surveys for a canal through Nicaragua or Panama, a member of the committee selecting the Subic Bay site in the Philippines, and director of a navy survey for a coaling station in Liberia. He must have been well trusted in U.S. naval circles in the age of Admiral Alfred Mahan (*Who Was Who in America*, vol. 1; CR, 12/25/1900, 20; LP, 12/8/1900, 363).

12. *Moody's* 1917, 55–56; LP, 10/12/1907, 226; Mark Spelman obituary, NYT, 7/20/1920.

13. Wood Report, 1900, table 22, 212. Santiago de Cuba's nineteen centrals were included in the 1901 report but not in 1900's.

14. Thompson to MR, 10/25/1900, Ser. 1; Van Horne obituary, NYT, 9/12/1915, and Dumas Malone, *Dictionary of American Biography* (henceforth DAB), 19: 197–99. For Van Horne, see Healey; Santamarina; Van Ness, "Sugar"; Vaughan; Zanetti and García.

15. MR to Rasco, Castaño, Muñoz, Bea, Angulo, Rabel, and Pelayo, 2/28/01, Ser. 2; Weigle, 252; MR to Rabel, 4/2/1901, Ser. 2; LP, 8/10/1901, 95; U.S. Senate Committee, *Cuban Sugar Sales*, 88–90. For MR's suspicions, see MR to Placé, 3/5/1902, MR to BBR and MER, 3/26/1902, MR to Henry R. Reed, 4/28/1902, MR to Rabel, 3/12, 5/9, 5/20, 3/12/1902, all Ser. 2.

16. MR to Leandro Rionda (henceforth LR), 11/15/1902, Platt to MR, 11/15/1902, MR to Placé, 5/16/1902, MR to Coma, 6/6/1902, all Ser. 2; G. Bryson in LP, 8/23/1902, 121–22.

17. MR to Placé, 1/22/1902, Ser. 2; Healey, 203; Porter, *Report*, 28; MR to Cz, M, 1/3/1903, Ser. 1; Ratner, 41; MR to Placé, 5/9/1903, Ser. 2; Mullins, 186–229.

18. MR to Cz, M, 1/3/1903, Ser. 1.

19. LP, 11/30/1912, 363; Rionda Family Genealogy; G. Braga, 3, 69, 92; MR to Parker, 8/3/1904, Ser. 2.

20. CR, 1905. Complete production figures for individual centrals become available in 1904 when the CR began to list all mills annually, by province, giving the output of each in 325-pound bags, with their addresses, owners, owners' nationalities, and administrators. In 1905, the figures from 1902 and 1903 were included to form an unbroken sequence from 1902 until 1931, when the magazine ceased publication and Farr's *Manual of Sugar Companies* took over. All subsequent references to production of individual mills are based on these figures.

21. G. Braga, 142–47.

22. *Moody's* 1908, 228–29; *Moody's* 1923, 98; MR to Placé, 9/10/1906, MR to Alonso, 9/11/1906, MR to Craig, 10/1/1906, MR to Allen, 10/20/1906, all Ser. 2.

23. *Mundo Azucarero*, August 1916, 26–28. Davis, born in Matanzas, had been secretary of the Cuban Tariff Commission and was sent to Washington in 1902 (Primelles, December 1915, 64; CR, 1915, 29; Lisagor and Lipsius, 71; "Voting Trust Agreement," Ser. 7, vol. 1; MR, "To the Cuba Cane Sugar Corporation," 4, Ser. 64). Rionda resigned on 3/29/1909, Cromwell replacing him.

24. G. Braga, 102–3.

25. Kelly obituary, NCAB, 14: 422; LP, 11/7/1908, 298; Catlin, 96–97; Mullins, Appendix K, 347–51, 283; Chandler, 328–29; Eichner.

26. *Moody's* 1909, 2704; MR to Parker, 8/31/1904, and MR to Craig, 6/10/1908, both Ser. 2.

27. MR to Placido, 4/17/1909, Ser. 2; NYT, 4/18/1909, 11; Janes and Sayers, 47; Lagemann to MacDougall, 7/30/1912, and MR to Lagemann, 9/7/1912, both Ser. 10A; Roberts, 130; BBC, RG III, Subgroup 1.

28. MR to LR, 6/25, 6/29, and 8/31/1909, Ser. 2.

Chapter 3. Tarafa and the Genial Shark

1. CR, June 1911, quoting *La Lucha*'s quotation from Van Horne; MR to C. Czarnikow, 11/11/1910, Ser. 2.

2. NYT, 8/26/1923, 1; Tarafa obituaries in Havana's *Mercurio*, 7/29/1932, FAS, August 1932, 328, and NYT, 7/25/1932.

3. Parker, 895–96; Primelles, 216.

4. Rubens obituaries in NYT, 4/4/1941, and *New York Herald Tribune*, 4/4/1941; Le Riverend, 211; Rubens, 298, 376.

5. Conklin obituary, NYT, 1/3/1938; Thomas, 545; Lagemann to Czarnikow-Rionda (henceforth Cz-R), 3/31/1911, Ser. 10A; LP, 9/2/1911, 151; LP, 9/9/1911, 167, 171–72; LP, 9/30/1911, 218; LP, 10/28/1911, 290.

6. MR to Truffin, 7/21/1911, Ser. 2; USDA, *Yearbook 1923*, 845–47; MR to Tarafa, 8/13 and 8/15/1911, Ser. 10A; MR to Tarafa, 8/18 and 8/22/1911, Ser. 2; Tarafa to MR, 8/29/1911, Ser. 10A.

7. MR to Hawley, 10/31/1911, and MR to Placé, 9/1/1911, both Ser. 2.

8. LP, 6/6/1914, 389.

9. Cleveland and Huertas, 54; Chernow, 152.

10. Cleveland and Huertas, 41; Chernow, 152, 176.

11. MR to Truffin, 4/18/1912, Ser. 2; Jaretzki obituary, NYT, 3/15/1925. Angulo was a Rionda attorney (Parker, 401).

12. MR to Truffin, 4/26/1912, Ser. 2; Jaretzki to MR, 5/15/1912, Ser. 1; MR to Craig, 5/26/1912, Ser. 2.

13. DAB, 571–72; Obituaries for Frederick Strauss, NYT, 8/12/1937, and Albert Strauss, NCAB, 22: 246.

14. MR to Truffin, 10/8 and 4/30/1912, Ser. 2.

15. Tarafa interview, NYT, 8/26/1923; Zanetti and García, 263; LP, 9/30/1911, 218.

16. LP, 2/3/1912, 7, and 10/19/1912, 258.

17. LP, 10/19/1912, 257–58. The story continues that attorneys for Cuban Central, which had bid $5,000 per kilometer for a shorter route, charged that "in granting the subsidy to Sr. Tarafa the President has . . . unduly discriminated against the British interests, to the displeasure of both Mr. Taft's and His Majesty's Government." Thomas, however, quotes U.S. State Department disapproval of "the prospect of English capital expansion in Cuba" (Thomas, 510; cf. Zanetti and García, 263–74).

18. MR to MacDougall, 7/8/1912, Ser. 2.

19. LP, 7/20/1912, 39.

20. NYT, 5/21/1912, 2; Wilson, "Tariff Reform Message of 1913," in Ratner, 140–41; MR to Miles, 4/24/1913, Ser. 2; MR to Schroeder and Company, 8/12/1913, Ser. 4.

21. MR to Lagemann, 8/4/1913, and MR to Westrik, 8/20/1913, both Ser. 4; MR to Lagemann, 8/10/1913, Ser. 2; MR to McDougall, 8/22/1913, Ser. 4; MR to V. Zevallos (henceforth cited as VZ), 5/27/1914, Ser. 2.

22. MR to Ogilvie, 4/7 and 5/5/1914, Ser. 2.

23. LP, 8/23/1913, 139, and 9/20/1913, 202.

24. LP, 9/20/1913, 203, and 10/4/1914, 237.

25. LP, 3/21/1914, 183, and 10/18/1913, 272.

26. LP, 8/30/1913, 157; LP, 1/31/1914, 78; LP, 12/6/1913, 382.

27. LP, 4/20/1914, 423; LP, 6/27/1914, 439; LP, 4/12/1913, 232.
28. MR to Truffin, 1/20/1914, Ser. 2.
29. "Comparative Statement—Crop 1913/14," attached to MR to Cz-R, 1/6/1914, Ser. 10A.
30. USDA, *Yearbook 1923*, 845, 852.
31. Mayer, 60–61; Cleveland and Huertas, 71–72; MR to Ogilvie, 7/1/1914, Ser. 2; MR to Lagemann, 8/13, 8/17, and 7/12/1914, Ser. 4.
32. MR to MacDougall, 6/5/1914, Ser. 4; MR to Ogilvie, 4/29/1914, Ser. 2.
33. LP, 8/8/1914, 87.
34. MR to Lagemann, 8/3/1914, Ser. 2.
35. MR to VZ, 8/7/1914, Ser. 2.
36. MR to Cz-R, 3/19/1914, Ser. 2. The Cuban total was 17,857,818 bags, 11,278,881 from the four western provinces.
37. Chalmin, 123–25.
38. W&G, 1/28/1915, 39; Hugill, 65.
39. MR to VZ, 8/3 and 8/5/1914, Ser. 2; MR to Lagemann, 8/13 and 8/17/1914, Ser. 4.
40. MR to LR and Doty, 8/7 and 8/20/1914, Ser. 2.
41. Roberts, 120; Ganzoni to MR, 1/7/1916, Ser. 4; *Who Was Who*, 5: 1088; MR to Baron Schroeder, 11/18/1914, Ser. 2; Roberts, 162.
42. MR to MacDougall, 8/7 and 9/9/1914, and MR to Ganzoni, 3/29/1915, all Ser. 4; MR to Lagemann, 8/24/1914, Ser. 2; MR to Nieburg, 11/9/1914, Ser. 4.
43. MR to Lagemann, 8/24/1914, Ser. 2.
44. MR to HF, 10/20 and 10/23/1914, Ser. 2.
45. MR to Lagemann, 7/12/1914 and 5/17/1915, Ser. 4; MR to Lagemann, 5/12/1920, Ser. 10.

Chapter 4. Cuba Cane

1. MR, "To the Cuba Cane Sugar Corporation," 7, Ser. 64.
2. MR to José B. Rionda (henceforth JBR), 9/20/1911, Ser. 2; LP, 7/31/1915, 72.
3. Atkins, 341; LP, 10/1/1921, 217; Catlin, 124; CR, August 1926, 27.
4. MR to F. Strauss, 10/21/1915, and MR to HF, 11/1/1915, both Ser. 2.
5. MR to HF, 11/26 and 11/15/1915, and MR to Truffin, 10/28/1915, both Ser. 2; MR to F. Strauss, 4/28/1916, Ser. 10A; MR to HF, 11/2/1915, Ser. 2.
6. MR to Lagemann, 12/27/1915, Ser. 2; MR, "To the Cuba Cane Sugar Corporation" (henceforth CCSC), 11, Ser. 64.
7. MR to Cz-R, 1/5/1916. A day later, he reported it "todo ilusiones" (MR to Cz-R, 1/6/1916, Ser. 2); MR to "NY Boys," 1/31/1916, Ser. 3; MR to F. Strauss, 4/28/1916, Ser. 10A.
8. MR to Cz-R, 1/25 and 2/11/1916, Ser. 126; *Wall Street Journal*, 3/15/1915; NYT, 3/16/1916.
9. A seventeenth, purchased only because Pote would not sell his *Conchita* without it, had been promptly resold at a slight loss.

10. Jencks, 244; Primelles, 54.

11. MR to Cz-R, Letter 22, 2/13/1914, Ser. 2. Five days later, Rionda added he had "agreed to take $100,000 in bonds of [Tarafa's] railway. . . . After all, I could not avoid it" (MR to Cz-R, 1/24/1916, Ser. 3); see also MR to Tarafa, 2/22/1916, Ser. 3.

12. James H. Westcott Jr., 4/2/1919, Ser. 126.

13. Thus the average price paid per bag (the customary way of comparing prices) had been $12.05. The average veils sizeable differences. Sugar from *Alava* and *Feliz* cost $7.74 per bag, from *Morón* $18.12 per bag.

14. Since many properties were incorporated, detailed searches of court records would be necessary to find the exact division of legal ownership. The names given are those of the men from whom MR reported he had made his purchases.

15. Lists dated 9/5/1916 of CCSC common and preferred stockholders owning 100 or more shares, Ser. 64; MR to Galbán, 1/20/1916, Ser. 3; Lincoln, 188.

16. MR to Jaretzki, Cable, 2/17/1916, Ser. 3; MR to A. Strauss, 3/27/1916, Ser. 64; FAS, 9/8/1917, 185; Primelles, 1918, 471.

17. *International Sugar Journal*, February 1920, 105; *Mundo Azucarero*, June 1919, 327; Primelles, ibid.

18. Thomas, 422, 1492, 506; MR to Jaretzki, 1/31/1916, Ser. 3. Manuel had cabled BBR, "Tell Jaretzki we believe it very desirable that he cable Ferrara asking him if he would accept a place on the Board of Directors." Jaretzki so cabled the same day. BBR to A. Strauss, 1/19/1916, Ser. 64; Jaretzki to Ferrara, 1/19/1916, Ser. 10A.

19. Lagemann to MR, 2/26/1916, Ser. 10A; Jaretzki to MR, 2/4/1916, Ser. 1, and 4/1/1916, Ser. 10A; MR to Jaretzki, 4/8/1916, Ser. 3; MR to "NY Boys," 2/5/1916, Ser. 10A.

20. MR to F. Strauss, 3/23/1916, MR to "NY Boys," 3/25/1916, MR to Cz-R, 2/6/1916, all Ser. 3; MR to F. Strauss, 4/28/1916, Ser. 10A.

21. LP, 10/7/1916, 227; *Mundo Azucarero*, November 1916, 103.

22. CCSC's First Annual Report states the contract was at 25 cents per 100 pounds and the average rate for others was 48 cents. Manuel later claimed a savings of 50 to 60 cents per bag. MR, "To the CCSC," 27, Ser. 64; MR to Cz-R, 1/31 and 2/5/1916, Ser. 3.

23. MR to MacDougall, 2/23/1916, Ser. 4; MR to Lagemann, 1/5/1916, Ser. 3, and 5/23 and 2/6/1916, Ser. 4; BBR to J. P. Morgan and Company, 4/21/1916, Ser. 64.

24. MR, "To the CCSC," 5, 7, Ser. 64.

25. MR to Lagemann, 4/3/1916, Ser. 3.

26. Undated and untitled, Ser. 64. It dates before November 1915 since the name "Cuba Cane" had not been agreed upon.

27. Many mills were slow to pay dividends at first. Cuban-American's common shareholders received nothing between 1906 and 1/1/1916 (*Moody's* 1919, 213–

15). The Guantanamo Sugar Company paid its first dividend on 7/23/1915 (*Moody's* 1923, 99).

28. The three banks controlled 25 percent of the voting shares.

29. Corey obituary, NYT, 5/12/1934; Jarvie obituary, NYT, 6/22/1929; LP, 7/15/1916, 42.

30. The report actually covered only nine months, since the corporation was created on 12/31/1915 and its fiscal year ended 9/30/1915. However, the former owners had turned over all profits from 12/1/1915, so the income represented a full grinding season.

31. MR to Ganzoni, 6/20/1916, Ser. 4; MR to Nieburg, 8/3/1916, Ser. 10A; MR to MacDougall, 6/19/1917, Ser. 4.

32. MR to F. Strauss, 4/28/1916, Ser. 10A.

33. MR to "NY Nephews," 2/2/1917, Ser. 12. The names in brackets are translated from the number code in the original using the key attached (MR to "NY Nephews," 2/22/1917, Ser. 4). I quote a typed English version in Ser. 12. Ganzoni to MR, 3/7/1917, Ser. 1.

34. "Prepared by Mr. Charles Lagemann," 7/30/1917, Ser. 10A ("*NY Evening World*" folder).

35. MR to MacDougall, 6/19/1917, Ser. 4; Gerard Smith to MR, 3/12/1917, Ser. 12.

36. MR to LR, 5/7/1917, Ser. 2; MR to Ganzoni, 5/11/1917, Ser. 4; MR to Nieburg, 4/5/1917, Ser. 3.

37. MR to Tarafa, 6/8/1917, Ser. 1; Tarafa to MR, 6/17/1917, Ser. 1 ("Sullivan & Cromwell" folder; English translation made in 1917); A. Strauss to MR, 6/13/1917, Ser. 10A; MR to MacDougall, 9/27/1917, Ser. 4.

Chapter 5. A Fixed Price

1. For Hoover, see Burner, Wilson, Brandes, and Barber.

2. Bernhardt, *Government Control*, 11, vii; MR to Ganzoni, 10/24/1917, Ser. 4, and 9/5/1917, Ser. 1; MR to MacDougall, 9/25/1917, Ser. 4.

3. Babst obituaries in NYT, 4/25/1967, and NCAB, 54: 471.

4. *International Sugar Journal*, February 1918, 53–54, and March 1918, 102; MR to Ganzoni, 11/15/1917, Ser. 1.

5. MR to Ganzoni, 10/24/1917, Ser. 4.

6. Lezama controlled the *Luisa, San Cayetano, Triunvirato,* and *Limones*.

7. Tarafa to MR, 6/8 and 5/24/1917, Ser. 1. Figures for 1917, blank in the typed "English version" of 5/24, have been supplied in ink in a Spanish copy.

8. MR to MacDougall, 9/25/1917, Ser. 4; U.S. Department of State, *Foreign Relations*, 1918, 344.

9. Dumoulin, 66–124.

10. MR to Ganzoni, 11/15/1917, and Ganzoni to MR, 12/3/1917, both Ser. 1.

11. MR to HF, 11/20/1917, Ser. 10A.

12. MR to Cuban Trading Company, 12/19/1917, Ser. 1; MR to Ganzoni, 12/16/1917, Ser. 4.

13. W&G, 1/9/1919, 19, adjusted for U.S. duty of 1.0048 cents.

14. CCSC Second Annual Report. NYT, 1/16/1918. The syndicate proffered $100 million, but only $16 million was ever borrowed. With 8.5 percent interest in New York, local and British capital was found after all. MR to F. Strauss, 1/21/1918, and MR to White-Todd, 1/21/1918, Ser. 3; NYT, 7/31/1918.

15. MR to F. Strauss, 2/3 and 2/6/1918, Ser. 2; F. Strauss to MR, 2/4/1918, Ser. 10A.

16. MR to Ganzoni, 5/4/1918, Ser. 2; MR to Arango, 6/6/1918, Ser. 10A.

17. MR to Ganzoni, 7/12/1918, Ser. 4; Bernhardt, *Government Control*, 44–45; NYT, 7/12/1918, 19; Hoover to Wilson, quoted in Bernhardt, ibid., 43.

18. MR to Ganzoni, 9/24/1918, Ser. 4; Bernhardt, *Government Control*, 54.

19. Ganzoni to MR, 11/9/1918, Ser. 10A; LP, 11/30/1918, 343.

20. Lyle to Lagemann, 1/6/1919, Ser. 12.

21. BBR to MR, 1/13/1919, Ser. 12; Agenda, Special Meeting CCSC, Ser. 64.

22. BBR to MR, 1/16/1919, Ser. 12; MR to F. Strauss, 2/7/1919, Ser. 2. I could not locate Strauss's letters.

23. MER to MR, 1/28/1919, BBR to MR, 1/21/1919, BBR to F. Strauss and Jaretzki, 2/14/1919, all Ser. 12.

24. MR to H. F. Kroyer, 2/7/1919, and MR to F. Strauss, 2/7/1919, both Ser. 12.

25. LP, 2/15/1919, 97, and 2/11/1919, 121; BBR to MR, 2/24/1919, Ser. 12.

26. BBR to MR, 3/10/1919, Ser. 12.

27. McCullough, 509; Goethals obituary, NCAB, 22: 6–7.

28. BBR to MR, 3/7/1919, and MER to MR, 3/21/1919, both Ser. 12.

29. Hayden obituaries in NYT, 1/9/1937, and NCAB, 14: 328; MR to F. Strauss, 3/15/1919, Ser. 12.

30. MER to MR, 3/26, 4/5, and 4/9/1919, MR to F. Strauss, 3/15/1919, all Ser. 12.

31. BBR to MR, 4/10/1919, Ser. 12; BBR, Part 2, section 7. The account is much extended in G. Braga, 139–40.

32. BBR to MR, 4/10/1919, Ser. 12; MR to "NY Nephews," 4/3/1919, Ser. 3; MER to MR, 4/9/1919, Ser. 12.

33. MR to "Boys," 4/30/1919, Ser. 3.

34. BBR to MR, 4/4, 4/29, and 4/21/1919, Ser. 12; MR to BBR and MER, 4/25/1919, Ser. 3; MER to MR, 4/9/1919, and BBR to MR, 4/21, 4/28, and 4/30/1919, all Ser. 12.

35. MER to MR, 4/5/1919, Ser. 12.

Chapter 6. Tail of the Lion

1. In his revised draft, he changed the final six words to "the stability of prices of Cuban sugar."

2. MR, "To the CCSC," Ser. 64.

3. MR to Salvador Rionda, 4/26/1919, and MR to JBR, 5/3/1919, both Ser. 3; BBR to MR, 5/8 and 5/9/1919, and MER to MR, 4/29/1919, both Ser. 12; MR to F. Strauss, 4/30/1919, Ser. 3.

4. "Report by Goethals," Ser. 64.

5. MR to VZ and HF, 7/15/1919, Ser. 3; Cz-R to Hayden, 9/3/1919, Ser. 64.

6. Cz-R to Hayden, 9/3/1919, Ser. 64, p. 16.

7. BBR to MR, 4/10/1919, Ser. 12; MR to VZ and HF, 7/9/1919, Ser. 2. Phrases in brackets are from attached keys to numerical codes.

8. Hawley to Menocal, 7/3/1919, attached to Hawley to MR, 7/3/1919, Ser. 12; MR to VZ, 7/2/1919 (an earlier draft had presumably been exchanged), Ser. 2; MR to VZ and HF, 7/15/1919, Ser. 10.

9. MR to VZ, 7/2/1919, and MR to VZ and HF, 7/15/1919, both Ser. 2.

10. NYT, 7/23/1919, 20; LP, 7/26/1919, 53; MR to Craig, 7/17/1919, Ser. 2.

11. MR to VZ and HF, 7/18/1919, Ser. 10.

12. Bernhardt, *Government Control*, 233–35.

13. LP, 8/23/1919, 119; Tarafa to Hawley, 10/14/1919, Ser. 12.

14. G. Braga, 140–41.

15. CCSC Fourth Annual Report.

16. MR to Tiarks, 5/14/1920, Ser. 2; MR to Ogilvie, 3/29/1920, Ser. 12; CR, November 1919, 32; MER to MR, 1/7/1920, Ser. 10.

17. MER to MR, 1/26/1920, Ser. 12.

18. MR to "NY Boys," 2/3/1920, Ser. 12. BBR reported that the Guaranty had been "very insistent" that the loan should be for $15 million instead (BBR to MR, 3/10/1920, Ser. 12).

19. CR, 9/5/1920, 157.

20. Lageman to MR, 5/11 and 5/12/1920, and MR to Lagemann, 5/11/1920, all Ser. 10B; MR to Westrick, 7/30/1920, Ser. 4.

21. BBR to MR, 1/2/1920, Ser. 12; Cleveland, 105–7.

22. LP, 11/22/1919, 328–29; MER to MR, 1/7/1920, Ser. 12; *Mundo Azucarero*, November 1916, 121–22, and June 1919, 327–28; Ogilvie to MR, 3/26/1920, Ser. 12; FAS, 7/16/1920, 23.

23. MR to "NY Boys," 3/11/1920, and BBR to MR, 3/22/1920, both Ser. 12; FAS, 3/27/1920, 244; LP, 9/4/1920, 157; CR, 9/4/1920, 158.

24. MER to MR, 2/1/1920, Ser. 12; De Mesa, 12–13; BBR to MR, 3/3/1920, and MR to "NY Boys," 3/5 and 3/11/1920, all Ser. 12.

25. BBR to MR, 3/22/1920, and MER to VZ, 3/22/1920, both Ser. 12.

26. MR to VZ, 6/24/1920, Ser. 2; MR to Nieberg, 7/30/1920, Ser. 12; "With our Javas we have done wonders" (BBR to MR, 10/31/1920, Ser. 12).

27. MR to Urquiza, 7/29/1920, Ser. 2; FAS, 7/17/1920, 41; MR to JBR, 9/10/1920, and MR to Laborde, 8/3/1920, both Ser. 2.

28. LP, 9/16/1920, 184; MR to Laborde, 10/5/1920, and MR to HF, 9/20/1920, both Ser. 2.

29. MR to Laborde, 10/5/1920, Ser. 2.

30. MR to HF, 10/4/1920, and MR to Laborde, 10/5/1920, both Ser. 2; CR, November 1920, 10; BBR to MER, 10/13/1920, Ser. 2.

31. FAS, 10/23/1920, cited in Jencks, 334; De Céspedes to Havana, 10/18/1920, Ser. 10; MR to HF, 10/14/1920, Ser. 4.

32. LP, 10/16/1920, 246; MR to Tiarks, 10/20/1920, Ser. 2; FAS, 10/30/1920, 344.

33. CCSC Fifth Annual Report. The 1919 deduction of marine freight from operating profits is consistent with the practice in 1917 and 1918 (*Anuario*, 1959, 107).

34. MR to Arango, 1/7/1921, Ser. 10, and 11/5/1920, Ser. 2.

Chapter 7. The Steel Gray Battleship

1. MR to "NY Boys," 1/28/1921, Ser. 12; CR, February 1921, 10; LP, 2/5/1921, 90; MR to Lakin, 5/13/1921, Ser. 2.

2. Cleveland and Huertas, 105–7.

3. Manach, 31–35; De la Torriente, 26–28.

4. MR to "NY Boys," 2/5/1921, Ser. 12; LP, 6/5/1920, 361; CR, 9/14/1920, 158.

5. LP, 2/19/1921, 119, and 3/5/1921, 153; Castaño to MR, 2/21/1921, and MR to Castaño, 2/23/1921, both Ser. 10B.

6. MR to Cz-R, Cable 8, 2/7/1921, Ser. 12; MR to "Boys," 3/25, 3/31, and 4/2/1921, Ser. 2; LP, 5/14/1921.

7. Castaño to Falla Gutiérrez (henceforth FG), 3/31 and 4/2/1921, MR to Castaño, 4/6/1921, Castaño to MR, 4/9/1921, MR to Castaño, 4/13/1921, all Ser. 10B; LP, 4/23/1921, 264; typed obituary in Ser. 10C; Dumoulin, 137, 149, 258; FAS, 3/30/1929, 293; FG to MR, 4/16/1921, Ser. 10B.

8. Ogilvie to Kroyer, 4/29 and 5/1/1921, and MR to Ogilvie, 5/2/1921, all Ser. 10B; Ogilvie to MR, 5/10/1921, Ser. 64; MR to Ogilvie, 5/16/1921, and Ogilvie to Kroyer, 5/16/1921, both Ser. 10B.

9. MR to VZ, 5/16/1921, Ser. 2; MR to FG, 5/16/1921, Ser. 10B; FG to MR, quoting a letter from Castaño, 6/1/1921, Ser. 10B; MR to Doty, 6/11/1921, Ser. 2.

10. FG to MR, 6/13/1921, Ser. 10B; MR to Doty, 6/14/1921, Ser. 2; MR to FG, 6/20/1921, FG to MR, 6/20/1921, MR to Castaño, 6/24/1921, all Ser. 10B.

11. NYT, 6/4/1921. It was a six-inch story, stressing the strong reaction in the market and a very quick sale in which "a group of traders" acquired 4,000 shares. NYT, 6/23/1921; LP, 8/6/1921, 89, and 7/30/1921, 71; FAS, 7/30/1921, 81.

12. Castaño to MR, 7/1/1921, and MR to Castaño, 7/12/1921, both Ser. 10B.

13. Ratner, 47–49; Smoot to William E. Bird, 12/10/1921, Ser. 2.

14. LP, 6/16/1921, 65; FAS, 7/30/1921, 81, 95; MR to A. Strauss, 6/13/1921, Ser. 2.

15. In addition to expanding in Cuba, Vanderlip had heavily committed the National City Bank in Russia. When Lenin replaced Kerensky, National City's losses were some 40 percent of its capital (Cleveland and Huertas, 41–44, 62–77,

99–103, 106–9; Mitchell obituary, NYT, 12/15/1955). Mitchell admitted that writing off the Cuban loans might have "meant pretty nearly the destruction of our institution" (Cleveland and Huertas, 106–7).

16. Rentschler obituaries in NCAB, 38: 54–55, and NYT, 3/5/1948.

17. A. Thompson to MR, 1/3/1922, Ser. 10C. For an example of the mix of creditors, MR reported that Atkins held a first mortgage on the *Santo Tomás* mill, while the National City Bank held one on its land ("and consequently on its cane") for $500,000. *Santo Tomás* also owed $300,000 in floating debts plus an additional $400,000 to a Cuban Development Company, which Ceballos had organized (MR to BBR and MER, 1/31/1921, Ser. 12).

18. Cleveland and Huertas, 109.

19. CCSC Sixth Annual Report; NYT, 9/28/1921; FAS 10/1/1921, 262.

20. Truffin to MR, 8/16/1921 (1921 translation), and MR to Truffin, 9/19/1921, both Ser. 2.

21. MR to Tiarks, 11/25/1921, Ser. 10B.

22. W&G, 11/19/1921, 648.

23. Farr, *Manual*, 1959, 284; USDA, *Yearbook 1942*, 150.

24. MR to VZ, 12/22/1921, Ser. 2; Smith, *United States*, 46–47.

25. CCSC Sixth Annual Report.

26. G. Braga, 154–59; MR to SR, 7/17/1922, Ser. 2.

27. MR to de Ulzurrún, 6/30 and 7/17/1922, and MR to HF, 8/29/1922, all Ser. 2

28. MR to LR, 3/16/1924, Ser. 3; MR to Manatí Sugar Company, 3/25/1924, Ser. 10C; MR to LR, 3/28 and 3/12/1924, Ser. 3.

29. Percentages as given in the CCSC's annual reports.

30. Deeds was an all-round entrepreneur who had designed baking machines for Shredded Wheat and invented the electrical self-starter for automobiles. Houston would become president of Wright-Martin Aircraft Corporation (Deeds obituary, NCAB, 49: 40–41; Houston obituary, NYT, 7/11/1949).

31. Atkins, 341–42; LP, 1/27/1923, 73; NYT, 1/15/1923, 17; Mrs. Edwin Atkins Jr., née Mary Coolidge, was rescued by a passing ferry and later married Gordon Rentschler.

32. CCSC annual reports for 1922–24.

33. MR to Truffin, 7/5/1923, Ser. 10C; see also MR to Tiarks, 7/12/1923, Ser. 2; List "Fondos para la campaña contra la ley Tarafa," undated, in Tarafa folder of Portuondo letters; MR to A. Strauss, 7/14/1923, MR to Aurelio Portuondo (henceforth AP), Cable 12, 7/17/1923, and Cable 16, 7/18/1923, all Ser. 10C; Zanetti and García, 282–96; NYT, 8/25/1923.

Chapter 8. Visible Hands

1. MR to MER, 12/5/1924, Ser. 3; CCSC 1923 Annual Report, 9, 10.

2. Primelles, 365; Thomas, 569–70; Jencks, 269–73.

3. Thomas, 571; W&G, 4/30/1925, 225–26.

4. Lockmiller, 247–48; *Moody's* 1927, 2354; CCSC 1925 Annual Report; Prinsen Geerligs in CR, July 1926, 6.

5. Reno in CR, December 1925, 10–11; CCSC 1926 Annual Report, 6.

6. MR to MER, Cable 1, 12/3/1925, "Memorandum re Colonos," 12/14/1925, G. Crawley to LR, 1/27/1926, all Ser. 3.

7. "Memorandum for Mr. M.R. for use in this week's circular," 4/28/1926, Ser. 2; W&G, 12/30/1926, 658–59; "Havana Correspondence," CR, May 1926; Alvarez Díaz, 241; W&G, 5/20/1926, 256; CR, July 1926, 22; *Anuario*, 1939, 53.

8. CR, May 1926, 8/18/1926, Ser. 10C; W&G, 4/29 and 5/20/1926.

9. MR to AS, 8/18/1926, Ser. 10C; *Moody's* 1928, 2489–90.

10. MER to AP, 10/19 and 10/14/1926, and Tarafa to Baroni, 10/9/1926, all Ser. 10C.

11. HF to MER, 12/17/1926, and MER to HF, 12/18/1926, both Ser. 10C; BBR, Part 2, 2.

12. MR, "Memorandum No. 38," 3/1/1927, Ser. 10C ("MER" folder).

13. MR, "Memorandum No. 16," 2/3/1927, and "Memorandum No. 28," 2/16/1927, both Ser. 10C.

14. MR, "Summary of Lunch—April 12, 1927," Ser. 10C ("MER" folder); Benjamin, *Hegemony*, 29–32.

15. MER to MR, Letter No. 5, 2/23/1927, Ser. 10C.

16. MER to MR, 2/22 and 2/23/1927, Ser. 10C.

17. Chadbourne, 210–12. This "autobiography" was ghostwritten by George Creel in 1928 (NCAB, 30: 308).

18. MER to MR, 1/27/1927, Ser. 10C; MR to SR, 5/2/1927, and MR to MER, 2/23/1927, both Ser. 2.

19. MR to MER, 2/28/1927, Ser. 2; MR, "Synopsis of Meeting of the Board of Directors, CCSC, 3/3/1927. Memorandum No. 41," Ser. 10C ("MER" folder). Vázquez Bello, Machado's campaign manager, was currently his secretary of the interior.

20. MR, "Memorandum No. 47, Cuba Cane Meeting held today, 3/10/1927," Ser. 10 ("MER" folder). CCSC's 1927 Annual Report would show a net operating profit of only 0.35 cent per pound, or about $1 per bag (MER to MR, Cable, 3/14/1927, Ser. 10C ["C. Hayden" folder]).

21. W&G, 1/5/1928, 3; Babst, in W&G, 1/6/1927, 5; NYT, 1/4/1927.

22. MR, "Memorandum No. 51, 3/30/1927," and MR, "Lunch-4/12/1927," both Ser. 10C ("MER" folder) with key to number code attached. According to Chadbourne (p. 212), he had plotted with his brothers Wilbur and Humphrey "a combination that would put together España, Cuba Cane Sugar and General Sugar."

23. W&G, 1/3/1928, 3.

24. MR to Hayden, 8/22/1927, Hayden to Machado, 9/1/1927, MR to Machado, 9/8/1927, all Ser. 10C ("CC. Crop Restriction" folder).

25. MR, "Memorandum of conversation with . . . Rubens, today, November 2,

1927," Ser. 10C ("MER" folder); Alvarez Díaz, 242; W&G, 10/20/1927, 525. The shares were distributed among the six provinces: Piñar del Rio, 914; Havana, 1,568; Matanzas, 2,714; Santa Clara, 5,049; Camagüey, 7,493; Oriente, 7,235. Thus the four western provinces held 10,245 shares, and the two eastern held 14,728 (Reno, CR, November 1927, 17).

26. W&G, 10/6/1927, 500, and 10/20/1927, 524; MR to AP, 11/3/1927, Ser. 2; Molinet obituary, NYT, 5/24/1959; MR to Hayden, 8/22/1927, Ser. 10C.

27. See Tarafa to MR 9/7, 9/24, 10/3, and 10/14/1927, Ser. 10C.

28. CCSC 1927 Annual Report; MR, "Memorandum No. 454, 3/9/1927," Ser. 10C ("MER" folder); W&G, 1/5/1928, 4.

29. Lincoln, 150–52, 184–92; MR, "Memorandum of conversation with Rubens, 11/22/1927," Ser. 10C ("MER" folder); W&G, 10/20/1927, 524.

30. MR, "Memorandum," 10/21/1927, Ser. 10C.

31. MR to Tarafa, 12/27/1927, Ser. 2; MR to AP, 12/30/1927, Ser. 10C.

32. W&G, 4/5/1928, 190.

33. MR, quoted in W&G, 10/11/1928, 531; MR to LR, 3/12/1928, Ser. 10C.

34. MR to AP, 8/22/1928, Ser. 2.

35. Simpson obituary, NCAB, 44: 124–25; unsigned and undated letter to Machado, and Simpson to Hayden, 8/3/1928 (copy in "CCSC. Simpson" folder), both Ser. 10C.

36. MR to Rentschler, 8/16/1928, Ser. 2.

37. José Gómez Mena to V. Gutiérrez (henceforth VG), 8/1/1928; Anonymous, "Comments upon Letter . . . from . . . Gómez Mena to . . . Gutiérrez," 8/23/1928; MR to VG, 8/28/1928; all in "V. Gutiérrez" folder, Ser. 10C (all are 1928 translations).

38. W&G, 10/4/1928, 518; MER to MR, "Memorandum to Uncle," 2/18/1929, Ser. 10C.

39. Hayden to MR, 8/23/1927, and MR to Hayden, 8/31/1927, both Ser. 10C (both are 1927 translations).

40. "Memorandum to Manolo," 5/7/1928 ("CC. Colonos. Renewal of Contracts" folder), and MR to JBR, 3/27/1928, both Ser. 10C.

Chapter 9. Receivership and Reorganization

1. CR, February 1930, 16; NYT, 2/1/1929; MR to AP, 1/4/1929, Ser. 2; Costello to General Sugar Estates, 2/15/1929, and Rosenberg, Treasurer, General Sugar Estates, to MR, 2/14/1929, both Ser. 10C ("General Sugar Estates" folder).

2. MR to AP, 4/12, 4/22, and 4/16/1929, Ser. 2; Alvarez Díaz, 325.

3. USDA, *Yearbook 1935*, 441, 446.

4. MR to HF, 6/7/1929, Ser. 2; "Synopsis of Exec. Mtg., CCSC, 1/24/1929," Ser. 10C ("CCSC Synopsis of Mtgs." folder); Ogilvie obituary, NYT, 9/26/1956.

5. MER, "Memorandum to Uncle," 2/18/1929, BBR to Rook, 2/26/1929, MR to Stoker, 2/28/1929, MR, "Synopsis of Talk with Hayden Feb 18," 2/19/1929, and "Synopsis of Mtg. of Exec. Comm. of Manatí," 2/21/1929, all Ser. 10C.

6. "Synopsis of talk yesterday with Col. Simpson," 5/21/1929, "Synopsis of two Meetings of Cuba Cane, 5/2/1929," and "Synopsis of Mtg. of Exec. Com. of CCSC, 5/9/1929," all Ser. 10C; MR to SR, 5/16/1929, Ser. 1.

7. Tarafa to Machado, 6/17/1929, Ser. 10C (1929 translation); MR to AP, 6/24 and 6/26/1929, and MR to Tarafa, 6/27/1929, both Ser. 2; Lippitt to MR, 7/13/1929, Ser. 10C ("Great Western" folder); Lockmiller, 255–57.

8. The *Andreita, San Agustín, Reforma, Patria, Adelaida,* and *Manuelita.* CR listings, 1930; Rook to MR, 7/12/1929, Ser. 2.

9. AP to MR, 5/29/1929, and MR to AP, 6/4/1929, both Ser. 10C.

10. "Synopsis CCSC Exec. Comm., 6/13/1929," Ser. 10C; MR to BBR, 6/14/1929, MR to AP, 6/26/1929, "Synopsis CCSC Exec. Comm., 6/17/1929," all Ser. 2.

11. "Synopsis CCSC Exec. Comm., 6/19/1929," Ser. 2; NYT, 7/26/1929. Cuban-American common stock fell from $60\frac{3}{8}$ in 1920 to $6\frac{7}{8}$ in 1929 (*Moody's* 1927, 2355; *Moody's* 1930, 343).

12. U.S. Cane Refiners Association, table 56, 71, shows the value of sugar exports as actually falling by $8 million if the values of refined sugar, molasses, syrup, alcohol, and cane brandy, plus local consumption, are taken into account.

13. MR to HF, 7/16/1929, and MR to AP, Cable 405, 7/17/1929, and Cables 654 and 655, 10/1/1929, all Ser. 2; *Diario de la Marina,* 7/20/1929, 1; AP to MR, Cable 415, 7/22/1919, Ser. 10C; Foreign Policy Association, 243–44; Alvarez Díaz, 326; MR to AP, 10/3 and 10/17/1929, MR to de Ulzurrún, 10/17/1929, and MR to AP, 10/17/1929, all Ser. 2.

14. NYT, 7/26/1929 and 8/7/1929; "Synopsis CCSC Exec. Comm., 10/31/1929," Ser. 2.

15. MR to AP, 10/29/1929, Ser. 10C ("CCSC-Reorg." folder); "Synopsis of CCSC Mtg.," 10/29/1929, Ser. 2; Doscher obituary, NCAB, 30: 204.

16. MR, undated draft "Memo with reference to allegations made by Doscher" attached to MR to AP, 10/29/1929, and Memorandum from Mr. Young, 12/6/1929, with "Data for Reply," both Ser. 10C ("CCSC-Reorg." folder).

17. Decision, 12/14/1929, Ser. 10C ("CC: Record of Infante, 1929" folder).

18. MR to HF, Cable 37, 1/10/1930, and MR to HF, 1/2, 1/3, and 1/8/1920, all Ser. 2.

19. MER, "Synopsis of CCSC Mtg.," 2/6/1920, Ser. 10C; Simpson to Cz-R, 2/11/1920, Ser. 2.

20. "Memorandum of MR's Transactions covering Cuba Cane Stock, 8/19/1935," Ser. 10C ("CCSC-Re-org 1934–35. CC Common in vaults of Cz-R Co." folder).

21. MR, "Synopsis of Exec. Comm. Mtg., 2/13/1930," MR to Knapp, 3/27/1930, MER to MR, 2/21/1930, all Ser. 10C.

22. MR to MER, 2/18 and 2/16/1930, and MR to MER, Cable 20, 2/21/1920, all Ser. 2.

23. W&G, 1/8/1931, 3; MR to AP, 2/26/1930, Ser. 2; NYT, 1/19/1930, 3; MR to

MER, 1/16/1930, Ser. 2. See MER to MR, 2/15/1930, Ser. 10C, for a summary of Gómez Mena's point of view. MR to HF, 2/17/1930, Ser. 2; MER to MR, 2/21/1930, Ser. 10C.

24. MER to MR, 2/5/1930, Ser. 10C; MR to HF, 2/27/1930, and MR to AP, Cables 95 and 96, 1/2/1930, all Ser. 2.

25. NYT, 4/15/1930, 48; MR to AP, 4/24/1930, and MR to Doty, 4/30/1930, both Ser. 2.

26. MR to Simpson, 4/21/1930, Ser. 2; MR to Hayden, 4/24/1930, Ser. 10C ("CCSC Simpson" folder).

27. MR to AP, 7/9/1930, Ser. 2; FAS, March 1931, 141; VG to Prinsen Geerligs, 7/9/1920, Ser. 10C.

28. MR, "Memorandum re Sta Clara Commission," 7/16/1930, and MR, "Synopsis of Talk with Chadbourne," 7/16/1930, both Ser. 10C ("Chadbourne Comm." folder).

29. Alvarez Díaz, 326–30.

30. MR to SR, 7/1, 7/31, 10/27, and 11/8/1930, Ser. 2; MR to de Ulzurrún, 12/18/1930, Ser. 1; MR to SR, 12/19/1930, MR to AP, 12/19/1930, MR to SR, 12/29/1930, and MR to AP, 12/31/1930, all Ser. 2.

31. MR, "Synopsis of Luncheon with Mr. Hayden Today," 11/15/1930, Ser. 10C.

32. MR to AP, 11/25/1920, Ser. 2; MR to Rook, 11/14/1930, Ser. 10C ("Tarafa, sugar, 1930" folder); Manatí, Annual Report, 1930, 13; MR to Rook, 4/30/1930, Ser. 2.

Chapter 10. Empty Saddlebags

1. Foreign Policy Association, 247; Alvarez Díaz, 327–28.

2. *Fortune*, February 1931, 23–28, 112–14; MR to Chadbourne, 11/19/1930, Ser. 10C ("V. Gutiérrez" folder); "Telephone conversation between Chadbourne and MR, 11/20/1930," Ser. 10C ("Chadbourne Comm." folder); Powell obituary, NCAB, 31: 449–50.

3. Farr, *Manual*, 1933, 87–88; MR to AP, Cable 9, 2/9/1932, Ser. 2; MER to Rentschler, 2/19/1932, Ser. 10C; MR to AP, 2/26/1932, Ser. 2. Also cf. MER to HF, 4/5/1932, Ser. 10C; NYT, 3/26/1932; MR to Doty, 1/13/1932, Ser. 2.

4. MR to SR, 1/14/1932, and MR to Doty, 1/18/1932, both Ser. 2; *Moody's 1935*, 1917–18; MR to SR, 4/21/1932, and MR to AP, 5/26/1932, both Ser. 2.

5. MER to HF, 4/5/1921, Ser. 10C; "Synopsis of matters discussed at lunch at Guaranty Trust Co. today," 4/15/1932, Ser. 10C ("CC. Financing" folder); Sample obituary, NYT, 10/17/1954; MR to "Havana Boys," 4/15/1932, Ser. 2.

6. MR to AP, 5/11/1932, and MER to HF, 5/23/1932, both Ser. 10C; MR to HF, 7/5 and 7/19/1932, Ser. 2.

7. MR to Root, 9/6/1932, Ser. 2; Tarafa to MR, 6/26/1932, Ser. 10C; MR to HF, 7/21/1932, Ser. 2; MER to HF, 9/6/1932, Ser. 10C.

8. MR to Tarafa, 7/23/1932, and MR to Pasco, 7/27/1932, both Ser. 2; Tarafa obituaries in NYT, 7/25/1932, 15, *New York Herald Tribune*, 7/25/1932, 13, and

FAS, August 1932, 328; Cuban newspaper clippings in BBC, Ser. 10C ("Tarafa" folder); MR to HF, 8/1/1932, Ser. 2.

9. MR to SR, 10/29/1932, Ser. 2; MER to HF, 9/6/1932, MER to Stoker, 9/19/1932, MER to HF, 9/6/1932, all Ser. 10C; MR to HF, 2/10/1933, Ser. 2. In another letter, he mentioned that "the competition of white sugars from Cuba and Porto Rico . . . may affect our estimates" (MR to HF, 1/24/1933, Ser. 10C).

10. "Conference held on Feb 1st, 1933," "Memorandum of interview with VG. 2/2/1933," "Memorandum about lunch at Higinio's house, 2/3/1933," "Conference Between Stetson, Sample, Fanjul, 2/8/1933," "Conference of Mtgs. at Viriato's House at 9:30 P.M. February 8, 2/9/1933," all Ser. 10C ("HF Crp. 1923–43" folder).

11. "Memorandum of Mali's interview with Canel Feb. 9, 1922," 2/10/1933, Ser. 10C ("HF Crp." folder). "Mali" and "Canel" were code for VG and Machado.

12. NYT, 2/11/1933; "Memorandum of Mtg. at Viriato's House," 2/9/1933, Ser. 10C; MR to Doty, 2/14/1933, Ser. 2; MER to HF, 2/15/1933, Ser. 10C.

13. MER to HF, 2/15/1922, and HF to Lehman, 2/28/1933, both Ser. 10C.

14. NYT, 3/12/1933, 20; Moley, 47; Tugwell, 201. For Taussig, see NCAB, 36: 78–79. For Berle, see NCAB, D: 26, and NYT obituary, 7/19/1971, 1; Schwartz, 91; Berle and Jacobs, 88; NYT, 9/11/1933, 3.

15. MR to Rentschler, 8/17/1933, and MR to BBR, 8/8 and 8/18/1933, all Ser. 2. A NYT headline read, "Rumor That Machado Carried $2,000,000 on Flight Denied" (NYT, 8/16/1933, 2).

16. MR to AP, 8/22/1933, and MR to BBR, 8/31/1933, both Ser. 2; Rodríguez Blanca to National City Bank and to de Céspedes, 8/23/1933, Ser. 11; MR to BBR, 8/24/1933, Ser. 2.

17. NYT, 9/11/1933; Carr, "Mill Occupations," 139–40; G. Braga, 27–30; MR to BBR, 9/9/1933, Ser. 2; HF to AP, 9/12/1933, Ser. 11.

18. JBR to MER, 9/12 and 9/13/1933, Ser. 11; NYT, 9/14/1933, 1; HF to AP, 9/14, 9/23, and 9/25/1933, Ser. 11.

19. NYT, 10/8/1933, 1; HF to AP, 10/24/1933, and AP to HF, 11/15/1933, both Ser. 11.

20. Phillips, 119; HF to AP, 12/9/1933, and HF to MER, 12/16/1933, both Ser. 11; NYT, 1/31/1934, 5; 1/14/1934, 12; 12/31/1933, 15; 1/11/1934, 4.

Chapter 11. From the Wolf, a Pelt

1. NYT, 1/17/1934, 3; Benjamin, *Hegemony*, 174–76.

2. AP to HF, 1/23/1934, and HF to AP, 1/25/1934, both Ser. 11.

3. Aguilar, 157–58; NYT, 1/31/1934, 5; HF to AP, 1/26/1934, MR to HF, 5/23/1934, and MR to AP, 7/23/1934, all Ser. 11.

4. HF to MER, 2/3/1934, Stetson to HF, 2/5/1934, HF to AP, 2/7/1934, AP to HF, 2/9/1934, all Ser. 11.

5. MR to HF, 4/3/1934, Ser. 10C ("CCSC-Re-org 1934–35" folder); HF to AP, 4/9 and 4/30/1934, Ser. 11.

6. HF to MER, 4/29, 4/20, and 4/30/1934, Ser. 11.

7. Sumner Welles to Wilson, 6/20/1934, Welles to J. R. Baker, 6/18/1934, Baker to Welles, 6/19/1934, Matthews to Sec'y of State, 4/25, 6/6, 6/8, and 7/19/1934, all National Archives, 337.1153 Cuba Cane Products/33.

8. MER to HF, 5/4/1934, Ser. 10C; MR to HF, 5/8/1934, MER to HF, 5/8/1934, HF to MER, 5/9, 5/10, and 5/11/1934, all Ser. 11 ("CCSC-Re-org 1934–35" folder).

9. MER to HF, 5/15/1934, "Memo of Interview of 5/19/1934," MR to HF, 5/23/1934, MR to AP, 7/23/1934, all Ser. 11.

10. HF to MER, 7/3/1923, HF to AP, 7/7/1934, HF to MER, 7/19/1934, all Ser. 11; MR to HF, 7/24/1934, Cable 11, Ser. 2; Garrett to HF, 7/26/1934, and Stetson to HF, 7/26/1934, both Ser. 11; MER to HF, 7/26/1934, Ser. 10C.

11. "Memorandum for Mr. Miller," 8/6/1934, Ser. 11 (1934 translation).

12. MER to HF, 8/1/1934, Ser. 10C. Anonymous memo of 8/3/1934 "Cía Az Atlántica del Golfo, S.A.," copy 8/5/1934 in Ser. 10 ("CCSC Re-org 1934–35" folder). What the Guaranty promised the U.S. State Department is not explained (MR to AP, 8/2/1934, Ser. 2).

13. HF to MER, 8/11, 8/17, and 9/11/1934, Ser. 11; MR to AP, 8/22/1934, Ser. 2. (There are two significant letters on this date). MR to de la Torriente, 9/5/1934, and MR to Mrs. Doty, 8/31/1934, both Ser. 2.

14. "Life is very long." MR to HF, 8/30/1934, Ser. 2; HF to AP, 9/10/1934, and HF to MER, 9/21/1934, both Ser. 11; MER to HF, 9/26/1934, Ser. 10C.

15. MR to Tiarks, 12/19/1934, Ser. 11; *Moody's* 1936, 333; "Plan of Campaign Toward Solving the Problems of the Former Cuba Cane," 4/27/1935, Ser. 10C ("CCSC-Re-org 1934–35" folder).

16. "Copy from Financial Notice published in Press of NYC, 5/17/1934," Ser. 10C.

17. "Memo of MR's Transactions covering Cuba Cane Stock," 8/19/1935, Ser. 10C; NYT, 8/24, 8/28, and 8/30/1935.

18. MR explained the difference between $7 million and the $4,135,025 paid at the final foreclosure sale as "apparently accounted for by the interest accrued, foreclosure charges and the current bank loans." He added that the consolidated balance sheet of 9/30/1935 showed buildings and equipment carried at $4,523,520, with current net assets of $2,648,696 and property liens of $260,853. Current liabilities were $268,760; net working capital, $2,378,936; and equity per share, $11.22. "Memorandum 3/14/1935," Ser. 10 ("CCSC-Re-org 1934–35" folder).

19. Sample to HF, 2/14/1936, HF to Sample, 2/21/1936, Stetson to HF, 2/26/1936, MR to HF, 3/3/1936, HF to MR, 3/2/1936, MR to HF, 3/9/1936, HF to MR, 3/12/1936, HF to MER, 3/12/1936, all Ser. 10C.

20. MR to HF, 3/2 and 3/10/1936, HF to MR, 3/10/1936, MR to HF, 3/19/1936, all Ser. 10C; MR to Doty, 4/3/1936, and MR to Rook, 3/30/1936, both Ser. 2; MR to LR, 4/1/1936, Ser. 10C.

21. MR to Rook, 12/7/1936, and MR to P. G. Clay, 12/31/1935, both Ser. 2; MER

to HF, 10/1/1936, HF to MR, 10/21/1936, MR to HF, 10/5 and 11/30/1936, and MR to MER, 12/29/1936, all Ser. 10C; MR to Young, 12/14/1936, Ser. 2.

The Roads Taken

1. MR to HF, 2/10/1943, Ser. 2; HF to G. S. Messersmith, 9/16/1940, Ser. 10C ("HF Crp." folder); HF to MER, 5/28/1938, Ser. 10C ("Gutiérrez, Dr. V., Crp." folder).

2. W&G, 12/26/1940, 449–50; MR, "Sugar Review for 1942," 2–5; *Moody's* 1944, 204, 297–98, 224.

3. In addition to the *Tuinucú, Céspedes, Francisco, Elía,* and *Manatí, Anuario* listed three small mills, the *Limones, Sta. Amalia* (which the Cuban Trading Company had just foreclosed), and *La Vega*, as under Rionda control (*Anuario*, 1939, 50–51). Atlántica figures do not include *Violeta*, nor do Cuban-American's include the *Guantanamo*.

4. MR to Doty, 3/24/1943, Ser. 2; *Francisco Annual Report*, 1942, 8; MER to LR, 3/30/1943, Ser. 10C; MR to Manuel Lamar, Ser. 2.

5. W&G, 10/14/1943, 379.

6. MR to Young, 9/1/1943, Ser. 2; BBR, "Experiences," Part 2.

7. *Sugar*, December 1943, 30.

8. "Quien es Manuel Rionda," 4/22/1939, Ser. 2 (88: 891–94); W&G, 11/4/1943, 400.

9. MR to HF, 2/10/1943, and MR to AP, 8/20 and 6/3/1943, all Ser. 2.

10. MR to Salvatore Rionda, 12/27/1935, Ser. 10C; mention of the younger Manuel's death in Rionda Family Genealogy; NYT, 5/19/1959, 1.

11. Padula, 593; Pérez-López, Appendix 2, 241–45.

12. G. Braga, 256–57; M. J. Callejo, "Memorandum," 7/14/1960, and Alfonso Fanjul Sr. to Richard Liddiard, 12/28/1961, both RG III, Ser. 63; G. Braga to Rook, 12/7/1956, RG III, Ser. 61.

Bibliography

Aguilar, Louis A. *Cuba 1933: Prologue to Revolution*. Ithaca, N.Y.: Cornell University Press, 1966.
Alvarez Díaz, José, chairman. *Cuban Economic Project: A Study on Cuba*. Coral Gables, Fla.: University of Miami Press, 1965.
Alvarez Díaz, José, et al. *Cuba: Geopolítica y Pensamiento Economico*. Coral Gables, Fla.: University of Miami Press, 1964.
Anuario Azucarero de Cuba. Havana: Ministerio de Hacienda, 1937–60.
Atkins, Edwin F. *Sixty Years in Cuba*. Cambridge, Mass.: Privately printed, 1926.
Ayala, César J. *American Sugar Kingdom: The Plantation Economy of the Spanish Caribbean*. Chapel Hill: University of North Carolina Press, 1999.
Barber, William J. *From New Era to New Deal: Herbert Hoover, the Economists and American Foreign Policy, 1921–1933*. Cambridge: Cambridge University Press, 1985.
Benjamin, Jules R. *The United States and Cuba: Hegemony and Dependent Development, 1880–1934*. Pittsburgh: University of Pittsburgh Press, 1977.
———. *The United States and the Origins of the Cuban Revolution*. Princeton, N.J.: Princeton University Press, 1990.
Bergad, Laird W. *Cuban Rural Society in the Nineteenth Century: The Social and Economic History of Sugar Monoculture in Matanzas*. Princeton, N.J.: Princeton University Press, 1977.
Berle, Adolph A., and Gardiner C. Means. *The Modern Corporation and Private Property*. Rev. ed. New York: Harcourt, Brace and World, 1968.
Berle, Beatrice B., and Traves B. Jacobs. *Navigating the Rapids, 1918–1971: From the Papers of Adolph A. Berle*. New York: Harcourt Brace Jovanovich, 1973.
Bernhardt, Joshua. *Government Control of the Sugar Industry in the United States*. New York: Macmillan, 1920.
———. "How the U.S. Quota System Developed." *Sugar* (April 1955): 33–34, 63.

———. *The Sugar Industry and the Federal Government: 1917–1947.* Washington, D.C.: Sugar Statistics Service, 1948.
Bidwell, Percy W. *The Invisible Tariff: A Study of the Control of Imports into the United States.* New York: Council on Foreign Relations, 1939.
Bonnet, William. *The World's Sugar Production and Consumption, 1800–1900.* U.S. Department of the Treasury, Bureau of Statistics. Washington, D.C.: GPO, 1902.
Braga, George A. "A Bundle of Relations." Ms., Braga Brothers Collection, University of Florida, Gainesville.
Braga, Michael Marconi. "No Other Law but Supply and Demand: Institutional Change and the Cuban Sugar Economy, 1917–1934." Master's thesis, University of Texas at Austin, 1993.
———. "To Relieve the Misery: Workers and the 1933 Cuban Revolution." In *Workers' Control in Latin America, 1930–1979*, edited by Joseph C. Brown, 16–44. Chapel Hill: University of North Carolina Press, 1997.
Braga Rionda, Bernardo. "Personal and Business Experiences." Ms., Braga Brothers Collection, University of Florida, Gainesville.
Brandes, Joseph. *Herbert Hoover and Economic Diplomacy: Department of Commerce Policy, 1921–1928.* Pittsburgh: University of Pittsburgh Press, 1962.
Brooks, John. *Once in Golconda: A True Drama of Wall Street, 1920–1938.* New York: Harper and Row, 1969.
Buell, Raymond Lesley. "The Caribbean Situation: Cuba and Haiti." *Foreign Policy Reports* 9, no. 8 (June 21, 1933): 82–87.
Burner, David. *Herbert Hoover: A Public Life.* New York: Alfred A. Knopf, 1979.
Carr, Barry. "Mill Occupations and Soviets: The Mobilization of Sugar Workers in Cuba, 1917–1933." *Journal of Latin American Studies* 28 (1996): 129–58.
———. "Omnipotent and Omnipresent: Labor Shortages, Worker Mobility and Employer Control in the Cuban Sugar Industry, 1910–1934." In *Identity and Struggle at the Margins of the Nation State*, edited by Aviva Comsky and Aldo Lauria-Santiago, 260–91. Durham, N.C.: Duke University Press, 1998.
Catlin, Daniel, Jr. *Good Work Well Done: The Sugar Business Career of Horace Havemeyer, 1903–1956.* New York: Privately printed, 1988.
Chadbourne, Thomas L. *Autobiography.* New York: New York University School of Law, Ingram Documents in Legal History, 1985.
Chalmin, Philippe. *Tate and Lyle: Géant du Sucre.* Paris: Economica, 1983.
Chandler, Arthur D., Jr. *The Visible Hand: The Managerial Revolution in American Business.* Cambridge: Harvard University Press, 1977.
Charadán López, Fernando. *La Industria Azucarera en Cuba.* Havana: Editorial de Ciencias Sociales, 1982.
Chernow, Ron. *The House of Morgan: An American Banking Dynasty and the Rise of Modern Finance.* New York: Atlantic Monthly Press, 1990.
Cleveland, Harold Van B., and Thomas F. Huertas. *Citibank: 1812–1970.* Cambridge: Harvard University Press, 1985.

Cruz de Del Pino, Mary. *Camagüey: Biografía de una Provincia*. Havana: Academia de la Historia de Cuba, 1955.
Cuba Review. New York: Munson Steamship Lines, 1903–31.
Dalton, John E. *Sugar: A Case Study of Government Control*. New York: Macmillan, 1937.
Day, Clive. *The Dutch in Java*. New York: Macmillan, 1904. Reprint, New York: Oxford University Press, 1966.
De Abad, Louis V. *Azúcar y Cana de Azúcar: Ensayo de orientación cubana*. Havana: Editorial Mercantil, 1945.
Dean, Arthur H. *William Nelson Cromwell, 1894–1948: An American Pioneer in Corporation, Comparative and International Law*. New York: Privately printed, 1959.
Deerr, N. *The History of Sugar*. London: Chapman and Hill, 1950.
De la Torriente, Lola. "Homenaje a Cosme de la Torriente." In *Libre Homenaje al Coronel Cosme de la Torriente*, 26–28. Havana: Editorial Cultural, 1951.
De Mesa, Hannibal. "Informe de Azúcar sobre la Industria Azucarera del Mundo." Havana, October 1919. Reprint, *Louisiana Planter* (January 3, 1920): 12–13.
Dumoulin, John. *Azúcar y Lucha de Clases: 1917*. Havana: Editorial de Ciencias Sociales, 1980.
Dunn, Robert W. *American Foreign Investments*. New York: B. W. Huebsch and Viking Press, 1926.
Dye, Alan. *Cuban Sugar in the Age of Mass Production: Technology and the Economics of the Sugar Central, 1899–1929*. Stanford, Calif.: Stanford University Press, 1998.
Edson, Hubert. *Sugar: From Scarcity to Surplus*. New York: Chemical Publishing, 1958.
Eichner, Alfred S. *The Emergence of Oligopoly: Sugar Refining as a Case Study*. Baltimore: Johns Hopkins University Press, 1969.
Elliott, Perry. *Production of Sugar in the United States and Foreign Countries*. U.S. Department of Agriculture, Bulletin No. 473. Washington, D.C.: GPO, 1917.
Ely, Roland T. *Commerciantes Cubanos del Siglo XIX*. Bogota: Aedita Editores, 1963.
———. *Cuando Reinaba Su Majestad El Azúcar*. Buenos Aires: Editorial Sudamerica, 1963.
———. "The Old Cuba Trade: Highlights and Case Studies of Cuban-American Interdependence during the Nineteenth Century." *Business History Review* 38 (1964): 456–78.
Facts about Sugar. New York: Domestic Sugar Producers, 1914–56.
Farber, Samuel. *Revolution and Reaction in Cuba, 1933–1960: A Political Sociology from Machado to Castro*. Middletown, Conn.: Wesleyan University Press, 1976.
Farr & Co. *Manual of Sugar Companies*. New York: Farr & Co., 1934–60.

Ferrer, Ada. *Insurgent Cuba: Race, Nation and Revolution, 1868–1898*. Chapel Hill: University of North Carolina Press, 1999.

Figarola, Joel James. *Cuba 1900–1928: La República Dividida Contra Su Misma*. Havana: Editorial Arte y Literatura, 1974.

Foreign Policy Association. *Problems of the New Cuba: Report of the Commission on Cuban Affairs*. New York: Foreign Policy Association, 1935.

Galloway, J. H. *The Sugar Cane Industry: An Historical Geography from Its Origins to 1914*. Cambridge: Cambridge University Press, 1989.

García Alvarez, Alejandro. *La Gran Burguesía Commercial en Cuba, 1899–1920*. Havana: Editorial de Ciencias Sociales, 1990.

———. "Una saga azucarera entre dos siglos." In *Asturias y Cuba en Turno al 1898*, edited by Jorge Uría, 43–55. Barcelona: Editorial Labor S.A., 1994.

Gardner, Lloyd C. *Economic Aspects of New Deal Diplomacy*. Madison: University of Wisconsin Press, 1984.

Garray, John A., and Mark C. Carnes, eds. *American National Biography*. New York: Oxford University Press, 1999.

Gellman, Irwin F. *Roosevelt and Batista: Good Neighbor Diplomacy in Cuba, 1933–1945*. Albuquerque: University of New Mexico Press, 1973.

George W. Goethals and Company. "Report on the Cuba Cane Sugar Corporation, July 11, 1919." Record Group II, Series 64, Braga Brothers Collection, University of Florida, Gainesville.

Goizueta, Felix. *Azúcar Amargo Cubano: Monocultura y Dependencia Economica*. Madrid: Filadelfia, 1972.

Guerra y Sánchez, Ramiro. *Azúcar y Población en Las Antillas*. 3d ed. Havana: Editorial Cultural, 1944.

———. *La Industria Azucarera de Cuba*. Havana: Editorial Cultural, 1940.

———. "Sugar: Index of Cuban-American Cooperation." *Foreign Affairs* (July 1942): 743–56.

Guggenheim, Harry F. *The United States and Cuba*. New York: Macmillan, 1934.

Hatch, Louis C. *Maine: A History*. Centennial ed. New York: Privately printed, 1919.

Havemeyer, Louisine W. *Sixteen to Sixty: Memoirs of a Collector*. New York: Privately printed, 1961.

Hazard, Samuel. *Cuba with Pen and Pencil*. Hartford, Conn.: Hartford Publishing Co., 1871.

Healey, David F. *The United States in Cuba, 1898–1902: Generals, Politicians and the Search for Policy*. Madison: University of Wisconsin Press, 1963.

Heitmann, John Alfred. *The Modernization of the Louisiana Sugar Industry, 1830–1910*. Baton Rouge: Louisiana State University Press, 1987.

Heston, Thomas J. *Sweet Subsidy: The Diplomatic Effects of the U.S. Sugar Acts, 1934–1974*. New York: Garland, 1987.

Hoernel, Robert B. "Sugar and Social Change in Oriente, Cuba, 1898–1946." *Journal of Latin American Studies* 8 (1976): 215–49.

Hoover, Herbert. *The Memoirs of Herbert Hoover*. New York: Macmillan, 1951.
Hugill, Anthony. *Sugar and All That: A History of Tate and Lyle*. London: Gentry Books, 1978.
Ibarra, Jorge. *Un análisis psicosocial del Cubano: 1898–1925*. Havana: Editorial de Ciencias Sociales, 1994.
———. *Prologue to Revolution: Cuba, 1898–1958*. Translated by Marjorie Moore. Boulder, Colo.: Lynne Rienner, 1998.
Ibarra Cuesta, Jorge. *Cuba, 1898–1958: Estructura y procesos sociales*. Havana: Editorial de Ciencias Sociales, 1995.
Iglesias García, Fé. *Del Ingenio al Central*. San Juan: Editorial de la Universidad de Puerto Rico, 1998.
James, Ariel. *Banes: Imperialismo y nación en una plantación azucarera*. Havana: Ediciones de Ciencias Sociales, 1976.
Janes, Hurford, and H. T. Sayers. *The Story of Czarnikow*. London: Harley Publishing Co., 1963.
Jencks, Leland. *Our Cuban Colony: A Study in Sugar*. New York: Vanguard Press, 1928.
Lauriault, Robin N. "Virgin Soil: The Modernization of Social Relations on a Cuban Sugar Estate: The Francisco Sugar Company, 1898–1921." Ph.D. diss., University of Florida, 1995.
Le Riverend, Julio. *Historia Económica de Cuba*. Havana: Editorial de Ciencias Sociales, 1985.
Lincoln, Freeman. "Julio Lobo, Colossus of Sugar." *Fortune* (September 1958): 150–52, 184–92.
Lisagor, Nancy, and Frank Lipsius. *A Law Unto Itself: The Untold Story of the Law Firm Sullivan & Cromwell*. New York: William Morrow, 1988.
Liss, Sheldon. *Roots of Revolution: Radical Thought in Cuba*. Lincoln: University of Nebraska Press, 1987.
Lockmiller, David A. *Enoch H. Crowder: Soldier, Lawyer and Statesman*. Columbia: University of Missouri Studies, 1955.
López Segrera, Francisco. "Algunos Aspectos de la Industria Azucarera Cubana: 1925–1937." In *La República Neocolonial*, 2: 167–293, edited by Juan Pérez de la Riva. Havana: Anuario de Estudios Cubanos, 1979.
Lord, Russell. *The Wallaces of Iowa*. Boston: Houghton, Mifflin, 1947.
Louisiana Planter and Sugar Manufacturer. New Orleans: Louisiana Sugar Planters Association, 1888–1929.
Lynsky, Stuart. *Sugar Economics: Statistics and Documents*. New York: United States Cane Sugar Refiners' Association, 1938.
Malone, Dumas, ed. *Dictionary of American Biography*. New York: Charles Scribner's Sons, 1935.
Manach, Jorge. "Torriente y la Memoria Pública." In *Libre Homenaje al Coronel Cosme de la Torriente*, 31–35. Havana: Editorial Cultural, 1951.
Marcosson, Isaac F. *Colonel Deeds, Industrial Builder*. New York: Dodd, Mead, 1948.

Martínez-Alier, Juan. *Cuba: Economía y Sociedad*. Paris: Ruedo Ibérico, 1972.

———. *Haciendas, Plantations and Collective Farms: Agrarian Class Societies—Cuba and Peru*. London: Frank Cass, 1977.

Martínez-Vaillant, Facundo. *El antiguo Central Francisco: Símbolo de una sombría historia poca concocida*. Havana: Editorial de Ciencias Sociales, 1972.

Mayer, Robert. "The Origins of the American Banking Empire in Latin America: Frank A. Vanderlip and the National City Bank." *Journal of Interamerican Studies and World Affairs* 15, no. 1 (February 1973): 60–76.

McCullough, David. *The Path between the Seas*. New York: Simon and Schuster, 1977.

Mendoza, Luis G. *Revista Seminal Azucarera: Seleciones, 1935–1945*. Havana: Bolsa de la Habana, 1945.

Mikusch, Gustav. *Kuba, Haiti und Louisiana als Zuckerlander*. Berlin: P. Parey, 1930.

Moley, Raymond. *After Seven Years*. New York: Harper and Brothers, 1939.

Moody's Manual of Investments, American and Foreign. Industrial Securities. New York: Moody's Investors Service, 1900–1953.

Moreno Fraginals, Manuel. *El Ingenio: Complejo económico cubano del azúcar*. 3 vols. Havana: Editorial de Ciencias Sociales, 1977.

———, et al., eds. *Between Slavery and Free Labor: The Spanish-Speaking Caribbean in the Nineteenth Century*. Baltimore: Johns Hopkins University Press, 1985.

"Mr. Chadbourne Makes a Plan." *Fortune* (July 1931): 23–28, 112–14.

Mullins, Jack S. "The Sugar Trust: Henry O. Havemeyer and the American Sugar Refining Company." Ph.D. diss., University of South Carolina, 1964.

El Mundo Azucarero. 1913–44. [Spanish monthly edition of the *Louisiana Planter*].

The National Cyclopaedia of American Biography. New York: James T. White, 1958.

Neal, John. *Portland Illustrated*. Portland, Maine: U. S. Jones, 1874.

Ortiz, Fernando. *Cuban Counterpoint: Tobacco and Sugar*. Translated by Harriet de Onís. New York: Alfred A. Knopf, 1947.

Padula, Alfred L. "The Fall of the Bourgeoisie: Cuba, 1959–1961." Ph.D. diss.: University of New Mexico, 1974.

Parker, William Belmont. *Cubans of Today*. New York: G. P. Putnam's Sons, 1919.

Parrini, Carl P. *Heir to Empire: United States Economic Diplomacy, 1916–1923*. Pittsburgh: University of Pittsburgh Press, 1969.

Pérez, Louis A., Jr. *Cuba between Empires, 1878–1902*. Pittsburgh: University of Pittsburgh Press, 1987.

———. *Cuba between Reform and Revolution*. New York: Oxford University Press, 1988.

———. *Cuba under the Platt Amendment*. Pittsburgh: University of Pittsburgh Press, 1993.

———. *Intervention, Revolution and Politics in Cuba, 1913–1921*. Pittsburgh: University of Pittsburgh Press, 1987.

Pérez de la Riva, Juan. "Los Recursos Humanos de Cuba al Comenzar el Siglo: Inmigración, economía y nacionalidad, 1899–1906." In *La república neocolonial: Anuario de Estudios Cubanos*, 1: 7–44. Havana: Editorial de Ciencias Sociales, 1973.

Pérez-López, Jorge F. *The Economics of Cuban Sugar*. Pittsburgh: University of Pittsburgh Press, 1991.

Pérez-Stable, Marifeli. *The Cuban Revolution: Origins, Course and Legacy*. New York: Oxford University Press, 1993.

Phillips, R. Hart. *Cuba: Island of Paradox*. New York: McDowell, Obolensky, 1959.

Pollitt, Brian H. "The Cuban Sugar Economy: Collapse, Reform and Prospects for Recovery." *Latin American Studies* 29 (1997): 171–210.

———. "The Cuban Sugar Economy and the Great Depression." *Bulletin of Latin American Research* 3, no. 2 (1984): 3–28.

———. "The Cuban Sugar Economy in the 1930s." In *The World Sugar Economy in War and Depression, 1914–1940*, edited by Bill Albert and Adrian Graves, 97–108. London: Routledge, 1988.

Porter, Robert P. *Report on the Commercial and Industrial Condition in the Island of Cuba*. Washington, D.C.: GPO, 1898.

Primelles, L. *Cronica cubana, 1915–1918*. Havana: Editorial Lex, 1955.

Prinsen Geerligs, H. C. *Cane Sugar Protection, 1912–1937*. London: N. Rodger, 1938.

———. "Protective Duties in Sugar Production." *Cuba Review* (July 1926): 27–30.

———. *The World's Sugar Cane Industry, Past and Present*. Manchester, England: Norman Rodger, 1912.

Ratner, Sidney. *The Tariff in American History*. New York: Van Norstrand, 1972.

Rionda, Manuel. "The Cuban Colono System." *Cuba Review* (December 1925): 20–28.

———. "Sugar Review for 1942" *Czarnikow-Rionda Annual Review* (1942): 2–5.

"Rionda Family Genealogy." Record Group II, Series 23, Braga Brothers Collection, University of Florida, Gainesville.

Roberts, Richard. *Schroeders: Merchants and Bankers*. London: Macmillan, 1992.

Rowe, J.W.F. *Studies in the Artificial Control of Raw Material Supplies*. No. 1, *Sugar*. London: London and Cambridge Economic Service, 1932.

Rowe, William H. *The Maritime History of Maine*. New York: W. W. Norton, 1932.

Rubens, Horatio. *Liberty: The Story of Cuba*. New York: Brewster, Warren and Putnam, 1932.

Santa Cruz y Mallen, Francisco Xavier de. *Historia de familas cubanas*. 8 vols. Havana: Editorial Hércules, 1940.

Santamarina, Juan-Carlos. "The Cuba Company and Cuban Development, 1900–1959." Ph.D. diss., Rutgers University, 1995.

Scheiber, Harry N. "World War I as Entrepreneurial Opportunity. Willard Straight and the American International Corporation." *Political Science Quarterly* (September 1969): 486–511.

Schwartz, Jordan A. *"Liberal": Adolph A. Berle and the Vision of an American Era.* New York: Free Press, 1987.

Scott, Rebecca J. "Fault Lines, Color Lines and Party Lines." In *Beyond Slavery: Explorations of Race, Labor and Citizenship in Postemancipation Societies,* edited by Frederick Cooper et al., 61–106. Chapel Hill: University of North Carolina Press, 2000.

Silva León, Arnaldo. *Cuba y el Mercado Internacional Azucarero.* Havana: Editorial de Ciencias Sociales, 1975.

Smith, Robert Freeman. *Background to Revolution: The Development of Modern Cuba.* New York: Alfred A. Knopf, 1966.

———. *The United States and Cuba: Business and Diplomacy, 1917–1960.* New York: Bookman Associates, 1960.

Sobel, Robert. *The Big Board.* New York: Free Press, 1965.

SUGAR. New York: R. Palmer, 1899–1929.

Sulroca D., Federico, and Bernardo de la Peña. "Evolución de la Organizacíon Territorial en la Agricultura Cañera." *Cañaveral* (January–March 2000): 43–47.

Swerling, Boris C. *International Control of Sugar, 1918–1941.* Stanford, Calif.: Stanford University Press, 1949.

Swift, Jonathan, and Luzminda Bartolome Francisco. *Conspiracy for Empire: Big Business Corruption and the Politics of Imperialism in America, 1876–1907.* Quezon City, Philippines: Foundation for Nationalist Studies, 1985.

Tabares de Real, Louis A. *La Revolución del 30: Los Dos Ultimos Años.* Havana: Editorial de Ciencias Sociales, 1973.

Thomas, Hugh. *Cuba: The Pursuit of Freedom.* New York: Da Capa Press, 1998.

Thompson, Charles A. "The Cuban Revolution: Reform and Reaction." *Foreign Policy Reports* 11, January 1, 1937.

Tugwell, R. G. *The Brains Trust.* New York: Viking, 1968.

U.S. Cane Refiners Association. *Sugar Economics, Statistics and Documents.* New York: U.S. Cane Refiners Association, 1939.

U.S. Department of Agriculture. *Statistics of Sugar in the United States and its Insular Possessions, 1881–1912.* Bulletin No. 66. Washington, D.C.: GPO, 1914.

———. *Yearbook.* Washington, D.C.: GPO, 1900–1943.

U.S. Department of Commerce. *Historical Statistics of the United States: Colonial Times to 1970,* Parts 1 and 2. Washington, D.C.: GPO, 1971.

———. *The Sugar Cane Industry: Agriculture, Manufacturing and Marketing Costs in Hawaii, Puerto Rico, Louisiana and Cuba.* Washington, D.C.: GPO, 1917.

U.S. Department of State. *Foreign Relations of the United States.* Washington, D.C.: GPO, 1917–40.

U.S. House Committee on Ways and Means. *Reciprocity with Cuba: Hearings before the Committee on Ways and Means.* 57th Cong., 1st sess., 1902, H. Doc.535.

U.S. Senate Committee on Banking and Currency. *Stock Exchange Practices: Re-*

port of the Committee on Banking and Currency pursuant to S. Res. 84. 72d Cong. and Senate Res. 56 and 97. 73d Cong., 2d sess., 1934. S. Rept. 1455.

U.S. Senate Committee on Finance. *Sale of Foreign Bonds or Securities: Hearings.* 72d Cong., 1st sess., 1931.

U.S. Senate Committee on Relations with Cuba. *Cuban Sugar Sales: Hearings.* 57th Cong., 1st sess., 1902.

Vagts, Alfred. *Deutsch-Amerikanische Ruckwanderung.* Heidleberg: Carl Winter Universitatsverlag, 1960.

Valdés, Nelson P. "La Diplomacia del Azúcar: Estados Unidos y Cuba." *Aportes* (Paris) 18 (October 1970): 99–119.

Van Hook, Andrew. *Sugar: Its Production, Technology and Uses.* New York: Ronald Press, 1949.

Van Ness, Carl. "Guide to the Braga Brothers Collection." Ms., Braga Brothers Collection, University of Florida, Gainesville.

———. "Sugar, Railroads and Dollar Diplomats." Master's thesis, University of Florida, 1984.

Vaughan, W. *The Life and Work of Sir William Van Horne.* New York: Century Company, 1920.

Vogt, Paul L. *The Sugar Refining Industry in the United States.* Philadelphia: University of Pennsylvania, 1908.

Wallich, Henry C. *Monetary Problems of an Export Economy: The Cuban Experience, 1914–1947.* Cambridge: Harvard University Press, 1950.

Weigle, E. D. "The Sugar Interests and American Diplomacy in Hawaii and Cuba, 1893–1903." Ph.D. diss., Yale University, 1939.

Weitzenhoffer, Frances. *The Havemeyers: Impressionism Comes to America.* New York: Harry M. Abrams, 1986.

Whitney, Robert. *State and Revolution in Cuba: Mass Mobilization and Political Change, 1920–1940.* Chapel Hill: University of North Carolina Press, 2001.

Willett and Gray's Weekly Statistical Sugar Trade Journal. New York: Willett and Gray, 1888–1978.

Wilson, Joan Hoff. *Herbert Hoover: Forgotten Progressive.* Boston: Little, Brown, 1975.

Winkler, John K. *The First Billion: The Stillmans and the National City Bank.* New York: Vanguard Press, 1934.

Wood, Major General Leonard. *Report of the Work Accomplished.* Washington, D.C.: GPO, 1900, 1901.

Wright, Philip G. *Sugar in Relation to the Tariff.* New York: McGraw-Hill, 1924.

Wright, Stephen J. "Cuba, Sugar and the United States: Diplomatic and Economic Relations during the Administration of Ramón Grau San Martin, 1944–1948." Ph.D. diss., Pennsylvania State University, 1983.

Yglesia Martínez, Teresita. *El Segundo ensayo de república.* Havana: Editorial de Ciencias Sociales, 1980.

Zanetti, Oscar, and Alejandro García Alvarez. *Sugar and Railroads: A Cuban History, 1837–1959.* Translated by Franklin A. Knight and Mary Todd. Chapel Hill: University of North Carolina Press, 1998.

Zanetti Lecuona, Oscar. "El Comercio Exterior de la República Neocolonial." In *La Republica neocolonial: Anuario de Esudios Cubanos,* 1: 45–126. Havana: Editorial de Ciencias Sociales, 1973.

———. *Comercio y Poder: Relaciones Cubano-Hispano-Norteamericanas en Tomo a 1898.* Havana: Casa de la Américas, 1998.

Zerbe, Richard. "The American Sugar Refining Company, 1887–1914: The Story of a Monopoly." *Journal of Law and Economics* (October 1969): 339–75.

Index

ABC Party, 247, 264–65, 270
Adelaida, 165, 241
Administration cane, 137–38, 185–86, 236
Agrarian League (1912–13), 60, 71, 143
American Beet Sugar Ass'n, 45, 69
American Sugar Refining Co., 20, 26, 38, 52, 59, 105, 148–49, 162–63, 180–81, 191, 200, 215, 296
Amistad, 70, 149, 189
Apezeguía, Marquis de, 31, 33
Arango Mantilla, Miguel, 71, 143; and Cuba Cane, 84–85, 88, 90. 98, 124, 129, 177; as political emissary, 110, 114, 142, 166; and *Violeta*, 146, 150; and *Cunagua*, 149; and *Andorra*, 176
Arenal, Pedro, 31, 79, 84, 87, 88
Asociación de Colonos y Agricultures (1933), 251–52
Aspuru, Manuel, 161
Association of Planters and Sugar Manufacturers (1913–14), 71–72
Atkins, Edwin Farnsworth, Jr., 82, 179, 310n.31
Atkins, Edwin Farnsworth, Sr., 15, 32, 59–60, 107, 150, 163, 179; and reciprocity, 16, 18, 20; and Punta Alegre, 81–82
Atkins, Elisha and Company, 15, 16, 187
Atkins, Robert, 82, 179, 187, 250
Atkinson, G. H., 35
Atlántica del Golfo, Compañia Azucarera, 262–72, 274. *See also* Cuban Atlantic Sugar Company

Babst, Earl, 105–7, 110, 145, 183, 193–94, 273, 291–92; tribute to MR by, 286–87, 289
Bailie, Earle, 209, 218
Banco Internacional, 148, 160
Banco Nacional, 86, 125, 148, 154, 159–60, 162
Barceló, José, 191
Baró, Juan Pedro, 31, 50
Batista y Zaldívar, Fulgencio, 252, 256–57, 259, 270
Bay State Sugar Refinery, 16, 19
Bea and Co., T., 28, 75, 79
Benjamin, Lewis, 8
Benjamin, Sophie (Mrs. Joaquín Rionda, d. 1877), 8, 10
Beola, José H., 63
Berle, Adolf A., Jr., 248–49
Blaine, James G., 16, 18
Bliss, Col. Tasker, 37, 44
Boston, 40, 47, 50, 51, 163
Braga, Bernardo Rionda ("Ronnie," MR's grandnephew, son of Bernardo Braga Rionda, 1911–1960), 47, 274, 295
Braga, George Atkinson (MR's grandnephew, son of Bernardo Braga Rionda, 1904–1985), 14, 47, 144, 174, 274, 295

Braga, Maude Atkinson (Mrs. Bernardo Braga, d. 1922), 35, 47, 174
Braga Brothers Collection, 3–4
Braga Rionda, Bernardo (MR's nephew, 1875–1960), 13, 14, 25,29, 33–34, 47, 154, 162, 175, 284, 286; and Czarnikow-Rionda, 33–35, 51–52, 54, 68, 80, 148; and Cuba Cane, 94, 97, 117–19, 121–22, 124–26, 131, 139, 146, 151, 197, 199, 253, 256
Brandeis, Louis D., 62, 291
Brown Brothers, 209
Brussels Agreement (1902), 15, 44, 225, 233

Cabrera, Juan, 181
Caffery, Jefferson, 257, 259, 266
Caracas, 41, 47, 50, 150
Carl W. Loeb, Roades and Company, 297
Casanova, José Manuel, 268
Castaño, Nicolás, 28, 31, 45, 109–10; as banker, 31; and clan connections, 64, 150, 165; on refining, 71; as Czarnikow-Rionda client, 75, 79, 188; and government restrictions on selling, 162, 166, 168–69
Catlin, Henry, 182
Ceballos, Juan M., 14, 15, 20, 22–24, 32
Central Cuba, 58, 108, 200, 209, 240
Central Cuba Sugar Company, 59, 64, 75, 102–3
Central Hanover Bank and Trust Co., 96, 218, 262, 272
Central Railroad, 41–42, 45, 58, 303n.17
Centrals: system of, 17; incorporation of, 18–19; Cuban vs. U.S., 47, 50, 55; western vs. eastern, 137–38; source for production figures of, 302n.20
Cervera Falla, Ricardo, 212, 251
Céspedes, 153, 238–39, 241
Céspedes, Carlos Miguel de, 107, 110, 141, 183, 250–51
Chadbourne, Thomas L., 190–91, 194, 225–27, 230, 232–33, 239, 251, 258, 311nn.17, 22
Chadbourne Plan, 226–28, 232
Chaparra, 38–40, 47, 50, 51, 140, 144, 257, 261, 301n.11

Chase National Bank, 61, 96, 149, 160, 212, 218, 226, 279–80, 283
Chiriqui Sugar Mills Corp., 297
Clark, Juan M., 20, 33, 36–37, 51
Clarke, Harriet (Mrs. MR, d. 1922), 14, 31, 33–34, 47–48, 119, 124, 126, 131–32, 174
Clarke, Joseph I.C. (Mrs. MR's brother, 1846–1925), 14, 35, 42
Colonial Sugars Co., 40–41
Colonos: strike threat (1918), 114; strike (1925), 185–86; dissatisfaction of, 205–6; group action by, 212, 228–29, 251–52; support for Atlántica, 265–66, 269–72
Colono system, 17, 37, 137–38, 178
Compañia Azucarera Atlántica del Golfo. *See* Atlántica
Conchita, 50, 87, 124
Conklin, Roland, 59
Consolidated Railroads, 187, 241, 243–45
Constancia, 31, 40, 47, 72
Cooperative Export Agency (1929–30), 211, 214–16, 217–18, 221–22
Craig, John F., 35, 63
Cromwell, William Nelson, 62, 286. *See also* Sullivan & Cromwell
Crosby, Lawrence, 245, 261–62, 265, 270, 279–80
Crowder, Gen. Enoch, 159–60, 162, 167, 183, 193, 211–12
Cuba: under Spain, 9–12, 15; sugar production in, 10, 18, 21, 24, 31, 35, 47, 56, 64, 69, 213–14; War for Cuban Independence, 21; Spanish-Cuban-American War, 25–28, 61; U.S. occupation of, 42–44; Second American Intervention, 50; 1917 insurrection, 100–102, 112; marketing restrictions, 140–43; "Dance of the Millions," 148, 152–53; banking crisis, 153–54; changes of 1920s, 182–84; crop restrictions, 186–89, 195, 200–202, 211, 232, 234, 312n.25; quotas for centrals, 190–95, 199–200; 1933 Revolution, 242, 245, 248–59; 1959 Revolution, 295. *See also* Cooperative Export Agency (1929–30); Joint Foreign Sales Syndicate (1929); National Sugar Ex-

330 Index

porting Co. (1930–33); Sugar Export Corporation (1927)
Cuba Cane Sugar Corporation (CCSC), 109, 178, 200, 289–90; incorporated, 1, 81–83; acquisition of centrals, 83–88, 304n.9, 305n.13; and colonos, 93; development of, 93–98; Board of Directors, 96–97; Executive Commitee, 97; Goethals investigation of, 118–27, 132; Goethals Report, 132–41, 143–44, 165; support for Association of Hacendados, 143–44; financing, 145–46, 156–57; during Ogilvie's presidency, 165–66, 168, 170–71, 176–77, 179–81, 188; during Simpson's presidency, 201–2, 209, 214, 218; reorganization process, 210–13, 216–20; sold at auction, 219
—annual reports: first, 98–99, 306n.30; second, 103, 111–14; third, 116–18; fourth, 144–45; fifth, 156–58, 309n.33; sixth, 173–74; for 1925, 184; for 1927, 198–99, 311n.20
Cuba Company, 41, 45–47
Cuban American Sugar Company, 1, 38, 50, 51, 55, 96, 107, 133, 143–44, 149, 160–63, 178, 184, 189–91, 193, 198, 200, 248, 257, 261, 284, 296; dividends paid by, 305n.27
Cuban Association of Hacendados and Colonos (Asociación de Hacendados y Colonos de Cuba) (1919), 143, 154
Cuban Atlantic Sugar Company: acquisition of Atlántica by, 274–75; history of, 276, 278–79, 295–97; profits of, 283–84
Cuban Cane Products Company, 219–20, 229–30, 235–38, 241–46, 248–49, 258–59, 263, 274–76, 286, 296; sale of, 261
Cuban Dominican Sugar Company, 191, 198, 212, 235, 269
Cuban Electric Company, 165, 182
Cuban Trading Company, 51, 78, 99, 124–25, 131, 136, 229–30, 238, 241, 250, 274, 278
Cuervo, Dr. Manuel Froilán, 70, 72
Cunagua, 90, 109, 149, 163, 180–81, 191, 193, 200

Czarnikow, C., Ltd., 22, 31, 77
Czarnikow, Julius Caesar, 22, 24, 27–28, 48, 53
Czanikow, MacDougall and Company, 22–24, 53
Czarnikow-Rionda, 2; early history of, 53–54, 66, 77–80; and clients, 73, 75, 79–80, 150, 152, 176; and Cuba Cane, 85, 93, 99, 124, 131, 137; later history of, 144, 147–50, 159, 197, 218, 200, 220, 253, 295; and Cuban Cane Products, 223–30

Davis y Owen, Octavio, 50, 302n.23
Davison, George W., 216, 273
Deeds, Col. E. A., 179, 207, 211, 215, 226, 261, 310n.30
Delicias, 144, 257, 261
Díaz, Miguel, 31, 79, 88, 90
Díaz Pardo, Dr. Rogelio, 64, 212
Doscher complaint, 216–17
Doty, John, Jr. (MR's grandnephew, b. 1916), 284
Doty, Oliver (Elena Rionda's husband, 1885–1942), 68, 77, 167, 256
Douglas, William C., 187, 193, 201–2, 215, 226
Dulles, John Foster, 193
Du Pont, Irénée, 216, 250, 276

Eastern Cuba Sugar Corporation, 146, 177, 210, 213, 218, 237, 274, 279
Elía, 117, 151
España, 90, 191, 226
Estrada de Fanjul, María (Mrs. Higinio Fanjul, b. 1881), 47
Evans, Mr. and Mrs. Henry, 119–21, 127, 141
Export Corporation. *See* Sugar Export Corporation

Falla Gutiérrez, Juan, 212
Falla Gutiérrez, Laureano, 71, 79, 110, 153, 164–69, 178, 188, 209; clan connections of, 165, 196, 212
Fanjul Estrada, Alfonso (MR's grandnephew, Higinio Fanjul's son, b. 1909), 248, 295–96

Index 331

Fanjul Fernández, Alonso (María Rionda's husband), 13, 79
Fanjul Gómez-Mena, Alfonso, Jr. (Alfonso Fanjul Estrada's son, b. 1937), 296
Fanjul Gómez-Mena, José (Alfonso Fanjul Estrada's son, b. 1944), 296
Fanjul Rionda, Higinio (MR's nephew, 1877–1963): early history of, 13, 23, 29, 37, 47, 54; and Cuban Trading Company, 79, 110, 142–43, 150, 153–54, 175, 185, 188, 190, 199, 239; and Cuba Cane, 83, 239, 241–46; and 1933 Revolution, 246–48, 252–57; and Right of Tanteo, 259–65, 270–74, 276, 280, 294–96; and Atlántica, 262–64; and Reciprocity Treaty, 273, 282; and Guaranty Trust Company, 276, 278–81; and 1959 Revolution, 296
Farr and Company, 220, 227
Farrel, Franklin, 11–13, 15
Federal Sugar Refining Company, 63, 97, 194
Feliz, 88, 90, 124
Ferrara, Orestes, 91, 97, 109, 163
Fleming, Stephen B., 96, 122
Flora, 58, 103, 108
Fowler, G. R., 31, 72
Francisco, 27, 31, 34–37, 40, 41, 46, 47, 52–55, 60, 72, 96, 101, 117, 147, 151, 178, 180, 184, 248, 261, 283–86, 295–96; bankruptcy of, 256, 281
Francke, Hijos y Cía., 27, 75
Futures trading, 70, 73–74, 217. *See also* manipulation of market; New York Coffee and Sugar Exchange

Galbán, Lobo y Cía., 75, 90, 197, 200, 207, 220, 274, 280
Galbán, Luis, 88, 90
Ganzoni, Julius Charles, 23, 53–54, 68, 78, 100, 110, 113–14
García, Laurentino, 75, 153, 159–60
Garrett, Tom, 261, 270
General Sugar Company, 178–79, 189–91, 198, 207, 211, 235, 261, 269
Goethals, Gen. George W., 122–27, 141, 146, 217, 291. *See also* CCSC "Goethals report"
Goin, Ellen (Mrs Manuel E. Rionda), 47
Gómez, José Miguel, 57, 59–60
Gómez Mena, 149, 189
Gómez Mena, Alfonso, 70, 71, 75, 114, 159, 183, 189
Gómez Mena, Andres, 70, 71, 75
Gómez Mena, José, 159, 183, 189, 207, 212, 215, 220, 221, 251, 255, 296; proposes single seller, 202–3; mission to Europe, 232
Gómez Mena, Lillian (Mrs. Alfonso Fanjul, b. 1917), 296
Grau San Martín, Ramón, 252, 255, 257–59
Guantanamo Sugar Company, 50–51, 55, 96, 149, 306n.27
Guaranty Trust Company, 61–62, 81, 96, 113–14, 118, 126, 146, 148, 160, 166, 173, 212, 218, 235–37, 241–45, 249–50, 261–64, 272, 281, 308n.18
Gutiérrez Valladon, Carlos Felipe, 150, 165
Gutiérrez Valladon, Dr. Viriato, 165, 200, 224–25; on Sugar Defense Committee, 196; as Machado's secretary, 202, 241–48, 283; missions to Europe, 212, 232; on Cooperative Export Agency, 215, 217, 221

Havemeyer, Henry Osborne, 4, 10, 19, 20, 23, 28, 36, 38, 43, 45, 50, 52, 66, 301n.7
Havemeyer, Horace, 52, 62, 97, 187, 286
Havemeyer, Louisine (Mrs. Henry O. Havemeyer), 19, 52
Hawaii, 30, 32, 121, 163, 194, 197, 203–4, 208
Hawley, Robert Bradley: launching Cuban-American, 37–38, 40, 50, 71; and World War I controls, 105, 107, 110, 115; and postwar controls, 140–43, 155, 160–63; death of, 171–72
Hayden, Charles, 122–23; and Cuba Cane, 127, 141, 145–46, 177, 185, 188, 190, 194–95, 201–2, 205, 207, 209; and reorganization process, 210–11, 216, 218–19,

229, 237, 239, 250, 258, 261; and Securities and Exchange Commission, 263–64, 269–70, 272; and Cuban Atlantic, 274, 276, 280–81; death of, 283
Hayden, Stone and Co., 82, 123, 212, 274, 276
Hershey Co., 150, 200, 214, 225, 256, 296
Hoover, Herbert: in World War I, 104–6, 108, 115; as secretary of commerce, 172–73; as president, 208
Houston, G. H., 179, 310n.30
Howell, B. H., Son and Company, 28, 38, 47, 55, 100
Howell, Frederick H., 38, 40, 301n.10
Howell, Thomas A., 50, 141, 301n.10

Ibáñez, Francisco Feliciano, 17, 40
Infante. *See* Cuba Cane Sugar Corporation and its successor companies
International Sugar Committee, 106, 109–11, 115
International Sugar Conferences: of 1929, 212, 224; of 1930, 232–34; of 1932, 239
International Sugar Council, 233–34, 258
Irving Trust Co., 216, 235

Jagüeyal, 64, 97
Jamison, William A., 105–6
Jaretzki, Alfred, 62–3, 82, 92, 97, 103, 118–20, 122, 124, 177
Jaretzki, Alfred, Jr., 209, 295
Jaronú, 163, 180–81, 191, 193, 200
Jarvie, James N., 96, 97, 122, 209, 212–13
Java, 30, 76, 121, 152, 184, 193, 196, 203–4, 212, 225, 226, 232, 234, 239
Joint Foreign Sales Syndicate (1929), 207–8
Jones-Costigan Law, 266, 282

Keiser, George E., 192, 273
Kelley, Henry, 262, 265–66, 270
Kelly, Hugh, 12, 15, 21, 32, 40, 52
Kuhn, Loeb, 61, 69

Labor, 109, 155, 167, 169, 185, 221, 228, 261

Laborde, Pedro, 75, 79, 84, 86, 88, 90, 91, 153–54
Ladenburg, Thalmann and Co., 279
Lagemann, Charles, 23, 44, 48, 53, 54, 59, 68, 73, 74–75, 78, 80, 85, 92, 99, 101, 116, 147–48
Lagemann, Eric, 68, 77, 113
Lagemann, Walter, 68, 77
Lamar, Mario, 267
Lamont, Thomas, 61, 245
Leonard, M. L., 215, 222
Lezama, José, 107, 306n.6
Lobo, Heriberto, 90, 197
Lobo Olavarría, Julio, 90, 197, 218, 222, 225, 226, 284, 297
Longa, Ernesto A., 38, 72, 109, 183
López, José M. (Lito), 225, 227, 232
López Rodríguez, José (Pote), 87–88, 90, 148, 164, 191
Louisiana Planter and Sugar Manufacturer, 52, 74, 91–93, 121, 141, 143, 153, 155, 163
Lowry, Frank, 187, 194, 212
Lugareño, 36, 40, 88, 101, 118, 132–33, 136, 297, 301n.7
Lyle, Robert Park, 76, 116

MacDougall, George, 23, 53, 68, 78, 105, 108
Machado, Gerardo, 165, 182–83, 185, 187, 189–95, 197, 200–201, 204, 211, 214, 221, 224, 232, 241–46, 249–50
Manatí, 60, 62–64, 72, 96, 147, 163, 166, 171, 176, 180, 184, 187, 191, 211, 229, 235, 248, 283–84, 295–96
Manipulation of market, 102–3, 121, 188
Marchena, Moises B. de, 88, 90, 131–32
Martí, José, 21–22
McCahan Sugar Refinery, 28, 35–36, 151–52, 188, 194
Méndez Peñate, Roberto, 260, 264
Mendieta, Carlos, 259, 261, 264–65, 270
Mendoza, Anthony G., 191, 271–72
Mendoza, Antonio, 31, 71, 88, 183
Mendoza, Miguel, 90, 109, 149, 175, 183
Mendoza, Victor G. and Co., 237
Menocal y Deop, Mario García, 38–39, 66,

Index 333

71, 100, 107–8, 110, 114, 140, 142, 160–62, 196, 301n.11
Mercedes, 59, 84–85, 88
Mercedita, 38, 72, 109
Merchant, W. A., 86, 154
Mesa, Hannibal de, 109, 146, 151, 183
Miller, Edward G., 271, 274
Mitchell, Charles E., 169–70, 198
Molinet, Gen. Eugenio, 191, 196, 215
Morgan, J. P., and Co., 60–62, 85, 94, 96, 173, 183, 190, 226, 244–45
Morgan, J. Pierpont, 10, 51, 61, 65
Morón, 64, 86–88, 93, 97, 101, 118, 136, 145, 149, 297
Morrow, Dwight, 173, 190

National Bank of Commerce, 61, 77
National City Bank, 10, 18, 60–62, 71, 73, 77, 82, 96, 120, 148, 159–61, 169–70, 178, 198, 211, 212. 215, 226, 244, 309n.15
National Sugar Exporting Corp. (1930–33) 232, 251–52, 258
National Sugar Refining Co., 38, 55, 149, 194
Nazabal, Domingo, 65, 88, 90, 212
Negra, Francisco, 70, 72
New York Coffee and Sugar Exchange, 70, 105. *See also* futures trading; manipulation of market
Northern Railroad, 58, 64–65, 136, 146, 149, 180–81

Ogilvie, George, 77, 209
Ogilvie, Walter, 59, 73, 77, 86, 96, 145, 158, 165, 177, 188, 209
Oxnard Brothers, 69

Pelayo, Ramón, 26, 33, 42, 44, 53, 75, 110, 150, 152
Pelegrin, Pedro, 205–6
Philippine Islands, 32, 48, 57, 152, 163, 194, 196, 203, 206, 208, 221
Placé, Louis, 37, 42, 50, 60
Platt, Orville, 43–44
Polledo, Rionda y Cía., 10, 12

Polledo y Alvarez, Joaquín (MR's uncle), 7, 10, 12
Ponvert, Louis, 21, 31
Porter, Robert Percival, 32, 45
Portuondo Barceló, Aurelio, 176, 181, 185, 187, 196, 209, 214, 234, 239, 253, 259, 263, 295
Post, James Howell, 38, 40, 43, 50, 62, 141, 194
Pote. *See* José López Rodríquez
Prinsen Geerligs, H. C., 186, 225, 233–34
Puerto Rico, 32, 163, 168, 197, 203–4, 208, 221
Punta Alegre Sugar Co., 1, 81–82, 96, 123, 143–44, 157, 178, 181, 187, 189, 198, 211, 235

Quotas. *See* Cuba, quotas

Reciprocity, 16–18, 21, 43, 246–47, 248, 263
Reciprocity Treaty: of 1903, 44–45, 59; of 1934, 264, 273–74, 282
Refineries, U.S., 193–94; vertical integration by, 55, 149–50
Refining, in Cuba, 70–71, 150–52, 159, 241
Rentschler, Gordon S., 170, 178, 189–90, 194, 198, 201–2, 252, 261
Revere Sugar Refinery, 55, 162
Right of Tanteo, 258, 260–61, 264–70, 279–81
Río Vista, 47–48
Rionda, Mrs. Manuel. *See* Clarke, Harriet
Rionda, Silvestre (MR's half-brother), 28, 254–55
Rionda Benjamin, Manuel Enrique ("Manolo," MR's nephew, 1877–1950), 10, 13–14, 23, 29, 47, 174–75, 284; and Czarnikow-Rionda, 54, 68, 80, 162, 168, 187–90, 193, 198–99, 221–22, 235; and Cuba Cane, 97, 117, 119, 125, 132, 141, 146, 149, 151, 209–10; and Cuba Cane Products, 246, 252; and Cuban Atlantic, 263, 268, 272
Rionda Chaumont, José Andres (MR's grandnephew, b. 1913), 285

Rionda Polledo, Bibiana (Mrs. José Braga, MR's sister, 1848–1883), 13
Rionda Polledo, Concepción ("Aunt Conchita," MR's sister, 1855–1935), 252, 254
Rionda Polledo, Francisco ("Pancho," MR's brother, 1844–1898), 7, 8, 10, 23, 27–28, 33
Rionda Polledo, Gregoria (Mrs. Nicasio Fernández, MR's sister, d. 1926), 13
Rionda Polledo, Isidora (Mrs. Alberto Noriega, MR's sister, 1846–1937), 23, 126, 252, 254
Rionda Polledo, Joaquín (MR's brother, 1850–1889), 7, 8, 14
Rionda Polledo, Manuel (1854–1943), 173, 177, 182, 187, 260, 280–81, 287; and dual allegiances, 2, 25–26, 111, 128, 199, 224, 226, 232, 236–37, 288–91, 293; youth of, 7–15; marriage of, 14; joins Czarnikow-MacDougall, 23–25; and Spanish-Cuban-American War, 25–26; as head of clan, 28–29; uplifting Cuba, 30–35, 42, 45, 128–29; and *Tuinucú*, 33–37, 46; and *Francisco*, 34–37, 46; business success of, 47–48; and group action, 71–72, 95, 200; and World War I, 74–80, 106, 111, 290; and Cuba Cane Sugar Company, 81–99, 188–89, 192, 201, 209; and Goethals investigation, 128–44; and banking crisis, 154–55; and Sugar Finance Commission, 161–72; and "invisible hand," 184–86; and colonos' strike, 185–86; and "survival of the fittest," 189, 204, 231, 235, 239; and crop restrictions, 195, 202, 292; and Cuban Cane Products Company, 219, 235–38, 241, 249, 275; and Chadbourne, 226–27, 230, 232–33; and Cuban Atlantic, 264, 272, 274–76; final years of, 282–86; death of, 286; memorial for, 286–89
Rionda Polledo, María (Mrs. Alfonso Fanjul, MR's sister, 1857–1909), 13
Rionda Polledo, Ramona (Mrs. Pedro Alonso, MR's sister, 1852–1948), 13
Rionda y de la Torriente, Elena (Mrs. Oliver Doty, MR's niece, 1882–1944), 13, 25
Rionda y de la Torriente, Esperanza (Mrs. George E. Crawley, MR's niece, 1890–1960), 13, 25
Rionda y de la Torriente, José (Pepe, MR's nephew, 1878–1962), 10, 13, 29, 33, 47, 68, 80, 98, 118, 125, 129, 177, 241, 244, 252–53, 255–56, 284
Rionda y de la Torriente, Leandro (MR's nephew, 1880–1952), 10, 13, 29, 47, 54–55, 68, 80, 83, 98, 118–19, 124–25, 129, 177, 256, 284
Rionda y de la Torriente, Salvador (MR's nephew, 1888–1961), 13, 29, 68, 80, 125, 175–76, 214, 252, 284, 295
Rionda y del Monte, Manuel (Manuel's grandnephew, 1925–1961), 295
Risley, Wallace, 37, 301n.8
Rodriquez Blanca, Walfredo, 251, 268
Rolph, George M., 105–7, 110, 115
Roosevelt, Franklin Delano, 241, 246, 248–49, 256, 259, 263, 266–67
Roosevelt, George, 216, 237, 276
Root, Elihu, 41, 97, 181
Rosario, 26, 33, 41
Royal Bank of Canada, 71, 82, 149, 160–61
Royal Sugar Commission, 76, 79
Rubens, Horatio, 58–59, 197
Ryan, John D., 96, 122

Sabin, Charles H., 81–82, 96–97, 114, 118, 127, 166
Saladrigas, Carlos, 264–65
Sample, John J., 235, 237–38, 242, 259, 262–64, 269, 276, 278
San Augustín, 31, 164
San Ignacio, 124, 236
San Vincente, 55, 118, 240
Schroeders Bank, 53–54, 71, 78, 269
Seligman, Isaac Newton, 63, 81
Seligman, J. & W., 1, 63, 87, 96, 97, 118, 127, 166, 212, 276
Simpson, John Roy, 201–2, 209–11, 214, 218, 219, 223, 226, 227
Single Seller. *See* Cooperative Export Agency

Smith, F. Gerard, 193, 205–6, 215, 222, 243–45, 262
Smoot, Sen. Reed, 169, 172, 254
Socorro, 84, 86–88, 93, 132–33, 136
Speyer and Co., 59
Spreckels, Claus August, 63, 97
Staples, Percy, 225
Steinhart, Frank, 183
Stetson, Eugene, 126, 192, 202, 209, 220, 235–36, 242–45, 249–50, 261–63, 268–71, 276, 278
Stewart, 50–52, 60, 64, 75, 96–98, 101, 109, 118, 131, 136, 139, 145
Strauss, Albert, 63, 81–82, 96–97, 103, 166, 177, 189, 198, 209
Strauss, Frederick, 63, 96, 113, 119–20, 132, 145, 158, 176, 209, 216, 219
Sugar: prices for, 11–12, 15, 23–24, 69–71, 73, 74–76, 79, 94, 101–4, 106–11, 115–16, 148–52, 155, 160, 172, 177, 182, 184, 186–87, 194, 214, 248; production of, U.S., 65, 73; worldwide crop restrictions on, 73, 184, 196–97, 211, 223–24. See also, Cuba, crop restrictions on; Cuba, sugar production in
Sugar beets: in Europe, 11–12, 15, 23–24, 47, 76, 196, 226; in the U.S., 18, 24, 65, 100, 172, 184, 203, 208, 226; in England, 196, 203, 283
Sugar Defense Committee (1927), 195–96
Sugar Export Corporation (1927), 195, 197–98, 200, 202, 205
Sugar Finance Commission (1921), 161–72, 199–200
Sugar Restriction Law. *See* Tarafa Law (1927)
Sugar Trust, 18–19, 43, 52, 70–71. *See also* American Sugar Refining Co.
Sullivan & Cromwell, 51, 62, 97, 106, 146, 181, 261, 280, 295

Tarafa, Col. José Miguel: and business activities, 58–60, 72, 85–86, 88, 90, 102–3, 180, 187–88, 200, 209; and wartime sugar prices, 107–9, 140–41, 143, 161, 180, 183; supports crop restrictions, 195–98, 204–5, 211–12, 214–15, 226, 231, 234; death of, 239–41
Tarafa Law: of 1923, 180–81, 198, 209; of 1927, 195, 202–3
Taussig, Charles W., 248–49
Thayer, Eugene V. R., 82, 187, 207
Thompson, Alfred J., 33, 170
Tiarks, Frank, 53, 78, 180
Torriente, Lola de la, 161
Torriente y Hernández, Elena de la (Mrs Francisco Rionda, d. 1926), 8, 23, 34
Torriente y Peraza, Cosme de la (Elena's nephew, 1872–1957), 25, 160–61, 250, 259–61, 265, 272–74
Trinidad, 20, 82, 191
Truffin, Regino, 58–59, 62–63, 75, 83–85, 88, 97, 146, 148–50, 166, 170–71, 176–77, 187
Tuinucú, 13, 20, 22–23, 31, 33–34, 41, 45–47, 52, 72, 113, 117, 124, 131, 147, 248, 279, 284, 295–96

Ulzurrún, Eduardo de, 63, 171, 176, 191–92, 200
United Fruit Co., 40, 55, 107, 143–44, 162, 190, 194, 212, 215, 223, 296
United Railways, 57–58, 96
United States: bounties on domestic sugar, 18; exports to Cuba, 21, 247; government control of sugar in World War I, 76, 105; Food Administration, Sugar Division, 105; Sugar Equalization Board, 115, 141–42; Sugar Control Board, 140; sugar quotas, 266, 282. *See also* International Sugar Committee
—tariffs, 300n.14; Morrill (1883), 12; McKinley (1890), 18, 20; Wilson-Gorman (1894), 21; Dingley (1897), 24, 42; Payne-Aldrich (1909), 57–58; Underwood (1914), 66, 70–71, 73, 99–100, 151; Hawley-Smoot (1930), 169, 208, 211, 217, 223, 247, 260

Van Horne, Sir William, 41, 51
Vanderlip, Frank A., 61, 120, 148

Vázquez Bello, Clemente, 193, 247, 311n.19
Verdeja Act (1926), 186
Violeta, 146, 150, 274, 279–80, 283

Warner Sugar Refinery, 149, 163, 189
Washington, 55, 118, 147
Welles, Sumner, 248, 250, 257, 261, 266
Wertheim and Co., 279, 283
Westrik, Theodore, 53, 68
Whitmarsh, Theodore F., 141–42
Wilson, Woodrow, 65–66, 70, 100–101, 104, 141
Wood, Leonard, 41, 44

Worcester, Harry, 273
World War I, 74–80, 99, 102–3, 116
World War II, 283
Wright, Irene, 64–66

Zabriskie, George A., 115, 141–42
Zayas, Alfredo, 100, 164, 166, 176
Zayas Bazán, Cristóbal, 191
Zevallos y Chiriboga, Rafael, 51–52, 54
Zevallos y Chiriboga, Victor, 51, 54, 69, 75, 77, 83, 135, 142, 151, 166, 176
Zulueta, Enrique, 31, 86, 90
Zulueta y Gamiz, 41, 88

Muriel McAvoy was professor emerita at Fitchburg State College, Massachusetts.

www.ingramcontent.com/pod-product-compliance
Lightning Source LLC
Chambersburg PA
CBHW031755220426
43662CB00007B/409